SCOTLAND YARD

SCOTLAND YARD

A History of the London
Police Force's Most
Infamous Murder Cases

SIMON READ

PEGASUS CRIME

NEW YORK LONDON

SCOTLAND YARD

Pegasus Crime is an imprint of
Pegasus Books, Ltd.
148 West 37th Street, 13th Floor
New York, NY 10018

First Pegasus Books cloth edition September 2024

ISBN: 978-1-63936-639-2

10 9 8 7 6 5 4 3 2 1

Printed in the United States of America
Distributed by Simon & Schuster
www.pegasusbooks.com

For my mum,
who loves 'a good murder'.

And my dad,
who sleeps with one eye open.

Truth will come to light; murder cannot be hid long.

Shakespeare
The Merchant of Venice, Act II, Scene 2

'There's the scarlet thread of murder running through the colourless skein of life, and our duty is to unravel it, and isolate it, and expose every inch of it.'

Sir Arthur Conan Doyle
Sherlock Holmes in *A Study in Scarlet*

Contents

Prologue

The Yard

The Ratcliffe Highway Murders. The New Police.

The highway, the main eastbound thoroughfare out of London, was not for travellers faint of heart. Even its name, 'Ratcliffe,' derived from the red sandstone cliff above Wapping Marsh, spoke of something sinister. Tenements and run-down cottages, homes to sailors and those who worked the harbours and ships that plied the Thames, lined its many cramped alleys. Its reputation by the nineteenth century was firmly established as a filthy gauntlet 'of unbridled vice and drunken violence – of all that is dirty, disorderly and debased.'[1]

Taverns and shops crowded the narrow byway that ran from the Tower of London, past Wapping – 'the usual place of execution for [the] hanging of pirates and sea rovers' – to Shadwell. The river, with its ships from abroad and up north bringing goods in and out of London, was its primary source of commerce. Indeed, one contemporary account referred to the highway as 'the Regent Street of London sailors.'[2]

Timothy Marr, a twenty-four-year-old linen draper, owned a modest shop at 29, Ratcliffe Highway. A one-time sailor for the East India Company, he had abandoned life at sea in 1808 for a more settled existence. He married his wife, Celia, and in April 1811 opened what he hoped would become a thriving business. A bay window, trimmed in green paint, offered passers-by a glimpse of the stocked shelves within and Marr a view of the traffic up and down Ratcliffe; the horse-drawn wagons and carts hauling tobacco and spices, sugar and rum, coffee and tea.[3]

It was just shy of midnight on Saturday, 7 December 1811, when Marr – busy behind the counter and hungry after a long day – asked his servant girl, Margaret Jewell, to fetch some oysters and pay the baker's bill. She wrapped herself in a shawl and stepped into the cold night. The terraced shops along the road were mostly dark, the soft, yellow glow of lamplight spilling from the odd window. Margaret hurried to Taylor's Oyster Shop, several doors to the left, and found it closed. So, too, was the baker's at this late hour. 'I was out about twenty minutes,' Margaret said, 'and when I returned, I found my master's shop and door closely tight, and there was no sign of light.'[4]

Margaret, puzzled, rang the bell but got no response. Surely, they hadn't shuttered for the night and gone to bed in her short absence. Marr had not yet finished arranging the store's inventory for the next day's business – and Celia had just gone down to the basement kitchen to feed their three-month-old son. Margaret rang the bell with increasing urgency. From behind the door came the soft but distinct sound of a footfall on the stairs. 'I also heard the child cry in a low tone of voice,' she said. 'I rang then again and again, and knocked at the door with my foot.'[5]

An eternity seemed to pass until about 1 a.m. when Night Watchman George Olney walked by on his rounds and asked Margaret what the commotion was about. He thought her story odd and pounded on the door, calling to Marr as he did so. The storefront remained dark and silent. The noise in the street had now attracted the attention of John Murray, a pawnbroker who lived next door. Appraised of the situation, he hopped a wall into the Marrs' back garden and saw a light flickering in an upstairs window. He entered through the shop's back door.

'Marr,' he called. 'Marr, your shutters aren't fastened.'

Silence.

He walked up the stairs and found a lit candle on the landing. He picked it up and in its pallid light noticed 'the two doors of the chamber in which Mr Marr usually slept were open'. Decorum stopped him from peering into the room. He went back downstairs to look in the shop and stumbled into a gore-splattered nightmare.[6]

Six feet from the bottom step he found the Marrs' errand boy, fourteen-year-old James Gowen, 'lying on his face . . . with his brains knocked out, part of them actually covering the ceiling, and blood on the wall and counter'. In a fit of terror, he staggered towards the door and found Celia face down in a widening pool of blood. A crowd of onlookers, aware by now something was amiss, loitered outside the shop. They drew closer as the door swung open and Murray, his pale face gleaming in the candlelight, appeared in the entrance.[7]

'For God's sake come in,' he cried, 'and see what dreadful murder is here!'

The crowd pushed forward into the shop. They stepped over Celia's 'mangled and bleeding body' and saw the errand boy lying near the back. Timothy Marr lay behind the counter, 'bleeding very much about the head'. They went in search of the baby, Timothy Jr, and descended the stairs to the basement kitchen. He lay there dead in his crib, blood seeping from his mouth and throat.[8]

Margaret, seeing the horror, began to scream.[9]

The coroner's inquest took place at the Jolly Sailor pub, across the street from the murder house, on the afternoon of Tuesday, 10 December. Surgeon William Salter, having examined the bodies, testified as to his findings and detailed a savagery that went far beyond initial newspaper reports:

Timothy Marr the younger had the left external artery of the neck entirely divided; from the left side of the mouth, across the artery, the wound was at least three inches long; there were several marks of violence on the left side of the face. Cecilia [sic] Marr, the wife, had the left side of the cranium fractured, and the temple-bone totally destroyed . . . Timothy Marr the elder had his nose broken. The occipital bone was fractured, and the mark of a violent blow was over the right eye. James Goin [sic], the apprentice boy, had several contusions on the forehead and nose. The occipital bones were shattered dreadfully, and the brains were partly protruded and partly scattered about.[10]

Margaret Jewell, asked to recount that awful evening, 'was so much convulsed by her feelings, that she fainted away; and every effort to restore her was used for a considerable time without effect. She was not examined further.' The jury, having visited the murder scene, viewed the bodies, and listened to the testimony of watchman George Olney and neighbour John Murray, returned a verdict of 'wilful murder against some persons unknown.'[11]

The inquest did nothing to elucidate the *who* and *why*, but the crime was not without its clues. The killer or killers left in the house a bloody eight-pound ship carpenter's maul, a hammer-like tool with the head rounded at one end for pounding in ship bolts and sharpened to a point at the other 'for driving the bolt deeper beneath the surface of the wood.' A twenty-inch iron-ripping chisel was also found in one of the bedrooms, but it was clean.[12]

An 'immense crowd' showed up for the Marr family funeral at St George-in-the-East on Sunday, 15 December. Mourners lined the route from the Marrs' shop to see 'the murdered family conveyed to the dreary mansions of mortality.' Those assembled in the church bowed their heads at the urging of Reverend Dr Farringdon but could not resist 'the impulse of strong language in the universal prayer of the vengeance of Heaven upon the heads of the unknown murderers.' The family was interred in a single grave, 'Mr Marr in one coffin, and those of the mother and infant placed together.'[13]

The aftershock of the murders had yet to subside when, five

days later on Friday, 20 December, the papers carried news of another slaughter. *The London Chronicle* struck an almost apologetic tone in having to break the tragedy to its readers:

> It is with equal terror and concern we have to state that three more persons have lost their lives by the hands of midnight murderers within two-minutes' walk of the very spot where the family of the late unfortunate Mr Marr perished a few days ago by the same means.[14]

Heads smashed to pulp and throats cut to the bone, the latest savagery occurred at the King's Arms tavern at 81, New Gravel Lane. The victims were fifty-six-year-old proprietor John Williamson, his sixty-year-old wife Elizabeth and a servant in her fifties named Bridget Harrington 'who collected pots and waited in the tap room.' The Williamsons, 'characters highly respected in the neighbourhood', had run the King's Tavern for fifteen years, welcoming locals and 'foreigners of every description.' The murders happened sometime between eleven o'clock and midnight on 19 December after the tavern had closed. A tenant named John Turner, a lawyer by trade, heard the trio being 'inhumanely massacred' from the safety of his room two floors up.[15]

The King's Arms had been Turner's home for eight months. He considered the Williamsons 'a peaceable couple' and pleasant landlords. He said goodnight to them a few minutes before eleven and went upstairs as they locked up.

'I went to bed and had not been there above five minutes before I heard the front door banged-to very hard,' he said. 'Immediately afterwards, I heard the servant exclaim, "We are all murdered!" or "We shall be murdered!" two or three times.'

There followed the sound of three violent blows striking home – 'with what weapon, I cannot say' – and John Williamson's desperate cry of 'I am a dead man!' Turner remained in bed, his room dark and now silent. It took him several minutes to muster the courage to investigate.[16]

'I got out of bed and listened at the door but could hear nothing,' he said. 'I went down to the first floor, and from below I heard the sound of three heavy sighs. I heard some person walk across the middle room on the ground floor very lightly. I was then half-way down the last pair of stairs, and naked.'

Turner tiptoed to a door, slightly ajar, at the bottom of the stairs. He squeezed himself between the door and its frame, worried the hinges might whine if he opened it further.

'By the light of a candle burning in the room, I saw a man – near six-feet high – in a large, rough Flushing coat of a dark colour, which came down to his heels,' he said. 'He was standing with his back towards me, apparently leaning over some person, as if in the act of rifling the pockets.'

Turner heard the distinct sound of coins being rattled and watched as the man stood and pocketed his ill-gotten gains.

'I did not see his face, and I only saw that one person. I was fearful, and went upstairs as quick – but as softly – as I could.'

Back in his room, Turner felt the onset of panic. He dismissed hiding under his bed as being too obvious, and instead tied two sheets together and wrapped one end around a bedpost. He threw on his nightcap, a shirt and waistcoat and lowered himself out the bedroom window, which overlooked the street. His descent coincided with the passing of a night watchman, whose curiosity was naturally piqued. Upon hearing Turner's story, the watchman 'sprang his rattle' and sounded the alarm.

Several men, including neighbour George Fox, heeded the call and forced their way through the front door and a cellar window when their knocks and shouts went unanswered. The tavern's front room was dark, but a soft glow from the middle room – the kitchen – drew their attention.

'There was a light burning on a table,' Fox said. 'There, I saw Mrs Williamson lying upon her face, along the hearth, with her head towards the door, with her throat cut and blood flowing from the wound.'

The gash extended ear to ear and through her windpipe. The whole right side of her head lay open, smashed to pieces with 'a large poker, or some such instrument.' It looked as though the killer had gone through her pockets. Bridget Harrington, the servant, lay between Elizabeth and the fireplace, blood pooling around her from a four-inch gash in her neck and a hole in the right side of her head about four inches long and two inches wide.

'Where is the old man Williamson?' Fox called out, his voice thick in his throat.

'Here he is,' one of the men who entered through the cellar window called out from below, 'with his throat cut.'

'Cut' was an understatement. The killer's blade had opened Williamson's throat from ear to ear, 'penetrating through the trachea, or wind-pipe, and down to the vertebrae of the neck.' His right leg was broken just above the ankle, indicating he perhaps tumbled down the stairs during the attack.[17]

The killer escaped through a rear window, leaving a bloody handprint on the open shutter, and dropping eight feet to 'a large piece of waste ground belonging to the London Dock Company.' The only route he could have taken was up a sloping bank of wet clay. He would have had to scale the slippery summit on his hands and knees, splattering himself in the stuff, before making his getaway. Despite a desperate search, the clay-covered killer remained at large.[18]

The Ratcliffe Highway Murders, 'the most superb of the century by many degrees,' generated a panic not seen in London before and wouldn't be seen again until Jack the Ripper – but, as one history notes, 'the Ripper was hunted in a city with 14,000 Metropolitan Police officers . . . In 1811, London had no effective police force at all.'[19]

What constituted law enforcement in the capital at the time consisted primarily of an inadequate and fragmented system of parish-based constables and night watchmen. The night watch patrolled 'London's cluttered cobblestone thoroughfares and dank alleys' between 10 p.m. and sunrise. Armed with a lantern and rattle, they were expected to confront any suspicious character they encountered, but were more likely to be drunk on the job. Indeed, the London journal *Englishman* described the typical watch-house as a place with 'the night constable asleep, and perhaps intoxicated, and empty pots and glasses, lately filled with gin and water, gracing the table and seats, and the whole place the picture of licentious debauchery rather than of stern justice.'[20]

The East End parish of St George, where the highway murders occurred, relied on 'up to a dozen unpaid constables' and 'thirty-five watchmen at two shillings a night'. It was not enough. 'The frequent instances of murder committed in the eastern part of the metropolis, which no vigilance has been successful to detect . . . call for the solemn attention of those immediately entrusted with the administration of Government,' noted one East End official in the wake of the killings. 'The latest and present murders are a disgrace to the country and almost a reproach on civilization. While the exertions of the Police . . . are found insufficient to protect men's persons from the hands of violence [and] without the possibility of delivering the perpetrators to justice and punishment, our houses are no longer our castles, and we are unsafe in our beds.'[21]

The closest thing London had to a police department was the brainchild of barrister, novelist and playwright Henry Fielding, who in 1748 became the city's chief magistrate. He set up his office at No. 4 Bow Street, where eight years prior a justice named Sir Thomas de Veil established a magistrates' court. It was, according to *The Illustrated London News*, comprised of 'dingy, fetid close smelling rooms, for the most part, places like a cross betwixt a bare, neglected, decaying school room, and a squalid sponging house, approached by low-browed intricate passages.'[22] It continued:

The walls greased and stained by the ceaseless friction of the forlorn, ragged groups of witnesses and prosecutors, and friends of prisoners, who lounge about in every avenue and approach which winds and crosses betwixt the Justice Room and the loathsome box-like cells.[23]

It was here – adjudicating matters amongst the 'swarms of poverty-stricken, squalid men and women who come with summonses, or with complaints, or to make distracted enquiries after missing friends or strayed children' – that Fielding, possibly 'the first Englishman to consider the causes of crime', sought a means to combat it. In 1753, he organized a constabulary force of seven honest men that became known as the Bow Street Runners. Paid a small weekly retainer, the Runners wore no uniforms and identified themselves with a short club topped with a gold crown. More proactive than the typical parish constable or drunken night watchman, the Runners 'actively sought to detect the perpetrators of crimes, not merely to impede those who might be contemplating some villainy.'[24]

Fielding's younger half-brother, John, soon joined him as an assistant at Bow Street. Although blinded in an accident at nineteen, John excelled in his law studies and earned a reputation as an energetic social reformer. The brothers believed the fear of capture to be a powerful deterrence to those considering unlawful acts. Through the Runners and informants, they kept abreast of criminal activity in the city. They published the information in the illustrated *Police Gazette*, overseeing from Bow Street an underworld intelligence network. In many ways, the Fielding brothers had evolved the concept of the thief-taker – a more suspect form of crime fighter.[25]

Thief-takers, mercenary-type characters with knowledge of London's underworld, operated much like bounty hunters and tracked down the likes of thieves, murderers and highwaymen for monetary rewards. They operated 'in a world of shadows' often in concert with their quarry, negotiating fees between victim and criminal for the return of stolen goods. Many, not surprisingly, exploited the system for their own benefit. The wily Jonathan Wild made a small fortune buying stolen property from those he was supposedly hunting and then returning it to the rightful owner for an inflated finder's fee. Soon, he was collaborating with thieves to target individuals for theft and then 'recovering' the goods for hefty rewards.[26]

The plan worked like a charm until it didn't. Two of Wild's minions, arrested on other matters, turned against him in exchange for leniency and helped send the once-admired 'Thief-Taker General of England and Ireland' to the gallows on 25 May 1725. Wild's cunning and deceit threw a harsh glare on the duplicity of thief-takers and was immortalized in the 1743 novel *The Life and Death of Jonathan Wild, the Great* by non-other than Henry Fielding.[27]

Fielding died in 1754 and was replaced as Bow Street Magistrate by his half-brother John, who, it was rumoured, could identify 'more than 3,000 criminals merely by the sound of their voices.' Known as 'The Blind Beak of Bow Street,' he advanced the work started by Henry and advocated for an organized police force. To keep track of criminal activity, he established a record-keeping system that became a forerunner to Scotland Yard's Criminal Records Office. Briefly, in the early 1760s, he got the government to fund ten mounted officers to patrol the approaches to London and combat the scourge of highwaymen. The patrols, although successful, fell victim to 'Treasury parsimony' after a mere eighteen months. Horse patrols would not resume on a permanent basis until 1783.[28]

All the while, the Bow Street Runners continued their duties with other magistrate offices adopting the Fielding system of running their own constables to detect crime. To the mix was added the Thames River Police in 1800 to patrol the city's waterways. None of this helped solve the Ratcliffe Highway Murders, for the various police forces viewed one another with suspicion. As one

London magistrate noted, 'different police officers keep their information to themselves and do not wish to communicate it to others, that they may have the credit and advantage of detecting offenders.'[29]

London, the heart of Empire, lacked the professional police force it so desperately needed – a fact the Ratcliffe killings underscored with a gruesome urgency. 'Hardly a week passed without a plain-spoken article in one of the newspapers on the increase in crimes of violence, the corruption of the police, or the ineptitude of the magistrates,' notes one history. 'The general, if vague, feeling of dissatisfaction might, however, have died down, as similar agitations had died down before; an impulse was needed to give it substance, and the appalling tragedies in Ratcliffe Highway supplied it.'[30]

The murder investigation, such as it was, reached an unsatisfactory conclusion after two lodgers at a pub called The Pear Tree informed on their roommate, a sailor named John Williams. Williams was arrested three days after the King's Arms massacre on circumstantial evidence: the maul found at the Marr house matched the description of one that went missing from the Pear Tree; Williams had recently shaved his beard, inexplicably come into money, and once served on a sailing brig with Timothy Marr; the women who laundered his clothes said 'twice in the past fortnight' they found blood on his shirt; finally, in Williams's waistcoat, constables found 'a bloodstained knife of peculiar shape' that 'might have caused the throat-wounds' in the Marr killings.[31]

Williams, who 'underwent a very long and rigid interrogation,' maintained his innocence. Remanded to Coldbath Fields Prison to await trial, he hanged himself in his cell with 'a white neck handkerchief' from a railing used for draping clothes and linens. 'On inspecting the body, it was supposed that he had not long committed the act,' reported *The* (London) *Star*. 'His eyes and mouth were open, and the state of his body clearly demonstrated that he struggled very hard.'[32]

Having deprived the public of its vengeance, Williams's body was paraded 'on a high cart, past the houses of Marr and Williamson, and afterwards thrown, with a stake through his breast, into a hole dug for the purpose where the New-road crosses and Cannon-street-road begins.'[33]

The Ratcliffe Highway Murders convinced a 'thoughtful section of the public to the urgent need of a complete overhaul of the police system'. The idea of a professional, centrally organized police department had been contemplated before but withered under public and political fears that such a force might curtail civil liberties and prove militaristic in nature. These fears now began to wane amongst the populace but not so among members of Parliament, 'who remained blinkered to the social collapse around them.'[34]

In March 1822, thirty-four-year-old Home Secretary Robert Peel – the wealthy Eton- and Oxford-educated son of a printing manufacturer – organized a Select Committee to study in London the creation 'of as perfect a system of police as was consistent with the character of a free country.' Peel was no stranger to the issue of policing. In his previous government post as Chief Secretary for Ireland, he had established the Irish Peace Preservation Police, 'forerunners to the Royal Irish Constabulary.'[35]

Peel's London committee pondered the matter for three months before issuing its final report, saying it was 'difficult to reconcile an effective system of police with the perfect freedom of action and exemption from interference which are the great privileges and blessings of society in this country.' The curtailment of such privileges, it said, 'would be too great a sacrifice for improvements in police, or facilities in detection of crime.'[36]

Disappointed but determined, Peel spent the next several years working on judicial reform and simplifying the nation's cluttered criminal code before introducing a bill in April 1829, 'For Improving the Police in and near the Metropolis.'[37] It declared:

The local establishments of nightly watch and nightly police have been found inadequate to the prevention and detection of crime, by reason of the frequent unfitness of the individuals employed, the insufficiency of their number, the limited sphere of their authority, and their want of connection and co-operation with each other.

And that:

It is expedient to substitute a more efficient system of police in lieu of such establishments of nightly watch and nightly police.[38]

'It is the duty of Parliament to afford to the inhabitants of the Metropolis and its vicinity, the full and complete protection of the law,' Peel argued in presenting his bill, 'and to take prompt and decisive measures to check the increase of crime which is now proceeding at a frightfully rapid pace.'[39]

One could hardly argue with such sentiment. Rioting and crime in London, fuelled by unemployment and an economy that hardly favoured the poor, had become major concerns. This time around, opposition to the bill proved light. It became law on 19 June, 1829, and established the London Metropolitan Police, the world's first professional and centrally organized police department. The new force would cover an area known as the Metropolitan Police District. It encompassed a twelve-mile radius from the centre of London at Charing Cross and was divided into '17 Divisions lettered A through T,' each of which would have 165 men. Two magistrates, soon to be called Commissioners, would oversee the force and report to the Home Secretary.[40]

Within weeks, Peel recruited forty-six-year-old Colonel Charles Rowan, an Army veteran who served under Wellington at Waterloo and was an expert on the military system of patrols; and Richard Mayne, a thirty-two-year-old Irish lawyer who brought a legal background to the department's leadership. Both men would have to learn on the job how to run a fledgling police service, as neither 'really had any idea what they were supposed to do or how they were supposed to do it.'[41]

The same could probably be said for its undertrained rank and file. The New Police, as the press called it, initially consisted of 8 superintendents, 20 inspectors, 88 sergeants, and 895 constables. A constable earned three shillings a day. In its first six months, the service recruited 3,200 men – half of whom were quickly dismissed for drinking on the job or not showing up at all. Peel 'borrowed the organizational structure of the London police from the military, including uniforms, rank designations, and the authoritarian system of command and discipline.'[42]

The primary objective of the New Police would be the prevention – not the detection – of crime. 'To this great end,' noted the service's first Instruction Book, 'every effort of the Police is to be directed. The security of persons and property, the preservation of public tranquility, and all the other objects of a Police Establishment will thus far be better effected than by the detection and punishment of the offender, after he has succeeded in committing the crime.'[43]

In 'a forerunner of the modern performance-related pay system' an officer's career trajectory 'would be linked to crime reduction.' Constables would patrol the streets in a uniform that, although it clearly identified them as agents of the law, left a lot to be desired when it came to comfort. 'I had to put on a swallow-tail coat, and a rabbit-skin high-top-hat, covered with leather, weighting eighteen ounces,' remembered one early member of the force, 'a pair of Wellington boots, the leather of which must have been at least a sixteenth of an inch thick, and a belt about four inches broad, with a great brass buckle some six inches deep.'[44]

The New Police established its headquarters at 4, Whitehall Place, the back of which 'faced a small street called Great Scotland Yard.' The origins of the name are not entirely known, although the most common story is that the land may have once housed a residence for kings of Scotland on their annual pilgrimage to bend the knee to their English counterparts. Another is that a man named Adam Scott owned the land in the Middle Ages. Whatever the true provenance, the name 'Scotland Yard' soon became a metonym for both the London Metropolitan Police and its headquarters.[45]

By September, with recruitment efforts still underway, Scotland Yard was ready to go with six divisions. At six o'clock on the evening of Tuesday, 29 September, the first constables – nicknamed 'Bobbies' and 'Peelers' after Robert Peel – emerged 'from the still-unfinished station-house in Scotland Yard, and from five of the old watch-houses.' Having reviewed their beats earlier that day, they marched 'in single file and on the outer side of the pavement and "proceede" on duty'.[46]

'How far their numbers, when distributed on duty, may compare with those of their lethargic and undisciplined predecessors, we cannot now conjecture,' pondered one paper. 'But if, as is probable, they fall short in that respect, the public, we trust, will not fail to be indemnified by their superior fitness and their skilful organization as a corps.'[47]

The force wasted little time in letting its presence be known. 'Since the new police have been on service,' one reader wrote to *The Times* on 6 October, 'I can bear testimony to the quietness of our western streets . . . It is to be hoped that the police-men will steadily persevere in clearing the streets of all disorderly and drunken people; and in doing so they will improve the vicious, be a terror to the simple uninitiated youths, and a security to the peaceable inhabitants of this great metropolis.'[48]

But not everyone was thrilled. Many still believed the new force to be agents of the government intent on establishing a police state. Such distrust manifested itself in 'verbal and physical attacks on policemen'. In the early morning hours of Sunday, 11 October, 'crowds of drunken and disorderly persons of both sexes assembled, as usual,' in the notorious Seven Dials neighbourhood of

Camden. When a small contingent of constables appeared, the crowd assailed the officers with cries of 'There go the bloody policemen!' and 'There go the *gens-de-harms.*'[49]

The drunken mob grew ever-more volatile, and the 'men who were on duty found themselves in a situation of considerable peril from inferiority of numbers.' A reinforcement of fifty officers soon arrived 'from the adjacent stations' and dispelled the mob, taking nearly thirty people into custody. Within a quarter of an hour, the neighbourhood was – in the words of one witness – 'as quiet and orderly, comparatively, as St James's-square.'[50]

The episode, reported *The Times*, offered 'a practical example of the spirit and determination with which the new civil force appear resolved to act in the performance of this disagreeable but necessary duty.' Disagreeable, indeed. On 29 June 1830, Police Constable (PC) Joseph Grantham tried to break up a fight between two drunks. He became the first Scotland Yard officer killed in the line of duty when, in the melee, he was knocked to the ground and kicked in the temple. His wife had given birth to twins the day before. Two months later, on 16 August, a thief fatally stabbed PC John Long in the heart near Gray's Inn Road.[51]

Scotland Yard was learning its lessons, tough and bloody, in the school of hard knocks. Although it seemed improbable in those early days, it would – through the 1800s to the eve of the Second World War – set new standards for policing. It advanced the application of forensics, from fingerprints to ballistics to evidence collection, made the first attempt at criminal profiling, and captivated the public on both sides of the Atlantic with feats of detective work that rivalled any fiction. It would, in short, become the most recognized name in policing – one gruesome case at a time.

1

The Unhallowed

Resurrectionists. Crime scene tours.

They worked by flickering lamplight, prowling from one grave to the next, digging and heaving, leaving in their wake a trail of rot and desecration. Come morning, the cemetery gates opened to reveal, scattered among the lopsided tombstones, 'coffins with their once-living and moving tenants exposed in all the horrors – the revolting horrors – of decomposition and putrefaction.' Four other coffins, hauled from the earth, lay 'emptied of all their contents, save the clothes of the deceased.' And so it was on a November night in 1830, the Resurrection Men plied their morbid trade in a Cambridgeshire cemetery.[1]

Body snatching, the plundering of graves for fresh corpses, was prevalent and profitable in nineteenth-century Britain. Against this macabre backdrop, Mary Shelley published *Frankenstein, or the Modern Prometheus*. Its dark exploration of death and the morality of scientific experiment touched on topics very much in the public consciousness at the time. 'To examine the causes of life,' Dr Frankenstein writes, 'we must first have recourse to death. I became acquainted with the science of anatomy, but this was not sufficient; I must also observe the natural decay and corruption of the human body.' To find the raw material necessary for his grim experiments, Frankenstein confesses to having 'dabbled among the unhallowed damps of the grave.'[2]

As in the novel, originally published in 1818, the advancement of medical studies and a flourishing desire to understand human anatomy fuelled the real-life and gruesome crime of grave robbing. Ten medical schools opened in and around London between 1824 and 1834. A report at the time from the Select Committee on Anatomy 'suggested that there were around 800 students at medical schools in London, of whom 500 practised dissection.' Meeting this demand required an annual supply of '450–500 corpses'. Cadavers proved a hot commodity.[3]

The bodies of those hanged for murder traditionally provided fodder for medical studies – a result of the Murder Act of 1751, which stipulated such corpses 'be conveyed . . . to the hall of the Surgeons Company . . . [and] shall be dissected and anatomized by said surgeon.' But in the 1800s, as the number of executions decreased and the number of medical students increased, supply could not meet demand.[4]

'The absolute necessity of having a good supply for the use of students, so as to prevent them going off to rival schools,' notes one contemporary history, 'caused the teachers to offer large prices, and thus made it worthwhile for men to devote themselves entirely to obtaining bodies for this purpose.'[5]

Enter the Resurrectionists, so named because they 'resurrected' the dead. Often thieves by trade, they represented 'the most desperate and abandoned class of the community'. They worked in gangs and stalked graveyards at night in search of recently filled graves and fresh product. Some dug up the coffin, while others went about it with a bit more – for lack of a better word – finesse. They'd dig down to the casket, pry it open with a crowbar, tie a rope around the neck or secure it beneath the armpits, and haul the corpse from its place of eternal slumber. It was, decried one paper, a 'dreadful crime by which the tables of the dissecting-rooms have been so wastefully covered with subjects.' Dreadful it might have been, but it proved lucrative. A fresh body might fetch as much as 16 guineas (roughly £2,200 or $2,800 today).[6]

To prevent such abominations, churchyards and cemeteries employed night watchmen and built 'high walls topped with broken glass or iron spikes.' It was not uncommon for the bereaved to stand sentry, night after night, at the graves of their recently deceased loved ones until certain the body had turned to rot.[7] One innovative gentleman with a mind for engineering pitched his idea to the press. Reported *The Northampton Mercury* on 27 February 1830:

> **Preservation of the Dead.** – A country mechanic, for the preservation of the bodies of deceased persons from the hands of resurrectionists, says, 'I can fit a 6lb grenade, to which is attached a single spring and percussion cap, to the inside of a coffin, in such a manner to preserve it free of moisture, and keep it effective for three months; during which period, should the resurrectionist attempt the removal of either the corpse or the coffin, instant death would in all probability be the result.' Resurrectionists beware![8]

Some went beyond robbing graves. Sixteen people died at the hands of the infamous William Burke and William Hare in Edinburgh over a ten-month period in 1828. Smothering and suffocation – what became known as 'burking' – was their preferred method of killing, as it left no signs of violence. A local anatomist, ignorant of where the bodies came from, purchased them for his lectures. Upon the duo's capture in October, Hare turned Crown's evidence and escaped the gallows. Burke swung on 28 January 1829. Anatomy Professor Alexander Monro at the University of Edinburgh publicly dissected Burke's body four days later.[9]

The bell of the dissecting room at London's recently established King's College in the Strand rang at 11:45 a.m. on Saturday, 5 November 1831. William Hill, the room's porter, answered the door to Jonathan Bishop and James May. He knew both men, as he had purchased corpses from them in the past. May asked Hill if he was in need of any dissecting material.

'Not particularly,' Hill replied – but, out of curiosity, asked, 'What have you got?'

'A male subject,' May said, his voice slurred with drink. The body was that of a fourteen-year-old boy they'd be willing to part with for twelve guineas.

Hill balked at the price. He said the school had no present need for cadavers, but he would check with the demonstrator of anatomy to be sure. He invited May and Bishop inside, out of the wet November gloom, and fetched Richard Partridge. Like Hill, Partridge refused to pay the asking price but countered with nine guineas.

'I'll be damned if it should go under ten guineas,' May spat and staggered outside.

'Never mind him,' Bishop said, 'he's drunk. It shall come in for nine guineas.'

Bishop and May wandered off into the grey afternoon and returned between two and three o'clock. They brought with them two colleagues – Thomas Williams and Michael Shields – and a large hamper. Hill invited them in. Bishop and May lugged the hamper into an adjoining room and opened it to reveal a body wrapped in canvas. May, in his drunken stupor, 'turned the body very carelessly out of the sack.'[10]

The body, both men said, was 'a good one.' Hill noticed it looked 'particularly fresh' and wondered aloud what took the life of one so young. Bishop and May shrugged. 'It appeared different from a body that had laid in a coffin,' Hill later said. 'The left arm was turned up towards the head, and the fingers of the hand were firmly clenched.' A cut on the dead boy's forehead aroused Hill's suspicions, but Bishop said it had just occurred when the body fell from its wrapping. Hill, not sure what to make of things, summoned Partridge to have a look.[11]

Partridge, accompanied by some of his students, entered the room and examined the delivery. 'The eyes seemed very fresh, and the lips were full of blood,' Partridge recalled. 'The chest looked as if blood had recently been wiped from it.' Partridge excused himself and his colleagues under the guise of collecting the funds to complete the transaction. One of the students couldn't help but notice the body 'corresponded with the description of a boy said to be missing, given in handbills posted up about the streets.'[12]

Partridge returned and told Bishop and May he only had a £50 note and some change – but, if they were willing to wait, he'd break the larger bill.

'Give me what money you have,' Bishop suggested, 'and I shall call on Monday for the remainder.'

May offered to take the £50 and get it changed somewhere.

'Oh no,' Partridge said, smiling, and left the room. He returned fifteen minutes later with an inspector and several constables from F (Covent Garden) Division, who took the four men into custody. May, emboldened by liquor, struck one officer several times before being subdued. The constables dragged the men – and the hamper with the body stashed back inside – to the Covent Garden station, where a battered May crawled in on all fours 'with his smock frock over his head'. The division's senior officer, Superintendent Joseph Sadler Thomas, ordered the four prisoners placed in a room together.[13]

'What do you have to say?' Thomas asked May. 'You're being charged with having come into possession of the subject in an improper manner.'

May scoffed. 'I have nothing to do with it. The subject is that gentleman's,' he said, jabbing a finger in Bishop's direction. 'I merely accompanied him to get the money for it.'

Thomas asked Bishop whose body it was.

'The body is mine,' Bishop said, 'and if you want to know how I got it, you may find it out if you can.'

Thomas asked Bishop what he did for a living.

'I am a bloody body snatcher.'[14]

Thomas left the men and went to the back of the station house to view the corpse. Two constables lifted the dead boy from the hamper, gently removed his body from the sack and laid him on a table. 'It struck me as the body of a person who had recently died,' Thomas said. 'I perceived that the teeth had been extracted from it.'[15]

Beyond that, it had no tales to tell.

A heavy police guard conveyed the prisoners to Bow Street Magisterial Court that evening. 'From the appearances on the body of the deceased and the fact that two of the prisoners are well known body-snatchers, the rumour almost instantly spread that the unfortunate boy was "burked" by the prisoners,' reported *The Times.* 'The crowds which surrounded the office and pressed forward to hear the examination were far greater than we ever remember to have seen on any former occasion.'[16]

The morbidly curious packed the room to capacity. Thomas, sworn in, stood at the bar and said he was charging the four men in custody with 'the murder of a boy aged about fourteen years whose name I am unable to state.' Although he had no evidence at present, he said, representatives from King's College would attest to the prisoners trying to sell the body. Thomas told the court that Bishop, since his arrest, had made a statement saying he had acquired the body from Guy's College.

'I sent a message to Guy's Hospital with a request as to know whether a boy answering the description of the deceased had died there lately,' Thomas explained. 'I received for answer a slip of paper stating that since the 28th three persons had died there, that one was a woman and the other two were males aged 33 and 37. Bishop's statement as to where he obtained the body cannot be true.'

Asked if they had anything to say in their defence, Bishop said nothing. May, 'dressed in a countryman's frock and who appeared perfectly careless during the examination,' played ignorant. 'It is not my subject,' he said, 'and I know nothing about it.' Williams and Shields both asserted their innocence.

The magistrate ordered the prisoners be remanded into custody and asked that an autopsy be performed 'to come to a positive conclusion as to the cause of death.'

'The prisoners were then removed to the cells at the back of the office,' wrote one reporter, 'and as they passed from the bar, they were groaned and hissed at by some persons in the office.'[17]

Dr George Beaman, a local surgeon, performed a cursory examination of the body that night at the station. The boy, in Beaman's estimation, appeared to have been dead no more than thirty-six hours. 'The face appeared swollen,' he noted, 'the tongue swollen, the eyes prominent and bloodshot, and the tongue was protruding between the lips.' He observed a wound, about an inch long, above the left eyebrow. Blood still oozed from the cut, but the forehead showed no sign of fracture. 'The teeth had been all extracted,' he observed, 'the gums bruised, and portions of the jawbone had been broken and removed with the teeth.'[18]

The next morning, Saturday, 6 November, a sad and desperate procession filed past the child. Thomas had already received eight requests to view the deceased from parents of missing boys 'aged thirteen to fourteen.' 'The parents could in no way account for their absence,' he said, 'and they all appeared in the greatest distress of mind. One of the boys so lost was deaf and dumb.'[19]

Not one of the distraught parents claimed the mystery boy as their own. An Italian couple, however, claimed they recognized him but didn't know his name. A street musician named Joseph Paragalli and his wife said they had known the boy in passing for the last two years. He was Italian and often wandered the streets carrying a cage suspended from his neck with two white mice in it. They last saw him strolling down Oxford Street at quarter past noon on Tuesday, 1 November.[20]

It wasn't much, but it was something.

That evening, Beaman – in the company of Richard Partridge and King's College anatomy professor Herbert Mayo – performed the post-mortem. The body showed 'not the slightest marks of violence' to the throat or chest. Examining the upper part of the skull, however, Beaman detected blood right beneath the scalp indicative of 'violence or accident'. He turned the body over and peeled away the skin from the lower part of the head to just beneath the shoulders, revealing 'three to four ounces' of coagulated blood 'amongst the muscles there'. The spine was not fractured but, removing a vertebral arch to examine the spinal marrow, Beaman found 'a quantity of coagulated blood . . . within the spinal canal, pressing upon the marrow.'[21]

The heart had no blood in it; an indication of sudden death. The stomach contained the partially digested contents of a meal, which reeked of rum. 'Digestion was going on at the time of death,' Beaman said. 'I should think that death occurred about three hours after the meal.' He wiped his bloody hands on the front of his leather apron. 'From the whole of my observations on the body,' he said, 'I ascribe the death to a blow given on the back of the neck.'[22]

On the morning of Tuesday, 8 November, Superintendent Thomas responded to a summons from a dentist named Thomas Mills, who had a practice at 39, Bridge House Place. Mills had read about the dead boy in the newspaper – particularly the details regarding the missing teeth. He produced a small cloth pouch and emptied it onto a table. Thomas looked down and saw a scattering of teeth. Mills said that on Friday, 4 November, a man walked into his practice and offered to sell twelve human teeth, 'six for each jaw', for a guinea. Mills examined the teeth, noticed one was chipped and questioned whether they all came from the same mouth.

'Upon my soul to God,' the man replied, 'they all belonged to one head and not long since.'

The man explained the teeth had come from the fresh body of a boy fourteen or fifteen years old, who hadn't been buried. Mills offered twelve shillings for the set. The man accepted the offer and left.[23]

'On examining them afterwards,' Mills said, 'I found that some part of the flesh of the gums was so firmly attached to them that I imagined they had been violently taken from the head. I found great difficulty in detaching it from them.'[24]

With most likely the dead boy's teeth in his possession, Thomas headed back to the station house. The coroner's inquest was scheduled to begin that afternoon at the Unicorn pub in Henrietta Street.

'The room in which the inquest took place,' remarked one spectator, 'was crowded almost to suffocation.' Three days of medical testimony and a recitation of the facts by Thomas failed to shed any light on the boy's identity and how he suffered such a fate. The four accused certainly did nothing to elucidate the matter. Bishop strayed from his previous statements and said he had not acquired the body from Guy's Hospital, but had actually pilfered it from a grave. 'The reason I don't like to say the grave I took it out of,' he said, 'is because the watchmen about the grounds entrusted me – and, being men of family, I don't wish to deceive them.'[25]

Unmoved, the jury returned a verdict against all four of 'wilful murder against some person or persons unknown' and urged Scotland Yard to conduct 'a strict inquiry into the case.'[26]

The investigation moved with surprising rapidity, confined mostly as it was to the house Bishop and Williams shared at 3, Nova Scotia Gardens, Bethnal Green, and the drinking establishments they frequented. One such watering hole was the Fortune of War at 4, Giltspur Street opposite St Bartholomew's Hospital and a known gathering place for resurrectionists. Here, grave robbers sold their wares in a back room 'where, on benches round the walls, the bodies thus obtained by the snatchers were placed, duly labelled with their names, and awaiting the appraisement of the surgeons.'[27]

A waiter said the accused spent the evening of 4 November in the pub. Sometime around 9 p.m., May approached the bar holding something wrapped in a handkerchief. 'I saw him pour water upon the handkerchief and rub it with his hand,' the waiter said. 'He afterwards opened the handkerchief, and I saw the teeth. I observed to him that they appeared to be young ones.' May agreed and told the waiter he hoped to fetch at least £2 for them. Bishop and Williams returned to the pub at eight o'clock the following morning and were joined by Shields. The waiter heard them discussing over pints of ale where to find a hamper. One of them suggested St Bartholomew's Hospital. Bishop left the pub and returned with a hamper a short time later. All three men then walked out together. 'I never saw them again until they were in custody,' the waiter said.[28]

Thomas and his team of officers followed the morbid trail from one witness statement to the next. They were directed to a coachman named James Seagrave, who said he'd been approached by the accused on the evening of 4 November outside a pub called the King of Denmark in the Old Bailey.

'Having put the nose-bag on my horse,' he said, 'I went into the watering house to take my tea.' He had just settled down at the bar when he heard someone call his name. He looked up to see Bishop, with May in tow, approaching. 'He took me on one side and said he wanted me to fetch a "stiff 'un", which I understood to mean a dead body,' Seagrave said, adding they offered to pay him a guinea for his efforts. He returned to his spot at the bar to consider the offer. 'Some person in the room jogged me by the elbow and hinted that the men were "snatchers", and I determined not to go with them.'[29]

Boiled down to the basics, the information Thomas acquired in the course of his inquiries was this: On Friday, 4 November, the accused had the body of a young boy they wished to sell. Sometime between nine and ten o'clock that morning, May sold the boy's teeth to dentist Thomas Mills. That evening, one of Bishop's neighbours saw the accused loading a sack into a yellow carriage in front of Bishop's cottage in Bethnal Green. 'The sack appeared to be heavy,' the neighbour said, 'as if there was something heavy in it.' The neighbour watched the men drive off 'to the city.' They attempted to sell the corpse to several institutions, only to be turned away. The dissecting room porter at Guy's Hospital told the men he wasn't interested. 'You know I can't take it,' he said. 'I purchased two from you yesterday, which I did not want.' He did, however, let them store the body at the hospital overnight. They retrieved it the following morning, packed it in the newly acquired hamper and crossed the river to King's College and their eventual arrest.[30]

None of this answered how Bishop and his crew came to possess the body. Who was the boy, where did he come from and how did he meet his end? He was buried in a pauper's grave in St Paul's, Covent Garden on Friday, 11 November. *The Times* voiced its outrage in a charged editorial, accusing Bishop and the others of multiple murders:

> If wretches have picked up from our streets an unprotected foreign child, and prepared him for the dissecting knife by assassination – if they have prowled about in order to obtain Subjects for a dissecting room – then we may be assured this is not a solitary crime of its kind.[31]

On the same day the boy was buried, Thomas and Police Constable Joseph Higgins went to Bishop's home and arrested Bishop's wife, Sarah, and their daughter, Rhoda, on the pretext they knew about the murder. Upon arriving at the run-down cottage, Thomas was struck by its appearance: 'It is a sort of cottage in a lonely situation; not a lamp within a quarter mile of the spot, and in a ruinous condition, the back door opening upon a sort of waste or commons.'[32]

A search of the home turned up several chisels and two wrenches, which Sarah admitted 'were used for opening coffins'. Higgins also found a bradawl – a hand tool not unlike a small sharpened screwdriver – caked in dried blood. 'I asked her for what purpose it was used,' Higgins said, 'and she made no answer; on which I observed it was used for punching out teeth.' The two women were subsequently charged with being accessories after the fact.[33]

Thomas, Higgins and other F Division officers, including 'one who has been bred a gardener', returned to the cottage on the morning of Saturday, 19 November, armed with shovels 'in the expectation that something more might be discovered connected with the horrible traffic in which the prisoners had been engaged'. The men spent more than six hours digging. From the scrap of wasteland that passed as a garden, the men dug up 'a jacket, a pair of trousers, and a small shirt'. In another area, they uncovered 'a blue coat, a drab-striped waistcoat, altered from man's size as to fit a boy, and a pair of trousers with the braces attached to them'. The items, buried a foot underground, 'were covered in cinders and ash'. The house had more secrets to reveal near the outside privy at the back of the garden, where the officers dug up bits of human flesh and a scalp – believed to be that of a woman – still covered in long, dark brown hair.[34]

The same day the house was searched and only eight days after the child's burial, the Yard disinterred 'The Italian Boy'. A man named Augustine Brun, 'an elderly Birmingham-based padrone', had come to London to view the body. He believed it to be that of a young lad named Carlo Ferrari he had brought to England two years prior. Brun had taken charge of the boy after Carlo's father signed him over 'for a fee'. Brun last saw the child in July 1830, when he signed the boy over to another master. Speaking through an interpreter, Brun peered hesitantly into the open coffin and said he believed it to be Carlo – although he couldn't be completely sure. 'The face was so disfigured,' he said, 'and the absence of the teeth so altered the usual expression of the boy's countenance.'[35]

That evening, Thomas reported the findings of his investigation to Magistrate Minshull at Bow Street. The report, notes one account, 'was of such a character as to strike the worthy Magistrate with astonishment and terror.' The accused appeared in front of Minshull three days later to hear the new evidence against them. Based on the discoveries at Nova Scotia Gardens, Bishop, May and Williams faced an additional count of 'wilful murder of a male person whose name is unknown.' Their one-day trial got underway at the Old Bailey on Friday, 2 December. Shields, luckier than his cohorts, was set free, as the evidence 'declared that all he knew of the matter was that he carried the hamper' containing the boy's body to King's College.[36]

'No trial that has ever taken place, whether in this or any other court of criminal judicature in this country, attracted more public attention or excited a deeper feeling of interest in the minds of individuals than the present,' reported one London paper. 'And certainly no persons ever stood at the bar of justice before a solemn tribunal, to answer a charge involving the grave question of life and death, respecting whom less commiseration was manifested than the three men who were put upon their trial this day.'[37]

They pleaded not guilty at 9 a.m., were convicted by 8:30 p.m., and sentenced to death thirty minutes later. The wheels of justice turned quickly with the execution scheduled for Monday, 5 December. The day before they hanged at Newgate Prison, Bishop and Williams confessed – with Bishop providing the lengthiest account of their crime. He said the boy was not Italian at all, but a Lincolnshire lad he and Williams picked up in the Bell pub in Smithfield on the night of 3 November. They lured him back to Bishop's place with the promise of work. At the house, with everyone else in bed, the men gave the boy rum laced with laudanum. He chased it down with some beer and was soon unconscious on the floor. The two men dragged the boy out back, tied cord around his ankles and then lowered him headfirst into a well in the garden. 'He was nearly wholly in the water in the well – his feet just above the surface,' Bishop said. 'Williams fastened the other end of the cord round the paling to prevent the body getting beyond our reach. The boy struggled a little with his arms and legs in the water, and the water bubbled for a minute.'[38]

They left him submerged for forty-five minutes before pulling him up, stripping him naked, and burying the clothes. They hid the body in the washhouse and retired for the night. They spent much of the next day, Friday, 5 November, at the Fortune of War and ran into May there that morning. 'I knew May,' Bishop said, 'but had not seen him for about a fortnight before.' The men drank rum and discussed the going price for a fresh body, deciding nine guineas seemed fair. They ventured out late that morning to find a cabman to help them transport their product around town. Unable to find a driver, they hired a yellow wagon in Farringdon Street and returned to Nova Scotia Gardens to show May what they had. May, unaware the boy had been murdered, asked if he could have the teeth. Bishop agreed and provided May the bradawl to knock them out.

'It is the constant practice to take the teeth out first,' Bishop said, 'because if the body be lost, the teeth are saved. After the teeth were taken out, we put the body in a bag and took it to the chariot.' Then off they went to try and sell what Bishop referred to as 'the thing' – an effort that met with dire consequences.[39]

Williams signed a statement attesting Bishop's confession to be true. The pair also admitted to murdering, in the same fashion, a homeless woman named Fanny Pigburn, who they found on the night of 9 October sheltering in a Shoreditch doorway. They sold her body to Grainger's Anatomical Theatre for eight guineas. Two weeks later, they stumbled across a boy named Cunningham

An 1831 sketch of John Bishop, Thomas Williams and James May
– the 'London Burkers'.

sleeping in the Smithfield pig market. They dispatched him in the usual fashion and sold his corpse to St Bartholomew's Hospital, pocketing another eight guineas.[40]

The fact May had not been involved in the actual killings earned him a twelfth-hour reprieve from the hangman. Bishop and Williams, blessed with no such luck, mounted the scaffold on the morning of 5 December outside Newgate Prison in front of a jeering crowd of thousands. 'In less than two minutes after they appeared on the scaffold,' noted *The Preston Chronicle*, 'the usual signal was given and the drop fell. Bishop appeared to die instantaneously, but Williams struggled several minutes.'[41]

The bodies were left to hang for an hour, as was customary, before being cut down. In death, the two men found a legitimate purpose. Bishop's body went to the dissection room at King's College; Williams's corpse provided raw material for medical studies at St Bartholomew's Hospital.

Some loose threads remained. Scotland Yard never established the identity of 'The Italian Boy'. Bishop's claim that the victim hailed from Lincolnshire is questionable, as there were no reports out of the county of a missing child. The number of victims who died at the hands of the 'London Burkers' – as Bishop and Williams became known – also riled the public. Rumours suggested Bishop wished to confess to as many as sixty murders, but that could very well have been hyperbole to sell newspapers. Despite these lingering questions, the case proved an early feather in Scotland Yard's cap.[42]

The crime so intrigued the public, the Yard convinced Bishop's landlord to open the murder house in Nova Scotia Gardens as a tourist destination to prevent it 'being rushed by the hundreds who were thronging the narrow pathways of the gardens and straining to get as close to the seat of horror as possible.' Admission booths were set up in front of the property, 'where only the genteel were admitted'. Souvenir hunters picked the house bare. Reported *The Examiner* magazine with more than a hint of dryness: 'The landlord upon whose premises a murder is committed is now-a-days a made man . . . If a Bishop will commit a murder for £12, which seems the average market price, the owner of a paltry tenement might find it worthwhile to entice a ruffian to make it the scene of a tragedy, for the sale of the planks and timbers in toothpicks, at a crown each.'[43]

The case had a lasting impact. Partly in response to the murder, Parliament passed the Anatomy Act of 1832 (an attempt to pass anatomy legislation four years prior had failed). It aimed to subvert the illegal corpse trade by tapping into a new market: the poor. It allowed for the unclaimed bodies of the destitute to be donated for legitimate medical research. Other laws followed until the Human Tissue Act of 2004 consolidated all previous amendments and legislation on the subject to regulate 'the removal, storage, use and disposal of human tissue.'[44]

2

Severed

'The Edgware Road Tragedy'. A decapitated head on display.

Scotland Yard, still in its infancy, ventured into the 1830s without a plainclothes detective branch. The concept of the civilian-dressed officer inflamed public paranoia and the fear of state surveillance. Police, the argument went, could easily act as 'spies'. The Yard, nevertheless, used plainclothes officers for security purposes on occasions such as the Lord Mayor's Show. This 'was only a small step away from using them to listen to conversations in public houses or even to infiltrate meetings of various kinds'. The issue sparked a controversy in May 1833 when a sergeant named Popay, posing as a starving artist, infiltrated the 'subversive' National Union of the Working Classes, an organization promoting socialist ideas for the betterment of the working man. Popay learned of an upcoming meeting to be held on 13 May at Coldbath Fields, 'a piece of waste land by the Clerkenwell House of Correction' in the borough of Islington.[1]

The Yard mobilized 600 constables, who, according to one witness, marched on the meeting 'in military order and in a dense array'. 'The contest while it lasted was terrific,' reported *The London Courier and Evening Gazette*, 'and some truncheons loaded with lead were brandished by the mob.' The police beat back the enraged crowd in less than five minutes, but not without casualties. In the wake of the tumult, Police Constable Robert Culley lay on the ground 'bleeding profusely from a stab wound in the left side, and in ten minutes afterwards the poor fellow breathed his last.'[2]

A coroner's inquest into Culley's death resulted in a verdict of 'justifiable homicide', much to Scotland Yard's disgust. A Parliamentary Select Committee convened in the aftermath also castigated police. It accused Popay of 'carrying concealment and deceit into the intercourse of private life'. Plainclothes officers, the committee opined, should be used only for detecting or solving crime, as opposed to merely preventing it. Any other reason 'was most abhorrent to the feeling of the people and most alien to the spirit of the constitution'. Even so, the idea of establishing a plainclothes detective branch remained a discomforting one. Scotland Yard was still very much on 'probation' and working to establish the public's trust. Indeed, as one early history of the Yard puts it, 'the Popay incident discouraged the Commissioners from venturing on what was felt to be dangerous ground.'[3]

Although primarily tasked with preventing but not detecting crime, the fledgling force was 'obligated to investigate any crime brought to [its] attention'. It had shown investigative prowess in the case of 'The Italian Boy' and would do so again in what came to be known as 'The Edgware Road Tragedy'.[4]

It began on the afternoon of Wednesday, 28 December 1836. A bricklayer named Robert Bond discovered something unpleasant beneath a paving stone at a construction site in Edgware Road at the end of Oxford Street. The stone, measuring four feet long and three feet wide, was leaning at an angle against a flagstone wall. Bond noticed 'something dark behind it' as he walked past. He bent down and saw a coarse canvas sack wrapped in cord.[5]

Bond heaved the paving stone aside and saw a pool of blood, about nine inches in diameter, had seeped from the mystery package. 'I at first thought it was meat,' Bond said, 'but on feeling it and pulling it about, I felt a hand.' He called over a colleague, who urged him to open it. He untied the cord, peered inside then scrambled back in disgust. 'We found it to be the trunk of a human body,' he said. 'The arms were folded across the breast and tied down.' His panicked cries of 'Police! Police!' drew the attention of Police Constable Samuel Pegler, S (Hampstead) Division, who was patrolling the opposite side of the road.[6]

Near the sack, Pegler observed what looked like part of a child's frock and a torn shred of towel, both soaked with blood and perhaps put in place to staunch the leaking. The men loaded the grisly heap into a cart and wheeled it to the nearby Paddington Workhouse, which provided employment and shelter to the poor. There, they deposited the remains in the 'dead-house'. The parish surgeon, Dr Girdwood, was promptly summoned. 'The body was tied round with a cord, binding the arms flat across the abdomen, squeezing them deep upon the surface,' Girdwood noted, 'and in this manner it was stuffed into the bag.'[7]

What remained of the body was that of a middle-aged woman. Her head had been severed three inches above the sternum and the legs hacked off right beneath the hip joint. 'The thigh bone on both sides,' Girdwood said, 'is sawn through from within, outwardly half through, and then broken off'. The doctor noticed superficial cuts on the left thigh and right side of the neck. Opening the body, he found it drained of blood but all the organs healthy in appearance. 'The bloodless state of the body induces me to consider that the mutilation must have taken place shortly after death,' he said. There was no evidence of disease or surgical scarring to suggest an underlying health concern, meaning the woman most likely died suddenly.[8]

Girdwood guessed the woman to be anywhere from thirty to forty years old. Based on the length of her arms and trunk, she probably stood about five feet eight inches tall. The fourth finger of her left hand bore the indentation of a ring – and the hands themselves, calloused with dirt beneath the nails, suggested she was 'engaged in household work'. It had recently snowed, and the frigid weather made it hard to determine the cause of death. The body showed no signs of decay. 'It might have lain in the situation in which it was found for three or four days,' Girdwood said, 'the severity of the frost and snow preserving the fresh appearance which it exhibits.'[9]

While Girdwood examined the body, PC Pegler braved the cold and returned to the construction site. On the other side of the flagstone wall where the body was found, workmen busied themselves putting up a row of nine detached homes called Canterbury Villas, four of which had not yet evolved beyond wooden frames. He searched the unfinished buildings and found nothing – but, sparked by the day's discovery, the memory of something he saw four nights prior on Christmas Eve flared with a sudden relevance.[10]

It was eight o'clock and Pegler was walking his regular beat past the construction site when he noticed 'an old chaise cart, covered with mud, drawn up, with the horse's head towards town'. It was parked alongside a footpath that ran parallel to the flagstone wall. He kept a distant watch on it for twenty minutes before it drove off into the night. Nothing, at that time, seemed amiss – but now he wondered. Had he seen the killer dumping the body? When the sack was found, snow had blown in at each end of the stone that concealed it from view. There was snow on top of the sack but none beneath it, and it hadn't started to snow until ten o'clock on Christmas morning.[11]

But even if he had seen the killer, what could he do about it now?

By ten o'clock on the evening of the twenty-eighth, Pegler and Inspector George Feltham of neighbouring T (Kensington) Division had been put in charge of the case. At a time when an officer's only investigative tools were his wits and powers of observation, Feltham and Pegler faced a daunting challenge. They had nothing on which to build an investigation. 'No discovery had been made of the other parts of the body,' it was noted two days after the initial discovery, 'nor had any clue been obtained likely to lead to the detection of the perpetrators of the horrid deed.'[12]

Reported *The Times* on Friday, 30 December:

> Since Wednesday afternoon, the greatest excitement has pre-
> vailed in the parish of Paddington and its neighbourhood in
> consequence of the discovery of the body of a female near the
> Pine Apple Toll-gate on Edgware Road in a horribly mutilated
> state, and under circumstances which leave no doubt that she
> has been inhumanely murdered, and her body afterwards
> mutilated to prevent its recognition.[13]

Indeed, not since 'The Italian Boy' had a murder caused such
sensation. A large crowd maintained vigil around the Paddington
Workhouse, and 'numerous applications were made by medical
gentlemen to view the remains.' Hundreds of people visited the
crime scene and chipped away pieces of the stone wall to keep
as souvenirs – but for all the intense curiosity and newspaper
coverage, not one viable lead presented itself. Feltham and Pegler
pursued numerous tips in the days that followed but could not
'obtain any trace as to who the ill-fated woman was.' The investigation limped along for more than a week, the Yard and the
press retreading the same ground, until the morning of Saturday,
7 January 1837.[14]

The Regent's Canal flows just north of central London from the
River Thames in the east to the Grand Union Canal in the west and
connected the capital by water to England's industrial north. At
around eight-thirty on the morning of 7 January, after a coal barge
passed through a canal lock in Stepney, east London, lock keeper
Mathias Rolfe noticed the sluice gates wouldn't close all the way.
Investigating, he discovered the obstruction was a human head
floating in the water.[15]

He retrieved a ladder and lowered himself into the canal. He
reached his hand beneath the water's surface expecting to feel the
body and 'discovered the head was quite detached from any thing

else, and that it was evidently the skull of a female, as there was a large quantity of very long hair upon it.' He grabbed a handful of sodden black hair and brought it ashore. Police took the head to the charnel house at Stepney Church. The surgeon to the hamlet of Mile End Town, acting on the local coroner's orders, examined it and issued the following report:[16]

> The face was very much disfigured from bruises. The lower jaw on the left side fractured; there was an extensive laceration of the left cheek as well as of the upper part of the head. These in all probability have been done since death, either by its being jammed in the locks or by boats in the canal. The right eye is knocked out, but that appears to have been done after death. The head had been very dexterously cut off with some sharp instrument . . . The hair is dark and slightly grey, and I should think her age to have been from forty-five to fifty.[17]

He guessed the head had been in the water four to five days. It was placed in a basket and delivered to Inspector Feltham at the Hermitage Road Police Station in Paddington at ten o'clock that evening. Early the next morning, the inspector brought the head to the Paddington Workhouse. [18]

The torso, having been interred in a pauper's grave in Paddington churchyard 'because the smell arising from it became very offensive', had to be exhumed. Dr Girdwood gave the head a good once-over. 'The eyebrows are well marked,' he wrote, 'and, with the eyelashes, which are not very long, are of a dark brown colour. The eye is grey with a shade of hazel in it. The nose is at the upper part flat and a short way above the point is depressed . . . The profile struck all of us as being very much that of the lower order of Irish.' The head had been sawn off at the fifth cervical bone and, when aligned with the torso's neck, matched perfectly. Still, it provided no answers as to her identity.[19] And so Feltham made a suggestion, as reported in *The Evening Standard*:

The head . . . which has been preserved in spirits by the parochial surgeon, is in possession of the authorities of Paddington, where all persons who have lost relatives or friends will be afforded every facility of viewing it for the purpose of identification.[20]

The head, its features decomposed and distorted, sat in a pickling jar on a shelf in the Paddington Workhouse to be gazed upon. Members of the public who had a legitimate reason to view the gruesome artefact could, though many wished to do so out of macabre curiosity. No one recognized her.

The investigation, in danger of stagnating, received another jolt on Thursday, 2 February. Two labourers clearing some marshy ground along Coldharbour Lane in Camberwell, south London, came across a coarse sack tied with rope 'concealed amidst a heap of weeds and rushes'. When they cut the binding, a pair of human legs fell from the bundle. The men scrambled from the brush and ran to the Brixton Police Station, a mere 300 yards away. Several constables went to retrieve the remains while another notified the local surgeon.[21]

One leg had been sawn off at the hip joint, close to the body, the other further down, 'so that a portion of the upper part of the thigh must have been left attached to the body in the form of a stump'. The legs appeared 'well formed' with neatly trimmed toenails. 'The upper portion of one of the thighs, near the hip joint, appeared to have been gnawed by a rat,' the surgeon noted, 'but the limbs were not much decayed.' They were taken to the Paddington Workhouse and examined by Girdwood, who had removed the upper thigh bones from the trunk and kept them in his possession should the legs ever turn up. Now, with the appendages on a worktable in front of him, he was most impressed. 'Altogether, in its general character,' he observed, 'it may be said to be a handsomely proportioned female limb.' He carefully aligned the left and right thigh bones with the corresponding legs and found they matched 'exactly in all irregularities of their half-sawn, half-broken surfaces.'[22]

The Yard now had a complete body but no name to go with it. Undaunted, Feltham and Pegler pursued one dead end after another. A steady stream of people requested to view the head, believing it to be that of a missing loved one, only to say they didn't recognize the lifeless face. They interviewed coachmen and bar-keeps, prostitutes and shop owners, in search of that one vital clue. 'The police,' reported *The Northampton Mercury* on 18 March, 'are constantly exerting themselves to the utmost, in order to trace out, if possible, the perpetrators of the sanguinary and inhuman act.'[23]

The break they desperately needed came on Friday, 24 March, when a man named William Gay met with Feltham at the Hermit-age Road Police Station. He told the inspector he had last seen his sister, Hannah Brown, aged forty-seven, the Thursday before Christmas and had heard nothing from her since. 'We did not agree,' he said, 'she being a very odd temper.' They had moved to the city from Norwich two years prior. He went to work in a broker's shop, while Hannah found employment with a hatter. She had plans to marry a cabinet-maker named James Greenacre, whom Gay didn't know much about. Greenacre had ended the engagement just before Christmas, Gay said, because he found out Hannah 'had deceived him in regard to money matters.'[24]

Although Gay and Hannah 'were at variance,' they saw each other often. Having not heard from her now in three months, he wondered if she might be the woman mentioned in the newspapers. Could he, by any chance, view the head? Feltham accompanied him to the workhouse and showed him the jar. Gay studied it for only a brief moment. 'Oh God,' he cried, 'my dear sister. She has been murdered.'

Feltham asked Gay if he was sure.

'The left ear is torn, as my sister's was,' Gay said, 'and the brown hair, mixed with a few greys, is like hers. I have no doubt of the head being my sister's.'[25]

Feltham secured an arrest warrant for James Greenacre on Saturday, 25 March, and – with Pegler at his side – tracked him to his home at No. 1, St Alban's Place, Lambeth. He entered on his own accord and found Greenacre in bed with his lover, Sarah Gale. It was one o'clock in the morning. 'I'm an inspector of police,' Feltham said, 'and hold a warrant for your apprehension on suspicion of having murdered Hannah Brown.'[26]

Greenacre, with a candle in one hand and wearing only his nightshirt, voiced surprise. 'I know no such person.' Searching the home, Pegler found a frock belonging to Gale's young daughter, who was sleeping in one of the bedrooms. The colour and fabric matched the torn fragment of dress found near the sack at the construction site. The officers took the couple and Gale's daughter into custody and placed them in cells at Paddington Station.[27]

'At an early hour,' Feltham said, 'a strange noise was heard in the cell in which the male prisoner was confined; and, on a constable repairing thither, he found him hanging by a handkerchief. He was cut down and life restored with much difficulty.'[28]

The suicide attempt could not stop the inevitable. At noon on Monday, Inspector Feltham escorted Greenacre and Gale to the Marylebone Public Office in Paradise Street to appear before the magistrates. Some 5,000 people crowded the thoroughfare to catch a glimpse of the accused. 'Greenacre is a man about fifty years of age, of middle height and rather stout,' reported *The Evening Standard*. 'He was wrapped up in a brown great-coat; and, without appearing to betray much emotion, gazed at all around.' His attempted hanging had left him 'in a very weak state.' Gale remained at Greenacre's side with her four-year-old in her arms. 'She seemed quite unconcerned about her situation,' the *Standard* observed, 'and was the subject of as much, if not more, attention and interest, if possible, as the other prisoner.'[29]

The inquest didn't go well for Greenacre. 'When I courted Mrs Brown, she told me she could at any time command from three to four hundred pounds,' Greenacre testified. 'I told her I was possessed of property of the same amount, which was not the case; so that there was duplicity on both sides.' He said Hannah came to his lodgings on Christmas Eve, got drunk on rum and confessed to lying about her wealth. Greenacre, in a fit of rage, kicked her chair and sent it and Hannah crashing backwards.

'Her head came with great violence against a lump of wood behind her, which I had been using,' Greenacre said. 'This alarmed me very much. I took her by the hand and lifted her up, and found, to my astonishment, that she was no more.'

Fearful he would be accused of murdering her, he decided not to summon help and instead 'dispose of the body in the manner which has so fully been before the public, thinking it would be the safest and most prudent plan.'[30]

The story caused a sensation in the courtroom. 'At this relation,' said one spectator, 'a thrill of horror ran through the office, and it was some time before silence could be obtained.'[31]

Greenacre told the court Sarah Gale knew nothing about the crime. The magistrate committed both to trial, which got under-way on 8 April. Friends of Hannah, and her brother, testified she was a sober woman and not prone to drinking. Medical experts told the court the injuries evident on the head were not indica-tive of someone simply falling out of a chair. She had most likely died 'from a blow to the front of the head, by which the eye of the deceased was knocked out'.[32]

The jury sat through two days of testimony before adjourning to reach the expected guilty verdict. For being an accessory to the crime by providing Greenacre shelter and comfort, Gale received the now-defunct sentence of exile 'beyond the sea to such a place as His Majesty . . . shall direct and appoint for the term of your natural life.' The judge, in dooming Greenacre to the gallows, did not mince words:

> The appalling details of your dreadful case must be fresh in
> the recollection of all who now hear my voice, and will live

long in the memory and (may I not add?) in the execration of mankind, and generations yet to come will shudder at your guilt. You have, indeed, acquired for yourself a revolting celebrity – an odious notoriety in the annals of cruelty and crime.[33]

Greenacre met his end outside Newgate Prison on 2 May 1837, before the celebratory masses. The night before his execution, he confessed to killing Hannah by throwing a rolling pin at her head, but still maintained the death was accidental. After realizing what he'd done, he pondered his predicament before setting on his grisly course. He cut the dead woman's throat with a bucket placed beneath the neck to catch the blood. When the wound stopped flowing, he dismembered the corpse, stuffed the various parts in a bag and dumped the bucket's contents down the privy. He left the house with the wrapped-up body parts at 7 p.m. and made his way to Stepney, where he tossed the head into the Regent's Canal. Asked how he disposed of the remaining portions of the body, 'he suddenly became very taciturn' and said no more on the matter.[34]

Another case solved.

Scotland Yard was establishing its reputation to the point that in February 1837 – in the midst of the Edgware Road investigation – it received a summons for help from the constabulary in Uxbridge. A fifteen-year-old boy named John Brill, having recently testified against two poachers before the local magistrates, had gone missing and was found beaten to death in the woods three days later. The man who found the body just happened to be the father of one of the poachers. The Yard dispatched Sergeant Charles Ottway to help the local constables. 'This,' notes a history of the force, 'was the first recorded request for a Metropolitan Police officer to be sent to assist an investigation outside the Metropolitan Police District.'[35]

Despite the apprehension of three suspects, the case fell apart due to a lack of evidence. It nevertheless underscored the Yard's growing stature; it was building a name for itself and achieving a certain level of prominence. Indeed, things appeared to be going well – but a series of unrelated and unsolved murders soon threw the Yard's standing into doubt.

3

Unsolved

A string of failures.

On Tuesday, 9 May 1837, four days after James Greenacre's plunge into eternity, another gruesome slaying seized the public's attention. The potboy, or server, at the King's Arms in Frederick Street found twenty-one-year-old barmaid Eliza Davies lying on the pub's first-floor landing, 'her throat cut in a most dreadful manner.' The lad ran to the landlord's bedroom in a panic. It was six-twenty in the morning; the pub had only just opened for the day. [1]

'Eliza is dead!' the potboy shrieked when George Wadley opened his bedroom door. Wadley peered over the boy's shoulder, down the stairs, at the sad wreckage on the landing. Eliza had only knocked on his door twenty minutes prior to get the keys to open the place up. He sent the potboy to fetch medical assistance and the police. A trail of bloody tracks led from the body to the bar downstairs. Wadley followed them and saw Eliza had served at least one customer that morning.[2]

On the edge of the bar was 'a glass half full of ale, a crust of bread and cheese, and a penny piece, as well as the instrument with which the horrid deed had been committed, namely, a table knife, which was smeared with blood.' A pool of blood nearly two feet across glistened on the oilcloth covering the floor. It appeared the killer slit Eliza's throat at the bar, the wound immediately haemorrhaging. She somehow staggered up the stairs, away from her assailant, and collapsed on the landing. 'One of her hands was covered in congealed blood,' notes a crime scene report, 'as if she had placed it to her throat to staunch the vital stream. The head was nearly severed from the body.'[3]

Surgeon Henry Barton examined Eliza within the hour and catalogued the horrific nature of the wound:

> The left side of her face was visible . . . there was a wound in her throat, beginning on the left side, and extending about six inches across the middle of the throat, dividing the windpipe and the whole of the muscles on that side of the neck; the carotid artery and jugular vein were also divided; the soft parts of the neck were cut through to the vertebrae.[4]

Barton believed the killer inflicted the damage with two strokes of the blade. 'I think it probable,' he said, 'that the first cut was inflicted at the bar, and that the man followed her through the kitchen and cut her a second time as she was going up the stairs.'[5] The murder occurred within the boundaries of S (Hampstead) Division. The task of figuring it all out fell to Inspector William Aggs and – fresh off the Greenacre case – Police Constable Samuel Pegler. The Yard's success with the Hannah Brown investigation elevated public expectations.

'The subject seems to have engrossed public attention so much, that nothing else is talked of,' reported *The Morning Advertiser*. 'But at present the affair is veiled in the greatest mystery, which in a few days will probably be cleared up.' Another paper, *The Bell's New Weekly Messenger*, suggested 'it is probable that within 24 hours [the murderer] will be secured.' Certainly, there was some cause for optimism. Unlike the Hannah Brown case, police had a complete body and knew the victim's identity. They also had the description of a possible suspect.[6]

Michael Hitchcock, the potboy, told Aggs and Pegler that a man frequented the pub each morning and took a keen interest in Eliza. He was always the day's first customer. It made her nervous.

'She felt pestered by his being there,' Hitchcock said, adding the man never spoke to Eliza but would watch her intently.

The mystery gentleman spoke with an English accent and said he was a modeller. He stood about five feet ten inches tall and was athletic in build with a fair complexion. Most mornings he wore a threadbare overcoat, a double-breasted waistcoat with dark stripes, fustian trousers and around his neck a black silk handkerchief.[7]

Aggs and Pegler spent the next several days visiting 'the factories of most of the principal modellers and decorators in London' but failed to turn up anyone matching the suspect's description. In the weeks that followed, the two officers covered a fifty-mile radius in their hunt for the killer, no small feat in a time of limited transit options, but their quarry remained elusive. The trail, littered with false leads and fleeting hope, turned cold within a month. Reported *The London Mercury* on Sunday, 11 June: 'Notwithstanding the strenuous endeavours of Inspector Aggs and Police-constable Pegler to discover the retreat of the man who is so strongly suspected of having been the perpetrator of the murder of Eliza Davies, whose diabolical murder has created such a sensation in the public mind, we regret to say that their efforts were, up to a late hour on Saturday night, unattended with success.'[8]

By July, without any new developments to report, the press had moved on to other matters and the case went unsolved.

Nearly one year to the day after the Eliza Davies murder, another Eliza suffered a similar fate. Known as 'the Countess' for her elegant manner, twenty-five-year-old Eliza Grimwood worked as a prostitute. She lived at 12, Wellington Terrace, near Waterloo Bridge, with her lover Matthew Hubbard. Her prowling ground was Drury Lane under the gas-lit theatre marquee. If she brought a man home, Hubbard would retreat to another room, as he did on the night of Friday, 25 May 1838. Eliza returned that evening with 'a well-dressed man, rather tall, and of a gentlemanly appearance'.[9]

Shortly after five the following morning, Hubbard peered into Eliza's bedroom. 'I saw what appeared to me to be a bundle of clothes, but which proved to be [Eliza], who was in a kneeling posture,' he said. 'She was against a chair, which was between the door and the bed. I stood at the door for about a minute. I stooped to pick up what I thought was a craw-fish – but it slipped out of my hand and proved to be the knee of the deceased clotted over with blood.'[10]

Inspector Charles Frederick Field of L (Lambeth) Division took charge of the investigation. The son of a publican, Field harboured theatrical ambitions before joining the Metropolitan Police upon its creation in 1829. He quickly ascended the ranks, 'having a higher standard of education and intelligence than the average recruit', and was soon assigned to the seedy district of Lambeth with its 'bars, theatres, prostitutes and other amusements.' Field entered Eliza's bedroom and watched the examining surgeon at work. He fought to keep his emotions in check, having known Eliza from his time patrolling the streets. 'When I saw the poor Countess (I had known her well to speak to) lying dead with her throat cut on the floor of her bedroom,' he recalled, 'you'll believe me that a variety of reflections calculated to make a man rather low in his spirits came into my head.'[11]

The blade had severed her windpipe and left carotid artery. The killer most likely struck first from behind, attempting to kill Eliza by piercing her spine. A knife wound on the back of the neck commenced 'just below the right ear, dividing the third cervical vertebra leaving the spinal marrow uninjured but lacerating its sheath.' The bone deflected the blade and sent it upwards, 'making a traverse wound.' Removing Eliza's blood-soaked dress, the surgeon uncovered another series of horrors. She had been stabbed just above her left nipple and suffered two deep wounds 'a short distance apart in the abdomen.' The stab wounds, the surgeon said, occurred after death. The weapon, most likely, was a long single-bladed knife.[12]

Field suspected Hubbard of the crime. One of the first constables on the scene noticed Hubbard 'take up seven shillings in silver, which were lying on the dressing table and quietly put them in his pocket.' If the man Eliza was last seen with indeed paid the seven shillings, would he have committed the murder – or, if he did, would he not have taken the silver with him? Try as he might, Field couldn't make the case against Hubbard, and the investigation petered out.[13]

The Morning Post called the slaying an 'inhuman massacre'. At least one paper compared the Grimwood murder and its lack of resolution to that of the 'unfortunate Eliza Davies, who was found with her throat deeply cut in the bar of the King's Arms'. The memory of the crime would resurface five decades later. Reported *The Telegraph* on 6 September 1888, following the death of Mary Ann Nichols at the hands of another knife-wielding maniac: 'Those with retentive memories may be comparing notes regarding the strange similarity existing between the Whitechapel case and that of Eliza Grimwood, who about half a century ago was found in a house in the Waterloo-road under circumstances of closely analogous horror, her murderer never having been discovered.'[14]

There's some speculation Eliza's killing inspired the bludgeoning to death of Nancy at the hands of the vile Bill Sikes in *Oliver Twist*, which Charles Dickens was writing at the time. Sikes eventually receives his comeuppance when he's fatally beaten by an angry mob, but things in fiction often work out. Reality is not so forgiving, and more failures for Scotland Yard followed.[15]

> SEARCH out the foulest, blackest crime,
> Since Abel fell by Cain,
> In any age, in any clime,
> Throughout the murd'rous train.
> And then your aching heart will bleed,
> whilst I the facts recite,
> Of this unequalled, bloody deed;
> Which happen'd on Monday night.[16]

The 'bloody deed' in question was the murder and attempted incineration of watchmaker Robert Westwood on Monday, 3 June 1839. At around midnight, the inhabitants of Princes Street in Soho awoke to the panicked cry of 'Fire! Fire!' Several engines responded to the blaze at No. 35, Westwood's home and business. Firemen found the proprietor 'partly enveloped in the flames' lying alongside his burning bed in the back of the shop. They pulled him into the parlour and doused the fire, only to discover Westwood was dead.[17]

It was evident the fire had not been the cause of death, but a means to get rid of the body. Someone had bludgeoned Westwood above the right eye with a heavy instrument and then gone to work with a blade. 'A dreadful gash' extended from the centre of the back of his neck, around the left side of his throat, stopping at his Adam's apple and severing all the arteries. Another deep wound, starting beneath the left ear, cut across his face and stopped just short of the mouth. Flames had severely scorched the left side of his body. In the passageway leading to the street entrance, police discovered a five-pound iron window weight, about a foot in length, with blood and hair on one end of it. In a sideboard drawer in the parlour, they found a white-handled table knife, 'the blade of which was much stained with blood, and which bore evident marks of having been wiped.'[18]

Westwood's wife, Mary, said her husband had started sleeping downstairs because of a recent burglary. She told Superintendent Baker of C (St James's) Division that she went to bed at eleven o'clock and left Robert downstairs. Shortly thereafter, she heard a scuffling noise she assumed was Robert 'turning the cat out of the room, as was his general custom before he went to bed.' There followed, several minutes later, loud groaning and the sound of the street door slamming. Alarmed, Mary got out of bed and asked her girl-servant to investigate. The girl went downstairs 'and on entering the parlour was almost suffocated by a dense cloud of smoke.'

She ran into the street and asked a passing gentleman to yell 'Fire!' – extreme shock having rendered her almost speechless.[19]

A review of the shop's inventory revealed a considerable amount of merchandise had been stolen: '41 gold watches, 45 silver watches, 25 gold watch chains, 42 silver ditto' and an assortment of gold and silver bracelets, rings and pins, all valued between £4,000 and £5,000. Baker obtained the serial numbers of the stolen timepieces and ordered his men to pass them out 'too all the pawnbrokers in the metropolis.'[20]

There was a sad irony to all this. Westwood had patented an iron shutter that business owners could pull across their store-fronts to deter would-be burglars. Indeed, Westwood had the contraption installed in front of his shop – and for the crowds that now gathered daily to gawk at the premises, it became a subject of great curiosity. It was reported 'the Duke of Wellington, and the leading gentlemen, bankers and others in London' used the shutters. Much to Westwood's misfortune, however, it seemed the contraption failed in its intended purpose to keep intruders out. 'It is a rather melancholy reflection,' noted *The Globe*, 'to find that the first inventor of additional means of preventing external aggression should himself be the first to find its insecurity.'[21]

Westwood's foreman, Charles La Roche, told Baker the culprit must have possessed some knowledge of the watch trade, for they only stole the valuable timepieces. Armed with such intelligence, they would not sell the watches in London but attempt to offload them on the continent. 'Holland,' he said, 'is the principal market for them.' A passenger could haul the freight to Holland in a trunk without having it inspected by customs.[22]

It seemed to Baker such expertise made La Roche an ideal suspect, but the man's alibi checked out. He was busy moving house on the day of the murder. The challenge in a typical investigation is identifying a suspect. The challenge in the Westwood murder proved to be winnowing the suspect pool down. In the course of his inquiry, Baker's suspicions would fall on Mary Westwood, the girl-servant, and a married couple who, until recently, had been lodgers in the building. And that proved just the beginning. It soon emerged Westwood was a man of 'rather peculiar habits . . . of an obstinate and irritable temper'. This extended not only to his wife, who had applied 'to the magistrates of Marlborough-street police office for protection from his violence', but also his customers.[23]

On one occasion, a sea captain returned a defective watch to Westwood's shop. Westwood 'flew into a violent passion', snatched the watch from the captain's hand, threw it on the ground 'and ultimately stamped on it with great violence.' Another customer who dared question the quality of Westwood's products found himself staring down the barrel of a pistol. The watchmaker 'threatened to blow out the young man's brains if he didn't instantly leave the place.' [24]

Finding someone who didn't have a grievance with Westwood proved a considerable task, as did finding the killer. The case went unsolved despite a promising lead that took one dogged investigator to Europe. An inspector named Nicholas Pearce learned someone had been shopping around a large collection of watches in the coastal town of Gravesend the night after the murder. That same evening, a boat was stolen from the nearby harbour at Ramsgate and seen heading for France. Pearce followed the lead across the Channel to Boulogne, where the trail went cold. His efforts, though futile, established Pearce's reputation for the thrill of the hunt. 'No matter where a criminal went,' notes one Yard history, 'it was believed that Pearce would follow.'[25]

The thirty-nine-year-old Pearce was given 'a roving commission as investigator in certain cases of murder or other serious crimes in the Metropolis.' He had joined the Yard in 1830 as a sergeant, worked his way up to inspector, and would soon be one of its most prominent investigators. Having started his initial career as a Bow Street officer, Pearce exemplified 'the best elements of the old force . . . carried forward by the new'.[26]

The role of Bow Street – London's 'prototype police force' – had by now diminished. Its 'Runners' were no more, disbanded by the Police Act of 1839, which aimed to improve 'the Police in and near the Metropolis' and reduce the city's number of competing forces. It established the Yard's marine division by bringing the Thames River Police into the fold and expanded the Metropolitan Police District, which now covered everything within a fifteen-mile radius of Charing Cross.*[27]

What the Yard still lacked, despite its greater responsibilities, was a detective branch – something that became a point of contention with the murder of Lord William Russell on 6 May 1840. Shortly after seven o'clock that morning, maid Sarah Mancer found Russell's study in disarray. 'His lordship's writing desk had been broken open,' she said, 'and a number of his letters and papers were scattered over the carpet and the hearthrug.' Likewise, in the kitchen, someone had forced open and rummaged through the drawers. She alerted the Swiss valet, twenty-three-year-old François Courvoisier, who rushed to Russell's chambers only to find the 'noble lord' had met an ignoble end. His lordship lay in bed, his 'head deluged in blood.' Russell's cook ran to the nearby police station in Marylebone Lane to raise the alarm. The slaying presented Scotland Yard its most sensational case yet.[28]

Word spread quickly, and a crowd gathered outside Russell's mansion at 14, Norfolk Street in fashionable Mayfair. 'Several noblemen' stopped by to nervously inquire if news of their peer's demise was true. Russell was the uncle of Lord John Russell, former Home Secretary, current Colonial Secretary and future Prime Minister. Considering the victim's social standing, Police Commissioner Richard Mayne oversaw initial inquiries at the scene, which before long thrummed with inspectors, constables

---

* The Bow Street Horse Patrol, vital to thwarting highwaymen on the roads in and out of London, had already merged with the Metropolitan Police in 1836 to create the Metropolitan Mounted Police.

and medical men. Soon, the Home Secretary and Under-Secretary of State would stop by to learn the latest. Mancer and the cook stood quietly in a passageway, watching police bustle back and forth. Courvoisier sat at the dining room table with his head in his hands. 'This is a shocking job,' he moaned. 'I shall lose my place and lose my character.'[29]

Inspectors Henry Beresford and Nicholas Pearce worked their way through the house. In the entrance hall, by the front door, they found 'a silver dish cover, an opera-glass gold mounted, a gold pencil case, a toothpick, and a silver thimble wrapped in a bundle.' Courvoisier told them he had locked the door the night before but, come the horrors of the morning, found it unbolted and only on the latch. More plunder – 'some silver articles and some plated articles' – was found piled in the front parlour. The inspectors entered the kitchen, where a door opened to a courtyard at the back of the house. Pearce noticed marks on the doorjamb.[30]

They were, he believed, a red herring designed to give the appearance of a break-in. 'The socket which receives the bottom bolt was on,' he explained. 'The upper one was forced off. That appeared to me to have been done by some instrument put into the socket when the door was open, and the instrument wrenched both ways to pry it off.'[31]

From the outset, the Yard believed it to be an inside job. 'Some of you in the house have done this deed,' one inspector told the servants.

'If they have,' Courvoisier sneered, 'I hope they will be found out.'[32]

Beresford searched the servants' boxes, the trunks in which they stored their personal possessions, and found in Courvoisier's a chisel. He took it into the kitchen, where the drawers had been pried open and the silverware taken. The chisel matched impressions found in the wood. Courvoisier admitted the chisel was his and that he used it for woodworking. In the pantry's fireplace,

Beresford and Pearce found a bent poker, which matched the markings on the doorjamb.[33]

Officers brought Sarah and the cook upstairs to question them in the attic, away from Courvoisier's accusing gaze. The maid told police Courvoisier had worked for Lord Russell no more than five weeks, but his performance left much to be desired. A recent example occurred the previous day. Lord Russell spent his final afternoon at his club, having left instructions for Courvoisier to send a carriage to pick him up at five. The valet forgot but didn't care. His attitude in general seemed to be one of disdain for Lord Russell's life of privilege.[34]

In the murder room, the blinds half drawn and the shutters closed, a scarlet stain continued spreading across the white bed-clothes. It pooled in the middle of the mattress, soaked through and now formed a puddle – drip by drip – beneath the bed. 'It was running partly from a large gash in the throat,' noted one inspector, 'extending from ear to ear.' A surgeon examined the body as Mayne looked on. The fatal wound cut a glistening red scar from his lord-ship's left shoulder to the trachea, about seven inches long and four to five inches deep, severing all the major vessels in the neck. A single stroke delivered with great force. The ball of Lord Russell's right thumb had been severed, most likely the result of the old man trying to defend himself.[35]

What struck the surgeon and police as odd was the lack of arterial spray and blood splatter elsewhere in the room. Nor, for that matter, was there blood elsewhere in the house. One would expect the killer to have left some trace on his way out the door. Furthermore, if robbery was the motive, why did the culprit abscond with such meagre pickings? Valuables ignored in the bedroom included 'silver dressing articles; a gold-handled cane; a gold pin; and a miniature portrait of a lady, painted on ivory'. In the study, the killer had piled by the door and then left behind 'a silver dish, a silver sugar dredger and a gold pencil case'. Police found it baffling. 'No thief would ever leave this property behind,' said one inspector, eyeing the discarded swag.[36]

The murder panicked London's upper crust. 'The excitement produced in high life by the dreadful event is almost unprecedented,' reported *The Times*, 'and the feeling of apprehension for personal safety increases every hour, particularly among those of the nobility and gentry who live in relative seclusion.' The shockwave packed enough power to rattle Buckingham Palace. 'This is really too horrid!' the twenty-year-old Queen Victoria scribbled in her diary. 'It is an almost unparalleled thing for a person of Ld William's rank, to be killed like that.'[37]

An ever-present crowd loitered outside the murder house, 'besieging the police constables on duty' with endless inquiries. Mayne and his officers returned to the scene the following morning. The pressure on Scotland Yard was intense. His Royal Highness Prince Albert and the Home Secretary dispatched messengers to the house for updates. The best Mayne could tell them was 'the inquiry was still in progress and that some important circumstances were likely to transpire in the course of the day.' Unfortunately, nothing transpired that could shed light on the mystery. Only two months prior, the Yard had failed to identify the killer of an old man named John Templeman, who was bound, blindfolded and beaten to death in his house. Now, two days after the murder of Lord Russell, with no arrests made, the press pounced. Davies, Grimwood, Westwood, Templeman and now his lordship – all unsolved. What, *The Times* wanted to know, were the police doing?[38]

> During no previous period of the modern history of London have five cruel murders been committed within two years without some of the perpetrators having been brought to justice. We feel convinced that it is not from any absence of abhorrence at the crime, that it is not from any desire to

screen or aid the escape of the offenders, that justice has been defeated, but merely from the inadequacy of the means employed to discover the guilty parties.

The focus on patrols and a military-like adherence to rules and regulations, the paper argued, rendered the Yard 'almost incapable of engaging in such inquiries as can alone lead to the discovery of offenders'. It was time for the police to establish a detective bureau. Argued the paper in closing:

This, we are convinced, will be allowed by everyone who considers the constitution of the present police force, a great portion of who are even strangers to the metropolis, and who, however ready to contend with and able to subdue all external demonstrations of criminal violence or riot, are for the most part quite ignorant of the various haunts of the London thieves, and destitute of that sagacity which long experience alone can give of the habits, and manoeuvres, and windings, and infinite intrigues of the pernicious 'corporations' (for so they may be called) of the thorough-bred villains who infest the metropolis and its environs.[39]

It was a most eloquent call to action – and though not untrue, it was premature to lump the Russell inquiry with the failed investigations before it. The same day *The Times* piece ran, Mayne and his men – Pearce among them – returned to 14, Norfolk Street. They brought with them 'several plumbers and other workmen' to search 'every chimney, cellar, drain and gutter attached to the premises, for the purpose of discovering either the weapon . . . or some portion of the stolen property.' While the workmen dismantled and searched, Pearce took another look in the butler pantry and noticed the mortar had been disturbed around the skirting board. He pried the board free and discovered, in a cavity behind it, five gold coins, five gold rings, a wedding band, a silver Waterloo medal and a £10 note. The inspector confronted the valet.[40]

'I have found these things concealed in your pantry,' Pearce said. 'Can you now look me in the face?'

'I know nothing about them,' Courvoisier said. 'I am innocent. My conscience is clear.'

Investigators now discovered other items stashed around the house, including a ring tucked behind a pipe and a gold locket beneath the pantry's stone hearth. The police had enough and arrested Courvoisier on Sunday night for 'the wilful murder of Lord William Russell.' In the weeks that followed, the Yard located the stolen silverware at the Hotel Dieppe in Leicester Square, where

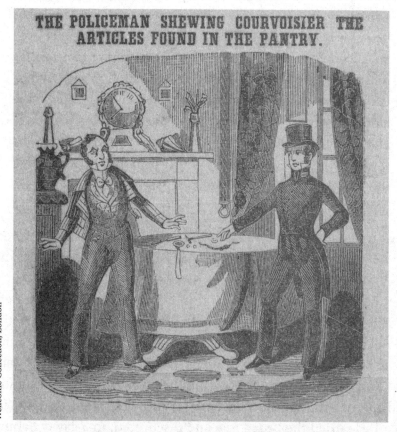

Wellcome Collection, London

The butler did it! From the *Trial, Confession, and Execution of Courvoisier for the Murder of Lord Wm. Russell,* 1840.

Courvoisier once worked as a waiter. In the days after the murder, it transpired, he left a wrapped parcel with the hotel's manageress that contained the stolen items. Despite such evidence, Courvoisier publicly maintained his innocence.[*41]

In the Norfolk village of Grimstone, far removed from events, a surgeon named Robert Blake Overton read in his local newspaper that a bloody palm print had been found on Lord Russell's bedding.

It so happened Overton 'had been doing some private study of handprints' and thought his findings might benefit the investigation. He wrote a three-page letter to Lord Russell's nephew, Lord John Russell, and shared his unique knowledge on the subject. 'It is not generally known that every individual has a peculiar arrangement [on] the grain of the skin,' he wrote. 'I would strongly recommend the propriety of obtaining impressions from the fingers of the suspected individual and a comparison made with the marks on the sheets and pillows.'[42]

He dabbed his fingertips in ink and left his own prints on the paper to prove his point. He posted the letter, which eventually made its way to Scotland Yard. Ignored, it got shovelled in with other paperwork and wasn't found again until the 1890s. One can only imagine, had the Yard acted upon receipt of the letter, its possible impact on Victorian criminal investigations and the eventual pursuit of Jack the Ripper.[43] As it was, Scotland Yard would not adopt the use of fingerprints until 1901.

Francois Courvoisier's three-day trial commenced at the Old Bailey on Thursday, 18 June 1840. 'The prisoner appeared pale, but perfectly composed,' reported *The Morning Chronicle*. 'He was

---

[*]   After the trial, it emerged Courvoisier had confessed his guilt to his lawyer 'but had no intention of changing his plea.' (See Harman, p. 122).

respectively attired in a suit of mourning, and bowed respectfully to the court and bar upon his introduction to the dock.'[44]

In the gallery sat members of London high society and aristocracy – 'persons of distinction' – including one Member of Parliament; the Portuguese ambassador; and a royal, Prince Augustus Frederic, Duke of Sussex. The valet's lawyer argued no physical evidence linked his client to the murder and called into question Pearce's integrity. Defence counsel put forth that Pearce only 'found' the stolen items in the house after the government offered a £400 reward for information leading to an arrest. Officers in those days shared such rewards, but the argument carried little weight and the jury found Courvoisier guilty.[45]

Forty thousand people watched Courvoisier hang outside Newgate Prison on 6 July. Among the spectators were Charles Dickens and William Makepeace Thackeray, both repulsed at what they saw. 'I did not see one token in all the immense crowd; at the windows, in the streets, at the house-tops, anywhere; of any one emotion suitable to the occasion,' Dickens wrote. 'No sorrow, no salutary terror, no abhorrence, no seriousness; nothing but ribaldry, debauchery, levity, drunkenness and flaunting vice in fifty other shapes. I should have deemed it impossible that I could have ever felt any large assemblage of my fellow creatures to be so odious.'[46]

Thackeray closed his eyes as the executioner pulled the hood over Courvoisier's head and spared himself the horror of watching the condemned thrash at the end of the rope for nearly two minutes. Still, the execution inflicted mental scars. 'I can't do my work and yet work must be done for the poor babbies' [sic] sake,' he wrote to his mother two weeks after the event. 'It is most curious the effect his death has had on me, and I am trying to work it off in a paper on the subject. Meanwhile it weighs upon the mind, like cold plum pudding on the stomach, & soon as I begin to write, get melancholy.'[47]

4

Detective Days

'A murder of the most appalling nature.'
The Bermondsey Horror.

The letter in *The Times* was signed 'DETECTOR' and ran on Saturday, 30 May 1840, prior to Courvoisier's trial. It argued that while the Yard excelled 'as a preventive force', it was 'an unequivocal failure as a detective police'. One had to look no further than 'the recent dreadful murders and extensive robberies, which still remain undiscovered.' It continued:

> I would suggest that 25 or 30 officers of the metropolitan police be selected with the greatest care and attention as to their activity, talent and integrity, to form a detective force only, and that it would be advisable that to this body some few of the most active, able, and respectable of the unemployed police-officers should be added, who might by their great skill and local knowledge render most important information and assistance . . . They should not wear a uniform unless it was thought necessary for them to do so upon state occasions or Royal processions . . . These men should not be required to do any of the ordinary patrol duty of the other part of the forces, but be allowed to employ their time in the investigation and detection of offences . . .[1]

It would take another two years and a public fiasco before the Yard deemed a detective branch necessary.

At eight-thirty on the evening of Wednesday, 6 April 1842, Daniel Good entered a pawnbroker's in the Wandsworth High Street and asked to see a pair of black breeches he wished to purchase. The shopkeeper, Mr Columbine, knowing Good, allowed him to take the clothing on the promise of paying for them later. On his way out the door, Good picked up a pair of black trousers and tucked them into his great coat – a transgression that did not go unnoticed. He shoved both items under a seat cushion in his four-wheeled chaise, gave his pony a snap of the reins and drove off.[2]

Columbine ran into the street, flagged down PC William Gardiner and directed him to the nearby village of Roehampton and the home of one Mr Shiells, who employed Good as a coachman. Gardiner inquired at the main house as to Good's whereabouts and was directed to the stables a quarter-mile away. There, the constable confronted the errant coachman about the stolen trousers.[3]

'Why, yes, I bought a pair of breeches from Mr Columbine, but I have not paid for them yet,' Good said. 'I will give you the money we agreed on, and you can pay him for them.'[4]

Gardiner dismissed the suggestion. He searched the chaise for the missing merchandize before turning his attention to the stables. Good, having until now displayed 'the utmost apparent coolness', appeared restless. The first three stalls surrendered nothing. The fourth, 'at the further extremity of the stable and very dark', was filled with hay trusses. Gardiner pulled two of them out and, in the light of his lantern, discovered a mound of loose hay beneath them. He scattered the hay with this foot and was startled to find what he believed to be a dead goose.[5]

'My God!' the constable cried. 'What is this?'

Good, deciding it best not to stick around, dashed from the stall. He slammed the door shut in his wake, locked it and fled with the key. Gardiner lowered his lantern to get a better look at what he'd found. 'On a more close examination,' he reported, 'it was found to be the trunk of a human body, which had been divested of the head, arms and legs. It was lying with the back upwards; and, when turned over, was discovered to be the trunk of a female, and the abdomen was found to have been cut open, and the entrails extracted.'[6]

Gardiner managed, with some difficulty and the use of a pitch-fork, to free himself from the stall and get help. Investigation at the scene stretched through the night and into the early-morning hours. The victim was in her mid- to late-twenties. She had been decapitated after death, the severing blow landing 'at about the third or fourth cervical vertebrae.' Both arms had been hacked off at the shoulder joints and the legs chopped away just below the hips. Peering into the gaping wound of the abdomen, the examining surgeon noted the stomach, intestines, liver and uterus had been ripped out. The whereabouts of the viscera, head and appendages posed a mystery – albeit a temporary one.[7]

A constable named Tye picked up an unpleasant scent and traced it to the harness room next to the stall. The smell inside the room 'was most overpowering' and turned the stomach. 'I never smelt such before,' Tye said, 'but it appeared to me like rind of bacon.' Trying not to gag, he approached the fireplace, sifted through the ashes and found 'a number of fragments of human bones in a highly calcined state.' The surgeon identified them as pieces of 'skull, arm and thigh bones.'[8]

Other items turned up that night included a bloodstained axe, knife and – stuck to the side of the gig box of Good's chaise – a piece of flesh 'about half the size of a pea.' Police also found a rent book with the name Jane Jones written inside it. Jane was Good's common-law wife. A 'mole just above the collarbone' on the right side of the butchered neck confirmed her identity.[9]

She was last seen alive over the Easter weekend 'dressed in a blue bonnet, black ground shawl, with flowers on it of different colours, and a mingled cotton dress.' The press equated the killing with a crime still fresh in the collective mind of Londoners, calling it 'a murder of the most appalling nature, and which, in the annals of crime, has only been equalled [sic] in atrocity by that of Hannah Brown by the miscreant Greenacre.' The crime scene became a must-see attraction. 'Vehicles of every description, from the aristocratic carriage to the costermonger's cart, were seen wending their way towards the scene of the awful tragedy,' reported *The Times*. Many of those who gathered, the paper sniffed, 'were, we regret to state, numerous females, some of whom, we doubt not, would aspire to be considered respectable women.'[10]

That Daniel Good, a man of known violent reputation, so easily escaped capture proved a grave embarrassment to the Yard. The fifty-year-old Irishman had multiple convictions for theft and a history of brutality. Once, 'in a fit of ungovernable rage', he supposedly ripped a horse's tongue from its mouth. Why, the press asked, was he not immediately arrested the night police confronted him? A game of cat-and-mouse lasting more than a week played out across the city and in the papers, much to the Yard's humiliation. How could a force of now 3,800 men 'constantly on active duty' not deliver one man 'into the hands of justice?' Failure to capture Good, *The Times* warned, would inflict upon the police an 'indelible disgrace, and the public will be led to suspect that there is something wrong in its government.'[11]

Nine divisions, all working independently and not communicating with one another, scoured the breadth and width of London without result. Despite police 'exerting themselves to the utmost to catch the monster', Good proved elusive. Opined *The Planet* newspaper: 'The conduct of the metropolitan police in the present case, as in those of the unfortunate Eliza Grimwood, Lord William Russell and others is marked with a looseness and want of decision which proves that unless a decided change is made in the present system, it is idle to expect it can be an efficient detective police, and that the most desperate offender can escape with impunity.' On one occasion, Inspector Pearce tracked down the fugitive's actual wife, 'Old Molly Good', and questioned her as to Daniel's whereabouts. She said she knew nothing, but speculation is Good may have been hiding in her house at the time.[12]

It wasn't skill on the part of the Yard but dumb luck that resulted in Good's apprehension. He took a job – under the name Connor – as a labourer at a construction site in Tonbridge, where a number of cottages were being built near the South Eastern Railway. On the morning of Saturday, 16 April, Thomas Rose, a fellow labourer and former police constable stationed in Wandsworth, recognized Good from a previous encounter and turned him in. Justice moved quickly, as it did in those days, and Good swung from the gallows at Newgate Prison three weeks later on 23 May.[13]

On 14 June, prompted by the Good fiasco, Commissioners Mayne and Rowan sent to the Home Secretary a 'Memorandum relative to the Detective Powers of the Police'. It laid out plans for a new branch of Scotland Yard comprised of two detective-inspectors and eight sergeants. The document has been lost to history, but in a follow-up letter they made clear that when not working a case, members of the proposed branch were to learn 'the habits, haunts, and persons or parties known or suspected to live by the commission of crime, so as to prepare themselves for tracing and detecting offenders when any case occurred.' The Home Secretary gave the proposal his stamp of approval for six sergeants, rather than eight, in the name of economy. [14]

Although the Yard kept the plan under wraps, the press caught wind of it on 12 July when *The Morning Post,* under the headline 'New Police Arrangement', reported:

> Several cases having lately occurred, in which criminals have not been taken into custody so promptly as the public had a right to expect, the commissioners of police have arranged that a new company shall immediately be raised out of the present police, to be called the 'Detective Force' . . . We doubt not that

the choice of the commissioners will fall upon men whose vigilance and industry in their vocation will entitle them to the preferment.[15]

On Monday, 15 August 1842, the Yard announced in its internal *Police Orders* the creation of its plainclothes Detective Branch – the first of its kind.* Inspector Nicholas Pearce oversaw the new detectives with Inspector John Haynes, a ten-year veteran and one-time chemist, as his second-in-command.[16]

In 1840, Haynes successfully tracked down a team of looters who picked clean a wrecked ship off Margate along England's southeast coast. He calculated how fast their horse-drawn carriage could travel and deduced from that what inns they stayed at on their run to London. As the two senior detectives, Pearce and Haynes earned a yearly salary of £200 – '£84 more than uniformed officers'. The six sergeants included veterans of the Westwood, Good and Russell murder investigations. Two constables recently promoted to Sergeant, including Jonathan Whicher, destined to become the most celebrated and then ostracized detective of his day, rounded out the team. The sergeants earned £73 a year, £10 more than their uniformed colleagues.[17]

The branch, in its early days, went through several personnel changes that saw Pearce promoted to Superintendent of F (Covent Garden) Division and Inspector Charles Frederick Field named Senior Detective. The press, which had long criticized Scotland Yard for its lack of investigative prowess, initially paid it little attention. Some histories contend it's because the Yard and Home Office made no public announcement, while another argues it 'was more probably due to the dearth during this period of spectacular cases'. Not 'until the end of the decade' did the Detective Branch 'come into the news with a crime of the more sensational sort.'[18]

---

* American police departments wouldn't establish detective units for more than a decade, with the New York Police Department doing so in 1857 and the Chicago Police Department in 1860.

In 1849, a cholera outbreak ravaged London 'with a large scale loss of life'. More than 14,000 people in the capital succumbed to violent cramps, vomiting and severe diarrhea after drinking contaminated water from the city's pumps.[19]

On Monday, 24 September, *The Morning Chronicle* ran an article by journalist Henry Mayhew under the headline 'A Visit to the Cholera Districts of Bermondsey'. Along 'the southern shores of the Thames', a hotbed of disease, some 6,500 people had died 'within the last three months'. Mayhew wanted to see for himself the conditions that bred such a 'fatal fury'. 'The masses of filth and corruption round the metropolis are, as it were, the nauseous nests of plague and pestilence,' he wrote:

> As we passed along the reeking banks of the sewer the sun shone upon a narrow slip of water. In the bright light it appeared the colour of strong green tea, and positively looked as solid as black marble in the shadow – indeed, it was more like watery mud than muddy water; and yet we were assured this was the only water the wretched inhabitants had to drink. As we gazed in horror at it, we saw drains and sewers emptying their filthy contents into it; we saw a whole tier of doorless privies in the open road, common to men and women, built over it; we heard bucket after bucket of filth splash into it, and the limbs of the vagrant boys bathing in it seemed, by pure force of contrast, white as Parisian marble.[20]

Against this nauseating backdrop, the Detective Branch tackled its first major case. For London's weary inhabitants, the sordid love triangle that became known as 'the Bermondsey Horror' proved a welcome distraction from endless stories of disease. 'At this time,' reported *Punch* that September, 'refined, civilized, philanthropic London reeks with the foulness of the Bermondsey murder.'[21]

It all began when colleagues at the London Docks reported Patrick O'Connor missing. An official with Her Majesty's Customs department, he was last seen by an acquaintance on the evening of Thursday, 9 August, strolling across London Bridge from the Surrey side towards Bermondsey. The two exchanged brief pleasantries, during which O'Connor mentioned he planned to spend the evening with a couple called the Mannings. He then bid farewell and vanished into the ether. 'Sinister apprehensions began to be entertained respecting his fate' when, by Monday, he had not shown up for work.[22]

O'Connor made no secret of his friendship with the Mannings, although it seemed an odd relationship. Marie Manning, née De Roux, was born in Switzerland in 1821. As a lady's maid to the aristocracy, she grew accustomed to the sumptuous surroundings of country manors, the comfort of fine clothes and the trappings of high society. She benefitted from the generosity of her mistresses, acquiring in the course of her service '11 petticoats, 9 gowns, 28 pairs of stockings, 7 pairs of drawers and 19 pairs of kid gloves'. Her outfit of choice was a black satin dress that accentuated her figure. She was a pleasure for the eyes with her long, dark hair. 'She . . . is an extremely fine woman,' notes one contemporary account, 'handsome, and of almost muscular stature.'[23]

She moved to England in July 1846, adopted the more English-sounding name Maria, and went to work 'in the household of the Duchess of Sutherland'. Along the way she met O'Connor. The fifty-year-old Irishman 'was excessively fond of money and endeavoured at all times to increase his store.' He had in recent years acquired a reputation for wealth through shady money lending and become known as 'The Customs' money lender'. His stature made him an attractive proposition – one who enjoyed the 'society of ladies'. Although he and Maria shared a mutual attraction, he never proposed. She instead married Frederick Manning, a one-time guard for the Great Western Railway Company, in May 1847, believing he was due a substantial family inheritance.[24]

A step down from the financially secure O'Connor, Manning was not, as he claimed, destined for wealth. A failed publican, his lack of business acumen drove the couple to the financial brink.

She kept them afloat as a dressmaker, but just barely. They moved into a respectable home at No. 3, Miniver Place, Bermondsey, and struggled to maintain appearances. 'The Mannings, through their extravagance and dissipation,' states one report, 'had got rid of nearly all their property, with the exception of the furniture, and their circumstances became critical.' Through all this, O'Connor stuck around and paid the couple frequent visits if only to be close to Maria. Neighbours often spotted the two smoking 'in the back parlour window' and 'the small garden at the rear of the house.' Friends urged O'Connor to keep his distance, but he dismissed their concerns, to his great detriment.[25]

Police Constable John Wright of M (Southwark) Division, accompanied by one Mr Flynn, O'Connor's cousin, questioned Maria at her home on Monday, 13 August, as to the missing man's whereabouts. She claimed she had invited him to dinner several nights prior but he never showed up. 'Poor Mr O'Connor,' Maria said. 'He was the best friend I had in London.' Maria's response struck Wright and Flynn as strange, as there was nothing yet to suggest O'Connor had met with foul play. They thanked her for her time and proceeded to O'Connor's rented room at 21, Greenwood Street, where the landlord let them in. In a trunk, they found the cashbox in which O'Connor kept his cash and railway share certificates. It was empty.[26]

When police returned to the Manning residence the next day, they found it abandoned. 'The nest was there but the birds had flown.' Police Constables Henry Barnes and James Burton returned three days later on Friday, 17 August, to search the place. Barnes noticed a damp mark on the kitchen floor between two flagstones. Closer inspection revealed the stones had recently been moved. The two constables pried the heavy stones up with a crowbar to expose a layer of earth beneath. 'I proceeded to remove a portion of the earth,' Barnes said. 'When I had got down about a foot, I discovered the toe of a man – and when I got about eighteen inches down, I discovered the loins of a man, the back of a man.'[27]

DISCOVERY OF O'CONNOR'S REMAINS (p. 368).

A gruesome discovery is made beneath the kitchen flagstones at No. 3, Miniver Place, Bermondsey.

Chronicle/Alamy

    The constables cleared away the remaining earth to reveal the naked body of a man, hogtied, covered in lime and lying face down in a pit about three-feet deep, two and a half feet wide, and six feet long. The head, slightly lower than the torso, was caked in dried blood. Breathless from their excavation, they hauled the corpse from its makeshift grave and laid it, still bound in heavy cord, on the kitchen floor. Two surgeons joined them at the house. Their examination found the victim had been shot above the right eye and the back of his skull caved in by at least sixteen blows from a sharp, heavy instrument. 'The fractures were quite sufficient to have caused death,' they reported. 'And no doubt the wound from the bullet would have eventually caused death.' One of the surgeons removed a set of false teeth from the corpse's mouth. Checking with dentists, the Yard soon found one in Osborne Street, Whitechapel, who had sold the teeth to O'Connor.[28]

In reporting the murder, the press dredged up Greenacre and Good and argued the nation had been scared 'from its propriety' by the savagery of O'Connor's death. The Detective Branch, under pressure to quickly resolve the matter and not yet tested to such a degree, moved with surprising rapidity. Detective Sergeant Frederick Shaw began knocking on doors in the Mannings' neighbourhood and learned Maria was seen getting into a cab on the afternoon of Monday, 13 August with three large trunks. One eagle-eyed neighbour provided the hackney-cab number, 1186. Shaw traced the driver, a man named Kirk, who remembered Maria and her excessive amount of luggage. He said she directed him to the London Bridge terminus, where she deposited two of the trunks in the luggage office under the name Mrs Smith. She next asked to be dropped off at the London and North Western Station in Euston Square, which Kirk did at quarter to six that evening. He watched her disappear into the crowd with the remaining trunk and a carpetbag.[29]

Shaw returned to Scotland Yard and reported his findings to Inspector Haynes. In the early morning hours of Tuesday, 21 August, detectives located the trunks left in the cloakroom of the London Bridge terminus. Both pieces of luggage had a white label attached. Scrawled across one in green ink was 'Mrs Smith, passenger to Paris, to be left till called for.' Across the other was 'Mrs Smith, passenger, to be left till called for.' Haynes and his men forced the trunks open and found 'a quantity of wearing apparel' – including a bloodstained gown – marked with the name De Roux, 'a quantity of articles belonging to the deceased Patrick O'Connor' and several letters from O'Connor to Maria.[30]

Haynes hurried to the London and North Western Station and began asking porters and ticket-takers if they'd encountered anyone matching Maria's description and going by the name of Smith. The odds played in his favour. He learned 'a female passenger, whose luggage was marked with the name of Smith, had left the . . . Station on the morning of Tuesday the 14th, by the 6:15 a.m.

train, having booked herself through to Edinburgh in a 1st class carriage.'³¹

Haynes pushed his way through the crowd to the station's telegraph office. Telegraphy was first used to capture a criminal in 1845, when police in Berkshire learned John Tawell, wanted for murdering his mistress, had fled by train to London. Much to the fugitive's bad luck, 'he was travelling along one of the only stretches of railway in the world to have telegraph wires running beside the railway lines.' A message, alerting police and describing Tawell, was telegraphed to Paddington Station, where he was arrested upon his arrival. 'Had it not been for the efficient aid of the electric telegraph, both at Slough and Paddington,' reported *The Times* 'the greatest difficulty, as well as delay, would have occurred in the apprehension.'³²

By the time Maria Manning fled by train to Scotland, electric telegraph connected 'about a third of the railway network' across Britain. Presently, from the North Western Station's telegraph office, Inspector Haynes sent a message through to Edinburgh addressed to the city's superintendent of police, cluing him into the situation and providing a description of Maria. All he could do now was be patient. He had 'scarcely arrived at Scotland Yard' when a messenger boy delivered the telegraphed response from Superintendent Richard Moxey. Maria Manning had attempted that very morning to sell O'Connor's railway shares to a local stockbroker who recognized the numbers on the certificates from a printed police bulletin. She was now in custody.³³

Moxey put Maria on a train under escort and had her back in London three days later on Friday, 24 August.

Frederick Manning's whereabouts remained a mystery. 'Every day that passes diminishes the chance of his arrest,' *The Times* unhelpfully pointed out, 'and unless the most strenuous exertions are now made a deed of the most extraordinary atrocity may be suffered to go unpunished.'[34] The couple who killed together didn't stay together. Maria told police her marriage to Frederick was a volatile and unhappy one, strained as it was by financial matters. The day she fled, Frederick had left the house to pawn their furniture. Maria, seeing her chance, took off with the railway shares and cash she'd taken from O'Connor's room, leaving Frederick with the proverbial shirt on his back.[35]

On Thursday, 23 August, coincidence and luck intervened when the Yard received a wire from the Crown Solicitor in the Channel Islands off the French Normandy coast. A local woman who knew Manning had seen him on a steamer the previous week travelling from Southampton to Jersey. At the time, the murder had yet to be discovered, so Manning's presence on the boat was no cause for alarm. The wire, dated Saturday, 18 August, had taken five days to reach London. Haynes, fearing Manning might be making a run for France, sent Sergeant Edward Langley to put an end to the chase. Langley traced Manning to a rented room in a cottage called Prospect House on Jersey and took him by surprise on the night of 27 August. The two men knew each other by sight. The detective had previously investigated 'extensive robberies' on the Great Western Railway line and interviewed Manning, who, employed as a railway guard at the time, had been a suspect.[36]

'Ah, sergeant, is that you?' Manning said when Langley entered his room. 'I am glad you are come. I know what you are come about. If you had not come, I was coming to town to explain all. I am innocent!'

Langley ordered Manning out of bed and told him to get dressed.

'Is the wretch taken?' Manning said as he pulled his clothes on. 'She is the guilty party. I am innocent as a lamb.'[37]

He had a lot to say and wasted no time blaming Maria. She 'had caused the grave to be dug some time before,' he said. On the night of the murder, she had laid the table for dinner and 'invited O'Connor downstairs to wash his hands.' As O'Connor did so,

Maria snuck up from behind and shot him in the head. Of O'Connor's multiple skull fractures, Frederick had nothing to say – but he expressed continued satisfaction with Maria's arrest, as she had left him 'in total ignorance of her destination, without money'.[38]

The Mannings stood trial together at the Old Bailey, the proceedings getting underway on 22 October with both blaming the other for O'Connor's death. The Yard tracked down a medical student who lived with the couple until shortly before the murder. He testified Frederick had once inquired as to 'what part of the head was most vital or tender' and whether murderers go to heaven. 'I told him, "No",' the student said. He also testified that Frederick, with Maria present, had asked, "What drug would produce stupefaction, or partial intoxication, so as to cause a person to put pen to paper?"' It was their intent, according to the young man's testimony, 'to get O'Connor to sign a promissory note for a considerable sum of money, £500.' One plan the couple floated was getting O'Connor drunk by telling him brandy would protect him from cholera.[39]

The guilty verdict on 26 October surprised no one. Frederick declined his opportunity to address the court, but Maria had a few things to say. She'd been scorned throughout the trial for her unwomanly lack of emotion and stoicism. In his closing argument, Frederick's defence lawyer all but levelled Maria's sex against her as a crime. 'History teaches us that the female is capable of reaching higher in point of virtue than the male, but that when once she gives way to vice, she sinks far lower than our sex,' he said. 'My hypothesis, then, is, that the female prisoner Manning premeditated, planned and concocted the murder, and that she made her husband her dupe and instrument for that purpose.'[40]

Maria, having her say, raged against the British justice system and England in general. 'There is no law for me,' she said. '. . . I think, considering that I am a woman and alone, that I have to fight against my husband's statements, that I have to fight against the prosecutors, and that even the Judge himself is against me – I think that I am not treated like a Christian, but like a wild beast of the forest; and the Judges and Jury will have it upon their consciences for giving a verdict against me.'[41]

The sentiment fuelling Maria's anger was lost on the press, who labelled her a 'Jezebel' and 'The Lady Macbeth of Bermondsey'. 'The terrible excitement under which she laboured,' reported *The Evening Mail*, 'may be conceived from the oath which she frequently uttered – "Damnation seize you all!"'[42]

The couple met the hangman on the rooftop of Horsemonger Lane Gaol on 13 November before some 30,000 people. The event had the atmosphere of a carnival; the enthusiastic crowd sung a ballad penned just for the occasion:

> Old and young, pray like a warning
> Females lead a virtuous life.
> Think upon the fateful morning,
> Frederick Manning and his wife.[43]

Charles Dickens attended the execution and, as with the Courvoisier hanging, found it an appalling spectacle. 'I believe,' he wrote to *The Times*, 'that a sight so inconceivably awful as the wickedness and levity of the immense crowd collected at that execution could be imagined by no man and could be presented in no heathen land under the sun.' He was nevertheless impressed by Maria's stoicism and appearance on the gallows. Her body, he wrote, presented 'a fine shape, so elaborately corseted and artfully dressed, that it was quite unchanged in its trim appearance as it swung slowly from side to side.'[44]

He would go on to use Maria Manning as the basis for the murderous Mademoiselle Hortense in *Bleak House*. The novel also featured 'Inspector Bucket of the Detective', modelled after Inspector Frederick Field. While murder and the desperate plight of the lower classes was nothing new to Dickens's work, he developed in

1850 a strong fascination with Scotland Yard's detectives, who, he wrote, 'perform the most difficult operations of their craft.'*[45]

As editor of the weekly journal *Household Words*, he published a series of articles that bestowed upon the detectives an elite status, elevating them above that of the typical policeman. There was something of the creative intellectual in the way they assessed a crime scene. 'As a connoisseur can determine the painter of a picture at the first glance, or a wine-taster the precise vintage of a sherry by the merest sip,' declared one glowing piece, 'so the Detective at once pounces upon the authors of the work of art under consideration, by the style of performance; if not upon the precise executant, upon the "school" to which he belongs.'[46]

Dickens invited the detectives to the *Household Words* office in Wellington Street 'to have some talk' over brandy and cigars. 'The Detective Force,' he wrote '. . . is so well chosen and trained, proceeds so systematically and quietly, does its business in such a workmanlike manner, and is always so calmly and steadily engaged in the service of the public, that the public really do not know enough of it, to know a tithe of its usefulness.' They sat together in a semicircle, the inspectors on the outside and the sergeants in-between, and discussed 'the most celebrated and horrible of the great crimes that have been committed within the last fifteen or twenty years.'[47] Naturally, the Mannings were a topic of considerable interest:

> One of our guests gave chase to and boarded the emigrant ship, in which the murderess last hanged in London was sup-posed to have embarked. We learn from him that his errand was not announced to the passengers, who may have no idea of it to this hour. That he went below, with the captain, lamp

---

* 1850 also saw a change in the Yard's leadership with Commissioner Charles Rowan's retirement. A superintendent named Captain William Hay took his place. He and Mayne spent the next five years arguing over matters of seniority. When Hay died in 1855, it was decided one commissioner was plenty.

in hand – it being dark, and the whole steerage abed and sea-sick – and engaged the Mrs Manning who was on board, in a conversation about her luggage, until she was, with no small pains, induced to raise her head, and turn her face towards the light. Satisfied that she was not the object of his search, he quietly re-embarked in the Government steamer along-side, and steamed home again with the intelligence.[48]

Through his pen, Dickens introduced to readers the Detective Branch's key personalities, slightly altering their names for the purpose of publication. Inspector Field, for example, became 'Inspector Wield' – 'a portly presence, with a large, moist knowing eye, husky voice, and a habit of emphasizing his conversation by the aid of a corpulent fore-finger, which is constantly in juxtaposition with his eyes or nose.'[49]

In a subsequent profile, Dickens would describe the 'sagacious, vigilant' inspector as a 'guardian genius' as he made the rounds in a notorious city slum. 'How many people may there be in London, who, if we had brought them deviously and blindfolded, to this street, fifty paces from the Station House, and within call of Saint Giles's church, would know it for a not remote part of the city in which their lives are passed? How many, who amidst this compound of sickening smells, these heaps of filth, these tumbling houses, with all their vile contents, animate, and inanimate, slimily overflowing into the black road, would believe that they breathe *this* air?'[50]

Dickens described Sergeant Jonathan Whicher, profiled as 'Sergeant Witchem', as being short, thick-set, and possessing 'something of a reserved and thoughtful air, as if he were engaged in deep arithmetical calculations'. Whicher was happy to detail for Dickens his adventures going up against 'the swell mob' – pick-pockets and thieves who concealed their criminal bent behind a façade of gentility and respectable airs. One story told involved Whicher and Field getting jumped by members of the mob at

'Epsom one Derby Day'. The detectives were sitting at the bar, each enjoying their fourth glass of sherry, when their assailants – 'four of 'em' – took them by surprise: 'There we are, all down together, heads and heels, knocking about on the floor of the bar – perhaps you never see such a scene of confusion!' Justice triumphed, however, and the detectives got the better of their adversaries.[51]

A bright and ascending star, the thirty-five-year-old Whicher had spent the past decade honing his craft in pursuit of counterfeiters and conmen, killers and thieves, establishing himself as 'Commissioner Mayne's favourite officer'. He took part in the hunt for Daniel Good, working in plainclothes and keeping an eye on one of Good's female acquaintances. He joined the ranks of the Detective Branch upon its formation in 1842 and was promoted to Sergeant. During the Bermondsey Horror investigation, he travelled to France 'to search Parisian hotels and keep watch at railway stations' for Maria Manning.[52]

He made Inspector and was appointed co-lead of the Detective Branch in 1856, moving from one high-profile success to the next. He recovered da Vinci's *Virgin and Child*, stolen from the Earl of Suffolk in 1856, and helped track down the would-be killers of Napoleon III after a failed assassination attempt in Paris. A man of stellar reputation, he was considered 'the Prince of Detectives', an investigator known for his keen insight and cautious approach.[53]

And then came the murder of young Francis Saville Kent.

5

A Murder in the Manor

The slaying at Road Hill House. A detective's downfall.

On Tuesday, 10 July 1860, *The Morning Post* ran the following editorial:

> The moral sanctions of an English home are, in the nineteenth century, what the moat, and the keep, and the drawbridge were in the fourteenth . . . And yet, in spite of all these proverbial sanctities, a crime has just been committed which for mystery, complication of probabilities, and hideous wickedness, is without parallel in our criminal records. A family retired to bed at night with the usual sense of peace and security. Yet before the time for rising next morning one of the children has been seized and murdered, and not a soul in the place can give the slightest evidence on the subject.[1]

The violated sanctum was Road Hill House. Built sometime around 1800 of light amber-coloured limestone, the elegant, three-storey Georgian home, with its sweeping lawn, curved drive and columned entrance, sat on a hill above the Wiltshire village of Road. Hidden and protected behind high walls and foliage, it was the residence of Samuel Kent, a factory inspector for the Home Office, his wife, Mary, their large brood and several servants.[2]

Between 10 p.m. and 11 p.m. on Friday, 29 June, the family and staff retired to their rooms, the housemaid having performed her nightly inspection of doors and windows to ensure all were fastened. Twenty-two-year-old nursemaid Elizabeth Gough slept in the first-floor nursery with the two youngest children, three-year-old Francis and one-year-old Eveline. Elizabeth had put Francis to bed at eight o'clock that evening and checked on him in his cot at five past eleven. 'He was well and happy,' Elizabeth said. Mrs Kent came in and kissed the children good night before heading to her bedroom across the hall. Elizabeth got into bed and soon fell asleep.[3]

She awoke at five and noticed the nursery door ajar. She checked the children in their cribs and was surprised to find Francis missing. 'The impression of his body still remained,' she said, 'and the bed clothes were placed neatly, as if I or his mother had done it.'[4]

The nightshirt and flannel waistcoat she had put him to bed in were gone. When she didn't find the boy in Mr and Mrs Kent's bedroom, she began searching the house – all to no avail. In the drawing room, the window and shutter were partially open despite the housemaid having secured them the night before. Panicked word quickly spread outward from the house and into the village that young Francis was missing. Concerned locals soon descended on the house and grounds to conduct a full-scale search.[5]

Those looking for the boy included a farmer, the village shoemaker, the parish constable and PC Samuel Urch. Walking his beat the night before, Urch heard the Kents' dog barking at something in the garden, but the policeman thought little of it at the time. The men now searched the shrubbery that bordered the property but found nothing. Not until they checked the water closet at the edge of the garden did the mystery of the child's disappearance end and a new one begin.[6]

'I noticed some blood of a dark colour on the floor,' said farmer Thomas Benger. He raised the lid of the privy and stuck his hand in the opening. 'I felt a blanket, which I pulled out. I then discovered the body of the deceased, dressed in the nightshirt, laying across the splashboard on his side. The splash board prevented the body falling lower down.'[7]

Benger and William Nutt, the village shoemaker, pulled the small, soiled corpse from the hole. 'Blood,' said Benger, 'was splashed all over his face.' 'When it was lifted up,' said Nutt, 'its little head almost fell off the body.' The two men wrapped Francis in a blanket and carried him into the kitchen, where Mary Kent and her twenty-eight-year-old stepdaughter Elizabeth saw what had happened. 'I can't describe the horror and amazement they seemed to be in,' Nutt said. 'I thought they would fall and I took them both round the waist. I went through with them into the passage.'[8]

Joshua Parsons, the local surgeon, arrived at about eight o'clock. 'The throat was cut to the bone by some sharp instrument, from left to right,' he said. 'It completely divided all the membranes, blood-vessels, nerve vessels and air tubes. It was no doubt done by one sharp, clean incision.' The boy had also been stabbed through the chest with a 'broad, sharp, long and strong instrument . . . passing below the pericardium and diaphragm, severing the cartilage of two ribs, and extending three-fourths across the chest.' The skin around Francis's mouth was black. 'It was likely to be produced by the violent thrusting of a blanket into the mouth to prevent it crying,' Parsons said, 'or it could have been done with a hand.'[9]

Parsons estimated death had occurred at least five hours prior and noted an oddity about the killing. 'A child of that size would have sent out with a gust at one jet a quantity of blood not less than three pints,' he said, 'whereas I do not think we have seen anything like a pint.' Stephen Millett, the parish constable and village butcher, guessed there to be roughly three-quarters of a pint of blood on the boy's clothes, blanket and the floor of the water closet. No stranger to the bleeding of carcasses, he had his own theory about the killing.[10]

'My impression is that the child was held with his legs upwards,' he said, 'and his head hanging down, and his throat cut while in that position.' In short, the killer drained the child's blood into the privy. Outside the water closet, Millet found a bloody scrap of newspaper, which appeared to have been used to wipe some sort of blade.[11]

From the outset, the crime exceeded the competency of the local constabulary under the command of Superintendent John Foley. A thorough search of the house by police on the evening of 30 June uncovered a woman's bloodstained chemise shoved down the kitchen boiler hole. Foley assumed the stains were menstrual blood and that an embarrassed servant girl had hidden the garment from view. He ordered the chemise be returned to the kitchen, where it soon went missing.[12]

The county coroner convened an inquest at the Temperance Hall in the village on Monday, 2 July and questioned all the servants from Road Hill House. The jury was then taken to the house itself, where they heard from Francis's sixteen-year-old sister Constance.

'I knew nothing whatever of his death until he was found,' she said. '. . . I did not hear anything during the night. I slept soundly.' Asked about Elizabeth Gough, she said, 'I have found the nursemaid generally quiet and attentive, and perform her duties in every respect as could be wished.'

Fourteen-year-old William Kent echoed his sister's sentiment. 'I have always found the nursemaid very kind and attentive,' he said. 'I know nothing about the murder.'[13]

Without hearing from Samuel and Mary Kent, the jurors returned to Temperance Hall. 'There is a strong suspicion on my mind,' one juryman said, 'for it is clear no one could have got into the house from the outside.'

The coroner, wishing to protect the name of a well-to-do family, brushed the implication aside. 'I have no doubt in my mind but that sooner or later the mystery in which this crime is at present enveloped will be cleared away,' he said, 'and the author or authors of it be brought to light; for if no mortal eye saw the deed committed, the eye of Providence saw it, and punishment will await the guilty.'

The jury returned a verdict of 'Wilful murder against a person or persons unknown.'[14]

The investigation continued with nothing to show for it. 'The security of families and the sacredness of English households,' opined *The Morning Post*, 'demand that this matter should never be allowed to rest till the last shadow in its dark mystery shall have been chased away.'[15]

Suspicion naturally fell on Elizabeth Gough. 'I am a light sleeper,' she said, 'and generally hear any movement of the children or crying.'[16]

If that was the case, how did she sleep through someone entering the nursery and stealing the boy from his crib? One theory entertained by Foley and his men was that Francis awoke to the sounds of an illicit rendezvous between Elizabeth and Samuel Kent and was therefore permanently silenced.[17]

The press all but convicted Elizabeth of the crime. 'It seems almost incredible,' remarked one paper, 'that the child could be abstracted from the nursemaid's room without her knowledge, but not the slightest suspicion attaches to her.' Police took Elizabeth into custody on Tuesday, 10 July, and set her free shortly thereafter due to lack of evidence. 'Nothing,' lamented the local *Frome Times*, 'absolutely nothing, has been done towards the detection of the perpetrator of this dreadful crime.[18]

On the evening of Sunday, 15 July, at the request of Wiltshire authorities, Detective Inspector Jonathan Whicher arrived from London to take over the investigation. The case before him, dominant in the headlines, would soon provide the template for many a fictional murder mystery: the country manor, a slaughtered occupant and a pool of suspects – from the aristocratic to the lowly servants – all present in the home at the time of the killing. The press marvelled at the complexity of the puzzle. Observed *The Wiltshire Times and Trowbridge Advertiser*:

How an individual could have taken the child from his cot, placed the bed clothes tidily, carried him through the drawing room (which is on the ground floor), across the lawn, through a shrubbery and stable yard, where a watchdog was loose roaming about, thence into the water closet, deprive the child of life, and decamp without leaving behind them the smallest clue to their guilt, or disturbing the inmates, or awakening the child, or coming into collision with the dog – is a mystery indeed![19]

The route from the nursery to the water closet was 'a circuitous one, and, to a stranger . . . quite a labyrinth'. The murderer knew the terrain. The privy itself was about twenty yards from the kitchen door and 'surrounded by shrubs'. Its well, or cesspool, was of considerable size and measured 'ten feet deep and seven feet square'. On the night of the murder, it 'contained about six feet of water and soil'.[20]

Whicher theorized the killer, after cutting the boy's throat, dropped him into the well, expecting him to sink into the muck. Instead, the body landed on the splash board, a plank of wood affixed to the privy seat that slanted downwards into the well. Whicher believed the stab wound to the boy's chest, inflicted after death, 'was caused by a thrust intended to force the body down the aperture, and not with any view of completing a deed already too fully accomplished.'[21]

A dozen people slept in the house the night Francis died: Samuel and Mary Kent and their seven children – four from Samuel's first marriage – and three servants: the housemaid, the nursemaid and the cook. But Whicher quickly settled his sights on Constance. Realizing Francis's killer must have been covered in blood, he examined the night attire of everyone in the house at the time of the murder. On Monday, 16 July, the day after his arrival, Whicher searched the dresser in Constance's bedroom and found in one of the drawers a handwritten inventory.

'Is this a list of your linen?' Whicher asked.

'Yes,' said Constance.

'In whose writing is it?'

'It is my own writing.'

'Here are three nightdresses. Where are they?'

'I have two,' Constance replied. 'The other was lost at the wash the week after the murder.'

She showed him the two nightdresses still in her possession. Whicher pointed to a nightdress and cap on Constance's bed and asked who they belonged to.

'They are my sister's,' Constance said.[22]

Whicher surmised Constance had destroyed the missing nightgown to get rid of evidence. In learning what he could about the girl, he discovered that several years prior she had – 'in consequence of some family unpleasantness' – run away from home dressed as a boy with her younger brother, William. Before leaving, she discarded her normal attire down the same privy in which the body had been found. They made it as far as Bath before being returned home. Schoolmates of Constance told the detective she often spoke poorly of her stepmother and younger half-siblings. She would 'make use of expressions of dislike towards the children of Mr Kent and his present wife, owing to the partiality shown them by their parents,' said one friend. 'She had complained that Mrs Kent would not let her have the coloured dress she liked, but bought the very opposite to that she selected.'[23]

On the afternoon of Friday, 20 July, Whicher – accompanied by Superintendent Foley – summoned Constance to the drawing room of Road Hill House. 'I hold a warrant for your apprehension,' he said, 'charging you with the murder of your brother, Francis Saville Kent, which I will read to you.'

Whicher read the warrant aloud, during which Constance wept and said, several times, 'I am innocent.' He escorted her to her bedroom, where she put on her bonnet and cloak, and took her into custody.[24]

The case came before the local magistrates on Friday, 27 July, and it soon became apparent the charges would not hold. The backlash to Constance's arrest proved intense, with the press failing to believe such an upstanding young woman could commit so heinous an atrocity. The detective from Scotland Yard bore the brunt of the condemnation. 'A fortnight ago, there was great confidence in Mr Whicher's ability and sagacity,' reported the local *Frome Times*, 'but the events of Friday have not been such as to justify that opinion. An officer who can play at hap-hazard with such an awful charge as that of wilful murder, and can promise that which he must have known he could not perform, cannot expect to be looked upon otherwise than with distrust.'[25]

Constance's barrister, Peter Edlin, in his summation before the magistrates said Whicher had proved nothing. Having a couple of schoolgirls testify that Constance didn't like her half-siblings was hardly evidence of guilt. 'Where was the animus which Mr Whicher swore he could prove?' Edlin asked. '. . . Every Englishman would feel likewise that that young lady ought never to have been dragged from her home, that she ought never to have been assigned to a gaol . . . A more unjust, a more improper, a more improbable case had never been brought before a court of justice, than was this upon which so terrible a charge was sought to be fixed upon Miss Constance Kent.'[26]

The magistrates agreed and set Constance free on £200 bail to appear if called upon again. 'The decision of the Bench,' it was reported, 'was greeted with loud applause.'[27]

Whicher saw no reason to hang about and returned to London. The assault on his reputation, however, continued. '"Better that 99 guilty persons should escape than one innocent should suffer" is an excellent principle,' preached one Wiltshire paper, 'but Mr Whicher appears to think that better than 99 innocent should suffer than one guilty escape.' Gloated *The Portsmouth Times and Naval Gazette*: 'The case, as got up by Mr Inspector Whicher, has completely fallen through. A missing bed-gown . . . and some trifling childish gossip with a schoolfellow, literally proving nothing, was the evidence on which the Inspector relied to commit his prisoner for trial on the awful charge of murder.' *The Frome Times,* no fan of Whicher, used the inspector's failure to taint all detectives. 'With reference to the course pursued by "the Detective",' it noted in a haughty tone, 'we cannot refrain from observing it will be long before Detectives will be tolerated again in this part of the country.' And so it played out in papers across Britain.[28]

In the House of Commons on Wednesday, 15 August, one Member of Parliament dragged Whicher's name through the mud and suggested that police inspectors and superintendents pass an examination before assuming their senior rank. 'They had an instance,' reported *Bell's Weekly Messenger,* 'of the inferior intellect and attainments of the inspectors of police in the case of Whicher, the person employed to investigate the Road murder. That man arrested a young lady on a charge of murder, merely on account of a mislaid nightdress.'[29]

Some papers came to Whicher's defence. 'That Mr Whicher's zeal went beyond his discretion is a mild charge compared to the abuse which the press has almost unanimously flung upon him,' observed *The London Daily News,* 'abuse so virulent and unfounded that no public officer who conscientiously discharged his duty should be permitted to suffer.'[30]

It did little good. The class distinctions and prejudices of the day worked against Whicher, as did the resentment and jealousy of a local constabulary forced to call Scotland Yard for help. He was viewed as an interloper and had little official authority. Superintendent Foley and his men had bungled the case – finding and then losing the bloody chemise – before the Yard was even summoned. Foley hid the garment episode from his superiors. Not until a local police sergeant came clean in November did the fact become public knowledge. 'Not one word,' said Whicher, who believed the garment to be Constance's missing nightgown, 'was said to me or to the magistrates, or indeed to anyone, about the finding of this dress or shift . . .'[31]

Constance, meanwhile, had left the country for a convent in France, where she supposedly found religion. She returned to England in the summer of 1863 and went to live at St Mary's Home, 'a house for religious ladies', in Brighton. Whicher became 'increasingly depressed' as the months dragged on and took early retirement from Scotland Yard in 1864 after twenty-five years on the force. His discharge papers listed the reason as 'congestion of the brain' – or, as *The Official Encyclopedia of Scotland Yard* puts it, a 'mental breakdown'.[32]

In April 1865 – five years after the murder and the year after Whicher's retirement – Constance confessed to the crime and committed her vile deed to paper: 'I, Constance Emilie Kent, alone and unaided, on the night of the 29th June, 1860, murdered at Road-hill House, Wiltshire, one Francis Saville Kent. Before the deed was done no one knew of my intention, nor afterwards of my guilt. No one assisted me in the crime, nor in the evasion of discovery.'[33]

'Constance Kent has achieved a celebrity which eclipses the pacification of half the world, and will certainly last as long as the English language is spoken,' *The Times* noted on 27 April alongside news of President Abraham Lincoln's assassination. 'She is not only the heroine of a foul murder, but an example in the science of the mind. As a psychological type she will long survive the vulgar crowd of poets, philosophers and historians.'[34]

Constance detailed the crime for Dr John Charles Bucknill, who examined her to determine if 'there were any grounds for supposing that she was labouring under mental disease.' Bucknill shared Constance's horrific narrative at her trial in July 1865. On the night of the murder, after everyone in the house was asleep, she crept from her bedroom and went downstairs to open the drawing-room door and window shutters.

She then went up into the nursery . . . took the child from his bed and carried him downstairs through the drawing-room. She had on her night-dress and in the drawing-room put on her galoshes. Having the child in one arm, she raised the drawing-room window with the other hand, went round the house and into the closet, the child being wrapped in the blanket and still sleeping, and while the child was in this position she inflicted the wound in the throat. She says that she thought the blood would never come, and that the child was not killed, so she thrust the razor into its left side, and put the body, with the blanket round it, into the vault.[35]

Returning to her bedroom, she saw her nightgown had two spots of blood on it. She washed the gown, let it dry overnight and returned it to her dresser the following morning. It was subsequently inspected by Superintendent Foley who failed to notice the faint but still-visible bloodstains when he held it up to the light. Not wanting to take any chances, she hid the garment in multiple places throughout the house before burning it in her bedroom six days after the murder. She dumped the ashes down the kitchen grate. The bloody chemise found in the kitchen had nothing to do with the crime. As for the motive, 'she had no ill-will against the little boy, except as one of the children of her stepmother.'[36]

The confession was not without its problems. How did Constance, with Francis in her arms, manage to pull on her galoshes, open the drawing-room window and climb through? The child's head had almost been severed, so why was there so little blood? And how did she cut the boy's throat while holding him? These questions, devoid of answers, only heightened the mystery. Was she protecting someone? Whicher, in the course of his investigation, had speculated the following in a report to his superiors:[37]

As far as I am able to form an opinion, the murder was committed either by Miss Constance alone while in a fit of insanity, or by her and her brother William from motives of spite or jealousy towards the younger children and their parents, and I am strongly impressed with the latter opinion judging from the sympathy existing between the two . . .[38]

Whicher's instincts had served him well, even if the press and public had doubted his intuition. Constance was found guilty; her death sentence commuted to 'penal servitude for life'. She served twenty years and emerged a free woman in 1885 at the age of forty-one. She left England and, in 1886, moved to Tasmania with William's family. She eventually settled in Australia under the name Ruth Emilie Kaye and found her purpose in nursing and working with lepers. She died in April 1944, two months after her hundredth birthday, having successfully kept her true identity a secret. She was, reported a local newspaper at the time, 'a really wonderful old lady'.[39]

Constance Kent, murderess.

Whicher's perceived failure to solve the Road Hill House mystery prior to Constance's confession reflected poorly on the Detective Branch, tainting its supposed investigative prowess and – by extension – the effectiveness of Scotland Yard. What the Yard needed to set itself right was a high-profile success. It would soon have one with a sensational case that enthralled both sides of the Atlantic.

6

A Zealous Effort

A chase across the sea.

The Liverpool and Manchester Railway, the world's first modern railroad featuring timetables and stations for passengers, opened in 1830. It was, enthused *The Scotsman*, a 'magnificent and stupendous work, which is calculated to be of immense utility to the public'. Its grand opening on 15 September attracted such political scions as the Duke of Wellington and the prime minister, who crowded aboard the train for its inaugural journey. Not all went according to plan. At one stop, a locomotive ran over and killed Liverpool MP William Huskisson as he tried to cross the track. The accident, though tragic, symbolized the public's perception of this new means of transit. There was a pervasive fear it might be detrimental to one's health.[1]

In the years that followed, stories began appearing in newspapers and magazines about passengers in railway carriages driven to violent insanity by the noise and rhythmic motion of travel by train. The articles suggested railway-induced lunacy posed a significant threat to society's well-being. It got to the point that, in 1862, *The Lancet* medical journal appointed 'a scientific commission to conduct an inquiry into the influence of Railway Travelling on the Public Health'. It sought to put nervous Victorians at ease. 'The mental condition of passengers by train is commonly, perhaps, sufficiently placid and unconcerned,' it reported, 'but several eminently careful observers have, in their communications to us, alluded to an often experienced condition of uneasiness, scarcely amounting to actual fear, which pervades the generality of travellers by rail.'[2]

A late-running train or stopping in an unfamiliar location proved enough to upset one's piece of mind, according to the journal. Even the unexpected blow of a locomotive's whistle could heighten a passenger's discomfort. 'The pace, also, prevents the traveller from that observation of natural objects and sights of interest on the road, which made coach travelling a source of mental relaxation and a pastime,' it theorized. 'The passenger is forced into subjective sources of mental activity; and where the tendency to excitement exists, this also, *quantum valeat*, must be esteemed an undesirable feature belonging to this manner of locomotion.'[3]

The Lancet study did little to soothe Victorian nerves. Never mind the fact more than 10,000 miles of track crisscrossed Great Britain, cutting through rolling, green country and connecting cities, or that more than 200 million passenger journeys a year occurred with minimal interference from raving lunatics. A fear of insanity on the tracks persisted.[4]

'It is the glory of an age of scientific progress to have invented a perfectly new and unique description of social torture,' noted *The Saturday Review* on 16 July 1864. 'The English railway carriage – more especially the English first-class railway carriage – may be defined as an apparatus of unexampled efficiency for isolating a human being from the companionship and protection of his fellow creatures and exposing him as helpless prey to murderous outrage. It is a prison from which there is no escape but with the certainty of broken bones and the risk of being pounded into atoms.'[5]

Although the article made no mention of it, events a week prior certainly appeared to bolster its argument.

The 9:50 p.m. train from Fenchurch Street Station on the North London Railway line pulled into Hackney at 10:11 p.m. on Saturday,

9 July. Henry Vernez and Sydney Jones, both clerks in the City banking firm of Robarts, Curtis & Co. found an empty compartment aboard the No. 69 first-class carriage. The compartment's interior was polished wood and plush seats – two on either side, divided by an armrest – upholstered in blue cloth and American leather, illuminated in the soft glow of a single wall-mounted oil lamp.[6]

Vernez took a seat on the right-hand side of the carriage, facing the engine, and Jones took the seat opposite. No sooner had the latter got comfortable than he lifted his hand from the seat cushion and found it wet with blood; he showed his glistening palm to Vernez. The two men raised the alarm and got the attention of train guard Benjamin Ames, who trudged to the brake van and grabbed his hand lamp.[7]

Entering the clerks' compartment, his lamp held aloft to brighten the gloom, Ames at once noticed something amiss. 'There was a goodish drop of blood altogether about,' he said. 'There was a great many spots of blood on the carriage cushion.' Blood, still wet, pooled in the buttoned divots of the seats. The armrest between the two seats on the compartment's right-hand side was smeared in blood, as if someone 'had been dragged over it.' Blood splatter left a grotesque pattern across the window – the largest splotch being 'about the size of a sixpence.' Ames got down on his knees, peered under the seats, and found an empty leather bag with bloody fingerprints on the brass locks, a crumpled hat, and a 'thick cane with a heavy ivory knob' covered in blood.[8]

Ames gathered the items, locked up the compartment, and signalled the driver to proceed to Chalk Farm, the final stop on the North London line. Minutes later, at 10:20 p.m., the driver of a train returning empty carriages to Fenchurch Street noticed something lying 'on the six-foot way between the Hackney Street and Bow stations.'[9]

He pulled the brake lever and alerted his guard, William Timms, who disembarked to investigate. 'I found it was the body of a man lying there,' Timms said. 'He was lying on his back with his head towards Hackney.' His right leg was straight; his left one drawn up. He lay on top of his right arm with his left draped across his torso. The man, his eyes half open, was unconscious but still alive.[10]

Timms ran down the railway embankment towards the lights of the Mitford Castle Tavern in Wick Lane for help. Landlord James Hudson looked up from behind the bar when a man, in a considerable state of excitement, burst through the door and announced 'the mutilated body of a gentleman had been found on the railway close by, between the rails'. Five men abandoned their beer and followed Timms back to the scene. They hoisted the prostrate and bloody figure between them and hauled him back to the pub. Police Constable Edward Dougan of K (Stepney) Division, on patrol near the tavern and alerted by the commotion, joined them in their efforts.[11]

They stretched the man out on a sofa in a small room behind the bar. He moaned quietly but remained unconscious, his head a battered mess and his clothes soaked in blood. Dougan knelt down and searched the man's rumpled clothes. He found some keys, four sovereigns, a silver snuffbox, 'ten shillings and sixpence in silver and copper', a silk handkerchief and a first-class ticket for the North London Railway. From one pocket he pulled 'a number of letters and papers' that identified the victim as Mr Thomas Briggs, chief clerk in the bank of Robarts, Curtis & Co. in Lombard Street.[12]

At eleven o'clock, a local surgeon named Alfred Brereton arrived. The air in the small room was by now dank from the number of people crowding around the sad spectacle on the sofa. The doctor had Briggs moved to a larger room upstairs and placed on a mattress on top of a table. 'He was evidently suffering from compression of the brain,' Brereton recalled. '. . . I endeavoured to restore reaction by different methods, but failed.' It was astonishing Briggs was alive at all. His left ear had been severed in a jagged wound; another gash anterior to the ear had exposed the bone. 'The skull,' the doctor said, 'was found to be extensively fractured, the fissures extending in various directions, radiating as it were from the centre.' Brereton believed the wounds on the left side of the head resulted from Briggs being thrown to the ground, while a blunt instrument inflicted the damage to the top of the skull.[13]

A runner was dispatched to the Briggs home at 5, Clapton Square, Hackney, in the early morning hours of Sunday, 10 July. The bad news roused Thomas James (T. J.) Briggs, the family's second-eldest son, from bed. He arrived at the Mitford Tavern at around two o'clock in the morning and found his father in the upstairs room beneath a blanket on the makeshift bed. Briggs's personal physician, Francis Toulmin, arrived shortly thereafter. Nothing could be done for the patient. Examining the head wounds, Toulmin noted 'the temporal bone was driven in upon the brain'. The doctor pulled up a chair and settled in for a long night.[14]

Sunday, 10 July. Police constables, dim silhouettes in the morning's grey light, searched for clues on the railway embankment where Briggs had been found and the Duckett's Canal bridge that spanned the tracks. In charge of the investigation was Inspector Walter Kerressey, Bow Division's senior officer – a stout Irishman, former soldier, and twenty-five-year veteran of the Yard. Now, at forty-five, he 'supervised eleven first-class sergeants and over 300 police constables in his division.'[15]

Carriage No. 69, with its gore-splattered compartment, now sat in a railway shed at Bow Station. The hat, cane and bag had been turned over that morning to one of Kerressey's men, who took them to the Briggs home for identification. While Mr Briggs's wife and children recognized the bag and cane, none of them recognized the hat. It was a black beaver hat with a much shorter crown than the high hat Mr Briggs wore. A label inside the hat identified its maker – 'Mr J. H. Walker, 49 Crawford Street, Marylebone' – but offered no clue as to its owner. Kerressey, meanwhile, busied himself inspecting the murder compartment. Nothing had been disturbed from the night before. He theorized from the blood-stains, now dry, that perhaps 'Mr Briggs had been attacked while dozing, with his head against the corner of the carriage'.[16]

Blood covered the iron step beneath the compartment door and stained part of a wooden step that ran the length of the carriage. At the rear exterior, Kerressey noticed heavy blood spatter on the axle box and the 'framework supporting the body of the carriage'. This seemed to suggest the victim was 'dropped, as it were, out of the carriage with his head downwards.' But of particular interest was blood on one of the compartment's door handles. Kerressey left the railway shed and made his way to 5, Clapton Square, arriving at eleven o'clock. Briggs had by now been moved from the tavern back to his house. 'He was then alive,' Kerressey said, 'but insensible.' The inspector looked at Briggs's hands and noticed that although they were bruised, they did not have any blood on them, meaning it wasn't Briggs who opened the compartment door and got blood on the handle.[17]

Talking with the family, the inspector learned Briggs left home that Saturday morning wearing 'a gold watch with an Albert chain and a gold eye-glass attached to a hair guard.'[18] The watch and chain were both missing. The chain was attached to 'a large gold key with the figure of an animal on top' and a swivel seal with two stones, one light and one dark. The timepiece was 'a large old-fashioned gold chronometer' with a white dial. It bore the name of the watchmaker, 'S. W. Archer, Hackney, No. 1487, the case being numbered 2,974.'[19]

The day progressed. Details of Thomas Briggs's final hours came into focus as police traced his movements. He left the bank at three o'clock on Saturday afternoon and dined at his niece's home in Peckham. He stayed until half past eight and departed by coach for Fenchurch Street Station, arriving at twenty minutes to ten. He was well known to the ticket collectors, as he passed through the station on a daily basis. The collector on duty that night was Thomas Fishbourne. He sat on a stool near the booking office.

Fully absorbed in his dinner of bread and cheese, Fishbourne felt someone tap him on the shoulder and say, 'Good night.' He turned and saw Thomas Briggs, who gave him a friendly nod before heading up the stairs to the platform. Briggs was alone, and no one appeared to be following him. On the platform, Briggs nodded in greeting to the operator in the telegraph office and boarded the train at 9:45 p.m.[20]

What happened after that remained a mystery. The bag Briggs carried was 'of the class generally used by bankers' clerks in removing bullion.' Did the assailant target Briggs, believing the bag was full of money? The bloody finger marks on the bag's brass locks seemed to suggest the possibility. Why did the culprit leave the diamond ring on Briggs's finger, ignore the change in his pockets (totalling more than £4) and not take the silver snuffbox? How did the assailant, undoubtedly covered in blood, escape the train unnoticed? How did he dump Briggs onto the tracks without drawing unwanted attention? And what about the hat? It was 'flattened and crushed' when found, and smeared with blood inside the crown. Briggs's silk hat 'was a good "Paris nap"' from Digance and Co. in the Royal Exchange. In the panicked aftermath of the attack, did the assailant mistakenly flee with the wrong headwear?[21]

Such questions took on greater urgency at 11:45 p.m. that Sunday, when Thomas Briggs died without ever regaining consciousness.

The London Morning Herald, Monday, 11 July 1864:

HORRIBLE AND ATROCIOUS MURDER
IN A FIRST-CLASS CARRIAGE OF A TRAIN
ON THE NORTH LONDON RAILWAY

One of the most atrocious crimes that probably ever disgraced this country was perpetrated late on Saturday evening in a first-class carriage of a passenger train on the North London

Railway, when a gentleman, Mr Thomas Briggs, connected with the banking establishment of Messrs. Robarts, Curtis, and Co., of Lombard-street, was murderously assailed, plundered, and thrown from the train.[22]

The murder, being the first to occur on a British train, caused a sensation. 'It is some years,' reported *The Evening Standard*, 'since so much excitement was created in the metropolis as that produced by the publication of the details of the appalling murder of Mr Briggs.'[23]

Police Commissioner Sir Richard Mayne must have read the newspaper accounts with dismay that morning.* The public, nervous as it was about railway travel, would demand – and expect – a swift resolution. The last thing the Yard needed was another debacle like the Road Hill House investigation. 'Our police have a character to keep,' warned *The Daily Telegraph*, 'but they also have a reputation to regain. Excellently as their general work is done, it must be remembered that many of their cleverest admirers ascribed to them some more special and peculiar credit than that resulting from a fair performance of their duties.'[24] There was, in Mayne's opinion, only one detective for the job: thirty-one-year-old Inspector Richard Tanner.

Dick to his friends, Tanner – only recently promoted to the rank of Inspector – was considered 'the most brilliant officer then at Scotland Yard.'[25] Affable in manner and tall in build with brown hair and blue eyes, he had joined the Metropolitan Police in March 1851 at the age of nineteen. He was working out of 4, Whitehall Place within three years, earning a name for himself through street smarts and determination. No stranger to the spotlight, he had cut his teeth on a high-profile murder case four years prior.[26]

Mary Emsley, a wealthy property owner, was found beaten to death in her East End home on 17 August 1860. Police could

---

* Mayne was conferred Knight Commander of the Order of Bath in 1851 for his public service.

find no sign of forced entry and deduced she'd been killed by an acquaintance. The case seemed to be going nowhere until one evening, a man named James Mullins – a labourer who occasionally worked for Emsley – knocked on the door of Tanner's home and said he knew the killer's identity. He named William Emm, who collected the rents from Emsley's properties, and lived in a cottage near the victim's house. Mullins said he had spied Emm hiding a suspicious-looking package in a small shed behind the cottage.[27]

The next morning Tanner, accompanied by Mullins, searched Emm's shed and found a wrapped package containing silverware stolen from the dead woman's home and a cheque made out to her on the day of the murder. On a hunch, Tanner asked Mullins where he'd been when he saw Emm hide the package. Mullins said he'd been standing 'on the other side of the road'. Tanner politely pointed out it would have been impossible to see inside the shed from such a vantage point. When detectives searched Mullins's home, they found the same kind of tape used to wrap the package in the shed and a footprint that matched a bloody one found at the murder scene. Mullins's date with the hangman was all but guaranteed.[28]

Now, Tanner faced the greatest case of his career. Inspector Kerressey, an old friend, shared what information he had and passed along the cane, bag and mystery hat. Tanner circulated a description of the missing watch and chain to jewellers and pawnshops. He had the details, along with those of Briggs's missing hat, printed on some 2,000 posters with word of a £300 reward for information leading to an arrest. The posters went up across the city within days.[29] Observed *The Daily Telegraph* on 13 July:

> In many of the chief thoroughfares of London yesterday, little groups were to be seen anxiously reading a brand-new placard. It was not one of those documents in which Sir Richard Mayne elaborately ordains the routes by which carriages shall

approach a flower-show or a drawing-room; the word that caught their eye upon it was 'Murder'. As they looked all men knew the death-hunt was afoot; that society shocked by a hideous crime was alert and eager to avenge it.[30]

Letters and leads from all corners of the country inundated Scotland Yard, the majority being 'of the most absurd character and utterly useless'. And that wasn't all. 'At the police station at Bow there is a large collection of hats of all shapes and sizes found all over London since the murder,' reported *The Evening Standard*, 'and the police have received the names of a number of doubtless most innocent individuals who returned home hatless or with black eyes on the night in question.'[31]

One tip stood out from the others. A jeweller, aptly named John Death, came forward after reading newspaper accounts of the crime and said he may have done business with the killer. On the morning of Monday, 11 July, 'a gentlemanly foreigner' entered Death's shop at 55, Cheapside to exchange a gold chain. He was either German or Swiss, about thirty years old, with a thin build and sallow complexion, dressed in 'a black frock coat and waistcoat, dark trousers, and a black hat'. He spoke good English and exchanged a gold Albert chain for another chain and a gold signet ring with a white cornelian stone. The transaction's total value was £3 10s (roughly £470 or $600 today).[32]

Although 'he seemed perfectly collected in his manner during the transaction,' Death said the customer 'endeavoured to keep his countenance concealed' and kept his distance from the display case. The chain the mystery man exchanged matched the description of Briggs's missing jewellery. Death turned it over to Inspector Kerressey, who examined it under his magnifying glass. There 'was not the slightest trace of blood upon it, and by the dirt caused by wear still adherent to the links it does not seem to have been washed.' Kerressey thought the chain must have been yanked from Briggs's waistcoat before the fatal beating began.[33]

On the morning of Thursday, 14 July, Thomas Briggs's funeral cortege departed the family home in Clapton Square. It made its way slowly through quiet streets lined with mourners towards the Gravel Pit Unitarian Chapel. Shop owners along the procession route closed their businesses in solemn respect.[34]

Tanner felt the pressure. 'The police seem to feel that after their many failures of late years the present case puts them on their trial,' reported *The Evening Standard*, 'and if their exertions are not rewarded with success it will be a blot on the detective police system in this country.' Although the description of Death's mystery customer provided little to go on, Tanner ordered detectives to 'Folkestone, Dover, Southampton, Harwich, Hull, Liverpool and other ports' to monitor steamers bound for foreign shores. The Yard instructed police in port towns to 'keep a sharp eye on persons taking berths in outward-bound vessels'. Officers also kept an eye on lodging houses that catered to a foreign clientele, 'which abound in certain quarters of the metropolis.' Constables armed with photographs of the deceased questioned porters, ticket-takers and travellers at every station on the North London Railway between Fenchurch and Hackney. Tanner hoped the effort might open a new avenue of investigation, but the effort went nowhere.[35]

The only concrete clue in Tanner's possession was the battered hat found in the carriage, yet the hatter – when interviewed – could not identify the customer. All this played out against a daily influx of letters to Scotland Yard naming random Germans as the killer. 'It would seem,' reported *Reynolds's Newspaper*, 'that the foreigners resident in London are the objects of very close scrutiny.' On the evening of Friday, 16 July, a constable in the south London borough of Southwark arrested a German 'who answered in certain points to the description of the man who exchanged the chain at Mr Death's shop.' The jeweller, summoned from his home, arrived at the police station and cleared 'the unlucky individual' of any wrongdoing.[36]

That same evening, Inspector Kerressey received word 'a man wearing the late Mr Briggs's hat' had been taken into custody at the Wells Street Police Station in Hackney. Kerressey arrived at the station, only to discover the report had been a hoax. Indeed, 'fantasy sightings, tip-offs and distractions' proved rampant. On Saturday, Kerressey was informed a German who matched the description of Mr Death's customer had taken up residence in a lodging house in North Woolwhich 'a day or two after the murder.' The inspector's pursuit of the lead proved it to be 'rather a hopeless case'. It seemed any thin, sallow-faced individual with a hat, cane and accent became a target of suspicion.[37]

Londoners followed the case and its wild goose chases with rapt attention and chimed in via Letters to the Editor on everything from whether a crime had actually been committed (one *Times* reader suggested Mr Briggs had suffered a burst blood-vessel) to what steps should be taken to improve the safety of railway travel. Wrote one reader to *The Evening Standard*:

SIR, – Criminal deeds, being not unfrequently perpetrated in railway carriages, perhaps you will allow space in your widely-read journal for the following hint to railway companies.

Bells, or other means of communications with the guards, are obviously surrounded by many difficulties, and even if practicable cannot always be depended on.

Let, then, at once set to work and have a pane of glass placed in the division between each compartment of a carriage. If it so happens that only three persons travel in one carriage, and two should be in one compartment of it, let the third be compelled, if they do not ride altogether, to sit in the next compartment, so that there might be a means of seeing if anything wrong was going on, and thus affording means of identification, &c. Public safety will be sufficient compensation for any curiosity that might be exhibited by anyone.

The adoption of this plan, I am convinced, will give confidence to every traveller.

Yours, &c.,

An Occasional Traveller[38]

As it so happened, the Briggs murder would have a lasting
impact on railway safety.*

The big break came just shy of 10 p.m. on Monday, 18 July.

A cab driver named Jonathan Matthews – 'a man of very
moderate intelligence and certainly no great reader' – stopped to
water his horse outside Paddington's Great Western Hotel. As he
dismounted his cab, he noticed a police placard with its details of
the Briggs murder: the description of the hat found in the carriage,
the chain exchanged at Death's store and the £300 reward. It was,
he would claim, the first time he'd heard of the crime, but Death's
name sparked a memory.[39]

Matthews's sister had, until recently, been engaged to a young
German tailor named Franz Müller, a twenty-five-year-old native
of Cologne who'd arrived in England eighteen months prior. The
romance didn't last, but Müller's friendship with Matthews's family
did. In fact, Müller had visited the Matthews house several days
ago and given Matthews's daughter a small gift. That memory,
and perhaps the thought of £300 lining his pockets, prompted

---

* Two years after the crime, railway companies installed a communication cord
along the roofline of all carriages. This allowed passengers to ring a bell in the guard
carriage should trouble occur, although they had to lean out of the window to do it.
One safety fix was the installation of small windows – dubbed 'Müller Lights' – in
the walls between carriage compartments, but they were scrapped after passengers
complained about the lack of privacy. In the 1890s, railway companies began putting to use corridor-connected carriages, a design already employed in the United
States. By the turn of the century, many trains were equipped with a brake cord
passengers could pull in an emergency (see Colquhoun, p. 274).

Matthews to climb back in his hack and rush home. By ten o'clock that evening, he was sitting in front of Inspector Thomas Steer at the Paddington Green Police Station and relaying his story.[40]

'Last Monday week,' Matthews said, 'Müller visited my house and saw my wife. After paying her the usual compliments, he took a box out of his pocket and pulled out of it a gold chain, which he said he had paid £3 10s for that morning. He then fixed the chain on a watch and gave the box to my child to play with.'[41]

Matthews pulled from his coat pocket the jewellery box with Death's name and shop address on it, much to the detective's intense interest.[42]

'I remember one Sunday in October or November last,' Matthews said, '[Müller] came to my house and said to me, "You have a nice hat. Where did you get it from?" I told him I bought it from a man named Walker, a hatter in Crawford Street.'

Steer listened with growing excitement as Matthews said he purchased a hat from the shop and gave it to Müller. Matthews said he could easily identify the hat if he saw it again. The inside brim had 'a peculiar thumb mark, caused by the hat being put on and taken off by the hand at one particular spot.'[43]

Steer inquired as to Müller's current whereabouts. Matthews said Müller had worked as a shirt-cutter for a clothing outfit in Threadneedle Street but quit three weeks ago following some dispute. He had been living in a lodging house at 16, Park Terrace, Old Ford, Bow – but, on his last visit to the Matthews's, he said he was leaving London to try his luck in Canada. Nothing about Müller that day seemed amiss, although he was walking with a limp. He said a cart had run over his foot and sprained his ankle.

Steer escorted the cabman to Scotland Yard. The two men rode by carriage through London's gas-lit streets, past taverns and darkened storefronts, the sound of the horses' hooves echoing off the cobblestones. At the Yard, Matthews repeated his story for Inspector Tanner. The detective pulled from a cupboard the crumpled hat found in the murder carriage and showed it to Matthews. Inside the brim was the thumb mark. It was indeed the hat, Matthews assured the inspectors. 'I could swear to it,' he said.[44]

Tanner got an early start the next day, chasing down the new lead before the sun cleared the city's spires. At 16, Park Terrace, Bow, he interviewed Ellen Blyth, Müller's one-time landlady. 'He lodged with me seven weeks, but I have known him for more than twelve months,' Mrs Blyth said. 'I have always known him to be a quiet, inoffensive and well-behaved young man.' She said that on Saturday, 9 July, the day Briggs was assaulted, Müller left the house in the morning and stayed out until after she and her husband had gone to bed late that evening. He joined the couple for breakfast the next morning and seemed in fine spirits. Mrs Blyth noticed one peculiarity: Müller had acquired a limp.[45]

On the morning of Monday, 11 July, the day Müller visited the Matthews family, he showed Mrs Blyth 'a gold Albert chain' but didn't say where he got it. Three days later, he told the Blyths he was going to New York and moved out. The couple was sorry to see him go, but not surprised. He had been discussing his New York plans for at least two weeks. 'He was a well-conducted young man in every respect,' George Blyth told Tanner. 'A man of kind, humane disposition. When he left on the Thursday morning, he bade me good-bye. He told me what vessel he was going in, the *Victoria*.'[46]

Mrs Blyth handed Tanner a letter she'd received from their one-time lodger:

> On the sea, 16 July, in the morning. Dear friends, I am glad
> to confess that I cannot have a better time as I have, for the
> sun shines nice and the wind blows fair as it is at the present
> moment, everything will go well. I cannot write anymore only
> I have no postage.[47]

Mrs Blyth had one last thing to show Tanner. It was a hatbox Müller had in his possession when he moved in and left in his room when he departed. Inside was a label with the hat-maker's name and address: 'Walker, 49, Crawford-street, Marylebone.'[48]

Armed with a photograph of Müller, Tanner hurried to Death's shop. The jeweller confirmed the man in the picture was indeed the customer who exchanged Briggs's chain. Exhausted but determined, Tanner secured an arrest warrant from Bow Street Police Court that afternoon and 'passports for two witnesses and two members of the police force' from the Foreign Office, which also supplied 'dispatches . . . so that any proceedings in America will be facilitated to the utmost.'[49]

What Tanner hoped would be his final stop that evening was the Chester Square home of Sir Richard Mayne to report the latest developments. He arrived by carriage with Jonathan Matthews and John Death and found the commissioner dressed for a night at the opera. Mayne listened to the inspector's update and the information provided by the two witnesses. The commissioner nodded his approval and then ordered a shocked and put-upon Tanner – along with Matthews and Death – to leave at once for America.[50]

The chase was on.

'London and the world at large will be thankful that such a clue has at last been found to the track of the murderer of the late Mr Briggs as to leave no doubt that the miscreant will be brought to justice,' *The Times* declared.[51]

Tanner, perhaps, felt less enthralled. 'I was twenty days in the Harbour of New York, during which time I do not think I ever went to sleep, waiting for that ship,' he would later write, 'and then there was the anxiety of coming home with Müller, besides the trouble of getting him and going to law in New York.' Leaving Mayne's house, he had less than two hours to prepare for his transatlantic voyage. He departed London via Euston Station at nine o'clock in the company of Matthews, Death and Sergeant George Clarke, and travelled through the night to Liverpool. Booked on the Inman Line's steamer *City of Manchester*, they put to sea the following morning, Tuesday, 20 July.[52]

Müller had a four-day head start but was travelling by wind and sail. The 2,000-ton *City of Manchester*, by comparison, was 'a splendid ship' of more modern design. Three massive boilers – each weighing 30 tons – gave life to her 400-horse-power engines. Measuring 274 feet in length and nearly 38 feet in breadth of beam, she was a ship of 'beautiful proportions and graceful lines.' Tanner, weather permitting, would arrive in New York ahead of his quarry and arrest Müller before the man had a chance to step ashore. It wasn't all smooth sailing. On the third day at sea, Tanner took a nasty spill down a flight of stairs and wrenched his back. 'I was confined to bed for four days,' Tanner wrote, 'and when we got to New York I was very ill.'[53]

As the *Victoria* and the *City of Manchester* raced across the white-tipped waves of the North Atlantic, the press in Britain did its utmost to portray Müller in an unfavourable light. 'The personal characteristics of the murderer may be thus summed up,' noted one London rag. 'He is a man of great resolution and singular energy. He had a character for extreme violence, which caused him to be disliked by his friends. His forehead is low, his cheek bones prominent, and his general expression of face rather forbidding.' *Reynolds's Newspaper* all but convicted him. 'The conclusive evidence which has come to light pointing out the man Franz Müller as the actual murderer of Mr Briggs produced throughout the City and the metropolis a feeling of intense satisfaction and relief.'[54]

Such a feeling was not universal. The Yard began receiving letters from the public questioning Müller's guilt. In particular, Jonathan Matthews's story came under scrutiny. Was it really possible the man – for more than a week – knew nothing about a murder that enthralled the entire city? Perhaps he fabricated his story to claim the £300 reward. His tale of buying a hat for Müller rang untrue to many. It seemed unlikely one could purchase a hat for another that fit perfectly. 'In our opinion,' penned one suspicious citizen, 'it is very difficult to get fitted with a hat even by a professional hatter.'[55]

Tanner and his motley team reached New York Harbour ahead of Müller's ship and docked in Manhattan on Friday, 5 August. The men took rooms at the Everett House Hotel 'on the north side of Union Square'.[56]

The inspector's mind was a beehive of anxiety. There was much to do and little time to get it done. Still hobbled with a bad back, he set off that Saturday morning, navigating New York's bustling streets, to meet with Francis Marbury, the legal counsel for the British Consulate, and Chief of the New York Metropolitan Police, Superintendent James Kennedy. Because Tanner could not legally make an arrest on American soil, Kennedy placed an officer named John Tieman at the inspector's disposal. Tanner was much obliged. 'The police,' he later wrote, 'rendered me all the assistance possible.'[57]

The operation's success relied on taking Müller by surprise, something the New York press seemed keen to thwart. The United States was a country at war. News of the Confederate advance on Washington dominated the headlines, but the city's papers still made room for Tanner's adventure. The day before his arrival, *The New York Times* – under the headline 'GREAT BRITAIN: THE MYSTERIOUS MURDER. SUPPOSED DISCOVERY OF THE PERPETRATOR. HIS FLIGHT TO AMERICA. FURTHER PARTICULARS' – reprinted a summary of the case that appeared several days prior in *The* (London) *Times*. Such coverage inflamed Tanner's fears Müller might learn of Scotland Yard's presence in New York before the *Victoria* even docked.[58] Another article in *The Brooklyn Eagle* the day after Tanner's arrival stretched his exhausted nerves. Under the headline 'MURDER WILL OUT', the paper informed its readers in breathless prose:

Here was a case where discovery was at least very unlikely, and proof improbable. Yet but a few weeks elapse before the murderer is traced, the proof fixed upon, and notwithstanding his utmost ingenuity, his tact in making himself obscure, and the rapidity with which he got out of the way, the officers of justice are upon his tail, and will surprise him when he sets foot upon the pier in this city in the course of a few days.[59]

Tanner was not amused. 'In consequence of the publication in the papers of all my movements there is a possibility of Müller escaping,' he wrote to Mayne in a report dated 9 August, 'but I shall take every possible step in my power to prevent it.' As a precautionary measure, he sent Sergeant Clarke and NYPD Officer Tieman to the Quarantine Station on Staten Island to watch for the *Victoria*'s entry into New York Harbour. They were to inform Tanner immediately via telegram when the ship appeared.[60]

The days slipped by in a slow, hot tedium with no sign of the *Victoria*. On Friday, 12 August, the Confederate raider *Tallahassee* captured and sank the *Victoria*'s sister ship, the *Adriatic*, bound for New York from London. Another boat took aboard the ship's 163 passengers before the *Adriatic* was set alight. 'It was a sad sight to witness the trouble of these poor creatures, who, in many instances, had their all on board,' remembered one crewmember. 'Perhaps, one-half the number were able-bodied young men, who will be found in a month's time, in the Army of Virginia.'[61]

Tanner could only hope the *Victoria* did not suffer the same fate. A week passed and still the ship's whereabouts remained a mystery. 'Up to this date we have no tidings of the ship *Victoria*,' Tanner reported on 23 August. 'She is now forty days out and may be hourly expected.' His words proved prophetic.[62]

The *Victoria* entered the harbour late in the afternoon of Wednesday, 24 August. Tanner could do nothing but hope everything went according to plan. He had spent the past two weeks distributing handbills to the city's harbour pilots, offering a $60 reward to the first pilot to board the *Victoria* and ask the captain to make sure Müller didn't escape. Captain Champion 'cheerfully' complied and assigned two crewmembers to keep a discreet eye on the unsuspecting Müller. Tanner, meanwhile, rushed back to the British Consul to 'make an affidavit that Müller was in American waters'. Only then would the US authorities issue the necessary arrest warrant.[63]

New Yorkers had become just as enthralled by all of it as Londoners – so much so that an excursion craft carried curious onlookers across the harbour to see the *Victoria* for themselves. 'How are you, Müller?' they shouted as they passed the larger vessel. 'Throw the murderer overboard!' Müller, on deck, did not hear the taunting and remained oblivious to what lay in store.[64]

From Staten Island, Clarke and Tieman sailed out to the *Victoria* on a small medical boat. Captain Champion greeted the two officers and led them to the stern of the ship, where he pointed out Müller mingling with other passengers. Clarke approached and seized Müller by the arms.

'What is the matter?' a startled Müller asked.

'You are under arrest for the murder of Mr Briggs,' Tieman replied.

'Yes,' said Clarke, 'on the North London Railway Line between Hackney Wick and Bow on 9 July.'

Müller shook his head. 'I was never on the line.'

Clarke and Tieman informed Müller they were police officers and escorted him to the ship's saloon. Tieman searched the prisoner and found a key in his waistcoat.

'What is the key of?' Clarke asked.

'The key of my box,' Müller said. 'In my berth.'

Champion, playing audience to the proceedings, directed Clarke to berth No. 9, where he found a large, black storage trunk with brass nails. He hauled it back to the saloon, unlocked it with the key and rummaged through its contents: 'one or two shirts, some collars, a few of the implements of Müller's trade, such as shears and measure, a few scarfs, a few brushes and an umbrella.' Of considerable interest was a hatbox. In it, Clarke found a hat with a label in the crown bearing the name of hat-maker Digance and Co. At the bottom of the box, sewn into a piece of leather, was a pocket watch.

'What's this?' Clarke asked.

'It's my watch,' Müller replied.

The watch bore the same serial number as the one stolen from Thomas Briggs.

Clarke studied the hat and held it up. 'Is this your hat?'

'Yes.'

'How long have you possessed them?'

Müller said he had owned the watch for two years and the hat for twelve months. 'I told him he would have to remain in custody and be taken to New York,' Clarke recalled. 'I kept him on board all night. Inspector Tanner came on board in the morning and I then gave him over to him.'[65]

Tanner boarded the *Victoria* early the next morning with John Death. He arranged to have Müller stand in a line-up with eight other passengers below deck. The jeweller, when summoned, easily identified Müller as the customer he served the Monday after the murder. 'I took possession of the effects of the prisoner,' Tanner reported. 'I showed them to him . . . He said that they were the whole of his property, with the exception of the ring.'[66]

Müller told Tanner he had lost a ring at some point during the journey. Asked what it looked like, the prisoner described the very ring Death had sold him on 11 July. Tanner escorted Müller to a boat waiting alongside the *Victoria* to take them ashore. 'At this time, the excitement in New York was intense,' Tanner wrote in a case summary. 'There were hundreds of boats around the ship.'[67]

Their journey to police headquarters on Mulberry Street met with great fanfare, as crowds lined the route to catch a glimpse of the British detective and German killer. 'Up to this moment, he appeared perfectly indifferent to what was passing,' Tanner said. Once safely inside the police station, he offered to fetch Müller a meal – but Müller declined.

'I have a duty to perform and wish to do it kindly,' Tanner said. 'You had better have something.'

'No, I cannot eat,' Müller said and burst into tears. He sobbed loudly for twenty minutes before agreeing to some buttered bread and a cup of tea.[68]

From the station, police took Müller to the Bleecker Street gallery of famed Civil War photographer Mathew Brady to have his mugshot taken. The resulting image, noted *The New York Daily Herald*, 'will no doubt add materially to the collection of distinguished personages who figure in the Rogues' Gallery'. Officers bundled Müller, still dazzled from the flash, back into the police wagon and brought him to the Chamber Street courthouse to begin the extradition process. 'A number of reporters and others were anxiously awaiting his arrival,' wrote one news scribe. 'They were all disappointed in his appearance, as they expected to see a fierce looking individual, instead of the poor, cowering looking wretch, who seemed more dead than alive when brought face to face with the witnesses who are to appear against him when he is brought to trial on the charges which have been preferred against him.'[69]

Francis Marbury represented the British government in the extradition proceedings before US Commissioner Chas Newton. Müller sat behind his assigned counsel – funded by the German Legal Protection Society of London – and showed no emotion as Tanner, Death and Matthews testified against him. He was, said one courtroom spectator, 'an unmoved countenance . . . apparently the most uninterested and unaffected person in the densely crowded court.'[70]

The British highlighted the evidence against Müller, while Müller's lawyers denounced the British – to considerable applause

– for assisting the Confederacy. Such 'treachery and gross mis-
conduct,' they argued, 'made any Extradition Treaty a dead letter.'
Nationalistic sentiment did not sway Commissioner Newton, who
authorized Müller's extradition on Sunday, 27 August.[71] One final
task awaited Tanner before he could return home with his prisoner. He updated Mayne in a report the following day:

> It will be seen by the newspapers which I send also by this
> mail that strong language was used by the prisoner's counsel
> in reference to England and the applause it gained. When the
> papers are ready I go on to Washington to obtain the warrant
> from the President to take the prisoner home . . . I beg also
> to state that extraordinary as it may seem, strong sympathy is
> felt here for the prisoner and it is rumoured that an attempt to
> rescue him from my custody will be made.[72]

Police confined Müller to the City Prison – the Tombs –
while Tanner journeyed to Washington, D.C. to have President
Abraham Lincoln sign the paperwork authorizing the prisoner's
extradition. Müller spent three days in his cell, reading the city's
newspapers until Tanner returned on Saturday, 3 September.
With all the red tape cleared and sorted, Müller was officially
placed in Tanner's custody. The inspector and his entourage left
New York that afternoon on the steamship *Etna*.[73]

'The ship was literally crammed with people eager to see
Müller depart,' Tanner wrote. 'When I got him on board, I told him
it was customary to put such prisoners in irons, but that I had no
desire to do anything to give him unnecessary pain.' Tanner made
arrangements to confine Müller under guard in the ship's sick bay
'so that he might be kept away from the saloon passengers, as well
as those of the steerage.' He made Müller promise not to cause
any problems. 'I will do anything you please,' Müller said.[74]

The two men enjoyed a cordial relationship. Tanner lent
Müller his copies of *The Pickwick Papers* and *David Copperfield*
to pass the time. 'He has never complained during the whole

voyage,' Tanner noted, 'and apparently enjoyed himself as much as anybody on board . . . Throughout the whole voyage the demeanour of the prisoner has been quiet and entirely indifferent to his position.'[75]

The *Etna* docked in Liverpool on the night of Friday, 16 September. 'Anything like the excitement in the neighbourhood of the docks and landing-stage has seldom been seen in the great port on the Mersey,' reported *The Evening Standard*. 'Crowds thronged every point, whence a view of the *Etna* could be seen, until the darkness of the night had rendered it impossible to see anything but the black water which bore the vessel.'[76]

A police tender brought Tanner and Müller ashore. A carriage made its way through the excited crowd and drew up alongside the landing stage. Tanner guided Müller by the arm towards the waiting cab, prompting the gathered masses to push forward. A frenzied surge of humanity crashed against the carriage and threatened to upturn it in a desperate effort to see the killer. Tanner pushed Müller into the cab and yelled at the driver to go. 'Müller did not altogether appear to understand why a demonstration was made,' wrote one reporter, 'and upon gaining his seat in the cab he displayed great emotion.'[77]

Müller appeared in Bow Street Police Court on Monday, 19 September. Over the week that followed, he sat and listened passively to the evidence against him. Hat-maker Daniel Digance said the hat found in Müller's possession was indeed the hat he had made for Mr Briggs. It was clear, looking at it, 'that it had been cut down an inch and a half and sewn together again, but not in such a way as a hatter would have done it.' Digance said he always wrote the customer's name on the hat's inner lining and pointed out the lining had been cut away. On Monday, 26 September, the magistrate committed Müller to trial for the wilful murder of Thomas Briggs.[78]

The trial got underway at the Old Bailey on Thursday, 27 October, and lasted two days. The jury adjourned at 2:45 p.m. and returned to the courtroom fifteen minutes later to deliver the unanimous guilty verdict. Müller had maintained his composure in the dock throughout the proceedings and continued to do so as Judge Baron Martin, the traditional black cloth placed atop his white wig, sentenced Müller to hang. Müller asked if he could address the court. The judge allowed it.

'I am perfectly satisfied with my judges and with the jury,' Müller said, 'but I have been convicted on false evidence and not a true statement. If the sentence is carried out I shall die innocent.'[79]

He spoke in such a quiet voice, only those sitting near the dock heard him. Outside, in the grey and darkening afternoon, the crowds gathered around the Old Bailey roared their approval as word of the verdict spread. The muffled sound of jubilation could be heard inside the courtroom. Two guards approached Müller to escort him back to his cell. As he stepped clear of the dock, his emotions boiled to the surface and he 'dissolved in tears.'[80]

Franz Müller went to the gallows at eight o'clock on the morning of Monday, 14 November, despite efforts by the German Legal Protection Society to have the sentence commuted. Not even a letter to Queen Victoria from Wilhelm I, King of Prussia, urging leniency, could spare Müller from 'the doom awarded by the English law.'[81]

Fifty-thousand people swarmed the Old Bailey Road to watch the execution outside Newgate Prison. Reported *The Times*:

> There can only be one thing more difficult than describing this crowd, and that is to forget it. Far up even into Smithfield the keen white faces rose rank upon rank, till where even the houses were shrouded in the thick mist of the early dawn the course of streets could be traced by the gleam of the faces

alone, and all, from first to last, from nearest to furthest, were clamouring, struggling and shouting with each other to get as near the gibbet as the steaming mass of human beings before them would allow.[82]

Müller presented a calm figure as he mounted the scaffold with Dr Louis Cappel, a German Lutheran minister, at his side. The executioner positioned Müller on the trapdoor and pinioned his arms and legs – throughout which the condemned showed no hint of fear.

'In a few minutes, Müller, you will stand before God,' Cappel said. 'I ask you again, and for the last time, are you guilty or innocent?'

'I am innocent,' Müller said through the hood.

'You are innocent?' Cappel replied.

'God Almighty knows what I have done.'

'God Almighty knows what you have done?' Cappel asked. 'Does God know that you have done this particular deed?'

Müller replied in German: '*Ich habe es gethan*' – roughly translated, 'Yes, I have done it.'[83]

The trap beneath Müller's feet opened, and Müller said no more.

The execution was not without controversy. The only person to corroborate the exchange between Müller and Cappel – and Müller's last words – was Cappel himself, who provided details to the press right after the hanging. Even as Müller's body still dangled from the rope, prison officials cleaned out his cell and went through his papers, expecting to find a written confession. They found none. Questions lingered.

'He does not seem to have been a bad-hearted man,' *The Times* opined of Müller the following day, expressing some doubt as to his guilt. 'He had never been convicted of anything before, and his character was as good as that of most other young men in his condition of life . . . His general behaviour up to the time of his capture did not indicate a mind charged with so fearful a secret, and his conduct since his imprisonment, both previous to the trial and after it, appears to have been exemplary.'[84]

It didn't matter. Majority opinion agreed justice had been served.

The Briggs case earned Scotland Yard plaudits in the United States and laid the foundation for its international reputation. *The New York Times* hailed 'the zealous efforts that were made by the police of London . . . to ferret out and apprehend the criminal.' Tanner was celebrated for his impressive detective work – but while his career appeared ascendant, he would tackle just one more notable case before illness cut his life tragically short.[85]

7

A Death in Duddlewick

Bloodstain analysis. Tanner's last case.

An empty chair at the breakfast table was the first sign of trouble, but not until supper did John Meredith decide it might be worth looking for his nephew. The date was Sunday, 14 January 1866. Meredith, who operated the local mill, lived in the Shropshire village of Duddlewick, with its gentle curving lanes, thatched roofs and the soft burbling of the River Rea. Sitting in the middle of 'an exclusively rural district' with 'a thin population widely scattered', Duddlewick's bucolic surroundings seemed an incongruent back-drop to violent death.[1]

Meredith's orphaned nephew, eighteen-year-old Edward Edwards, had lived with him for the past twelve years. Every Sunday before breakfast, Edward visited the mill to balance the account book. He left the house that particular morning at eight and never returned. The young man's absence at first failed to alarm Meredith, who only grudgingly went in search of him late that afternoon. He trudged to the mill, 500 yards from his house, in the cold January dusk. The mill's key was in its usual place on a hook above the door. 'I unlocked the door of the mill,' Meredith recalled, 'and saw the flour-scoop and mill floor with spots of blood on them. I thought the lad had killed a rat. I went a little further and saw more blood on the floor.'[2]

He spotted Edward's bloody hat lying nearby. Afraid to pro-ceed on his own, he fled to the nearby farm of William Dorrell for help. Dorrell accompanied Meredith back to the mill. Inside, they approached an opening in the floor used to drop sacks of flour to the mill's lower level. A staircase descended through the opening to the floor below. Meredith went to the top of the stairs and peered down into the gloom.

'There is a lot of blood down there,' he said. 'I expect you will find him dead. I am afraid to go and look for him.'[3]

Dorrell went down and left Meredith at the top of the stairs. He found Edward sprawled in a pool of blood 'with his right arm doubled under his chest.' Blood ran in thick rivulets down a nearby wall and had splattered white sacks of flour stacked in the corner. A stick lay on the floor, its end splintered and sticky with gore. Dorrell gently rolled the body over and discovered the young man, although unconscious, was still alive – if barely.[4]

The two men hurried back to Dorrell's farm and retrieved a door to use as a makeshift stretcher. They carried Edward to Meredith's house and laid him down in the warm glow of the kitchen stove. George Hodges, the local surgeon, arrived and found Edward in a dreadful state, lying on a coat and sheet with several blankets piled on top of him. 'He was quite insensible,' Hodges said. 'His fingers were cut and scarred in many places.'[5]

The doctor noted heavy bruising on Edward's forehead; the young man's right eye was blackened and swollen shut. A thick crust of blood masked Edward's features and glued his hair to his shattered scalp. 'The skull was fractured on the left side,' Hodges said. 'There was a large opening in the skull and a portion of the brain protruding. I removed one small bit of bone. The other portion of the bone appeared to have been driven into the brain.' He poured some brandy down Edward's throat and had him carried upstairs to bed. The doctor had known Edward for a number of years. 'He was a delicate boy,' he remembered. 'He had a broken thigh and walked lame.' Hodges maintained a bedside vigil until Edward's laboured breathing ceased at one o'clock on the morning of 15 January.[6]

Edward's death shocked the tight-knit community. Why would someone want to harm the church warder's nephew? 'The object of the murder,' according to one report, 'would seem to have been plunder, for Edwards was known to have some little money with him when he went to the mill.' Although Edward often carried a purse, the only things found in his trouser pockets had been 'two pocket knifes, tobacco pouch, some gun caps, and some matches.'[7]

The Shropshire Constabulary, unaccustomed to such brutality, did what it could. They knocked on doors and asked if anyone had seen anything suspicious. No one had. The rural press, meanwhile, did its part to shield the respected Meredith from suspicion. 'Of the deceased,' reported a local paper, '[Meredith] was extremely fond and had cherished him since the age of six, since which time he had seen to him as his son.'[8]

Suspicion fell briefly on a farm labourer named James Childe, who was observed on the night of the assault downing pints in a local pub. The bartender couldn't help but notice blood on Childe's clothing. When asked how it got there, Childe replied he'd been in a fight. Police arrested Childe, but several witnesses came forward and said the accused had 'been sleeping off the drink in a pub barn 8½ miles from the mill' the morning of the crime.[9]

On 19 January, Shropshire Chief Constable Edward Cureton sent a request to Metropolitan Police Commissioner Sir Richard Mayne for Scotland Yard's assistance:

Sir:

On the morning of Sunday last, a murder was committed at the Duddlewick Mill near Bridgenorth. Up to the present time, no clue has been obtained as to who committed the murder, and the Magistrates of the District, in which the murder was committed, have authorized me to apply to you and to ask if you could spare a Detective from the Metropolitan Force, they would feel glad of his assistance in attempting to unravel the mystery . . .[10]

Mayne assigned the case to Inspector Richard Tanner, who departed London by train at 10 a.m. on Sunday, 21 January and arrived in Duddlewick that evening. His inquiry lasted only a week, but cognizant of being the big city detective in a close-knit village, Tanner went out of his way to make it clear he was merely assisting Shropshire police – and not leading the investigation.

'At the commencement of the enquiry,' Tanner wrote, 'I endeavoured to ascertain what motive could exist for any person to murder the deceased, and I could find none. He was a poor boy (an orphan) solely dependent on his uncle John Meredith since seven years old.' Edward was not entitled to any inheritance nor was he on bad terms with anyone in the village. He was, in fact, well liked. Nevertheless, Tanner believed Edward died at the hands of someone he knew. 'Duddlewick is a very small village,' he wrote in his report, 'and a stranger would almost sure to have been observed on the morning in question, but none was seen.'[11]

Tanner 'had very strong suspicions that the uncle was the person who committed the murder,' which caused consternation among the locals. The detective thought it improbable 'that a youth in a pair of corduroy trousers in a mill was likely to be regarded by a stranger as a prize worth murdering for plunder.' The nature of the wounds also suggested a motive other than robbery. 'The injuries,' Tanner believed, 'look more like those produced by a person acting under the impulse of violent rage'. And it seemed Meredith had frequent cause to be angry with Edward. 'He sometimes neglected to make entries in his account book at the mill, where he was in the habit of receiving money for me,' Meredith told the inspector. 'He neglected to make an entry on Saturday.'[12]

Tanner believed Meredith, enraged by his nephew's perceived negligence, lashed out at the boy and killed him. It was the only theory Tanner could come up with based on Meredith's 'manner when I spoke to him on the case and his conduct throughout the day of the murder.'[13]

Meredith told Tanner he got up at nine o'clock on the day in question, had breakfast 'and went out, returning in about half an hour.' Upon Meredith's return, his maid asked if Edward would be coming home for breakfast, to which Meredith replied, 'I don't know. I have been down to the mill but I cannot see anything of him. Give me my coat and vest and a cup of ale. I shall go to church.'[14]

Tanner was struck by Meredith's story. As he noted:

Now, the uncle knew well that the deceased should have brought his books from the mill to the house on that morning as was the custom every Sunday morning for the purpose of settling before going to church. Yet not seeing him, he went to church exhibiting no anxiety about deceased. And did he go to the mill as he said he had? If he did, he must have seen deceased, because one thing is certain. The deceased was found locked in the mill, the key put in its usual place, viz over the mill door.[15]

Meredith told Tanner he returned from church at 1 p.m. and was informed by a servant girl that Edward had still not come home. Meredith wondered if maybe, as the day was windy, Edward had been blown into the local brook. Instead of heading out to search for his missing nephew, he insisted on eating dinner. Tanner found this 'extraordinary' and couldn't help but notice Meredith appeared to be diverting attention away from the mill. Even after dinner, Meredith didn't rush from the house. He instead, Tanner noted, 'has a cup of ale and smokes his pipe for an hour, and then went and found the deceased insensible and nearly dead.'[16]

Tanner presented his evidence – circumstantial as it was – to the local magistrates, who authorized Meredith's arrest and had him remanded into custody. The detective, however, felt less than confident a conviction would follow. The community, as had happened during the Road Hill House investigation, rallied to the defence of one of its own. 'Against the supposition that Mr Meredith is guilty of this fearful crime,' reported the local paper, 'is the fact which is well known in the district in which he lives, that he is of a kind, hospitable and charitable disposition, ever-ready in purse and person to prove a Good Samaritan to his needy neighbours.'[17]

Tanner, considering his work done, boarded the next train to London.

There is nothing sensational about the Duddlewick murder; it lacks the behind-closed-doors mystique of Road Hill House and the transatlantic thrill of the Briggs investigation – but it's notable for its early foray into bloodstain analysis, resulting in 'probably the earliest surviving forensic science report.'[18]

Prior to Tanner's arrival in the village, Sergeants David Cox and Alexander Christy of the Shropshire Police searched Meredith's house. The officers went upstairs with Meredith following close behind. In his bedroom, Meredith pulled from the wardrobe 'an old coat and waist coat' he wore on the day of the murder.

'I picked up a pair of trousers which were by the side of the bed and saw a good many marks of blood upon them,' Christy said. 'There were upwards of twenty spots of blood on the left leg of the trousers.'

Christy held out the trousers in a questioning manner. Meredith said blood got on them when he helped carry his nephew home. Christy bundled the trousers under an arm while Cox removed the coats from the wardrobe. The officers went downstairs with Meredith again at their heels.

In the entry hall, Cox removed a coat from a hook by the door and noticed what appeared to be bloodstains on the fabric. He passed the coat to Christy, who pulled out a magnifying glass to have a closer inspection.

'You surely can't detect blood after being washed,' Meredith said, his utterance more a statement than a question.

Cox assured him they could.[19]

It was Tanner, before departing the village, who recommended Cox take Meredith's bloodstained clothing to London to be examined by Professor Alfred Swaine Taylor, Professor of Chemistry and Medical Jurisprudence at Guy's Hospital. An early pioneer of forensic science and a leading expert of the day in toxicology, Taylor had testified in several high-profile poisoning cases. His 1865 book, *The Principles and Practice of Medical Jurisprudence*, considered an early bible in the field of forensics (medical jurisprudence), went through numerous editions in his lifetime.

Bloodstain analysis was still very much in its infancy. The first modern study of bloodstain patterns would not happen until the late 1800s at the University of Krakow, when Eduard Piotrowski clubbed rabbits to death and then examined the resulting blood splatter. Four years before the Duddlewick murder, however, Dutch scientist J. Izaak Van Deen developed 'one of the earliest presumptive tests for blood.' It required the 'employment of the peroxide of hydrogen and the freshly precipitated resin of guaiacum,' a shrub from West India. A stain, when treated with a diluted mixture of the resin and peroxide, will turn blue if blood is present. The test 'was equally sensitive for old or fresh blood.' Van Deen originally developed the procedure to detect blood in faeces but 'pointed out its value as a test in forensic medicine.'[20]

Taylor had employed Van Deen's methods a number of times and, he wrote, 'found that under proper precautions the results are most satisfactory. The colouring matter of blood could be detected in cases in which the microscope and the ordinary means of research failed to show its presence.'[21] He applied the procedure to Meredith's clothing, confirming his findings with a spectral microscope, and summarized the results:

1. The stains on the overcoat have not been produced by blood.
2. The small spots or stains on the left sleeve and the flap of the shirt, have been caused by blood and are comparatively recent.

3. The pale red coloured stains on the front of the trousers have been caused by blood apparently removed while wet by a wet cloth or sponge. These have the appearance of fresh or recent blood.

4. The stains or spots found on the lining of the flap of the trousers and in the lining of the left pocket have been caused by blood, but they are apparently of old date.[22]

Taylor couldn't determine the blood's provenance. 'The blood of animals is so much like human blood,' he said, 'that you cannot distinguish between them.'[23] Not until 1901 would German scientist Paul Uhlenhuth develop a precipitin test that detects proteins found only in human blood – a major breakthrough in the field of forensics, but one that came too late to benefit Tanner in the Duddlewick investigation.

On Friday, 23 March 1866, the coroner's jury returned a verdict of 'wilful murder' against a person or persons unknown and acquitted John Meredith. Tanner had expected as much. He regretted not being called in sooner. 'Mystery,' he believed, 'will long hang over this even as it hung over the Road murder.'[24]

While not a rousing success like the Briggs case, Tanner's prestige escaped the public battering that doomed Whicher. His career, nevertheless, would soon be over. Rheumatism forced him to retire in 1869 at the age of thirty-seven. He moved to Winchester and took over the Swan Hotel, perhaps regaling guests with stories of his exploits at the Yard.

Though short, his career was not without impact. He had served, in his pursuit of Franz Müller, as a worthy ambassador and demonstrated on the transatlantic stage Scotland Yard's doggedness in pursuit of a killer. Certainly, Inspector Richard Tanner 'of the London detective squad' became 'a byword for a new breed of detective' – one who followed a case no matter where it led. He died four years into his retirement, age forty-one, of a stroke.[25]

8

Martyr and Monster

'The Clerkenwell Outrage.' A teenaged killer.

Guarded by a dozen mounted officers, the Black Maria – a police wagon with 'separate locked cubicles' used to transport prisoners – trundled its way from the police court in Manchester to the Belle Vue Gaol in Hyde Road on the opposite side of town. The date was Wednesday, 18 September 1867. In the back sat Thomas Kelly and Timothy Deasy, leaders of the Irish Republican Brotherhood – also known as the Fenians – a militant group 'violently opposed to British rule in Ireland'. Police had arrested the pair the previous week for loitering, believing them at first to be simple vagrants.[1]

Sergeant Charles Brett rode with the prisoners, a duty he had performed many times before. 'He appears to have been highly esteemed both by the public who knew him,' notes one contemporary account, 'and those who came more immediately under his notice as frequent passengers, both for his kindness and courtesy to all, whether prisoners or not.'[2]

The wagon proceeded without incident until it reached a railway bridge that spanned Hyde Road, where roughly fifty members of the Irish Republican Brotherhood waited in one of its three brick arches. Alerted to the wagon's approach by a lookout at the nearby Hyde Road Hotel, the raiding party stormed from its hiding place, according to one witness, 'as suddenly and in such numbers as a swarm of whasps [sic] from a nest into which a stone has been thrown.'[3]

The mob threw rocks and fired pistols. Outnumbered and out-gunned, the police – 'a miscellaneous lot, apparently embracing the long and short and the fat and lean of the Manchester force' – dismounted and ran for cover behind a nearby wall. One horse pulling the wagon took a round in the neck; another fell after being shot in the face. The wagon clattered to a halt.[4]

Two men scrambled onto its roof and began pounding on it with rocks. Others attacked the sides with sledgehammers and axes. One man rushed to the back of the wagon and tried to shoot out the lock. The bullet passed through the door and struck Brett in the face, 'the ball taking effect just above the eye and escaped near the top of the head'. Brett became the first Manchester police officer killed in the line of duty. A female prisoner snatched the keys off Brett's body and passed them to the outside mob through a ventilation slit.[5]

'It seems bordering on infatuation almost to send these officers to guard the prison van with merely their bare hands,' lamented *The Preston Chronicle*. 'It does not speak much for the judgment and foresight of the chiefs of police.'[6]

Kelly and Deasy escaped, never to be caught again, but the drama was far from over. Police arrested three men – William Philip Allen, Michael Larkin and Michael O'Brien – based on dubious eyewitness accounts for their involvement in what became known as the 'Manchester Outrages'. The fact none of them fired the fatal shot was of little consequence. 'In English law,' explains one Scotland Yard history, 'anyone taking part in an illegal act which results in someone being killed is deemed guilty of con-structive murder.'[7] The trio went to the gallows two months later in November.

The triple execution proved a gruesome affair. Hangman Wil-liam Calcraft miscalculated the length of rope necessary to do the job in a merciful fashion – a frequent lapse for which he had gained an unfortunate reputation. Allen died without drama, but Larkin and O'Brien thrashed in agony for several minutes before passing.[8] Their botched hangings, the result of a conviction based on less-than-solid evidence, made them martyrs to the Irish cause.

That same week, a series of related events began unfolding in London that would result 'in one of the worst instances of inefficiency in the whole history of [Scotland Yard].'[9]

One man wanted for helping plan the Manchester ambush was Ricard O'Sullivan Burke. An adventurer at heart, the thirty-year-old Irishman had been constantly on the move since the age of fifteen, travelling through the United States – 'my ideal of free government, the refuge of my race' – and journeying to such far-flung corners as 'China, Japan, the South Pacific Islands and the Arctic Circle'. He fought in the American Civil War on the side of the Union with the 15th New York Engineers and achieved the rank of colonel before joining the Irish Republican Brotherhood in 1867 in New York.[10]

He left the United States for England early that year to fight for Irish independence closer to home and established an operation providing arms to the cause. In February, he took part in a failed raid to seize weapons from the British armoury at Chester Castle in Cheshire. In the wake of Sergeant Brett's murder, Burke made his way to London under an assumed name. An informant tipped off Scotland Yard and alerted Detective Inspector James Jacob Thomson that Burke was in the city.[11]

Thomson was rare among his Yard colleagues, being fluent in French, Italian and Greek at a time when most constables could barely read. He had served a brief stint as a London officer in 1856 and then spent several years plodding the rural beat in Hampshire and Devonshire before joining Scotland Yard's Detective Branch in 1862. He wasted little time making a name for himself with headline-grabbing exploits. Most recently, he had solved 'The Great Stamp Office Robbery', tracking down a gang of thieves – including a one-legged culprit nicknamed 'Peg-leg Dick' – who stole £10,000 worth of stamps from the Government Stamp Office in Manchester.[12]

On the night of Friday, 20 November, Thomson and a constable tracked Burke and an associate to Woburn Square in Bloomsbury. He approached Burke from behind and tapped him on the shoulder.

'I want to speak with you,' Thomson said. 'I am Inspector Thomson of the detective police and hold a warrant for the apprehension of Richard Burke for a serious crime. I know you to be Richard Burke and must take you into custody. You must consider yourself my prisoner and must accompany me to the nearest police station.'

Burke feigned ignorance. 'I don't know what you mean,' he said. 'My name is George Berry, and I am a medical student just arrived from Hamburg.'

'Whether you're Berry or Burke you must come with me,' Thomson said. 'If I am under a mistake, I will abide the consequences.'

When Burke still refused to come along, Thomson and the constable each grabbed one of Burke's arms and began dragging him through the square. Burke's associate, a man named Casey, launched himself at the detective. '[He] struck me several blows,' Thomson said. 'He struck me in the chest.'

Burke wrestled himself free. Thomson reached into his coat and drew a revolver. 'By God, Burke,' he said, 'if you attempt to escape, I'll shoot you.'

'Don't do anything desperate,' Burke said, remaining calm.

The sight of the gun mellowed Casey. 'This is a mistake,' he said. 'It's an illegal arrest. Don't allow a gentleman to be taken in this way.'

By now a crowd had gathered but ignored Burke's pleas for help. Thomson and the constable arrested Burke on a felony charge and Casey for obstruction of justice and dragged them to the local police station. There, Thomson's informant – a one-time member of the Irish Republican Brotherhood who had tired of its violent tactics – confirmed Burke's identity.[13]

Three days later, on 23 November, a magistrate at Bow Street Police Court remanded Burke and Casey into custody at the Clerkenwell House of Detention in central London to await trial. Almost immediately, Burke's brothers-in-arms began plotting his escape. Around midday on Wednesday, 11 December, a letter from Daniel Ryan, superintendent of the Dublin Metropolitan Police, arrived at Scotland Yard:

> I have to report that I have just received information from a reliable source to the effect that the rescue of Richard Burke from prison in London is contemplated. The plan is to blow up the exercise wall by means of gunpowder; the hour between 3 and 4 p.m.; and the signal for 'all right' a white ball thrown up when he is at exercise.[14]

Commissioner Mayne ordered Thomson to notify the prison's chief warder. 'I am competent to protect the interior of the prison,' the warder told the detective in a rather sanctimonious fashion. 'I will be content if the commissioner affords the same protection to the outside of the prison, which he affords to ordinary homes.'[15]

Thomson reported back to Mayne and relayed the warder's haughty message. The Commissioner bolstered police activity in the area with 'a double patrol of two police-constables, and three police-constables . . . employed in plain clothes'. He placed an additional eight officers, with three in plainclothes, 'on duty round the prison walls.'[16]

One glaring question, however, remained: on what day would the rescue attempt take place?

At about four o'clock on the afternoon of Friday, 13 December, fifty yards of the prison's fourteen-inch thick north wall along Corporation Lane vaporized in a giant ball of flame. The noise thundered across the city. The explosion hurled scorched masonry up to eighty feet in all directions, the blast's concussion shattering windows within a half-mile radius, and the detonation's ferocity knocking down a neighbouring 'block of poor dwellings, counting from a dozen to fifteen houses'. [17]

The ear-ringing aftermath was one of smouldering devastation. 'The maimed and wounded being carried out,' recalled one witness, 'mothers carrying children bleeding in their arms, covered with dust, dirt and blood. The chemists' shops in the neighbourhood were filled with sufferers from this dreadful event, including persons of all classes, even policemen who were on their beat in the neighbourhood.' [18]

The screams and cries of the wounded and dying drifted upward from the row of wrecked and smoking tenements. Police and members of the fire brigade struggled to reach the scene, having to manoeuvre over rubble and broken bodies scattered about the street. A swirling cloud of dust veiled everything. 'Mothers,' reported *Reynolds's Newspaper*, 'were to be observed rushing wildly through the crowd with pale faces and uplifted arms, frantically inquiring for little ones whom they knew to be either lying in the debris of the shattered houses or to have been immediately prior to the calamity enjoying themselves in the neighbourhood.' [19]

Shortly before the explosion, witnesses saw two men and a woman approaching the prison wall with a large barrel loaded in a handcart. The men unloaded the barrel and positioned it against the wall, an activity that 'created no suspicion as to its contents'. Come nightfall, a large number of uniformed constables guarded the approaches to the prison with cutlasses in hand, as the curious in their thousands descended on the scene. By the time the dust settled, casualties numbered twelve dead and more than 100 injured in a district of working-class Londoners 'sympathetic to the Irish cause'. Papers on both sides of the Atlantic decried the attack. *The New York Times* lamented the suffering of 'women and children torn in pieces and sent by scores to the hospitals'. *The Dublin Evening Mail* labelled the atrocity a crime 'against society and humanity itself'. [20]

The devastation of the Clerkenwell explosion, as seen from the prison yard. Police and firefighters search the smoldering ruins for survivors.

The coroner's inquest into what the press now called 'The Clerkenwell Outrage' determined Sir Richard Mayne had not taken the threat seriously enough. 'The protection which ought to have been given for the prison had not been afforded by the Commissioner of Police,' read a summation of the coroner's findings a week later. 'If proper precautions had been taken . . . this dreadful calamity would have been avoided.' Mayne tendered his resignation, but Home Secretary Horatio Walpole refused to accept it. 'We told Mayne,' Walpole supposedly said, 'that he made a damned fool of himself, but that we weren't going to throw him over after his long public service.'[21]

Scotland Yard indeed looked foolish. Only finding those responsible could salve the wound to its reputation. Yard detectives worked feverishly over the next month, tracking down informants and pursuing every lead. Arrests were made and statements, whether voluntary or forced, pointed investigators to Glasgow. There, on 14 January 1868, officers arrested twenty-six-year-old Michael Barrett. Of the eleven individuals the Yard apprehended in connection with the bombing, Barrett would be the only one found guilty and the only one to hang. One of Barrett's co-conspirators, a tailor from Dublin named Patrick Mullany, said it was Barrett who 'put light to the fatal barrel.'[22]

In exchange for leniency, Mullany testified for the Crown when Barrett went on trial at the Old Bailey in April. Six witnesses for the defence said Barrett was in Glasgow at the time of the explosion. Their words carried little sway with the jury. Upon being sentenced to death, the dignified Barrett addressed the court with a powerful eloquence, pointing out inconsistencies in the prosecution's case, calling into question Mullany's character, and voicing sorrow for the loss of life.[23]

'I am far from denying, nor will the force of circumstances compel me to deny, my love for my native land,' he said. 'I love my country; and if it be murderous to love Ireland dearer than I love my life, then it is true. I am a murderer. If my life were ten times dearer than it is, and if I could by any means redress the wrongs of that prosecuted land by the sacrifice of my life, I would willingly and gladly do so.'[24]

Barrett's guilt was far from certain. 'Seldom has evidence more conflicting been submitted for the consideration of a jury,' London's *Morning Post* observed. 'And seldom has the current of opinion in respect to the guilt or innocence of at least one of the accused been subjected to such sudden or violent variations.'[25]

Originally scheduled for 12 May, the execution was postponed to give the Home Office time to investigate Barrett's Glasgow alibi. The inquiry turned up nothing to save him. Despite pleas for clemency from the public and some members of Parliament, Barrett went to the gallows outside Newgate Prison on the morning of 16 May 1868. He met his end in stoic fashion. 'He placed himself under the drop and the rope was adjusted,' said one witness. 'He then turned and shook hands with the chaplain and hangman, who, a moment afterwards, withdrew the bolt, and he died after a severe but short struggle.'[26]

Doubt lingered. 'Millions in the three kingdoms, as well as in the United States and British colonies, will continue to doubt that a guilty man has been hanged at all,' *Reynolds's Newspaper* stated four days later, 'and the future historian of the Fenian panic may declare that Michael Barrett was sacrificed to the exigencies of the police, and the vindication of the good Tory principle, that there is nothing like blood.'[27]

Michael Barrett's hanging was the last of its kind. Three weeks after his death, the British government outlawed public executions.

Seven months to the day after Barrett's death, on 26 December 1868, an exhausted and seventy-two-year-old Sir Richard Mayne passed away at his London home after serving thirty-nine years as Police Commissioner. He had, over the course of his long and active service, guided Scotland Yard from a fledging force of 1,000 men to a 'national institution' of nearly 8,000 and kept it free of corruption. Under his leadership, the 'policeman, like the post man and the engine driver, joined the universal British stereotypes of the parson, the clerk, the farmer and the squire.'[28]

Forty-eight-year-old Colonel Edmund Henderson was appointed Commissioner in February 1869. Although a professional soldier by trade, the past two decades had seen him serving as 'Comptroller-General of Convicts in Western Australia . . . and a few years spent in England as Surveyor-General of Prisons.' With a passion for painting and a sharp sense of humour, he was more relaxed than Mayne. He eased restrictions on facial hair and allowed officers to 'grow beards and moustaches, provided they did not conceal the Divisional Numbers on their tunic collars.' He also let them vote, something previously forbidden to 'safeguard

against public suspicion of the force as an instrument of government tyranny.' Not surprisingly, he proved popular with his men.[29]

Prompted by a Home Office review in the wake of Clerkenwell
that determined the Yard lacked the manpower to operate effectively, Henderson launched an aggressive expansion. 'In those
times, there were no divisional detectives as there are now,' wrote
one detective. 'If anything serious happened in a division, it was
notified to Scotland Yard, and a detective officer was ordered to
make enquiries and report.' Henderson changed this by authorizing the recruitment of 180 detectives to operate out of the now
twenty divisions, thus increasing the number of detectives on the
force to 207.[30]

He promoted Chief Inspector Frederick Adolphus ('Dolly')
Williamson to serve as the first superintendent of the Detective
Branch. The son of a police officer, Williamson first donned the
uniform in 1850 and wasted little time moving upwards. He joined
the Detective Branch and was promoted to Sergeant in 1852; he
made Inspector the following year and Chief Inspector in 1867. It
was Williamson who took Constance Kent into custody following
her confession.[31]

'No matter the intricacy of the case submitted to him,' one colleague said of Williamson, 'he immediately gripped its points and
required but ten words of explanation where others asked for fifty.
He was always most courteous and he had the faculty of inspiring
confidence in the most timid.' The men worked in close quarters
at 4, Whitehall Place. 'The detectives had three little rooms in the
building . . . on the right-hand side of Great Scotland Yard,' remembered one member of the branch. 'Mr Williamson had one room,
the inspectors the second, and the sergeants the third.'[32]

Divisional detectives – selected from what Henderson hoped
would be 'the most promising men in the service' – would have
the rank of constable and report to a local sergeant. This expansion of the investigative ranks marked 'a major achievement' but
was not immediately recognized as such. Lamented one Scotland

Yard official at the time: 'The divisional detectives consisted for the most part of illiterate men, many of whom had been put into plainclothes to screen personal defects which marred their smart appearance in uniform. They were but nominally controlled by a sergeant, little superior to themselves.'[33]

While detectives at the divisional level may at first have been frowned upon, it was such an investigator who brought to light in 1871 a series of child murders – a crime made all the more shocking because of the killer.

On Wednesday, 19 April, *The Morning Advertiser* informed its readers that Detective Sergeant Henry Mullard of L (Lambeth) Division, testifying at an inquest into the death of a toddler, 'stated a series of facts so startling as almost to exceed the bare possibility of belief.' The facts of the case were such: On the afternoon of the seventh, John Beer and his wife went out to dine with friends and left their three children in the care of fifteen-year-old nursemaid Agnes Norman, whom they'd hired three days earlier. The couple returned home at midnight to hear screaming upstairs. Rushing to investigate, 'they found a child undressed on the floor and another dead between the bedstead and the wall.'[34]

The dead child was fourteen-month-old Jessie Beer. The family physician was of the opinion the girl had suffocated but could make no determination as to the cause. Mullard, reciting the facts, elicited a collective gasp from the coroner's court when he said inquiries suggested Agnes had killed at least four other children, along with 'three dogs, a cat, a parrot, a number of gold fish and nearly a dozen fancy birds.' The press would have none of it. Noted *The Morning Advertiser*:

> Now, we do not wish for one moment to assert our belief in this catalogue of horrors. In the last instance, the child might have fallen out of bed and been suffocated between the bed and

the wall. Such things do occur. But either Detective-Sergeant Mullard has been listening to a number of romances and cruel groundless scandals, or the tragic suggestiveness of his story is of a nature to curdle the blood with horror and take away the breath.[35]

The coroner's jury also dismissed Mullard's story and returned a verdict 'that the deceased died, accidentally caused.' Jessie's father was less than satisfied, as was Commissioner Henderson. He assigned Inspector James Pay of the Detective Branch to make a 'careful inquiry' as the case had 'the horror-mongling population of London in a state of excitement'.[36]

Pay's investigation indeed confirmed that 'wherever [Agnes] went something died.' She first went to work for Ralph and Elizabeth Milner in Kennington Park in January 1869. The Milner's ten-month-old son, Thomas, was dead in less than a month. A coroner's inquest ruled the child died from natural causes.[37]

The Milners suspected nothing and kept Agnes in their employ. Three-year-old Minnie Milner was dead two weeks later. In the wake of this tragedy, the Milner's six-year-old son Arthur told his parents he'd seen Agnes lock Minnie in a wardrobe and paid him half-a-crown to keep quiet about it. Agnes eventually pulled the unconscious Minnie out and put her in bed. She felt the child's forehead, turned to Arthur and said, laughing, 'She's dead.' The Milners, unable to prove the story, let Agnes go – but not before Elizabeth warned her not to work with children again.[38]

'Do you like children?' Elizabeth asked her.

'No,' replied Agnes, 'not so much.'[39]

On 21 April 1870, Agnes went to work for the Gardener family. Ten days later, a family friend named Fanny Taylor paid a visit with her five-month-old son. Left for three hours that evening in Agnes's care, the baby, 'a perfectly healthy child', was dead by night's end. An inquest returned a verdict of 'natural death.' The Gardeners, unaware of the monster living under their roof, left

Agnes to watch their fifteen-month-old son James Alexander on 18 May. James 'was then quite well to all appearance' when they went out at eight o'clock that night. Returning three hours later, they 'found the child quite dead' in his cot.[40]

As little James 'suffered from bad health', an inquest was deemed unnecessary. Only Agnes and the family cook were home at the time of the death, but the grieving Gardeners suspected nothing. Their ordeal had not yet run its course. 'During the six weeks that Agnes Norman was in the service of Mr Gardener,' Pay wrote in his case report, '3 dogs, a cat, a parrot, 12 canaries and linnets, and some goldfish died very mysteriously.'[41]

It was Agnes who 'found them all dead'.[42]

With no more children in the home to care for, the Gardeners dismissed Agnes with a reference that highlighted her 'sobriety and civility'. She soon found work in August as a housemaid with George and Charlotte Brown. It didn't last long. Noted Pay: 'She was in service at Mr Brown's a fortnight, during which time a cat, a canary, a linnet and some goldfish died, and the parrot was thought to be dying. Mr Judd, a bird fancier, was called to see it, and he was of [the] opinion the neck had been pinched, it being swollen at the time.'[43]

The Browns had two houseguests, Elizabeth Parfitt and her ten-year-old nephew, Charlie, who was visiting for the school holiday. One morning, Elizabeth heard 'a stifling sort of cry, as it seemed, from a room upstairs.' Entering the bedroom, she found Agnes standing over the boy's bed.

'What's the matter?' Elizabeth asked.

'He's been dreaming and is frightened,' Agnes said.

'Oh, no, aunt!' Charlie cried. 'I have not been dreaming. Agnes tried to choke me!'

He said he woke up to find Agnes kneeling on his stomach with one hand over his mouth and the other pressed over his nose. Only when he managed a muffled scream did she get off him.

'Oh, Charlie, you naughty boy,' Agnes said. 'I did not!'

Elizabeth could see the boy's lips looked sore and noticed 'his neck swollen very much.'[44]

Agnes, deemed an undesirable presence in the house, once again found herself looking for work. It might seem strange by today's standards that a fifteen-year-old – a child – kept finding employment as a nanny, but such was the norm. 'Children taking care of children form one of the most curious spectacles of the London streets,' *The Daily Telegraph* reported at the time. 'One sees a little creature who, if her parents were rich, would not be allowed to stir a yard from her father's door without mama, or the governess, or the nurse, and yet, because her parents are poor, she is head nurse to three or four.'[45]

As for getting hired without references, as Agnes managed to do on multiple occasions, that, too, proved common. 'As a rule, it is almost impossible to get "characters" of the usual sort with girls of fourteen or fifteen,' the paper noted, explaining the difficulties of finding good domestic help. 'If they have "not been out before", they live with relations only too anxious to get rid of them, and who would swear that black is white to get them off their hands . . . but the ranks of domestic service are not choked by applicants; there is a steady demand and a rather fitful supply.'[46]

And so it was on 15 April 1871 that Agnes went to work for the Beers. The coroner's inquest may have found nothing suspicious about the death of the couple's child, but Detective Branch Superintendent Williamson – upon reviewing Pay's report – thought otherwise and authorized Agnes's arrest on suspicion of murdering Jessie Beer. She would also be charged, Pay warned her, on suspicion of murdering Thomas Milner, Minnie Milner, John Taylor, James Alexander Gardener, and the attempted murder of Charlie Parfitt.

'Me, murder the child?' Agnes proclaimed in disbelief.

It was about as vocal as she got.

'She treated the matter very quietly,' Pay recalled, 'declined to say anything.'[47]

Her silence only intensified the mystery of her character and, short of additional details, her background. Where had she come from and what, in her life, had twisted her in such an evil fashion? 'This extraordinary girl,' noted *The Irish Times*, 'is either insane or one of the greatest monsters of the age.'[48] Because medical experts could not agree on whether Jessie Beer's death was a homicide, the case failed to move forward. Lack of evidence also resulted in the other murder charges being dropped. Ultimately, she received a ten-year sentence for the attempted murder of Charlie Parfitt.[49]

9

The Trial of the Detectives

**More failures. A major scandal.
The rise of the Criminal Investigation Department.**

Charles Dickens was dead: to begin with. He died in June 1870, the dawn of a decade that saw his effusive praise of the Detective Branch begin to fade and wither. 'The omniscience of the London detective is a popular delusion,' *The Graphic* asserted in a scathing editorial, 'and Charles Dickens has done more than anyone else to foster it. Mr Bucket moves through the pages of *Bleak House* like a magician in an Eastern tale, and is sketched with so much skill and realism that we accept him as reality. It is only when the Londoner finds his house broken into or his property purloined, that he realizes that Scotland Yard can do very little to help him.'[1]

Igniting such scorn was a string of failures that – much like Jonathan Whicher's investigation at Road Hill House – called into question the Detective Branch's ability. And it began in the early hours of Wednesday, 26 April 1871.

Police Constable Donald Gunn, R (Greenwich) Division, found the woman in 'a lonely and isolated spot', a narrow hedge-rowed byway called Kidbrook Lane beneath the bucolic slope of Shooter's Hill in southeast London. It was four o'clock in the morning. The woman swayed on her hands and knees, 'bobbing her head up and down and knocking it on the ground.' Gunn looked around and saw no one else about. The nearest house was a quarter-mile away.

'What are you doing here?' he asked, crouching down beside her.

'Take hold of my hand,' she said, raising her left hand and turning her face up to him.

The first slate-coloured moments of daylight revealed the horrific damage done. Her face was covered in blood. Through the gore, Gunn could see a deep gash above the woman's smashed right eye. Part of her brain protruded from the shattered bone. Her left cheek and jaw had been slashed down to the gristle and her skull hammered in with a heavy object.[2]

'When I saw such a fearful sight,' Gunn recalled, 'I hesitated a moment to give her my hand. And as I stretched forth my hand, she fell flat on her face and said, "Let me die!"'[3]

Gunn stood up and noticed a partially clotted pool of blood ('I should say it would cover nearly a foot square') behind him. In the wet grass and mud along the side of the lane, he observed 'marks as though a scuffle had taken place'. He went in search of help and found his sergeant, a man named Haynes, on patrol nearby. The woman lay unconscious on her back when Haynes reached the scene. He searched her and found a handkerchief and blue purse with eleven shillings in it. More officers soon arrived with a stretcher and carried her to the home of Dr King, the local surgeon in Eltham.[4]

King took one look at the woman's injuries and declared them fatal. He told the officers to take her to Guy's Hospital, nine miles away in Southwark. They travelled by cab, the brightening day adding colour to the fields and hedgerows. The thatched roofs and quiet lanes soon gave way to 'the growing din and congestion of the metropolis'. It was 7:15 a.m. when they reached the hospital and passed the woman into the care of house surgeon Michael Harris.[5]

'She was quite unconscious,' Harris noted, 'and very cold.'

The bone above the right eye had been smashed into several fragments; her swollen brain protruded from a three-inch hole. A deep gash ran from her severed upper lip to her broken upper jaw. A heavy blow had caved in the left side of her skull and left the shattered bone hanging loose. Harris lifted one of the pieces and saw lacerations on the brain. Her arms and hands had been sliced with a sharp cutting instrument. 'They were such wounds as might have been produced in a struggle if she was defending herself against violence,' Harris said. With the exception of 'a light bruise' on her right thigh, which Harris estimated was no more than a few hours old, the lower body was free of injury.

The doctor guessed a sharp, heavy instrument – perhaps a hammer – had been used to inflict the wounds. Although her identity remained a mystery, rough skin on her hands and knees suggested she was 'a respectable and hard-working servant girl.' Harris could do little more than make her as comfortable as her condition allowed. He placed her in a ward and 'had several gentlemen of the hospital constantly sit by her to see if they could hear her say anything intelligible.'[6]

The crime scene surrendered few clues: large footprints leading away from where the girl was found, splotches of blood along a nearby brook, and an empty locket. On the grounds of Morden College, a mile and a half away in the direction of the city, the gardener found a plasterer's hammer with blood on the handle. Random pieces of a very incomplete puzzle. The mystery woman lingered in Guy's Hospital for four days without regaining consciousness. She died around nine o'clock on the evening of Sunday, 30 April. Dr Harris performed the post-mortem and made a startling discovery.[7]

'She was pregnant. I think she had been so two months,' he said. 'The embryo was dead and decomposed. It would be impossible to say how long it had been dead; I should say a week or two.'[8]

The case had by now passed into the hands of forty-two-year-old Inspector John Mulvany of Scotland Yard's Detective Branch. Mulvany had joined the force in 1848 and become an inspector in 1869. His career up until now had been varied and not uneventful, having chased jewel thieves, exposed con artists and pursued Fenians at home and on the continent. Never before, though, had he tackled a crime of such brutality and intense public interest. Working under the ceaseless gaze of London's merciless press may have been discomfiting, but it provided Mulvany his first solid lead.[9]

At quarter past nine on Sunday night – within minutes of the woman dying – William Trott, a mariner living near the river in Deptford, sat down by his hearth, opened a paper and read an account of the crime. What struck him, in addition to the savagery, was a description of the woman's clothing, which included a green hat with pink roses. 'It is of so common and gaudy a description,' reported *The Daily News*, 'as to stamp its wearer with the character generally called gay.' It so happened Trott's seventeen-year-old niece, Jane Clouson, wore such a hat. The last time he'd seen her was the previous Sunday, when she came for tea.[10]

Early the next morning, he visited the boarding house at No. 12, Ashburnham Place, where Jane lived. No, the landlady told him, she hadn't seen Jane in several days. His next stop was the Black-heath Road Police Station, from which Mulvany was overseeing the investigation. The inspector took Trott and his wife, Elizabeth, to Guy's Hospital, where they first identified a piece of muddy, bloodstained lace that Jane often wore around her neck. Then, they saw the body. The face was so battered, its features so obliterated, they hesitated putting Jane's name to such a horror – but the shape of the girl's mouth and a mole on her breast confirmed her identity. 'She was . . . a very clean, respectable young woman,' Elizabeth remembered. 'And a hard-working, industrious one, too. She was very stout, a fine-looking girl for her age.'[11]

Mulvany learned that Jane had been employed as a house servant for Ebenezer Pook, a Greenwich stationer and bookseller, but had recently been let go. She did not, however, cut all ties with the Pook family. On leaving her lodgings the night of the attack, she 'remarked that she was going to meet the son of her late master.' Further inquiries with those who knew Jane said she 'was on terms of intimacy' with twenty-year-old Edmund Pook and that he had recently professed his love in a letter. Jane's cousin, Charlotte, told Mulvany that Edmund showered Jane with gifts. On the night she disappeared, Charlotte said, Jane had supposedly visited Edmund to discuss plans to elope.[12]

At two o'clock on the afternoon of Monday, 1 May, Mulvany and Greenwich Police Superintendent James Griffin went to the Pook residence. Ebenezer told the officers he had recently dismissed Jane because of her slovenly habits and poor work ethic. Edmund appeared incensed when Mulvany asked him about any romantic entanglement with the girl. 'She was a dirty young woman,' he said, 'and left in consequence, and I cannot account for my time or nights last week.'[13]

'Have you written her a letter?' Mulvany asked.

'No, I have not.'

'People say you have.'

Edmund scoffed. 'Do they?' he said. 'Have you the letter? If it is in my handwriting, that will prove it.'

A search of Edmund's bedroom turned up the clothes he wore the night Jane was last seen alive. Griffin pointed out what appeared to be faded drops of dried blood on a shirtsleeve. Pook said it came from a scratch on his left wrist. When Griffin countered the blood was on the right-hand sleeve, Pook had no response.

'I shall have to take you into custody on suspicion of having murdered Jane Maria Clouson at Eltham,' Griffin said.

'Very well,' Edmund replied. 'I will go anywhere with you.'[14]

The case against Pook at first seemed solid: a young man from a well-to-do family, involved with a woman beneath his station, panicked when he found out she was pregnant. Not sure what else to do, he lured her to a lonely spot on the pretence of planning their future and instead beat her to death. The motive, coupled with the stains on the shirt, was enough for the coroner's court to find Edmund guilty of wilful murder and commit him for trial, but things began to fall apart once the case reached the Old Bailey on 10 July.

Much of the police evidence, based on things Jane had told others, was ruled inadmissible as hearsay. The defence explained away the blood found on Edmund's sleeve by calling witnesses who testified the defendant suffered seizures, during which he bled from the mouth. The public began to doubt Pook's guilt. On 15 July, the jury returned a not guilty verdict after twenty minutes of deliberations. 'The announcement was received with loud cheers,' reported *The Daily News*, 'which were immediately taken up and repeated by a crowd of two or three hundred persons who had been patiently waiting during the day in the thoroughfare outside the courthouse for the result of the trial.'[15]

Blame for the Crown's weak showing fell on Scotland Yard. *The Times* fired a savage broadside on 18 July, accusing the police of rushing to judgment and conducting too narrow an investigation:

> In the Eltham murder we find the Police, in spite of their experience, wholly at fault to the very rudiments of the detection of crime. They make a few inquiries, and they conceive that there are circumstances of suspicion against a particular young man. What these amounted to we know from the trial; they, at least, fell so far short of proof that the Jury was bound to find the prisoner *Not Guilty*, and did so find him. Yet these policemen chose, from the very first, to assume the guilt of Pook, and behaved as if the testimony they had sought out which had been volunteered in the neighbourhood was conclusive. The conduct of Inspector Mulvany and Superintendent Griffin was as stupid as it was reprehensible.

Detectives, the paper said, lacked 'the acumen with which their class is credited in fiction', with the end result being 'a failure of justice, for the murderer, whoever he might be, remains unpunished.'[16]

More high-profile failures followed in quick succession. On 10 July 1872, seventy-three-year-old Sarah Squire and her thirty-eight-year-old daughter, Christina, were found beaten to death in

their London home at 46, Hyde Road, Hoxton. The pair ran a stationery business from the address. Shortly after 1:30 p.m., a young
boy entered the premises to buy a newspaper and noticed blood
and hair smeared across the shop's countertop.[17]

The boy alerted Mrs Dodge, the proprietress of the coffee shop
next door, who found 'a horrible spectacle'. Sarah Squire lay welter-
ing in a pool of blood behind the stationery shop's counter. As Mrs
Dodge recoiled, her gaze settled on a door that led to the Squires'
parlour. Christina lay across the threshold, her head a smashed
and pulpy mass.[18]

Police found the house 'ransacked from top to bottom'. In the
parlour, the hands of a toppled-over clock sat frozen at twelve
o'clock. Every drawer had been rummaged through, every box
turned out and every shelf cleared. The responding surgeon sifted
through bloody, matted hair and probed the wounds. The killer
struck Sarah nine times on the top of her skull, forehead and
bridge of her nose with what appeared to be a plasterer's hammer;
each blow leaving a triangular wound about three-quarters of an
inch in length.[19]

'The features of the deceased presented an appearance of
repose that suggested the idea that she must have been suddenly
killed by the first blow inflicted by the sharp-edged hammer upon
the top of her skull,' police noted, 'and that the other eight wounds
were subsequently inflicted while she was laying upon the floor.'

Christina suffered at least fifteen blows. Blood still streamed
from her wounds, seeping 'through the boards of the passage,
dripping onto the ground below'. 'Death in each case,' the surgeon
determined, 'had been caused by injury to the brain, which had
been cut into after pieces of the skull had been broken with a sharp
instrument.'

The monetary sums recorded in the account books did not
match the amount found in the house, prompting police to believe
'that some must have been carried away'. Strangely, detectives
found no bloody footprints or splatter upstairs where the rooms

had been torn asunder. Had the killer entered the premises, snuck upstairs and surprised the two women when he came back down? From Christina's blood-smeared hand, police lifted one grey hair they believed she tore from her killer's head – a clue of little value in these days of primitive investigation.[20]

Public interest in the murders ran high, with more than 2,000 people congregating daily outside the shop. 'The audacity of the criminal in attempting a deed of violence so desperate in an open shop, in a public street, and at noon-day, has, indeed, sometimes, though, but rarely, been paralleled,' reported *The Times*. 'Nor is the mystery which still surrounds the event greater than envelopes some other famous murders. It is the combination of audacity with the apparent success in escaping which gives an exceptional interest to this attack on two lonely and helpless women . . . We are all of us interested in the detection of criminals. Life in a great city would be intolerable if it were to be overshadowed by the mystery of undetected and unpunished murder.'[21]

The detection of criminals appeared to be a problem for Scotland Yard. The double-murder went unsolved.

Five months later, on Christmas Day 1872, Harriet Buswell was 'found to be quite dead' in her rented room at 12, Great Coram Street. The landlady made the gruesome discovery when Harriet didn't show for breakfast. Entering the room, she found the walls splashed with blood and 'the bed exhibiting a dreadful appearance.' Harriet lay at the end of the bed, 'her throat having been severely cut.' A stab wound under the left ear and on the left side of her neck appeared 'large enough to put a man's fist in'.[22]

It was a tragic end to a sad life. A would-be ballet dancer, twenty-five-year-old Harriet dreamt of a career on the stage and 'eked out a living' performing in some local productions – but she earned the bulk of her livelihood between the sheets. The day of Harriet's murder, her eight-year-old daughter, cared for by another couple, showed up at the lodging house to spend Christmas with her mother.[23]

Inspector James Thomson, former member of the Detective Branch and now Superintendent of the local division, took charge of the investigation. Thomson, *The Times* noted, 'has had much experience as a detective officer'. The Coram Street crime scene provided no clues as to the motive. Harriet's body was 'drawn up as from the convulsion of the sinews caused by pain'. A bloody thumbprint stood out on her forehead. A little further down was a bloody palm print, 'as if after the first wound had been inflicted the poor creature had been held down by the left hand while the second cut was made'. The pillows on the bed were 'steeped with coagulated blood'. A large can in the corner of the room filled with pink water suggested the killer had washed his hands when done with his grisly work. A towel hanging near the washstand bore 'a mark as if a small pocket-knife had been wiped'. On the floor, near the washstand, Thomson counted ten large drops of blood.[24]

The killer locked the bedroom door from the inside when he left – yet there was no evidence of blood on the handle, door jamb or threshold. Thomson learned from another tenant in the building that Harriet returned home the night before from the Alhambra Theatre in Leicester Square and said she had met 'a very handsome German gentleman'. A neighbour saw the mystery man heading up the stairs 'as if he knew his way' to Harriet's bedroom, but stairwell shadows concealed his features.[25]

After a quiet night, the man was heard descending the stairs and leaving the building at six-thirty in the morning. His footsteps betrayed no sense of panic or hurry. 'He walked measuredly along the passage,' Thomson was told, 'and slammed the street door after him.'[26]

One tenant told Thomson that Harriet mentioned her German companion had purchased oranges and nuts for her from a fruit stand near the Alhambra. The inspector located the greengrocer and got a description of the suspect: roughly twenty-five years old, five feet nine, no facial hair, but several days' worth of stubble with a blotchy complexion. He wore a brown, knee-length coat over dark clothing with heavy boots. Further inquiries around Leicester Square led Thomson to Cavour's Restaurant and a waiter who saw Harriet in the company of a man on Christmas Eve. It seemed a promising start, but the investigation soon descended into farce.[27]

The German emigrant brig *Wangerland*, bound for America, had recently docked in Ramsgate for repairs. Several passengers and crewmembers, including a pastor named Dr Henry Hessel, his wife and a shipbroker named Wohlebbe, decided to spend the Christmas weekend in London and see the sights. They returned to the ship on 4 January. An inspector with the Ramsgate police, keeping an eye on the port, spotted Wohlebbe, thought he matched the circulated description of the man last seen with Harriet Buswell and arrested him on the spot.[28]

Duly notified, Thomson escorted the greengrocer and waiter to Ramsgate to pick Wohlebbe out of a line-up. Dr Hessel, insisting Wohlebbe to be innocent, volunteered to be part of the identification parade along with about thirty of the ship's crew. Things took an awkward turn when the greengrocer identified the pastor – and not Wohlebbe – as the man he saw with Harriet. The waiter, when summoned, did the same and requested Hessel say a few words. Before Hessel could comply, the waiter waved a dismissive hand. 'That's enough for me,' he said. 'He is the man who sat with the woman at supper.'[29]

Based on this evidence, police set Wohlebbe free and took Hessel into custody. 'The indignation of Dr Hessel's friends, and especially his wife, at his arrest,' noted *The Bristol Mercury*, 'may be better imagined than described.' Thomson escorted the stunned Dr Hessel to London, where he appeared before the Bow Street magistrate on a charge of murder. His lawyer proved, however, that on the night in question, Dr Hessel was bedridden in his room at Kroll's Hotel in America Square, several miles from Great Coram Street. The charge was dropped.[30]

Although the Bow Street magistrate saw nothing wrong in the way Scotland Yard conducted itself, the press thought otherwise.[31] *The Daily Telegraph*, on 31 January 1873, levelled a dry assessment:

> The public will learn with satisfaction that a step has actually been taken towards the detection of the Coram Street murder. The step though small, is certain. It has now been conclusively shown, by an indisputable chain of evidence, that, whoever murdered the woman Buswell, it was not Dr Hassel [sic]. We only have to pursue the same course of action with reference to every grown-up man who slept in London on Christmas Eve and, by process of elimination, we must at last arrive at the guilty man. The only objection to this process is the duration of mortal life.[32]

The investigation stumbled along for some time but ultimately went nowhere. If anything, it underscored the fallibility of eyewitness accounts. The case further tarnished Scotland Yard's reputation. It lost additional lustre in December 1874 when detectives failed to recover £20,000 of jewellery ('ornaments and so forth') stolen from the Countess of Dudley at Paddington Station. The following month, Russian Ambassador Baron Bulow had his dressing-case pilfered at Paddington – ironically, while awaiting a train to take him to visit Lord and Lady Dudley. Such failures of policing, however, proved insignificant when compared to the 1877 'Madame de Goncourt case' and the 'Trial of the Detectives'.[33]

Harry Benson, the son of a successful French merchant and well-educated in Paris, saw no need to make an honest living. He preferred the art of the swindle and thrill of the con, embarking down a crooked path at an early age. By his mid-twenties he had lined his pockets through various schemes that 'though small in scale, bore the stamp of genius'. In 1872, he took it a step too far. He went to Britain posing as an emissary from the town of

Chateaudun, heavily bombed in the Franco-Prussian War, and convinced London's well-to-do - including the Lord Mayor - to contribute £1,000 to finance the town's reconstruction. The scheme, when uncovered, earned Benson a twelve-month prison sentence. An attempt to kill himself by setting his cell bunk on fire left him severely burned and barely able to walk.[34]

Upon his release, the multilingual Benson responded to an advertisement in *The Daily Telegraph* 'for someone to write and translate articles into various languages'. He applied for and landed the job, thus meeting - through a twist of fate - William Kurr. The son of a baker, Kurr had abandoned the bread business for more colourful pursuits. He had a plan to print a fake publication called *Sports*. It would feature the story of one Mr Montgomery, who proved so lucky at the racetrack no British bookies would take his bets. Consequently, Mr Montgomery was looking for people in France willing to place bets on his behalf under their own name for a small commission.[35]

Benson and Kurr printed up betting sheets for non-existent races, established a bookmaking front, and issued the 'winnings' on cheques from the wholly made-up 'Bank of London'. Mr Montgomery's lucrative (and fake) winnings convinced those who fell for the scam to place their own wagers with what they believed to be a legitimate betting house. They were, in fact, simply sending money to Benson and Kurr. The 'complex and elaborate' plan worked like a charm - particularly on the wealthy Countess de Goncourt, who sent her solicitor into near apoplexy when she asked him to slap £30,000 of her family fortune on a horse race. The solicitor, not as naïve as the countess, sensed something amiss. His suspicions put Scotland Yard on the trail of the two conmen, but the pair proved hard to catch and were always one step ahead of detectives.[36]

Once captured and convicted, Benson and Kurr confessed to bribing senior officers of the Yard's Detective Branch to avoid apprehension. They named Inspector John Meiklejohn and three of the branch's four chief inspectors: George Clarke, Nathaniel Druscovitch and William Palmer. The allegations blindsided Superintendent 'Dolly' Williamson, who allowed the close friendships he enjoyed with his men to cloud his judgment. The four detectives, charged with 'conspiracy to defeat the ends of justice', went on trial in October 1877. Clarke was acquitted and resigned from the Yard; the other three men, all guilty, received two-year sentences.[37]

The so-called 'Trial of the Detectives' made international news. 'The British public,' reported *The American Law Review* after the verdicts, 'were soon made aware of the singularly disagreeable circumstance that all was not as it should be at Scotland Yard – that the force of skilled detectives . . . which existed as the possible protector of every capitalist and merchant in the realm, contained an unknown number of members in league with some of the most daring and successful depredators, who for a long time past had made booty of the property of honest men. Few discoveries could have been more odious.'[38]

In the scandal's wake, the Home Office assembled a commission 'to inquire into the state, discipline and organization of the Detective Force of the Metropolitan Police.' It worked quickly, assisted by a twenty-eight-year-old lawyer named Howard Vincent, who 'went to Paris and studied the centralized French detective system.' Based on Vincent's input, the commission recommended a single report structure for Scotland Yard's detectives. This meant ending the current use of divisional detectives and establishing 'a central detective force with some of its officers stationed in Divisions.'[39]

This reorganized force would 'take precedence over the uniformed branch of the service', evident by its higher salaries and the fact new recruits could join the detective ranks without first walking the beat. If this created a sense of elitism, so be it. 'The head of the new department was not to be a policeman but a lawyer' with a rank equivalent to assistant commissioner. Howard

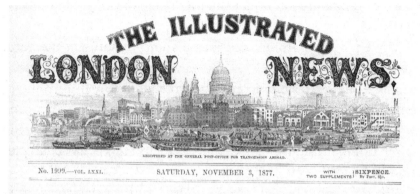

Scotland Yard's detectives go on trial.

Vincent landed the job under the title Director of Criminal Investigations.[40]

Vincent's appointment came as a shock to some at the Yard. 'He was young, comparatively speaking, unknown, inexperienced in police matters, with no previous record but a brief military service, followed by a call to the Bar,' wrote one contemporary. 'But he was energetic, painstaking, a man of order, with some power of organization; above all, a gentleman of high character and integrity.'[41]

Vincent channelled his organizational prowess into structuring the new department. At Scotland Yard headquarters, or Central Office, it would have three chief inspectors, twenty inspectors, and six sergeants and constables working in support. Across the divisions, the department would allocate fifteen inspectors and 159 sergeants. Frederick Adolphus ('Dolly') Williamson – having survived the recent scandal to be promoted from Superintendent to Chief Superintendent – would serve under Vincent and oversee the department's day-to-day operations.[42]

And so it was on 8 April 1878 that the Criminal Investigation Department, or CID, was born.

10

Human Wickedness

A major case for the CID. A body boiled to sludge.

The Criminal Investigation Department emerged from the blemished shadow of its predecessor with much to prove. 'The Detective' bore a heavy stain. 'Through the undetected murders and unpunished villainies of many years we know to our cost that the detective of the novelist and the real [thing] are as different as can be,' declared London's *Weekly Dispatch* in assessing the new department. 'Little or nothing escaped the detective of fiction, while still less is discovered by the detective of real life.'[1]

It was a discovery that could've spilled from the pages of a particularly gruesome detective story that initiated one of the CID's first major cases – a twisted crime, the sheer brutality of which stunned Victorian sensibilities. Indeed, the press called it 'one of the most sensational and awful chapters in the annals of human wickedness.' Sifting through the grisly details, the detectives of real life would prove themselves worthy of their fictional counterparts.[2]

Coal porter Henry Wheatley guided his horse-drawn cart along a narrow towpath that meandered the banks of the Thames. It was six forty-five on the morning of Wednesday, 5 March 1879. The tide retreating, the mud-coloured waters slowly pulled away from the shore to reveal a slime-thickened bed of trash and debris.

Wheatley rounded a gentle bend and saw the Barnes Railway Bridge spanning the river thirty yards ahead. He turned his gaze to the Thames; the pallid morning light played on the murky surface.

An object caught his eye. It appeared to be a box, white in colour, a stark blemish against the mud. A good portion of it remained submerged. 'The water was just ebbing away from the top of the box, which was stationary, and about seven yards from the bank,' Wheatley said.[3]

Wondering if maybe 'the box contained the proceeds of a burglary,' Wheatley brought his cart to a standstill, dismounted and trudged just far enough into the water to retrieve the mystery loot. As he got closer, his feet sinking into the sludge, he noticed a clothesline tied around the box. A torn page from a March 1877 edition of *The Daily Telegraph* floated alongside it 'as though the paper had, perhaps, been put around the box.'[4]

He hauled the plunder ashore. The box, a uniform white with a hinged lid, was not that big. He guessed it to be no more than a foot in length, width and depth. It had no address or markings of any kind stamped upon its smooth-planed surface and was missing a handle. He pulled a knife from his belt and cut through the tightly wrapped clothesline. The water had taken its toll.

'When I untied the box, it fell to pieces,' Wheatley said. What lay festering inside was not the spoils of a burglary. 'I saw a lot of what looked like cooked meat in it. It was quite full.'[5]

Realizing the sinister nature of his discovery, he hurried to the Barnes Police Station and alerted Sergeant Thomas Childs, who returned with Wheatley to the riverbank. 'I saw a box on the shore,' Childs said. 'The box was broken. It appeared to contain human remains.'[6]

Childs sent for local doctor James Adams, who showed up just before seven and confirmed Childs's suspicions. A cursory examination revealed the remains to be 'the trunk and other portions of the body of a woman.' They were taken to the Barnes Mortuary at the local cemetery. There, Adams spread the butchered anatomy out on a coffin lid for a more thorough study and made note of his findings:

The heart was in the cavity of the chest. I found a portion of the right lung, but the left lung was absent. Attached to the trunk was the right shoulder. The upper part of the left arm had been detached, and I found it to be perfect down to the elbow. A portion of the thigh of the right leg and the remainder of the leg down to the ankle was also among the remains. A part of the pelvis was present, as also a small portion of the spine – the rectum was divided. The head was absent.[7]

CID inspectors Henry Jones of T (Richmond) Division and John Dowdell from headquarters watched Adams as he worked. They inspected the trunk but found nothing to shed light on its origin or ownership. Likewise, its contents offered nothing in the way of a clue. All Adams could do was make an educated guess as to the dead woman's age and physicality, but even that proved a challenge considering the scarcity of body parts.[8]

'I should think the woman had been dead about a week,' he said, 'while the remains might have been in the water about two days.'

Making allowances for the missing anatomy, he estimated the woman's height to be 5ft 4in and placed her age between eighteen and thirty. He theorized the bones had been fractured 'after death' by an unskilled hand using 'very bad instruments.'

'The mutilation must have been a work of time,' he said. 'The bones must have been smashed with a blunt instrument.'[9]

For Jones and Dowdell, the investigation had no clear starting point. Officers scoured Barnes Common and the banks of the river, looking for missing body parts – or anything that might lend an identity to the victim. Constables knocked on doors trying 'to ascertain if anyone [was] missing from the neighbourhood.' Their efforts turned up nothing.[10]

'Now that the weather is about as bad as it could possibly be and people are heartily tired of the long winter,' *The Manchester Evening News* proclaimed, 'nothing could be more acceptable, as a means of producing a little stimulating excitement, than a "mystery" associated with an outrageous "deed of blood".' The press revelled in the grotesque find and compared it to Hannah Brown's slaying in 1836. *The Penny Illustrated* called it 'a brutal murder of the Greenacre type'. The discovery was not typical of leafy Barnes, which, according to one paper, 'blooms into a garden of girls on the morning of the Oxford and Cambridge Boat-Race.' [11]

The mystery deepened five days later when a labourer loading a manure cart on an allotment in Twickenham felt the tines of his pitchfork strike 'a soft substance'. He sifted through the muck and was startled to see a severed human foot still attached to the ankle. 'It had been sawn off recently,' he said. The foot wound up with the other remains at Barnes Mortuary.[12]

The next day, Thursday, 12 March, police summoned Dr Thomas Bond – assistant surgeon at Westminster Hospital and a lecturer of forensic medicine – to provide his opinion. He guessed the person had been dead no more than a fortnight due to a lack of decomposition. 'With the exception of one thigh,' Bond noted, '[the remains] were very dry, shrivelled, shrunken, and the soft parts were easily torn, the cartilage easily pulled off, and the tendons were very soft. I had no doubt that the parts had been boiled.'[13]

One theory floating around suggested 'the body had been put into the river by medical students after dissection,' but the savage nature of the wounds put such conjecture to rest. The papers christened Wheatley's find 'The Barnes Mystery' – and perhaps a mystery it would have stayed, if not for a nosy neighbour.[14]

Vine Cottages in Richmond was a grey-stoned, two-storey, subdivided villa with 'a small garden in front and at back'. Elizabeth Ives lived at No. 1. Next door at No. 2 lived Elizabeth's tenant, Julia Thomas, an older lady of prickly demeanour who had moved in the previous September. 'No. 2 is a small but very respectable house,'

The Times informed its readers, 'and its appearance would suggest that it was the dwelling of a person in good circumstances.'[15]

Shortly before seven o'clock on the evening of Tuesday, 18 March, Elizabeth peered through her window and saw, parked in front of Julia's house, two furniture vans and several men removing items from the home. Elizabeth stepped outside to find out what was happening. As she assailed one of the moving men with questions, a woman emerged from No. 2 and approached. Elizabeth recognized her as Julia's maid, Kate.

'Is it Miss Ives who wishes to know where the furniture is going to?' Kate asked.

'Well, I should like to know,' Elizabeth replied.

'Mrs Thomas has sold the furniture. Mr Weston,' Kate said, gesturing at one of the men, 'is going to take it to Hammersmith.'

Elizabeth found this odd, especially as two weeks had passed since she last saw her neighbour. 'Where is Mrs Thomas?' she asked.

'I do not know,' Kate said, and turned away.

Elizabeth could see the questioning had annoyed the woman. 'Her face,' she later recalled, 'was quite convulsed, and she could hardly speak to me.' When Elizabeth asked if Mrs Thomas had left a forwarding address, the maid replied with an adamant 'No.'

Elizabeth, her patience exhausted, went back inside. She had last seen Julia on the afternoon of Saturday, 1 March, in the garden planting flowers. Two days later, on the Monday morning, Elizabeth noticed 'a very strange smell' coming from her neighbour's place. Oddly, it seemed not to have piqued her curiosity. Nor did the sounds she heard that Monday night of a heavy object being moved and what she thought to be 'the chopping of wood on the hearth' and someone stoking a fire up until nine o'clock.[16]

Even now, with men loading furniture vans – 'a large one and a small one' – outside Julia's home in the gathering gloom, Elizabeth drew no sinister conclusions. 'Strange though it may seem,' *The Daily Telegraph* later mused, 'nobody thought of connecting the discovery of the remains at Barnes with the fact that Mrs Thomas had not shown herself while preparations were being made to remove her goods.'[17]

One of the men carrying furniture out to the vans was a painter and decorator named Henry Porter. He assigned nothing untoward to his task and believed he was merely helping a friend. He'd returned from work on the evening of Tuesday, 4 March, one day before the box was discovered in the Thames, and found Kate Webster waiting for him on his doorstep with a large black bag in her possession. The two were former neighbours, Kate having lived next door to him six years prior. 'I did not recognize her at once,' Porter said. 'She seemed a great deal more respectably dressed. We had tea together. At tea she said an aunt had died and left her a very comfortable home at Richmond.'[18]

Kate explained she was now widowed, went by the name Mrs Thomas and had a young son who was living with a caretaker. She wanted to clear out her dead aunt's house and sell off the possessions before returning to Ireland with her child to care for her ailing father. Could Henry help? Porter agreed, and the two of them decided to walk to the Oxford and Cambridge pub on the Hammersmith Bridge Road and discuss the matter over a glass of ale.

When Kate moved to pick up her black bag, Porter volunteered his fifteen-year-old-son Robert to carry it. It was a considerable size for the boy: about twenty inches long and twelve inches in depth. Robert noticed the bag was partially open and could see a package wrapped in brown paper. He lagged behind on their stroll to the pub, forcing Kate and Porter to wait for him. 'I thought he was looking at the shop windows,' Porter said. 'When he came up, I said, "What are you looking about for?" and he said, "Take the bag, father; it is rather heavy."'

Porter took the bag, which he guessed weighed about twenty-five pounds, and carried it the rest of the way. He didn't ask what was in it. At the pub, the three of them took a seat at the bar. Porter ordered a glass of ale for himself and one for Kate, who made quick work of it. She put the empty glass down and said she had to pay a quick visit to a friend in nearby Barnes, just across the river, without elaborating further. When she reached down to pick up the bag, Porter again said Robert would be happy to carry it for her.

'Oh, no,' Kate said. 'I can manage it myself. I shan't be gone long.'

It was nearing eight o'clock when she lugged the bag from the pub. She returned half an hour later, the bag no longer in her possession, and said she'd seen her friend. Over two more pints, Kate showed Porter pictures of her deceased aunt's house in Richmond and flashed several rings bequeathed to her. It was nine when they left the pub for Hammersmith Station so Kate could catch a train back to Richmond. As they walked, she inquired if Porter knew anyone who might want to buy her aunt's furniture. Porter said he would check around. She had one more favour to ask when they reached the station. Would Robert accompany her home for the night? She gave no reason as to why, but Porter nevertheless allowed it.[19]

Kate and the boy took a train to Richmond Station and, from there, walked in silence to Vine Cottages. Inside, the house was dark. Kate lit an oil lamp in the sitting room and offered Robert a glass of rum. They drank in the flickering, yellow light. Kate moved across the room to a piano in the corner and gently ran her fingers over the keys. 'It's a nice one,' she said, almost to herself.

She polished off the rum and pulled two £5 notes from her pocket.

'I want you to help me to carry a box to Richmond Bridge, because I have to meet a friend there,' she said. She left the room and returned ten minutes later dragging a box tied up in cord. 'This is the box I want you to carry.'

Robert hoisted one end. The two of them trudged from the house at eleven o'clock with the heavy cargo between them and made their way to the bridge, the Thames flowing swift and black beneath it. They crossed and stopped near the Twickenham end of the expanse.

'Put it down and you go on,' Kate said, her breathing heavy. 'My friend will be here directly. I'll catch you up.'

Robert started walking back towards the Richmond side of the river. 'I heard a slight splash,' Robert later said. 'I did not know whether it was the box or a barge coming under the bridge. I did not see a barge.'

Kate emerged from the darkness and caught up with the boy. She no longer had the box with her. 'Bob, I have seen my friend,' she said. 'Now, we'll keep towards the station and get home.'

Upon reaching the station, they found the last train back to Hammersmith had already departed, so Robert slept at Kate's house. Nothing about the night's events seemed peculiar to the boy. 'It did not strike me as very curious,' he said, 'that she should take a box and go and meet somebody on the bridge.'

He returned home the next morning.[20]

Several days later, on Sunday, 9 March, Porter and his wife happened to read in *Lloyd's Weekly Newspaper* an account of the coroner's inquest into 'The Barnes Mystery.' The morbid details sparked a lively conversation between the two – one overheard by Robert. He had not discussed the task he helped Kate with the night he went off with her, but now he shared the details.

'He described the size of the box,' Henry Porter said, 'and it answered the description in *Lloyd's* newspaper. I understood from him that he thought the box might have been the one found in the river.'[21]

Perhaps Henry Porter dismissed his son's story as the product of a boy's overactive imagination. Whatever the reason, he failed to act on the information. In fact, on that very Sunday, Porter brought Kate to the Rising Sun pub in Hammersmith and introduced her to proprietor John Church, who wanted to purchase new furniture for his establishment. The three had a drink before making their way to Kate's house, where Church agreed to purchase its contents for £68. He made arrangements with a moving man named Henry Weston.

And that's how Porter, along with Church and Weston, presently came to be loading furniture into the back of a van outside 2, Vine Cottages. He had just witnessed the strange scene of the lady next door asking Kate where Mrs Thomas had disappeared to – strange, because he thought Kate *was* Mrs Thomas. Porter noticed the encounter left Kate 'a little agitated'. She seemed eager to finish clearing out the house and helped by bundling some dresses into the back of the van.[22]

Even before the men finished loading the furniture, Kate busied herself with other matters. She left the house without explanation and walked to Richmond Station, where she hired a cab to Hammersmith. She put in a brief appearance at the Rising Sun and borrowed a sovereign from Church's wife. From there, she headed to the Porter residence, where her son was staying that evening. Robert answered when she knocked. He helped the boy into a 'suit of knickerbockers and a pea jacket' and carried him outside. Kate stood waiting near the cab.[23]

She bundled the child inside and thanked Robert for his kindness before ordering the driver on to Hammersmith Station. There, with her child in her arms, she boarded a train bound for King's Cross and vanished.[24]

Not until three days after Kate's departure by train did her story come under suspicion. Indeed, the strange thread running through this twisted saga is that no one suspected anything sooner. On the afternoon of Friday, 21 March, Church's wife, Maria, went through the pockets of the dresses taken from Vine Cottages. She found in one a letter addressed to 'Mrs J. Thomas' from a gentleman named Charles Menhennick, who lived at 45, Ambler Road, Finsbury Park.[25]

Church and Porter, having grown suspicious about Kate's disappearance the evening they cleared out the house, took the letter to the man who wrote it. It became apparent in conversation that the Mrs J. Thomas that Menhennick and his wife had known for ten years was not the supposedly widowed Mrs Thomas with whom Church and Porter had been acquainted. Whereas the real Mrs Thomas was elderly and greying, the imposter was in her late twenties or early thirties with a 'light freckled complexion [and] blue eyes'.[26]

And so it was, three weeks after Henry Wheatley found boiled human meat floating in the Thames, Church and Porter notified police that Mrs Julia Thomas of 2, Vine Cottages, Richmond, was missing.

Inspector John Pearman took initial statements from Porter and Church on Saturday, 22 May at the Richmond Police Station. He accompanied the men to Julia's house and was let in by Elizabeth Ives. It was six o'clock in the evening, the light fading from the sky. A deepening gloom crept across the rooms, up the stairs and down the hallways.

'The place was in great confusion,' Pearman said. 'The beds moved out, the carpet taken up. I saw three large boxes of bed linen ready to be taken away.' It was apparent the house had been vacated in a hurry. Over the next several days, officers dug up the garden and searched every nook and cranny for signs of Julia Thomas.[27]

They found bits of her.

Pearman noticed the brickwork around the laundry copper in the scullery had been scrubbed clean. He pried the grate beneath the copper free and found 'a quantity of charred bones' that weighed nearly three pounds. The larger bones had been splintered into smaller pieces. In the copper itself – which measured fourteen inches wide and thirteen inches deep – he found a thick, smeared 'fatty substance'. 'The copper had been wiped out, but, in a hurry,' he noted, 'the fatty matter attaching to it had escaped attention.'[28]

Under the sink in the scullery, he found a broken handle that subsequently fit the box found in the Thames. He also found some cord that matched the twine wrapped around the box. A razor-blade lay on the floor alongside a burned nightdress. Bloodstains throughout the house told a violent tale, one that played out on the staircase, in the hallway and in the scullery. On a table in the sitting room, Pearman found a day diary. Under the date of 28 February was this entry: 'Gave Katherine warning to leave.'[29]

Police interviewed Julia's friends and acquaintances. She was a woman of mercurial temperament. According to some, she 'held little intercourse with her neighbours but was generally known as an extremely bad-tempered woman'. And yet others described her as 'a genuine lady, ever endeavouring to please all about her even in the midst of her depression of spirits'. Her depression stemmed from being twice widowed, but her misfortune rendered her a woman of comfortable means – so much so she often employed help to manage the household. In this regard, many remembered her 'as very much a tartar to her servants'. This was to prove her undoing.[30]

The last servant she employed, detectives learned, was a woman named Kate Webster. Born Catherine Lawler in the Irish village of Killane in 1849, Webster was no stranger to law enforcement. She embarked on a criminal career in her teens and developed a proficiency in stealing from lodging houses. She served her first prison term when she was eighteen and, once free, fled Ireland for England. The change of scenery did nothing to set her straight. She 'connected and lived with criminals of the vilest class' and ultimately served another three prison terms 'varying from two months to two years'. In May 1875, she did eighteen months in Wandsworth Prison for 'no less than thirty-six robberies committed in the neighbourhood of Kingston'. Back on the outside, she resorted to old habits and was again locked away in February 1877 for a year.[31]

What legitimate living she occasionally earned, she did so as a servant, which proved useful in identifying her next targets. On 2 January 1879, she went to work for Julia Thomas, 'who appears to have engaged her without any character and without inquiring into her antecedents'. The last time anyone saw Julia was exactly two months later, when she attended two services at the Presbyterian Chapel in Richmond. She complained to several people that evening about her latest servant's lack of work ethic and surly attitude.[32]

Julia returned home between seven and eight. Later that night, Elizabeth Ives told police, she heard a noise 'such as would be caused by the falling of a heavy chair'. Early the next morning, she noticed the 'vile smell' from next door – 'but nothing was thought of this at the time.' On the morning of Tuesday, 3 March, it looked like laundry day at 2, Vine Cottages with 'the clothes-lines being filled and the copper chimney smoking as if the washing apparatus was in full work.'[33]

On Wednesday, 26 March, Scotland Yard released the following to the press:

> Wanted for stealing plates, etc., and supposed murder of her mistress, Kate — , aged about 32, 5ft 5in or 6in high; complexion sallow, slightly freckled; teeth rather good and prominent. Usually dressed in dark dress, jacket rather long and trimmed with dark fur round the pockets, light brown satin bonnet. Speaks with an Irish accent, and was accompanied by a boy aged five, complexion rather dark, hair dark. Was last seen at Hammersmith.[34]

Two days later, police brought the bones found under the laundry copper to Dr Bond's house in Westminster. 'I recognized pieces of the left thigh bone, the small bone of the left leg, the small bone of the right arm, the bones of the right hand, some pieces of the haunch bone or pelvis, and some fragments of the spinal column,' he said. 'I found a piece of the large bone of the leg and a part of the bone of the arm. I could not say to which side either of them belonged. They had all been burned to a cinder.'[35]

What remained missing was any sign of the head, without which police couldn't confirm the victim's identity. Reported *The Times*, 'Though it would be hardly possible to give legal proof of the identification of the body without the head, still there remains scarcely any doubt of the fact that the body is that of the missing Mrs Thomas.'[36]

Scotland Yard, in the meantime, canvassed train stations and shipping yards. It traced Webster's movements to Liverpool, where – on the nineteenth – she and her son boarded a coal vessel bound for Dublin. Police in Ireland, alerted to the Yard's hunt and acquainted with Kate Webster, found her hiding out with her boy at the home of an uncle, a man named Lawless, in Killane. The local constabulary locked her up in the Enniscorthy town jail and sent word to London.[37]

CID inspectors John Dowdell and Henry Jones hopped onto the first available steamer across the Irish Sea. They left London on 26 March and arrived in Enniscorthy, via Dublin, three days later and took Webster into custody. She showed no emotion when told she would be charged with murder. 'She appeared an amiable, pleasant sort of woman, as far as I can tell,' Dowdell said. 'She gave no trouble, and came back quite quietly and calmly.'[38]

The detectives wasted little time catching a ship for the sea-tossed crossing back to England. More than once Dowdell accompanied Webster to the railing on deck. She told the inspector her life had been a series of unfortunate events. She claimed to have married a sea captain named Webster when she was still a teen and mothered four children, all of whom – along with her husband, she said – subsequently died. The story was most likely a falsehood to earn the inspector's sympathy.

'Is there any other person in custody for the murder?' she asked at one point. 'If there is not, there ought to be. It is very hard the innocent should suffer for the guilty.'

'I hope you will not say a word against an innocent person,' Dowdell cautioned.[39]

She said John Church, proprietor of the Rising Sun, had been her lover for seven years and killed Julia Thomas for her money. She said she stumbled across the ghastly scene just after Church had done Julia in with a carving knife. 'If you say a word about it,' Church supposedly told her, 'I'll put this knife into you up to the handle.'

Church, she said, got rid of the body.[40]

They arrived in London on the morning of Sunday, 30 March, pulling into Euston Station a little before seven. Despite looking 'pale and haggard', Webster wore her Sunday best: 'a dark plum-coloured dress, black cloth jacket edged with fur, and a hat or bonnet with French grey feather.' Constables waited with a four-wheeled cab to take Webster to the Richmond Police Station. She walked past them 'bold and defiant'. No sooner had the cab departed the station than word of its infamous passenger got out. 'In a very few moments a large number of people were on the track of the vehicle,' wrote one reporter. 'To avoid interruption, the driver gave whip to his horse and ran into Richmond at full speed, the horse at the end of the journey being laved in perspiration.'[41]

At the station, seated across a table from Inspector Jones, she repeated the story she'd told on the sea crossing and fingered Church for the murder and the disposal of the body. 'I never laid a hand on Mrs Thomas and had nothing to do with murdering her,' she said, 'but I knew Church had done it. I don't see why I should be blamed for what Church has done. I wouldn't accuse my great-est enemy of anything wrong, let alone a friend, which Church has been to me up till now.' Jones summoned Church to the station and read him the statement. Church laughed at the absurdity of it but lost his sense of humour when told he was under arrest. 'The lying woman,' he cried. 'How can she say that about me? I know nothing of her!'[42]

Church and Webster appeared in magistrates court shortly after 2 p.m. the next day, 30 March, and stood side by side in the dock to be arraigned. A crowd waited hours outside 'the building, which at Richmond is used as a Vestry-hall and Justice-room'. A reporter for *The Times* said Webster looked 'pale, but she was firm and self-possessed.' The paper critiqued her looks and wardrobe: 'She has no characteristics of a criminal in her face, and, though not handsome, is not ill-looking. Her jacket was of shabby cloth, trimmed with imitation fur, and her dress of the material and cut usually favoured by respectable servants.' As for Church, *The Times* merely noted he 'has the appearance of an artisan'.[43]

The same afternoon Webster and Church appeared in magistrates court, 'all members of the local police force, as well as all the central divisional detectives who have had anything to do with the case, were called to Scotland Yard.' The case against Church was already in doubt. Statements by other witnesses, including the Porters, backed up Church's insistence he'd had no dealings with Kate Webster prior to being introduced to her by Henry Porter. Furthermore, witnesses and a signed registry placed him at a Slate Club meeting on the night and time he was supposedly committing the murder. There was also the fact he had been one of the individuals to alert police to Mrs Thomas's disappearance. The charge against him was subsequently dropped.[44]

Webster's trial at the Old Bailey began on Wednesday, 2 July, before Justice Denman. There was still no definitive understanding as to what transpired at 2, Vine Cottages. 'The prisoner was placed in the dock at a few minutes passed [sic] ten o'clock,' one court-room spectator wrote. 'The air of indifference which appeared to mark her conduct before the Richmond magistrates has altogether passed away, and has given place to an anxious, restless expression, intensified by her careworn appearance.'[45]

Six days of testimony followed. The prosecution's case, though solid, was not without its challenges. The missing head meant the body had not officially been identified, and there was no proof a murder had been committed. Crown Counsel Sir Hardings Giffard tried to prove foul play by establishing through Inspector Pearman's testimony that body fat had been found in Mrs Thomas's laundry copper. He tied that to the testimony of Dr Thomas Bond, who said the body parts found in the river had been boiled.[46]

In his closing argument for the defence, barrister Warner Sleigh put to the jury that Julia Thomas could have died from 'heart disease, apoplexy, or the bursting of a blood vessel'. There was, he said, no clear evidence of a crime. 'The gentlemen of the jury were the bulwarks of safety between the accused and an unjust conviction,' he said to the crowded courtroom. 'Upon them lay the power of sending a woman to the gallows or preventing a miscarriage of justice.'[47]

The jury retired at 5:12 p.m. and returned seventy-three minutes later with a guilty verdict. 'I am not guilty, my lord, of the murder,' Webster protested. 'I have never done it, my lord.' She apologized for trying to pin the crime on Church and said the man responsible, instead, was the father of her child who had left her to ruin. She tried to delay the inevitable by blurting out she was pregnant. The judge asked Dr Bond to examine Kate in the jury room and 'inquire into the truth of the allegation made by the prisoner'. She was not, it turned out, with child, and the sentence of death was passed.[48]

'The sentence is one with which the public will agree,' *The Dundee Evening Telegraph* reported. 'Involved, mysterious, and hidden as were the circumstances attendant upon the horrible crime, no one could doubt as the evidence proceeded that a verdict of guilty must be the inevitable result.'[49]

Webster spent her final three weeks in the condemned cell at Wandsworth Prison being watched over by two female attendants. She provided two more statements, blaming her child's father for the murder. Authorities dismissed both as utter falsehoods. She hoped the Home Secretary might issue a reprieve, but no show of mercy was forthcoming. On Monday, 28 July, the night before her 'untimely end', she revealed what happened at Vine Cottages. The story she told detailed, in the words of *The Pall Mall Gazette*, 'a crime of rare atrocity'.[50]

All seemed well when Kate Webster started working for Mrs Thomas in January. 'At first I thought her a nice old lady, and I imagined that I could be comfortable and happy with her,' Webster said. 'But I found her very trying. She used to do many things to annoy me.' Julia often inspected rooms once they'd been cleaned and pointed out areas that had been missed. 'This sort of conduct made me have an ill feeling towards her,' Webster said, 'but I had no intention of killing her – at least not then.'

The situation in the house continued to deteriorate, Webster said, with Mrs Thomas 'showing evidence of a nasty spirit towards me.' On the afternoon of 2 March, the two of them got into one of their frequent arguments – over what, Webster couldn't recall.

'She and myself were enraged,' Webster said. 'She became very agitated and left the house to go to church in that state, leaving me at home.'

The argument resumed when Julia returned that evening. Webster followed Julia up the stairs, where the disagreement 'ripened into a quarrel, and in the height of my anger and rage I threw her from the top of the stairs to the ground floor. She had a heavy fall.'

This accounted for the noise Elizabeth Ives thought was a chair being knocked over. Fearing Julia might scream, Webster threw herself on top of the stricken woman and choked the life out of her.

'I then became entirely lost and without any control over myself,' Webster said. 'I determined to do away with the body the best I could.' She scrounged about the house for the necessary tools and then got to work:

> I chopped the head from the body with the assistance of a razor, which I used to cut through the flesh afterwards. I also used [a] meat saw and carving knife to cut the body up with. I prepared the copper with water to boil the body to prevent identity; and as soon as I had succeeded in cutting it up I placed it in the copper and boiled it. I opened the stomach with the carving knife and burned up as much of the parts as I could.

She went about the ghastly business with a grim determination. 'When I looked upon the scene before me and saw the blood around my feet, the horror and dread I felt was inconceivable,' she said. 'I was bewildered and acted as if I was mad.' She almost succumbed to revulsion:

> I was greatly overcome, both from the horrible sight before me and the smell, and I failed several times in strength and determination but was helped on by the devil in this vile purpose.

She spent all night chopping, boiling and scrubbing. She lit a fire in the kitchen grate and burned the entrails. When the body parts in the copper had been sufficiently rendered to sludge, she dumped the contents out and cleaned the copper as best she could. She placed the parts that didn't boil down in the box that would subsequently be found in the Thames. When she was done packing it up, she realized she still had a foot in need of disposing, so she dumped it 'in the dunghill at Kingston.' She stashed Julia's head in the black bag that she carried to the Porters, for afternoon tea. She didn't say in her final statement where she ultimately dumped it.

Once she was free of all incriminating evidence and had scrubbed the house clean, she decided it would be best 'to sell all that there was in the house and go away.' And it was that decision that proved her undoing.

'I alone should be blamed,' she concluded in her statement. 'I am perfectly resigned to my fate and full of confidence in a happy eternity. If I had a choice, I would almost sooner die than return to a life full of misery, deception and wickedness.'[51]

Kate Webster's final moments as depicted in
The Illustrated Police News on 2 August 1879.

Kate Webster went to the gallows at nine o'clock the following morning. She offered no last words as the white execution hood fell across her face. Seconds later, hangman William Marwood dropped her six feet into oblivion.

Although mostly forgotten today, the horrific murder of Julia Thomas served as a fitting prologue to a decade defined by history's most infamous killer.

11

'From Hell'

The age of serial killers. The dawn of criminal profiling.

The decade began with a fiery terror campaign and followed a midnight path to the lamp-lit cobblestones of Whitechapel. Even as a madman stalked the East End, the Thames disgorged its own mutilated horrors along its muddy banks. The 1880s proved a dark and violent decade for Scotland Yard, marred by spectacular failures and public humiliation.

From 1881 to 1885, the Fenians set bombs off across London and Britain, targeting military bases, government buildings and public spaces. This prompted the creation on 17 March 1883, of the Special Irish Branch. Its twelve officers – all 'conversant with Irish affairs' – were placed under the command of Superintendent 'Dolly' Williamson, who was ordered 'to be relieved of the greater proportion of his regular duty and to devote his time entirely to Fenianism.' Reporting to CID head Howard Vincent and the Home Office, Williamson and his men were tasked with collecting 'intelligence on Irish Home Rulers and their sympathizers in parliament and the immigrant communities'. The branch itself became a target when an anonymous letter arrived at the Yard later that year, threatening to bomb all public buildings in London and blow 'Williamson off his stool'. The letter went so far as to provide the date of the pending attack: 30 May 1884. The warning went unheeded.[1]

Shortly after 9 p.m. on the day in question, three massive explosions battered London's West End. 'The whole of Pall-mall,

St James-street, and St James's-square was shaken by the sharp detonations,' *The Times* reported, 'which sounded as if three mortars had gone off, one after the other.'

Two bombs went off in St James's Square near the Junior Carlton Club, blowing up the pavement, shattering windows, knocking out the gas in the streetlights and injuring ten people. The third bomb went off less than a mile away at Scotland Yard, opposite the Rising Sun pub, blowing up a section of building that housed the CID and Special Irish Branch.

Someone had placed the bomb in a public restroom – 'a disgracefully dark place,' according to *The Times* – in the building's northwest corner and 'shielded by a large iron shutter'. The detonation hurled the shutter across the street. 'The wall of the building was burst outwards,' said one eyewitness, 'and the explosion wrecked the public-house opposite, injuring some persons who were there.' Among those hurt was a police constable and a cabbie struck by flying debris. Fortunately, no one was in the building at the time of the explosion. Remembered one Yard detective:[2]

> The very desk at which I'd been working was blown to pieces . . . We never discovered how the bomb was ignited, though of course the debris was searched with the greatest care; no traces were found that could help us to a conclusion. Neither have we ever been certain who the perpetrators were; but we suspected two men named Burton and Cunningham, who were arrested six months later for being concerned in a serious explosion at the Tower of London. Both men were sent to penal servitude for life. This affair caused some confusion at Scotland Yard for some months; we could not console ourselves in the same way as the proprietor of the Rising Sun.[3]

A fourth explosive, found at the base of Nelson's Column in Trafalgar Square, failed to detonate. The terror campaign continued. In December 1884, a bomb detonated on London Bridge and killed the two men planting it. The most brazen attack, however, came on 24 January 1885, when three bombs went off at the Tower of London, the House of Commons and Westminster Hall, all causing extensive damage without inflicting serious injury.

The Daily Telegraph demanded 'universal indignation' at the 'diabolical outrage' and questioned Scotland Yard's effectiveness. 'Are all its inspectors asleep and all its detectives tangled in those innumerable "clues" which they are always finding and never following up?' it queried with particular venom. '. . . Is this pestilence that walketh at noonday so mysterious that the Home Office is utterly in the dark until it sees the flash, and only wakes up when it hears the explosion?' Another publication, *The Referee*, took a more sarcastic approach: 'All things come to those who wait, and eventually the dynamitards will come to the police. The police are patiently waiting for them to walk into Scotland-yard and give themselves up.'[4]

There seemed no shortage of vitriol aimed at the Yard's inability to combat the scourge. It couldn't even safeguard its own offices. Its perceived incompetence, notes *The Official Encyclopaedia of Scotland Yard*, 'did much to lower the reputation of the Metropolitan Police in the years running up to the Jack the Ripper case.'[5]

The appointment of Sir Charles Warren as Commissioner of Police in March 1886 following the resignation of Sir Edmund Henderson did little to help matters. A 'military man by training and inclination', Warren faced accusations he was 'attempting to militarize the Force'. Almost from the outset, his tenure – tainted by civil unrest and high-profile blunders – was viewed as less than stellar. A riot at the 1886 Lord Mayor Show got things off on the wrong foot. Not long thereafter, police mistakenly arrested a seamstress named Elizabeth Cass for prostitution in Regent Street. Her public indignation and ultimate acquittal sparked considerable controversy, prompting Parliament to request an inquiry.[6]

And then came 'Bloody Sunday'. On 13 November 1887, a large crowd gathered in Trafalgar Square to demonstrate against unemployment and harsh government policies against Irish Home Rule.

The gathering was a slap in the face to Warren, who had recently banned such meetings in the square. The resulting clash between demonstrators and some 2,000 constables reinforced by mounted troops sent dozens to the hospital.

'During the melee, the police freely used their weapons,' *The Shields Daily Gazette* reported, 'and the people, who were armed with iron bars, pokers, gas pipes and short sticks, and even knives, attacked the police in a most determined manner.' Two officers were stabbed in the back with an oyster knife and another in the chin. By the time it was over, hundreds of people had been arrested or hospitalized. 'A police beyond the control of the ratepayers are used to extinguish the rights of the ratepayers,' *The Northern Echo* complained, 'and the people who have made no effort to govern themselves are governed despotically by Sir Chas. Warren.'[7]

Reeling from these public humiliations, the Yard soon found itself up against a killer unlike any encountered before.

The particulars are well known. In the late summer and autumn of 1888, five women – all prostitutes primarily in the East End district of Whitechapel – met horrifying ends within a one-mile radius. It began in the pre-dawn hours of Friday, 31 August, when at 3:45 a.m., two men on their way to work discovered the butchered body of forty-five-year-old Mary Ann Nichols in Buck's Row (now Durward Street). The deep cut to her throat had nearly severed her head. A 'long-bladed knife, moderately sharp, and used with great violence' had partially opened her abdomen. A week later, early in the morning of Saturday, 8 September, the mutilated body of forty-seven-year-old Annie Chapman was found in the yard behind a lodging house at 29, Hanbury Street. The killer cut her throat, opened her stomach and positioned 'a flap of the wall of belly' and 'the whole of the small intestines' above her right shoulder. He placed more viscera above the left shoulder before absconding with the womb, part of the vagina, and most of the bladder.[8]

'On Saturday morning,' reported *The Morning Post*, 'the neighbourhood of Whitechapel was horrified to a degree bordering on panic by the discovery of another barbarous murder.' Suspicions initially swirled around 'a noiseless midnight terror' known as 'Leather Apron,' so-called for a garment he wore and who was known to be violent towards the area's working women. Police identified the mystery figure as a tailor named John Pizer and arrested him but couldn't build a case.[9]

On 27 September, a letter from someone claiming to be the killer arrived at London's Central News agency. Postmarked two days prior and penned in red ink, it had a jaunty tone. 'Grand work the last job was,' it said. 'I gave the lady no time to squeal. How can they catch me now, I love my work and want to start again . . . My knife's so nice and sharp I want to get to work right away if I get a chance, good luck.' It was signed, 'Jack the Ripper.' Although police questioned the letter's authenticity, it bestowed upon the killer a name that would long outlast his atrocities.

Three days after the letter arrived, in the early-morning darkness of Sunday, 30 September, the Ripper struck twice. He slashed the throat of forty-three-year-old Elizabeth Stride in Dutfield's Yard, Berner Street, but did not mutilate her body. Less than an hour later and a short distance to the west in Mitre Square, he killed and butchered Catherine Eddowes, slashing her throat, cutting her face down to the bone and disembowelling her. He took with him her left kidney and part of her womb. In the wake of the double atrocity, the public's panic intensified. 'The anxiety is intense . . .,' reported *The London Daily News*. 'Everywhere [the] gas lights were most powerful papers were unfolded in the drizzle and fog, and little groups of eager listeners gathered round to learn what new horror had come so close on the heels of the old.'[10]

And what of Jack?

The criminal, who it is quite conceivable, and indeed extremely probable, is abroad in the streets, is no doubt watching the seething agitation, listening to the speculations and discussions of the awe-stricken people, gloating over the horrible details of his work, and chuckling at the discomfiture of a whole army of police, the clues they are supposed to be following up, the suggestions made to them, and the arrests from time to time.[11]

Two days after the double slaying, *The Times* published a letter from a reader named Percy Lindley. 'As a breeder of bloodhounds, and knowing their power,' Lindley wrote, 'I have little doubt that, had a hound been put upon the scent of the murderer while fresh, it might have done what the police failed to do.' Intrigued by the idea – and desperate for any sort of break in the case – Warren reached out to Edwin Brough, a reputable bloodhound breeder in Scarborough, and asked if he could bring a couple of hounds to London 'for the purpose of testing their capabilities in the way of following the scent of a man.'[12]

Brough came to London on 4 October with his two finest hounds, Burgho and Barnaby, 'magnificent animals', in the words of the London papers. On a frigid morning in Regent's Park, the ground 'thickly coated with hoar frost', the dogs successfully tracked the scent of a stranger with a fifteen-minute head start. A night-time trial at Hyde Park, with the dogs hunting on their leashes, also proved successful. Warren attended several trials one morning, even 'acting as the hunted man' on two occasions. The dogs worked slowly in the cold weather, 'but they demonstrated the possibility of tracking complete strangers on whose trail they had been laid.' Warren, observed one reporter, 'seemed pleased with the result of the trials, though he did not express any definite opinion on the subject to those present.'[13]

This is believed to be the first trial of sniffer dogs in modern police work. Plans were put in place 'for the immediate convey-ance of the animals to the spot in the event of another murder occurring', but Warren would not commit to purchasing the hounds for Scotland Yard. Frustrated, Brough left London and took Burgho and Barnaby with him. The news, soon to humiliating effect, did not filter its way to the CID.[14]

Turmoil in the upper ranks of the Criminal Investigation Department hindered its work on the case. James Monro, who succeeded Howard Vincent in 1884 as head of the department and the Yard's first assistant commissioner, retired in the early days of the Ripper case. Monro, a lawyer and civil servant who previously served as Inspector General of Police in Bombay, wanted the CID to have more autonomy and believed Warren 'ruled with a too iron hand to suit his men'. His replacement was Dr Robert Anderson, formerly an intelligence officer serving the Home Office in matters relating to Fenian violence. No sooner did Anderson assume his role at the head of the CID than he left on a two-month vacation to treat exhaustion. His timing proved unfortunate. The day Anderson departed for Switzerland, the Ripper killed Stride and Eddowes. The Home Secretary sent Anderson a desperate message, asking him to return. 'Of course,' Anderson wrote, 'I complied.'[15] Even then, he took a less than urgent view of the Whitechapel slaughter:

> On my return I found the Jack-the-Ripper scare in full swing. When the stolid English go in for a scare they take leave of all moderation and common sense. If nonsense were solid, the nonsense that was talked and written about those murders would sink a Dreadnought. The subject is an unsavoury one, and I must write about it with reserve. But it is enough to say that the wretched victims belonged to a very small class of degraded women who frequent the East End streets after midnight, in hope of inveigling belated drunkards, or men as degraded as themselves.[16]

On 16 October, George Lusk, Chairman of the Whitechapel Vigilance Committee – established in response to the Ripper killings – received a letter, the return address being 'From Hell.' It was delivered in a small cardboard box and included half a human kidney preserved in wine. 'Sor,' the letter read, 'I send you half the Kidne I took from one woman and prasarved it for you tother piece I fried and ate it was very nise. I may send you the bloody knif that took it out if you only wate a while longer. Signed Catch me when you can Mishter Lusk.' The curator of the London Hospital confirmed the piece of meat enclosed in the letter was indeed a human kidney – and not one 'charged with a fluid, as it would have been in the case of a body handed over for purposes of dissection to a hospital.'[17]

On 9 November, twenty-four-year-old Mary Jane Kelly was found carved up beyond recognition in her squalid room on the ground floor of 13, Miller's Court. Unlike the previous four victims, she had been killed indoors, providing the killer more time and privacy to do his awful work. Stretched out on the bed, her body presented 'a most horrifying spectacle . . . exceeding in ghastliness anything which the imagination can picture.' Her nose, cheeks, eyebrows and ears had been partially removed. The killer had skinned her thighs, opened her stomach and pulled the organs out of her abdominal cavity. Her breasts had been cut off.[18]

The medical report by the Yard's consulting surgeon, Dr Thomas Bond, is a catalogue of horrors. 'The viscera were found in various parts,' Bond wrote. 'The uterus and kidneys with one breast under the head, the other breast by the right foot, the liver between the feet, the intestines by the right side of the spleen by the left side of the body.' Other lodgers in the building last heard Mary Jane at 1 a.m. singing 'Sweet Violets.'[19]

Word of the killing drew a large crowd to Dorset Street. In its coverage, *The Daily Telegraph* reported the following:

> Amongst the populace there was very widespread disappoint-
> ment that bloodhounds had not been at once employed in an
> effort to track the criminal. The belief had prevailed through-

out the district that the dogs were ready to be let loose at the first notice of a murder having been committed, and the public had come to possess greater confidence in their wonderful canine instincts and sagacity than in all Sir Charles Warren's machinery of detection.[20]

When Detective Inspector Frederick Abberline and other investigators arrived at 13, Miller's Court on the morning of 9 November, he was 'told that the bloodhounds had been sent for ... and it would be better not to break down the door until the dogs arrived.' The men hung about aimlessly for two hours, unaware the hounds were no longer in London, before learning 'the order for the dogs had been countermanded.'[21]

The press lampooned the dog idea with merciless glee. 'Sir Charles Warren's bloodhounds were out for practice this morning and were lost,' *The Evening Standard* falsely reported. 'Telegrams have been dispatched to all the Metropolitan Police stations, stating that if seen anywhere, information is to be immediately sent to Scotland-yard.' The plan to use hounds, unique for its time, had ultimately gone to the dogs.[22]

Taunted by the killer, the press and an outraged public, Scotland Yard was at a loss.

Jack the Ripper, according to former FBI special agent and criminal profiling mastermind John Douglas, is 'generally considered the first modern serial killer' – but the term 'serial killer' did not exist in 1888 and did not enter the lexicon until the 1970s. The idea of such an individual, one who carries on slaughtering until they're captured or killed, was itself an alien concept.[23] Although serial killing most likely predates the Ripper, his crimes established the modern-day template for sex, murder and sensational news coverage.

'What makes it so easy for him,' remarked one inspector, 'is that the women led him, of their own free will, to the spot where they know interruption is least likely. It is not as if he had to wait for his chance; they make the chance for him. And then they are so miserable and so hopeless, so utterly lost to all that makes a person want to live, that for the sake of four-pence, enough to get drunk on, they will go in any man's company, and run the risk that it is not him.

'I tell many of them to go home, but they say they have no home, and when I try to frighten them and speak of the danger they run they'll laugh and say, "Oh, I know what you mean, I ain't afraid of him. It's the Ripper or the bridge with me. What's the odds?" And it's true. That's the worst of it.'[24]

The inability to capture the Ripper haunted those working the case. 'If I get into bed I think maybe he is at it now, and I grow restless,' admitted one detective three years after the killings. 'I finally get up and tramp the courts and the alleys till morning.'[25]

A considerable challenge facing the Yard was its lack of insight into the kind of individual committing the murders. The recently appointed head of the CID, Dr Robert Anderson, summarized the challenges in a letter to Dr Bond.

> In dealing with the Whitechapel murders the difficulties of conducting the enquiry are largely increased by reason of our having no reliable opinion for our guidance as to the amount of surgical skill and anatomical knowledge probably possessed by the murder or murderers . . . I brought up this matter with Sir C. Warren some time since and he has now authorized me to ask if you will be good enough to take up the medical evidence given at the several inquests and favour him with your opinion on the matter.[26]

Bond reviewed the autopsy records of the Ripper's first four victims. During this period of study, he also performed the post-mortem examination on Mary Jane Kelly. He replied to Anderson on 10 November with what's considered to be the first attempt at a criminal profile and 'medical analysis linking murders together on medical evidence.'[27]

Bond harboured no doubt the same person killed all five women. In the case of the first four, the Ripper cut their throats in a left to right slash. Mary Jane was so mutilated it was impossible to discern what wound she suffered first. Bond did not believe the killer possessed any medical knowledge. 'In each case the mutilation was inflicted by a person who had no scientific or anatomical knowledge,' he wrote. 'In my opinion he does not even possess the technical knowledge of a butcher or horse slaughterer or any person accustomed to cut up dead animals.'

Although Mary Jane had what could have been defence wounds on her hands, Bond theorized the killer – in all cases – moved with a sudden ferocity that took the women by surprise. 'In the Dorset Street case,' Bond wrote, 'the corner of the sheet to the right of the woman's head was much cut and saturated with blood, indicating that the face may have been covered with the sheet at the time of the attack.' The butchering of the victim 'showed clearly that in all the murders, the object was mutilation.' The weapon in each slaying 'must have been a strong knife at least six inches long, very sharp, pointed at the top and about an inch in width. It may have been a clasp knife, a butcher's knife, or a surgeon's knife. I think it was no doubt a straight knife.' It seemed clear, from the brazen nature of killing out in the open to the extent of the mutilations, 'the murderer must have been a man of physical strength and of great coolness and daring.'

Sitting in his lamp-lit study, the files and their horrific details spread out before him, Bond delved into the Ripper's psychology:

> He must in my opinion be a man subject to periodical attacks of Homicidal and erotic mania. The character of the mutilations indicate that the man may be in a condition sexually, that may be called satyriasis. It is of course possible that the Homicidal impulse may have developed from a revengeful or brooding condition of the mind, or that Religious Mania may have been the original disease, but I do not think either hypothesis is likely.

His ability to approach women, and the fact Mary Jane brought him back to her place, suggested he was normal in appearance, 'quite likely to be an inoffensive looking man probably middle-aged' and neatly attired. 'I think,' Bond wrote, 'he must be in the habit of wearing a cloak or overcoat or he could hardly have escaped notice in the streets if the blood on his hands or clothes were visible.' Bond concluded his assessment:

> He would probably be solitary and eccentric in his habits, also he is most likely to be a man without a regular occupation, but with some small income or pension. He is possibly living among respectable persons who have some knowledge of his character and habits and who may have grounds for suspicion that he is not quite right in his mind at times. Such persons would probably be unwilling to communicate suspicions to the Police for fear of trouble or notoriety, whereas if there were a prospect of reward it might overcome their scruples.[28]

Bond's analysis makes for a fascinating read, but one can only speculate as to its accuracy. Most likely the first document to derive a perpetrator's psychological traits and personality from a crime scene, the profile ultimately proved to be of little use as the police floundered their way through the investigation, arresting suspects, letting them go and making no progress. The blame, perhaps unfairly, fell on Commissioner Warren with resentment still lingering over the Bloody Sunday fiasco. 'Sir Charles Warren,' *Lloyd's Weekly Newspaper* proclaimed, 'seems to consider that his duty is to look after the morals of the people, to stamp out popular demonstrations, and generally to drill the population into good behaviour. But this does not lend to the prevention or detection of crime.'[29]

Warren responded to the criticism with an article in *Murray's Magazine* titled 'The Police of the Metropolis'. He highlighted Scotland Yard's efforts to capture the East End killer and then, unwisely, lashed out at the public and press for not doing more to help. He voiced his support for vigilante justice and, more egregiously, complained about his lack of direct control over the CID. The Home Secretary did not take kindly to the public airing of grievances and reprimanded Warren, who bristled at such treatment. Warren, ever the military man, preferred giving orders – not taking them. His patience exhausted, he resigned on 9 November 1888, the same day Mary Jane's body was discovered. Former Assistant Commissioner James Monro took Warren's place at the top.[30]

The Ripper case was part of a larger series of eleven unsolved killings, known as the Whitechapel Murders, which began with the slaying of Emma Smith in April 1888 and ended in February 1891 with the murder of Frances Coles. Most, if not all, the victims worked as prostitutes. Smith, sexually brutalized with a blunt instrument, survived her injuries just long enough to tell police she'd been assaulted by a gang – but all the killings have, at one time or another, been attributed to Jack.

One victim, her torso discovered beneath a railway arch on Pinchin Street in the pre-dawn hours of 10 September 1889, has never been identified. Police dismissed it as a Ripper killing. 'What becomes most apparent,' notes Chief Inspector Donald Swanson in his case report, 'is the absence of the attack upon the genitals as in the series of Whitechapel murders beginning at Bucks Row and ending in Miller's court. Certainly if it be a murder there was time enough for the murderer to mutilate as in the series mentioned. It appears rather to go side by side with the Rainham, Whitehall and Chelsea murders.'[31]

Collectively known as 'The Thames Torso Murders', the Rainham, Whitehall and Chelsea crimes were another series of killings that – like the Whitechapel slayings – puzzled Scotland Yard. They began in 1887 when, over the course of May and June, the severed parts of a woman's body, each individually wrapped in a parcel and tied with canvas, were found floating in the Thames near

Rainham. The recovered remains included the lower half of the torso, part of a thigh, both legs, but no head or upper-half of the body. The Yard never identified the victim but believed 'the dissection was performed by a man well versed in medical science.'[32]

At the time of 'The Rainham Mystery', work was underway on Scotland Yard's new headquarters on Victoria Embankment just down river from the Houses of Parliament. On Tuesday, 2 October 1888, a builder stumbled across the dismembered remains of a woman in one of the new building's basement rooms. 'The corpse,' reported The Daily Telegraph, 'was a mere trunk, both head and limbs having been severed in an apparently brutal and unskilful manner.' Someone had snuck onto the construction site sometime between Friday night and Monday night and dumped the body 'in a dark recess about 100 yards from the roadway'.[33]

News of the latest find – at the future headquarters of Scotland Yard, no less – caused considerable excitement, and large numbers of the curious gathered at the site. Only the building's basement and part of the ground floor had so far been built, the basement being 'a vast labyrinth of brick passages, archways and vaulted chambers.'[34]

A seven-foot-high hoarding fence surrounded the location, making access difficult. It would have been easier for someone to dump the body from the Embankment into the Thames than access the site. And yet, somehow, the killer had managed to do just that. 'When there,' it was noted, 'instead of throwing the body into the large open well dug to supply water, or secreting it beneath the countless heaps of soil and rubbish laying about, he conveyed it, almost fifty yards, through a network of partly underground passages to a remote corner of the building.'[35]

Even the workmen who toiled daily on the site told detectives they'd be hard-pressed 'to have readily found their way through the intricate vaults to the spot where the mutilated trunk was concealed.' The discovery, coming as it did in the midst of Jack the Ripper's spree and two days after the double-murder of Elizabeth

Stride and Catherine Eddowes, drove home the startling realization that two killers now prowled the city. Reported *The London Daily News* with dramatic flair:

> Last evening all down the chief thoroughfares the pavement seemed busier than ever. There was drizzling rain and fog in the air, and slush and mud underfoot, and the East-End of London has rarely looked more wretched. But high over all the din and hubbub of the traffic, the news vendors were shrieking out news of another 'Horrible murder' reported to have been discovered on the Embankment, and all through the dark streets for a long distance . . . the murky night was being made hideous by the same dismal banshee wail of further murder and mutilation . . . Never perhaps in the history of London has public feeling been so deeply stirred by stories of murder and maiming as during the past few days, and the universal fear is that the fiendish work is not yet done.[36]

The body, wrapped in 'two-thirds of a woman's dress made of black broche silk with a flounce about three inches wide at the bottom', was in an advanced state of decomposition. The workman who found it initially thought it to be 'a rotten ham wrapped in a petticoat'. The inspector in charge of the investigation, a man named Marshall, wondered if the killer had hauled the body to the Embankment to toss it in the Thames but changed course owing to 'the vigilance observed in all parts of the river.' Marshall examined all points of entrance and exit at the site. There was no policeman or watchman on duty at night. Workers told the detective a man carrying such a bundle would not have gone unnoticed during the daytime hours.[37]

'He could not have got over the gates, unbolted the gate, admitted the parcel, and then, after depositing the parcel in the dark recess, have escaped out of the door, for the doors have never been found unbolted. It is possible,' Marshall theorized, 'that the bundle was conveyed by the carts which enter at the side of the building and deliver materials.' Indeed, the location where the body was found – 'the most secret spot on the site' – most likely meant 'the person who placed the remains there must have been well acquainted with the place.'[38]

When Dr Thomas Bond arrived at the scene to examine the trunk, he turned to Marshall and said, 'I have an arm that will fit that.' Just three weeks prior, an arm and shoulder had washed ashore near the Grosvenor Road railway bridge in Pimlico. A medical examination determined it to be the right arm of a woman. It had been in the river at least two or three days and cleanly severed with a sharp blade. The examining surgeon told police the arm had been removed after death, 'for if it had been cut off in life the muscles would have been more contracted.'[39]

Presently, the trunk was conveyed by cart to Westminster Mortuary in Millbank Street. There, Bond – along with Marshall and Dr Charles Hibberd of Westminster Hospital – awaited the arrival of the severed arm from the mortuary in Pimlico. Upon the arm's delivery, the medical men placed the trunk on one of the dissecting tables and removed the limb from its canvas packaging. Although cut off with no medical skill, the arm had been severed with grim precision just above the shoulder with the armpit still attached. It fitted the trunk perfectly, 'the jagged edges of the flesh corresponding in every part.' The nails at the end of the 'plump fingers' had not been well maintained, suggesting the arm to be that of someone from the lower classes – but the dress used to wrap the trunk would have 'belonged to a person of good position in life.'[40]

The trunk was that of an 'exceedingly well-nourished' and 'very fine' woman. The lower extremities had been removed an inch and a half below the navel, taking part of the lower intestine with it. The other major internal organs were all intact with the lungs, heart and liver 'presenting a perfectly normal appearance.' Bond believed the dismemberment had occurred at least six weeks previously. The doctors conducted their examination alongside the miserable detritus of their trade. 'Added to the condition of

'

the remains,' *The Times* reported, 'there were in the mortuary the bodies of the woman who was murdered by her husband in Westminster on Saturday, of a man who had committed suicide by hanging, and of a woman who was killed on Sunday by a boiler explosion.'[41]

When finished, the doctors placed the trunk in 'spirits of wine' to preserve it in the event more butchered anatomy washed ashore. The post-mortem provided Marshall little to work with. He and several detectives and constables returned to the construction site the following day to further examine the basement vault.[42]

Scaffolding, topped by a two-ton steam derrick, towered sixty-five feet above the site. The derrick chugged noisily, hoisting a piece of heavy machinery, while Marshall and his men conducted their investigation. As the machinery neared the top of the scaffolding, the derrick's backstay cable snapped, sending the derrick and the machinery plummeting to earth. 'We all heard the crashing of timber and saw the mass falling,' said one witness. 'It crashed through the concrete flooring into the vaults below.'[43]

The derrick's boiler exploded in a steaming cloud of scalding water. Broken scaffolding and shattered stonework fell into the basement vaults, sending up massive plumes of dust. 'It was known to those on the works that the police-officers were underneath where the mass fell, and great consternation prevailed, as it was fully expected that there would be many fatalities,' the witness said. By some miracle, Marshall and his men heard the panicked screams of the workers above as the seven tons of machinery hurtled towards them and escaped with mere seconds to spare. One constable only became aware of the danger when the roof caved in above him. He leapt clear of the wreckage, which fell 'within two feet of him'. The construction workers and police officers all escaped serious injury – a fact, *The Times* said, 'regarded as providential.'[44]

Providence could not help Marshall with the case. In the days that followed, he checked missing persons reports and pursued countless leads, all of which led nowhere. The press dubbed the case 'The Whitehall Mystery'. On 17 October, detectives returned to the construction site with a terrier 'provided by a gentleman whose faith in its scenting powers induced him to offer its services to the police'. They took the dog to the vault, where it began nosing a pile of 'loose and broken bricks'. The detectives cleared away the rubble and started digging by lamplight. Six inches down they found a decomposed leg severed at the knee with remnants of a woollen stocking adhered to the rotting flesh. It was Dr Bond's opinion the leg went with the trunk. It would seem the Whitehall terrier proved a greater success than the Whitechapel bloodhounds, but the case soon went cold.[45]

Eight months passed before the 'Thames Torso Murderer' struck again. On 4 June 1889, some boys bathing in the river near Albert Bridge at Battersea Park noticed something floating nearby. It was a woman's upper leg, severed at the hip joint and ending at the knee. The day had more sickening discoveries in store.

'Officers of the Criminal Investigation Department had scarcely had time to commence their investigations,' reported *The Evening Standard*, 'when news reached Scotland Yard that other human remains had been found at . . . a spot below London Bridge about five miles from the scene of the first discovery'. The remains 'consisted of the lower part of a female body, including the abdomen and the uterus'. The victim had died no more than twenty-four hours ago, as 'blood was still flowing from the ragged edges where the knife or hatchet had been used'. Dr Bond matched the limb found at Battersea Park to the remains found at London Bridge. He determined the woman to be about thirty years old and nearly nine months pregnant. 'There is reason to believe,' Bond said, 'that the child to which she gave birth has also been thrown into the river.'[46]

Two days later, a labourer stumbled across a parcel in Battersea Park containing the upper part of a woman's trunk with two ribs missing and the organs removed from the chest cavity. Over the next several days, more pieces of the woman washed ashore along the Thames, including the liver, neck and shoulders, the severed arms and legs, and the buttocks and pelvis. Scraped flesh on the ring finger of her left hand showed signs of a band having been forcibly removed. 'The system of cutting up the body showed skill and design,' Bond noted. 'Not the anatomical skill of a surgeon, but the technical skill of a butcher or horse knacker or any other person accustomed to deal with dead animals. There was a great similarity of design in the cutting up in this case with that of the Rainham mystery and the more recent case in Whitehall.'[47]

Although her head never turned up, detectives identified the victim as Elizabeth Jackson, 'a homeless unfortunate well known in some of the common lodging-houses in the Chelsea district'. She was last seen alive on the evening of 31 May. A sister, concerned she hadn't heard from Elizabeth for some time, came forward to report her missing. She said Elizabeth had 'a peculiar scar on one of her wrists'. Bond, examining the decomposed flesh in Battersea Mortuary, 'arrived at the conclusion that a scar similar to that described by the sister had certainly existed.'[48]

Elizabeth frequented Battersea Park. Police dredged the river, searched the park's ornamental waters and shrubbery, and made inquiries across multiple counties – all to no avail. At an inquest on 25 July, a coroner's jury returned a finding of murder by person or persons unknown and expressed the opinion 'that the greatest credit was due to the police for the vigilance and activity they had shown in the case.'[49]

The female trunk found two months later beneath the Pinchin Street railway arch in Whitechapel was the last of the known Thames Torso Murders. Scotland Yard never identified the victim or the killer. Had the murders not occurred at the height of the Jack the Ripper slayings, they might have achieved greater infamy. As it is, they are a curious – and more gruesome – footnote to Jack's bloody deeds.

*

The Yard's inability to catch the Ripper, in particular, battered a reputation still bruised from Bloody Sunday. The press accused the Yard of withholding information that might have brought the killer to light and abandoning its 'duty of serious crime prevention in favour of harassing the unemployed . . . and spying on Irish Nationalist politicians.'[50]

The Yard cannot be entirely blamed for its hesitation in sharing details with the press. The papers revelled in the gruesome sensationalism of it all, preferring gory details to cold facts and casting Jack as a spectre for all midnights. 'Even now,' remembered one detective some years after the killings, 'I can recall the foggy evenings, and hear again the raucous cries of the newspaper boys: "Another horrible murder, murder, mutilation, Whitechapel." Such was the burden of their ghastly song.'[51]

Because the papers and public viewed Sir Charles Warren as a villain prior to the murders, the Yard was fated to be seen as incompetent no matter what it did. 'People are terrified and loud in their complaints of the police, who have done absolutely nothing,' reported the London correspondent for *The New York Times*. 'They confess themselves without a clue, and they devote their entire energies to preventing the press from getting at the facts.'[52]

To say the police had done 'absolutely nothing' was grossly unfair. Through no fault of its own, the Yard lacked the investigative skill to apprehend a killer who explored previously unchartered depths of depravity. It showed imagination with its bloodhound trials and foray into criminal profiling, and did what it could with its available expertise and knowledge. But its efforts paled against crimes of such a monstrous nature.

And so, tainted by its most infamous failure, the Yard staggered into a new decade and soon found itself up against another repeat killer – but one who preferred poison to the blade.

12

Dr Death

New headquarters. Old business.

Scotland Yard moved into its new headquarters on the Victoria Embankment in 1890. The granite used in its construction was, 'appropriately', mined by inmates from Dartmoor Prison. One Member of Parliament, noting the red-and-white brick pile of gothic design, described it as 'a very constabulary kind of castle'. Within the building's castle-like walls, the CID occupied more than forty of its 140 offices, all 'linked by a warren of corridors' measuring three-quarters of a mile in length. Commissioner James Monro held sway in the top of a turret overlooking the Thames and christened the building New Scotland Yard, a name that would attach itself to all future headquarters of the Metropolitan Police.[1]

Perhaps indicative of a decade that would see the first motor cars on the streets of London and the emergence of fingerprints as a means of identification, the Yard's new home was notable for its use of electricity.[2] Reported *The Times*:

> The first public building in which electric lighting has been adopted in its entirety is New Scotland-yard, which is situate between Whitehall and the Thames Embankment and consti-tutes the central offices of the Metropolitan Police. The original intention was to obtain the electric current from one of the public supply companies. Careful consideration, however, showed that it would be possible for the authorities to generate

their own supply at a cost per unit considerably lower than the 7½ d. per unit demanded by the supply companies. It was therefore decided to put down a special generating plant on a site, which, owing to neighbouring ancient lights, was not available for other purposes.[3]

A special wing was built onto New Scotland Yard, 'projecting from the side nearest Whitehall'. The floor was set ten feet below street level and allowed for a low glass roof that wouldn't 'interfere with ancient lights'. Four steam turbines, spinning at up to 5,000 revolutions per minute, each supplied juice to '500 16-candle power lamps, so that two of the large sets are sufficient to run as many of the lamps as are ever in use at one time'. The set-up, the paper noted with approval, made 'the police entirely independent of strikes or other troubles that might affect the electrical supply obtained from an outside source'.[4]

And so, fully ensconced in its new headquarters with its new-fangled lighting, New Scotland Yard got down to old business.

On the night of 13 October 1891, a nineteen-year-old prostitute named Ellen Donworth collapsed in excruciating pain near the Wellington Pub in Lambeth's Waterloo Road. A costermonger named James Style ran to Ellen's aid. 'Someone has given me a drink,' she said, her voice choked and features contorted. 'Take me home.' Style helped Ellen back to her boarding room in Duke Street, by which time her body heaved with convulsions. Her tortured thrashing became so violent, her landlord and another neighbour had to hold her down by the arms and legs. 'A tall gentleman with cross eyes, a silk hat and bushy whiskers gave me a drink twice out of a bottle with white stuff in it,' she gasped. A doctor arrived to find Ellen beyond help. She died on the way to St Thomas' Hospital. A post-mortem revealed strychnine poisoning to be the cause of death.[5]

The case took an odd turn six days later when G. P. Wyatt, the coroner conducting the inquest, received a letter:

I am writing to say that if you and your satellites fail to bring the murderer of Ellen Donworth . . . to justice, I am willing to give you such assistance as will bring the murderer to justice, providing your government is willing to pay me £300,000. No pay if not successful.

It was signed 'G O'Brian, Detective.'

MP William Smith, whose family owned the W H Smith news-agent and book retail chain, also received a letter. It claimed Ellen had died possessing correspondence incriminating him. The letter writer – one 'H. Bayne, Barrister' – offered to extricate Smith from this predicament for a considerable fee. When Smith failed to take the bait, another letter was sent to authorities naming Smith as Ellen's killer, but the identity of the real culprit and the fiendish scribe remained a mystery.[6]

Inspector George Harvey of L (Lambeth) Division found himself charged with the investigation. Although he had more than two decades' experience on the force, he'd only been an inspector for two years. He boasted an impressive track record of taking down 'burglars, coiners, an abortionist, a child stealer and an attempted murderer', but a poisoning case was something else entirely. And so the cross-eyed gentleman with bushy whiskers remained elusive prey.[7]

Early in the evening of Tuesday, 20 October, twenty-seven-year-old Matilda Clover returned to her boarding house at 27, Lambeth Road in the company of a gentleman. Live-in maid Lucy Rose let them in. 'At the time, there was a lamp burning in the passage, but it did not give out very good light,' Lucy said. 'Matilda and the man who was with her passed up the stairs. He was very tall and broad, about forty years of age. He was wearing a tall silk hat and no glasses.' Matilda, the mother of a two-year-old son, often brought men back to her room to make ends meet. The man remained upstairs for about an hour. Lucy retired to her room at ten o'clock only to be woken at three in the morning to 'Miss Clover screaming as if she were in pain'.[8]

Lucy alerted landlady Emma Phillips and ran to Matilda's room. Matilda lay across the foot of her bed with her head bent backwards between the bedstead and the wall. 'She was apparently in great agony,' Lucy said. Matilda managed to look up when Lucy entered the room. 'That wretch has given me some pills, which have made me ill,' she managed before another fit consumed her. Her 'eyes rolled about terribly' and her body 'was all of a twitch'.[9]

The fits continued. Moments of calm and clarity punctuated prolonged periods of excruciating pain. She managed to identify the man as 'Fred' and said he had given her four pills to take before bedtime to 'save her' from catching any disease. 'I think I am going to die,' she told Lucy. 'I should like to see my baby.'

Because no local surgeon was available, the best medical help Phillips could find was a doctor's assistant named Francis Coppin, who showed up at seven o'clock. Phillips told him Matilda 'had been in the habit of drinking,' so Coppin believed the affliction to be alcohol related.

'How much brandy did you drink last night?' Coppin asked.

'I don't know,' Matilda wheezed.

'Are you going to tell the doctor about the pills?' Lucy asked.

'No,' said Matilda.[10]

Coppin dismissed the talk of pills as a delusion brought on by the illness. 'I had no doubt that this woman was suffering from excessive drink,' he said later. He prescribed carbonate of soda to control the symptoms and left after ten minutes. When they gave Matilda the medicine, 'she turned black in the face.' She died around nine o'clock that morning and received a pauper's burial on 27 October at Tooting Cemetery. Because 'delirium tremens' caused by excessive drinking was ruled the cause of death, nothing linked it to Ellen Donworth's poisoning the week before.[11]

On Monday, 30 November, Dr William Henry Broadbent, a prominent physician living in Portman Square, was shocked to receive a letter accusing him of Matilda's murder. The missive, dated two days prior and signed 'M. Malone', read:

> Sir – Miss Clover who until a short time ago lived at 27, Lambeth Road, S.E., died at the above address on the 20th October (last month) through being poisoned by strychnine. After her death a search of her effects was made, and evidence was found which showed that you not only gave her the medicine which caused her death, but that you had been hired for the purpose of poisoning her. This evidence is in the hands of one of our detectives, who will give the evidence either to you or the police authorities for the sum of £2,500 sterling.[12]

The letter continued, saying if Broadbent didn't pay the money he would be ruined forever. The doctor was to post an advertisement to M. Malone in the *Daily Chronicle* acquiescing to the demand. Instead, Broadbent passed the letter along to Scotland Yard's CID, which – with Broadbent's blessing – placed an advertisement in the 3 December edition of the *Chronicle*. Detectives kept an eye on Broadbent's house for two days, but no one showed up and the matter went nowhere. Surprisingly, the Yard made no enquiries at 27, Lambeth Road about Matilda's death – nor did it notify Inspector Harvey, whose division included the Lambeth Road address. It was a glaring oversight, particularly as the letter attributed Matilda's death to strychnine poisoning.[13]

Death by poisoning terrified and fascinated nineteenth-century Britain. 'With the progress of chemical science the field of the poisoner is constantly extending,' noted one contemporary report. '. . . Death lurks in many unsuspected forms, and but for the parallel march of the science of detection, the poisoner would more often escape.' Indeed, Charles Dickens's weekly *Household Words* claimed without much proof that '249 people had been poisoned to death between 1839 and 1849 but that only 85 murderers had been convicted.'[14]

Perhaps had Sherlock Holmes and Dr Watson been around to investigate, the numbers would not have been so skewed. Watson concludes strychnine poisoning is the means of death in *The Sign of Four*, the victim having been found with a 'ghastly, inscrutable smile upon his face' and 'not only his features but all his limbs . . . twisted and turned in the most fantastic fashion.'[15]

Strychnine poisoning is a torturous way to die. It tastes bitter going down and within a minute to an hour after consumption, 'the person who has taken it is seized with a feeling of suffocation and great difficulty of breathing.' An 1878 medical treatise on the subject details an awful demise:

> The head and limbs are jerked; the whole frame shudders and trembles; tetanic convulsions then suddenly commence; the limbs are stretched out, the hands clenched, the head is bent backwards, and the body assumes a bow-like form, supported on the head and feet (opsithotonos); the soles of the feet are curved . . .

The victim's eyeballs appear 'prominent and staring' and 'a peculiar sardonic grin is noticed on the features'. In between the body-twisting spasms, 'the intellect is perfectly clear.' Such was the torment of eighteen-year-old Emma Shrivell and twenty-one-year-old Alice Marsh. Police were summoned to a brothel at 118, Stamford Street in the pre-dawn hours of 12 April 1892, six months after Matilda Clover's death, and found Emma and Alice in a terrible state. The two friends had come to London from Brighton three weeks prior, having pawned their possessions to pay the fare and telling loved ones they had found work in a biscuit factory. PC William Eversfield arrived at two-thirty in the morning and found Alice lying in the hallway in her nightdress and Emma, in her room, 'lying on a sofa on her face.'[16]

Both women 'seemed to go into convulsions from time to time.' Eversfield gave them mustard and water before carrying Emma outside to a waiting cab. As he did so, he encountered PC George Comley walking the beat. Eversfield called to him and said there was another stricken girl inside the house. Comley ran in and came out with Alice in his arms. She died on the way to St Thomas' Hospital. Emma, although in agony, survived the journey long enough to say she and Alice had spent the evening with a man named Fred, who gave them each 'three long, thin pills.' Fred left their company at about two o'clock that morning, after which the girls had some tinned fish for dinner and quickly became ill.[17]

It just so happened Comley had been walking past 118, Stamford Street at quarter to two and saw a man leave the building. He was about six feet tall and between forty and fifty, dressed in a dark overcoat and high silk hat. Light reflected off his spectacles as he passed beneath a streetlamp. He had a moustache but no beard. A woman waved him off from the doorway – a woman Comley now recognized as Emma.[18]

'Was that the man with the glasses I saw you let out about two o'clock?' Comley asked.

'Yes,' Emma said. She made it to the hospital but didn't survive the morning.[19]

Post-mortems revealed both women died of strychnine poisoning.

Dr Thomas Neill Cream was, according to one female acquaintance, a 'bald and very hairy man; he had a dark ginger moustache, wore gold-rimmed glasses, was well-dressed, cross-eyed, and spoke with an odd accent.' The forty-one-year-old Cream was Scottish by birth but had moved with his family to Canada as a teen. He earned his medical degree in 1876 from Montreal's McGill University and squandered it on a career of 'arson, abortion, blackmail, fraud, extortion, theft and attempted murder.'[20]

In 1876, he was forced to marry Flora Brooks after he attempted to abort her pregnancy. She died the following year of consumption while he was finishing his medical training in Edinburgh. Flora's doctor suspected she may have died from taking medicine Cream

McCord Stewart Museum

The nefarious Dr Cream in Montreal, 1874.

sent her from London, but a suspicion is all it remained. Cream returned to London, Ontario to start his residency. In May 1879, a young woman under his medical care died of chloroform poisoning. Although no charges were filed, he left Canada for Chicago and set up a practice at 434 West Madison Street. There, two more of his female patients died. He again escaped any consequences. In June 1881, the elderly husband of Cream's lover, Julia Stott, died of strychnine poisoning. There was enough evidence this time to charge and convict Cream of second-degree murder, resulting in a life sentence at the Illinois State Penitentiary at Joliet.[21]

In July 1891, his sentence was commuted for good behaviour and he returned to Canada. Using money his late father had left him, Cream decided to finance a trip to England and left Canada in September. It was at this time, based on his recent history, 'that there began to be a suspicion among his relations and intimates that Cream was insane.'[22]

He arrived in England on 1 October 1891. Ellen Donworth died twelve days later and Matilda Clover seven days after that. He got engaged to an unsuspecting woman in December and returned the following month to Canada, where he had 500 notices printed up. They warned guests at London's Metropole Hotel 'that the person who poisoned Ellen Donworth on the 13th last October is today in the employ of the Metropole Hotel and that your lives are in danger as long as you remain in this Hotel.' He signed the note 'W. H. Murray' but did nothing with it. He returned to London on 9 April, three days before Emma Shrivell and Alice Marsh died.[23]

He rented a room at 103, Lambeth Palace Road, an area rife with brothels, pubs and theatres of ill repute. It suited him just fine, as he enjoyed discussing women in the crudest terms with others. Residents in the boarding house noted Cream took a keen interest in the deaths of Shrivell and Marsh. He went so far as to accuse Walter Harper, a medical student staying at the same address, of the crime. At about this time, Harper's father received an anonymous letter threatening to expose Walter as the killer if

£1,500 was not paid immediately. The blackmail came to nothing, but Cream shared his suspicions about Harper with everyone.[24]

At the beginning of May, through sheer happenstance, a mutual friend introduced Cream to Detective Sergeant Patrick McIntyre of Scotland Yard's CID. Cream showed McIntyre a postmarked letter he said was originally received by Shrivell and Marsh, warning that Harper planned on poisoning them – just as he had done with Ellen Donworth, Matilda Clover and a woman named Louise Harvey. It was signed by a detective named W. H. Murray.[25]

Cream said he was leaving his lodgings one afternoon when he was approached by this Detective Murray and questioned about Harper and Harper's relationship with the poisoned women. It was Murray, Cream said, who gave him the letter. The story, in every respect, was ludicrous. Cream had overplayed his hand. Up until this point, Matilda's death was believed to be alcohol related – and the police had never heard of Louise Harvey or a detective W. H. Murray. The CID began keeping an eye on Cream, monitoring his address and shadowing him around town.[26]

Inspector George Harvey dispatched 'officers to all parts of London to make inquiries of prostitutes' and tracked Louise Harvey down. She told police she met a man matching Cream's description one night in late October at the Alhambra Theatre and spent the night with him. When they parted the next morning, 'he said I had a few spots on my forehead, and he said he would bring me some pills to take them away.' He gave her two pills – 'long and rather narrower at one end than the other' – later that evening as they strolled along the Embankment. 'He said I was to put them in my mouth then and there, one by one, and "not bite them, but swallow them", she said. He put the pills in her right hand, but something about his manner made Louisa uneasy. 'I pretended to take them,' she said, 'putting my hand to my mouth and pretending to swallow them.' She passed the pills to her left hand and dropped them behind her; a sleight of hand that saved her life. Satisfied she'd taken the medicine, Cream handed her five shillings for the music hall and bid her goodnight.[27]

Armed with these details, the Yard pushed forward with its inquiries and exhumed the body of Matilda Clover. McIntyre's superiors sent him to get a writing sample from Cream at his Lambeth Palace Road lodgings. 'I took a sheet of notepaper from his table, which he pointed out to me,' McIntyre said, 'and I read to him a few words from the *British Medical Journal*, which was just lying by. [Cream] wrote it at my dictation.' The doctor handed the paper to McIntyre, who made note of the watermark: 'Fairfield, superfine quality.'

'Doctor,' McIntyre said, 'you appear to be pretty well posted in these matters.'

'Yes. I have followed the matter closely in the *British Medical Journal*,' Cream replied. 'Being a medical man, I take an interest in matters of this kind.'

McIntyre's superior, Inspector John Tunbridge, paid Cream a visit at Lambeth Palace Road on 29 May and asked him what brought him to England. Cream said he had come to consult an oculist and that he was a doctor of medicine with a practice in America. As proof, he showed Tunbridge his doctor's bag filled with phials of medicine. Tunbridge noticed one bottle labelled '1/16th grain of strychnine.'

'What are these pills composed of?' he asked.

'1/16th grain of strychnine and the sugar coating only,' Cream said.

'This bottle contains quite a large quantity of strychnine,' Tunbridge said. 'It would be highly dangerous that they should fall into the hands of the public in any quantity.'[28]

Cream said he had no intention of dispensing it directly to the public and was in the business of supplying chemists and surgeons, though he could not provide the names of any customers. Tunbridge left the lodging house convinced of Cream's guilt. Back at his desk, he reviewed the statements provided by the victims before they died. They described a man matching Cream's height and being cross-eyed like Cream. And they said he was a doctor. 'We have Neill accusing Harper of being the murderer in no uncertain terms,' Tunbridge wrote in a case report. 'Now why would he do this? To me it appears to point to Neill being either mad or the murderer himself, as I do not think it can for one moment be entertained that Mr Harper is the murderer.'[29]

On 2 June, Tunbridge travelled by rail to the river town of Barnstaple in north Devon to interview the Harper family. He had, up until now, no idea they had received a letter threatening to expose Walter Harper as Matilda's killer. Not only did the writing match the sample McIntyre obtained from Cream, but the paper's watermark – 'Fairfield, superfine quality' – was identical. 'That Neill was the writer,' Tunbridge said, 'I have no doubt.' Tunbridge arrested Cream the following day at Lambeth Palace Road for extortion. 'You have the wrong man,' the doctor roared. 'Fire away!'[30]

On 13 July, the inquest into Matilda Clover's death concluded she had died from strychnine poisoning. Five days later, Tunbridge amended the charge against Cream to wilful murder.

'What,' said Cream, 'in the Clover case?'

'Yes,' Tunbridge replied.

'All right. Is anything going to be done in the other cases?'

'Not at present, I believe.'

'You will be sure and let me know if anything is to be done.'[31]

Cream went on trial at the Old Bailey on 17 October 1892 for Matilda's murder. Confident to the last, he never considered the jury might convict him. Even after being found guilty and sentenced to death, he refused to believe the punishment would be carried through. 'They will never hang me,' he said. He spent his remaining days in the condemned cell at Newgate Prison, never confessing to his crimes or the reasons behind them.[32]

A massive crowd assembled outside the prison on 15 November 1892 to await word of Cream's death. It was the largest assembly to gather for a hanging since Britain ended public executions in 1868 with the death of Michael Barrett. 'Probably no criminal was ever executed in London who had a less pitying mob awaiting his execution,' reported *The Quebec Morning Herald.*[33]

Arrogant to the end, Cream tried to have the last word. As he stood on the trapdoor, the noose around his neck and the execution hood pulled over his head, he addressed the hangman and gathered prison officials. 'I am Jack the . . .' he said, according to one apocryphal story (another claims he yelled, 'I am ejaculating!'), dropping to his death before he could finish the sentence.[34]

In one respect, Cream would achieve some lingering fame. The wax museum Madame Tussauds did big business in the macabre. Established in London in 1835 by French wax sculptor Marie Tussaud, who made a name for herself 'casting guillotined heads', the museum enthralled and repulsed visitors with its Chamber of Horrors – an exhibit featuring waxwork recreations of humanity's worst. In the immediate wake of the hanging, Madame Tussauds purchased Cream's clothes for £200 (approximately £30,400 or $38,700 today) and put his waxwork on display four days after his execution.[35]

Though he is sometimes mentioned as a Ripper suspect, Cream was in the Illinois State Penitentiary at the time of the Whitechapel murders. And his motives – as well as those of Jack the Ripper and the Thames Torso Killer – remain a mystery.

13

The Murder Squad

Fingerprints. Preserving the crime scene.

Far removed from the East End slums of Whitechapel, the squalid public houses of Lambeth and the murky flow of the Thames, in a distant corner of the British Empire, a murder took place. It would not generate international headlines or achieve the same level of infamy as Jack the Ripper or Dr Cream, but it would forever change the nature of police work.

While Robert Overton's 1840 letter informing Scotland Yard that 'every individual has a peculiar arrangement [on] the grain of the skin' sat forgotten and discarded in a filing cabinet, headway into fingerprinting was being made elsewhere. Since the late 1850s, William Herschel, the chief magistrate of the Hooghly District in Jungipoor, India, had been collecting 'fingermarks of native pensioners as receipt "signatures" to prevent fraudulent claims'. Herschel developed a fascination with these strange patterns and came to realize, through his own non-scientific study, that prints 'were unique and did not alter over the years'. A Scottish doctor and medical missionary named Henry Faulds advanced this notion three decades later, when he published a letter in the scientific journal *Nature*, stating 'bloody fingerprints or impressions on clay, glass, etc.' could prove useful 'in the scientific identification of criminals.' He spoke from experience, having used 'sooty fingerprints' at the scene of a hospital break-in in Japan to clear one suspect and identify another.[1]

Criminal identification at the time relied on the Bertillon system. Developed by French criminologist Alphonse Bertillon, it used skeletal measurements divided into 243 categories – the length of one's arm span, the width of the head, the length of an index finger, etc. – to identify an individual. French authorities adopted the system in the 1880s, and its acceptance gradually spread. Scotland Yard established its Anthropometry Department, 'which used five of Bertillon's proposed measurements of bones', in 1895. It was not, however, without its shortfalls. A criminal had to be captured first before his measurements could be taken, which resulted in other problems. One officer 'might apply more or less pressure on the callipers than another officer, thus producing two different sets of measurements that failed to match upon comparison.' An individual's base measurements might also be taken before they stopped growing, resulting in different measurements later in life.[2]

In 1892, Sir Francis Galton, cousin to Charles Darwin, published the first book on fingerprints (titled, not surprisingly, *Finger Prints*) and confirmed through scientific analysis that prints 'retained their unique details unchanged from birth to death.' He also realized print patterns could be classified into three specific categories: loops, whorls and arches. That same year, police in Buenos Aires, Argentina, matched a bloody thumbprint found at a crime scene with that of Francisca Rojas and arrested her for murdering her two children. Rojas confessed when shown the side-by-side comparisons and became the first person convicted based on fingerprint evidence. Argentina, consequently, 'became the first country to rely solely on fingerprints as a method of individualization.'[3]

In 1896, Inspector General of the Bengal Police, Edward Henry and two of his inspectors, Hemchandra Bose and Azizul Haque, devised a simple classification system that enabled prints to be 'easily filed, searched and traced through thousands upon thousands of others without prior scientific training.' The Henry

Classification System, as it came to be known, assigned 'numerical values to certain types of fingerprints.' This allowed prints to be organized into '1,024 primary groups, which in turn were sub-divided' by the physiological characteristics of the prints. Henry, believing fingerprints to be far superior to anthropometric meas-urements, requested the Indian government conduct its own review. Surveyor General of India, Charles Strahan and chemist, Alexander Pedler arrived in Bengal in early 1897 to do a compara-tive study.[4] They presented their findings in late March:

> We are of the opinion that the method of identification by means of fingerprints, as worked on the system of recording impressions and of classification used in Bengal, may be safely adopted as being superior to the anthropometric method – (1) in simplicity of working; (2) the cost of apparatus; (3) in the fact that all skilled work is transferred to a central or classifi-cation office; (4) in the rapidity with which the process can be worked; and (5) in the certainty of results.[5]

And so, in 1897, the governor-general approved fingerprinting as the sole means of criminal identification in British India. This led to the establishment of the world's first fingerprint bureau in Calcutta, which catalogued prints of all convicted criminals in the district. The timing proved prescient.[6]

On 15 August, Hridaynath Ghosh, manager of the Kathalguri Tea Estate, was found with this throat slit in the ransacked bed-room of his bungalow. The killer swiped several hundred rupees from a safe and rifled through Ghosh's dispatch box. Inspectors from the Bengal Police found 'a calendar in book form, printed in the Bengali character, with an outside cover of light-blue paper on which were noticed two faint brown smudges.' An examination under magnifying glass showed one smudge had been left by 'one of the digits of some person's right hand.' The police, using Henry's new classification system, matched the print to the right thumb of Kangali Charan, Ghosh's former servant, who had a previous conviction for theft.[7]

Charan went on trial in May 1898. He was found guilty of theft but acquitted on the murder charge. The court ruled that 'although the identity of the defendant is proved beyond all question' it did not equate to his being the killer. Said the judge:

> There is nothing suggestive beyond the blood-stained finger impressions of the defendant on the calendar to connect him with the murder. It is possible he was cognizant of the conspiracy against the manager, and knowing that the manager had been killed, to satisfy a grudge he entered the room immediately after the murder was committed and removed the keys from the manager's body and thus stained his fingers, not knowing that the impressions might be used against him at a trial.[8]

The court was uncomfortable convicting on the more serious charge based on a new method of identification. The case, nevertheless, is considered to be the first instance 'in which fingerprint evidence was used to secure a conviction.' Two years later, in 1900, the Home Office empanelled a five-man committee to weigh the benefits of fingerprints against the anthropometric system still used by British police. Dr John Garson, president of the Anthropometry Society, argued the case for Bertillon's method. Henry, on home leave from India, demonstrated the practicality and efficiency of fingerprinting using a catalogue of 7,000 prints he lugged from Bengal. Convinced, the committee issued a report recommending 'all criminal identification records be classified by the fingerprint system.' It was the first step in fingerprinting becoming 'adopted in most English-speaking countries.'[9]

Henry's work made an impression. In 1901, he was appointed Assistant Commissioner at Scotland Yard in charge of the CID and established the Yard's Fingerprint Bureau in July that year. 'It was,' remembered one senior officer, 'housed well towards the top of the building in a room which looked out over the Thames. I remember there was a round window which we used to call the "bull's-eye" window, because it reminded one of the bull's-eye on a target.' The bureau quickly proved its worth. Of 54 pickpockets arrested in 1902, fingerprints and the Henry Classification System proved that 29 of them – despite their assertions of being first-time offenders – had previous convictions.[10]

Sweat and oils secreted by the skin create latent fingerprints, impressions left by the friction ridges found on one's finger. The print becomes visible to the human eye when fingerprint powder is applied and adheres to 'the swirling patterns of grease and oil' deposited by touch. In September 1902, a British jury at the Old Bailey was schooled in the strange and visual language of 'arches and tented arches, ulnar and radial loops, and whorls'. The case at hand was that of forty-one-year-old labourer and small-time crook Henry Jackson, charged with stealing billiard balls from a home in south London. At 156, Denmark Hill, he planted his left thumb in a newly painted window sash. Detective Sergeant Charles Collins, future head of the Fingerprint Bureau, photographed the impression. With names of likely suspects provided by informants, he pulled a match from the ever-expanding catalogue of prints taken from known criminals at Scotland Yard.[11]

Police nabbed Jackson shortly thereafter in the act of burglarizing another home. He pleaded not guilty at trial but did not anticipate the 'remarkable evidence' against him. He was sentenced to seven years in prison and became the first person in Britain convicted on fingerprint evidence. As with anything new and different, it caused some controversy. In a letter to *The Times*, a reader identified only as 'A Disgusted Magistrate' wrote, 'Scotland Yard, once known as the world's finest police organization, will be the laughing stock of Europe if it insists on trying to trace criminals by odd ridges on their skins.'[12]

Others took a different tack. Observed the *Weekly Dispatch* in cringe-worthy fashion:

As an indication of the brotherhood of man that exists, it may be of interest to learn that the finger-prints of nations or classes of individuals present no peculiarities, nor can they be distinguished. There is no difference between the thumb-print of the Polish Jew and that of the American millionaire, neither is there any difference between the finger-print of the Heathen Chinese and a Bishop in the House of Lords.[13]

The following year, 1903, saw the forward-thinking Henry appointed Police Commissioner. He pushed hard to modernize the Yard and bring it into the new century. He established 'a small training school for detectives at New Scotland Yard' and had a telephone line installed at headquarters to enable easy contact with the divisions. Old-timers couldn't help but grumble. 'I don't know what we're coming to,' one detective moaned. 'If this sort of thing goes on, we'll have the public ringing us up direct.'[14]

In June 1904, the British government put the Crown Jewels on display at the World's Fair in St. Louis. Inspector John Ferrier, a protégé of Henry's, accompanied the jewels to America and demonstrated the Yard's fingerprinting methods for the nation's police chiefs, who gathered for a conference at the fair's Hall of Congresses. 'Many of the police chiefs who have been in St. Louis this week,' reported the *St. Louis Post-Dispatch* on 12 June, 'will carry home with them as souvenirs of the Fair prints of their fingertips taken by Detective John Kenneth Ferrier of Scotland Yard.'[15] The paper detailed for its readers the Yard's fingerprinting method:

> The finger tip system of making records is simple. A slab of metal covered with ordinary printer's ink 'does the business.' Mr Ferrier presses the tip of one of the subject's fingers on this surface. Then he presses the inked finger on a white surface. He repeats the operation several times, taking each finger and thumb separately. Then he makes an impression of the tips of the four fingers of each hand taken together.[16]

This caught the attention of the St. Louis Metropolitan Police, which – on 28 October 1904 – became the first American police department to adopt the use of fingerprints. Ferrier remained in the States for some time after the fair 'to teach fingerprinting, including how to use powder to develop latent prints'. His students, in turn, began 'to teach fingerprinting to law enforcement and military communities throughout the rest of America.' The same month the St. Louis Police adopted the new method, the federal prison at Leavenworth, Kansas, began printing its inmates. 'These fingerprint records,' notes a US Department of Justice history, 'became the beginning of the U.S. Government's fingerprint collection.'[17] Other American police departments soon followed suit.

At 8:30 a.m. on Monday, 27 March 1905, seventy-one-year-old Thomas Farrow was found beaten to death in his art-supply shop at 34, Deptford High Street. His wife, sixty-five-year-old Ann, severely battered about the head, lay bleeding in their small flat upstairs. She died at the hospital four days later having never regained consciousness. Scotland Yard detectives found at the scene two discarded masks made of women's stockings lying on the floor. An empty cashbox provided the motive and a subtle clue: a fingerprint on the inner tray. Detective Sergeant Collins obtained the prints of everyone who handled the cashbox at the scene – including those of the victims – but none of them matched.[18]

A search of the Yard's extensive print collection failed to produce a lead. 'We have now between 80,000 and 90,000 sets of fingerprints,' Collins would testify in court, 'which means between 800,000 and 900,000 impressions of digits.'[19]

Several witnesses told police they saw a pair of young men running down the High Street an hour or so before the bodies were discovered. Ellen Stanton was on her way to work when the pair dashed past her. 'I recognized one of the men as Alfred Stratton,' she said, explaining Stratton was the acquaintance of a man she was dating. 'On this morning, Alfred was dressed in a dark brown suit and dark cap. I don't know who the man was who was with him . . . he was dressed in a dark overcoat and a bowler. When I came home that night, I heard about the murder.'[20]

Alfred, twenty-two, and his twenty-year-old brother Albert did not have criminal records but were known as local troublemakers. Police arrested them on 2 April. The print lifted from the cashbox matched Albert's right thumb. Explained Collins:

> In comparing the impressions we proceed to classify them first by types and sub-types, and then by counting and tracing the ridges – that is, when we have complete prints of the whole finger. We then compare what are called the characteristics. In my experience, if . . . the number or tracing of the ridges differ, they cannot be the prints of the same finger. If those matters agree, we then compare the characteristics.[21]

Collins said he had never found two prints to have more than three points of similarities – until now. The print found in the cashbox and Albert Stratton's right thumbprint shared eleven characteristics. Collins detailed them for the jury using enlarged images of both prints when the case went to trial in May. 'From my experience,' he said, 'I should say that it is impossible that those can be prints of two different digits.' It was the first use of fingerprint evidence in a British murder trial.[22]

There was little doubt as to the brothers' pending fate. 'The day wore on, and the big clock over the prisoners' heads ticked towards ten at night before the drama spun itself out,' *The Woolwich Gazette* noted on the trial's last day. 'The heat of the place grew denser, and the light that came through the tall windows was supplemented by the dull gleam of gas. There prevailed always that stricken silence of the expectation of doom, in which the voice of counsel and the murmur of witnesses was like a tinkle in a well.'[23]

On 23 May, only seventeen days after being found guilty, the Stratton boys went to the gallows together. 'Has God forgiven you?'

Albert asked his brother seconds before the trapdoor fell. In death, the two men found lasting infamy – not so much for their crime, but for the role fingerprints played in their downfall.[24]

Commissioner Henry continued pushing the Yard into the new century. 'He, more than anyone else,' notes *The Official Scotland Yard Encyclopaedia*, 'set the Metropolitan Police service on the path away from the beloved Victorian institution of gentleman amateur "toffs" commanding humble, loyal and rather comic

National Portrait Gallery

A caricature of Metropolitan Police Commissioner
Edward Henry published in *Vanity Fair* in October 1905.

policemen, and into the age of modern up-to-date professional policing.' He 'squeezed' extra funding from the Home Office for more men and police housing, implemented a proper training programme for constables, worked to boost morale, and established a command structure that 'was to last fifty years.' In addition to the telephone and the streamlining of communications with and between the divisions, he introduced the typewriter to Scotland Yard and standardized the use of police call boxes for the public, which had never moved beyond the experimental phase under his predecessor.[25]

Some 700 detectives plied their trade on London's streets by 1907, while the rest of the country relied upon local constabularies that lacked both the resources and expertise to handle major crimes. 'The County Police, excluding a few large provincial cities, have no detective forces,' a Home Office memorandum stated that year. 'They deal well enough with the ordinary run of criminal cases, but when a case of special application arises, they almost invariably muddle it. Sometimes at a late stage, they ask for assistance from Scotland Yard, but by then the scent is cold and, moreover, the Scotland Yard detective gets very little help from the local men who regard his intrusion with great jealousy.'

The memorandum continued:

> In London we have many detectives of great experience who have, more or less, specialized in dealing with particular classes of cases. It would be of great advantage if the County Police could be induced to call in their services at an early stage, but we have no means of compelling them to do so.[26]

Cases of 'special application' referred to murder. Home Secretary Herbert Gladstone proposed Scotland Yard take command of all murder – and other violent crime – investigations in rural districts, bringing big city resources and experience to rural hamlets ill-equipped for such inquiries. Several detectives from the CID were placed under the command of the Home Office to be dispatched when needed. With no official title, this ad-hoc team of investigators earned the sobriquet the 'Murder Squad'.[27]

One member of the squad was Chief Inspector Walter Dew, who joined the Metropolitan Police in 1882 when he was nineteen. He spent his first five years as a uniformed constable patrolling Paddington before transferring to the squalor of the East End. In 1887, he was promoted to the CID as a detective constable and attached to the Commercial Street Police Station in Whitechapel. 'Even before the advent of Jack the Ripper a year later,' Dew recalled, '[Whitechapel] had a reputation for vice and villainy unequalled anywhere in the British Isles.'[28]

Only recently married, he worried about moving his young wife to a 'hot-bed of crime' – but a sense of elation counterweighted his foreboding. 'I had attained my first ambition as a police officer,' he wrote, 'being now a member of the famous Criminal Investigation Department – a detective officer.' And Whitechapel proved an ideal environment to learn his craft. 'Whitechapel, Spitalfields and Shoreditch were now my hunting ground, with hundreds of criminals of the worst type as my quarry,' Dew wrote. 'I knew Whitechapel pretty well by the time the first of the atrocious murders, afterwards attributed to Jack the Ripper, took place. And I remained there until his orgy of motiveless killing came to an end.'[29]

Dew spent eighteen months in the East End before transferring back to Paddington in December 1889. His rise through the ranks, which saw him serve as head of CID at the Hammersmith Division, brought him to the Central Office in 1906 as a detective chief inspector. 'The real detective is by no means like the detective of fiction, who is always successful – in the end,' he wrote. 'Hard thinking is necessary. But with hard thinking must go hard graft as well. Dogged perseverance has brought far more criminals to book than flashes of genius.'[30]

His casebook was not short on murder. 'Unfortunately there were many . . .' he wrote, 'brutal ones all of them, and most of the culprits found their way to the gallows. Whatever district I was in murders cropped up . . . Once I was sent to a distant town to investigate a most fiendish murder, which left a lasting impression on my mind.'[31]

On 1 November 1908, the Home Office sent Dew ninety miles west of London to Salisbury to investigate the murder of a one-legged twelve-year-old boy named Teddy Haskell. On the outward journey by train, Dew familiarized himself with the facts. The boy lived with his widowed mother, Flora, lived at 40, Meadow Road, Fisherton, 'amongst neighbours of the artisan class and railway workers, who had much affection for the afflicted boy.' At roughly ten-thirty, on the night of 31 October, Percy Noble – Teddy's cousin – called at the Haskell house to repay Flora a shilling she had loaned him. No sooner had he knocked on the back door, he heard her screaming, 'Stop that man! He has murdered my Teddy!' Percy, scared, ran into the street but didn't see anyone. Flora followed close behind, her frantic cries raising the alarm.[32]

Teddy was found in his bed 'with a deep gash in his throat.' The local doctor, 'who was promptly in attendance, stated that death must have been practically instantaneous.' The boy kept a box by his bed in which he'd been 'saving up all the odd pence he received' to someday 'purchase a cork leg to take the place of the limb he lost in early years.' His neighbours had contributed what they could, helping Teddy save £8. The killer fled with half of it.[33]

In her statement to local police, Flora said she bathed Teddy and put him to bed at 9:45 that night. She went into the kitchen, locked the back door and turned down the gas. Settling down at the kitchen table, she heard a noise in Teddy's bedroom above. As she got up to investigate, a man thundered down the stairs and ran out the front door, tossing aside a bloodstained knife before vanishing into the night. It was at that moment Percy knocked on the back door.

As news of the killing made its way up and down the quiet street, Flora's neighbours took action. 'Bands of men with lanterns at once set out to search on the downs and farm lands round the city,' reported *The Salisbury Times*. Flora's house was dark, so she couldn't provide a complete description of the killer. She did somehow manage to observe he was 'thirty to forty years of age, 5ft. 6 in. in height, clean shaven, and dressed in a dark suit, with a light cap, and without a collar or tie.'[34]

Salisbury Chief Constable Ernest Richardson 'telephoned to all the neighbouring towns, and called together the entire police force to watch all the exits from the city and scour the country roads on bicycles.' With the city cordoned off, he contacted Scotland Yard for assistance.[35]

When Dew arrived in Salisbury, there was little he could do. None of the neighbours reported seeing anything suspicious – and the scene itself provided no clues, as nothing had been preserved. The bedclothes had been laundered, the boy's body had been washed, and the house had been scrubbed clean of all traces of blood. All physical evidence had effectively been destroyed. Even had the crime scene not been cleaned, a number of people had traipsed through the house that night to lend Flora their support. Dew learned from two neighbours who had 'obtained sad confirmation of the little boy's fate' that 'there were no signs of disorder in the bedroom.' Teddy lay in bed 'with one small hand outside the coverlet', suggesting he had died in his sleep.[36]

The Salisbury Times played this detail to the hilt:

> It is some small consolation to think that this helpless little cripple, who by all accounts was ever bright and cheery under a heavy affliction, was saved the pain and terror of a violent end, and this one has reason to believe was the case, for there is every indication death was instantaneous. He was mercifully wrapped in a deep sleep and one hopes was dreaming of the innocent delights of the saving penalty kicks in the games of football, into which, though bereft of a leg and encumbered with a crutch, he entered with such zest.[37]

The blade's passage severed the boy's windpipe and carotid artery. The murder weapon was a recently sharpened knife taken from the scullery. It, too, had been cleaned. To Dew, the seasoned investigator, things seemed odd. No neighbours could say they saw a man running from the house that evening. In talking to Flora, he learned she didn't go upstairs after the supposed killer ran from Teddy's bedroom with a bloody knife. What mother wouldn't rush to check on her child's well-being? She told Dew that when she opened the door to Percy, she actually yelled at the boy to fetch a doctor. Why, Dew wanted to know, had she assumed a doctor was needed if she hadn't even gone upstairs? Flora had no answer.[38]

Dew arrested Flora on the evening of 3 November and charged her with murder. The coroner's inquest that followed found her guilty and committed her to trial. As it had done with Constance Kent, the press took pity on the suspect, who sobbed and fainted her way through the legal proceedings. Her first trial in December 1908 resulted in a hung jury with the judge blasting the police for not preserving the blood evidence. Her second trial in April 1909 resulted in an acquittal. Flora, upon hearing the verdict, burst into tears; the crowd gathered outside the courtroom roared its approval.[39]

Dew was unimpressed.

'[I] was absolutely satisfied that Mrs Haskell herself had committed a pre-meditated, coldblooded murder,' he said afterwards. Frank Froest, Dew's colleague and the Murder Squad's Superintendent, concurred. Dew, he wrote in a case summary, 'performed his duty with marked skill and ability,' adding it was 'more than surprising that the jury should have acquitted this woman.'[40]

The case had one significant impact. The Home Office, more than a little disgruntled at the laissez-faire handling of the Meadow Road murder house, issued instructions to local constabularies across the country 'that all such crime scenes must be preserved in the condition they were found, and a guard should be posted until experienced personnel could arrive.'[41]

And while the Haskell outcome frustrated Dew, he would soon be hailed as 'the most celebrated and written about detective in the world.'[42]

14

Chasing Crippen

'The first internationally known fugitive from justice.'

On the afternoon of 30 June 1910, Chief Inspector Walter Dew was at his desk in Scotland Yard when he received a summons to the superintendent's room. CID Superintendent Frank Froest sat at a table with a couple he introduced as Mr and Mrs Nash, members of the theatre set.

'They have called to see me in connection with the disappearance of a friend of theirs, a Mrs Cora Crippen, a member of the Music Hall Artists' Guild, and known on the stage as Belle Elmore,' Froest said. 'She is the wife of a Dr Crippen living out Holloway way. Mr and Mrs Nash are not satisfied with the story the husband has told. Perhaps you had better listen to the full story.'[1]

The Nashes told Dew the Crippens hosted a small dinner party on the night of 31 January. Although nothing seemed out of the ordinary, no one had seen or heard from Cora since. Crippen, a doctor of homeopathic medicine, maintained an office in Albion House, New Oxford Street, the same building as the Music Hall Ladies' Guild of which Cora served as treasurer. In early February, Crippen tendered his wife's resignation from the guild after she had departed suddenly for America. This struck the bohemian circle in which the Crippens moved as odd. Bella cherished her guild work and had never once mentioned any plans to visit the States.

Suspicion among Cora's friends intensified, when, on 20 February, Crippen attended a ball for the Music Hall Benevolent Fund with his young 'typist', Ethel Le Neve, attached to his arm. This raised eyebrows, but the fact Ethel wore a brooch belonging to Cora set tongues aflutter. When asked as to Cora's whereabouts, Crippen merely repeated she'd gone to America on some personal matter. Then came the shocker. On 26 March, an obituary ran in the theatrical paper *The Era*, announcing Cora's death in California from pneumonia.[2]

'Naturally,' John Nash said, 'we were very upset.'[3]

Cora's friends wanted answers, but Crippen proved evasive and would only say Cora had died in Los Angeles. At the end of March, Mrs Nash – under the stage name Lil Hawthorne – embarked on a music hall tour of North America. While there, the Nashes sent an enquiry to the Los Angeles Police Department. They received a letter in response that said no one by the name of Cora Crippen or Belle Elmore had recently died in the city. Upon returning to England, John Nash confronted Crippen.[4]

'He told me the same story, but there was something about him I didn't like,' Nash said of his conversation with the doctor only two days prior. 'I do wish you could make some enquiries and find out just when and where Belle did die. We can't get details from Dr Crippen.'

The Nashes fell silent.

'Well, Mr Dew, that's the story,' said Froest. 'What do you make of it?'

'I think it would be just as well if I made a few inquiries into this personally,' Dew replied.[5]

Dew launched his inquiry that afternoon. Rather than go directly to the doctor, he started at the periphery and worked his way inwards, learning what he could about the Crippens. 'I saw a lot of people,' Dew said, 'and took a large number of statements.'[6]

Melinda May, Secretary of the Music Hall Ladies' Guild, told Dew that Cora loved being Guild Treasurer and, for the last two years, had attended every Wednesday meeting.

'I last saw her alive at the meeting on Wednesday, 26 January,' Melinda said. 'She was then in her usual health. As regards her spirits, she was quite bright, and she was in her usual spirits when I saw her.'

The next guild meeting was 2 February at the Crippen home at 39, Hilldrop Crescent.

'I expected Mrs Crippen to come,' Melinda said, 'but she did not attend.'

Present was Ethel Le Neve, Crippen's typist, who gave Melinda two letters supposedly from Cora. The first one read:

> 39 Hilldrop Crescent, 2 February
>
> Dear Miss May,
>
> Illness of a near relative has called me to America on only a few hours' notice, so I must ask you to bring my resignation as treasurer before the meeting to-day, so that a new treasurer can be elected at once. You will appreciate my haste when I tell you that I have not been to bed all night packing, and getting ready to go. I shall hope to see you again a few months later, but cannot spare a moment to call on you before I go. I wish you everything nice until I return to London again. Now, good-bye, with love hastily.
>
> Yours, Belle Elmore

The second letter, addressed to the Committee of the Music Hall Ladies' Guild, echoed the first. 'I hope some months later to be with you again,' it read, 'and in [the] meantime wish the Guild every success and ask my good friends and pals to accept my sincere and loving wishes for their own personal welfare.'

'I knew Mrs Crippen's writing,' Melinda told Dew, 'but I could not say in whose writing that letter is in.'

Crippen told Melinda that Cora was 'away up in the hills of California – right up in the mountains' and hard to reach. 'I saw Dr Crippen several times during the following month of March,' she said. 'I remember seeing him on Wednesday, March 23, when he told me that Mrs Crippen was very ill – very ill indeed – and he was waiting for worse news.'[7]

Paul and Clara Martinetti, the couple the Crippens hosted for dinner on 31 January, said nothing seemed out of the ordinary that evening. They arrived at eight and spent most of the night playing whist. 'It was quite a nice evening,' Clara said. Cora appeared in good humour and fine health. 'When we left at 1:30, Mrs Crippen stood at the top of the steps, and I said, "Good night, Belle" and, of course, kissed her,' Clara said. 'She wanted to come down the steps with me, but I said, "Don't come down, Belle, you will catch a cold."'

No one outside the Crippen home saw Cora again.

A couple of days later, the Martinettis learned of Cora's sudden departure to America. They castigated Crippen for not telling them about Cora's travel plans. Crippen said everything happened so fast, they didn't have time to notify friends. Clara thought Cora might send a postcard once she reached the States, but no such card arrived. Crippen stayed in touch with the Martinettis, often visiting their flat in Shaftesbury Avenue. On one visit in late February or early March, he said Cora had taken ill in America. 'I cannot make it out,' he said. 'I have a letter from my relations to say she is very ill and had something the matter with one of her lungs. At the same time I also got a letter from Belle to say that I must not worry, she is not as bad as they say.'

On 23 March, Crippen told Clara 'that Belle was very dangerously ill' and not expected to live much longer. He said if she did pass, he would go to France for a week 'for a change of air'. The next day, Crippen wired Clara a telegram from Victoria Station: 'Belle died yesterday at six o'clock . . . shall be away for a week.' Clara confronted Crippen upon his return for more details. He said she'd died in Los Angeles and had been cremated. Not long after Cora's passing, Clara saw Ethel Le Neve – Crippen's 'lady typist' – wearing the dead woman's furs.[8]

Initially, based on 'the Bohemian character of the persons concerned', Dew thought the story of Belle's disappearance 'capable of explanation'. Now, having spoken to her friends, he thought otherwise. 'Mrs Crippen appears to have been a great favourite with all whom she came in contact with,' Dew wrote in a case report dated 6 July, 'always cheerful, and apparently in excellent health, and does not seem to have expressed any intention of leaving England to her intimate friends . . . We should continue our enquiries.'[9]

Hawley Harvey Crippen was born in Coldwater, Michigan in 1862. The son of a successful dry goods merchant, Crippen enjoyed a pampered youth before embarking on his medical studies as a young man. He enrolled at the University of Michigan in 1882 to pursue homeopathic medicine. His studies brought him the following year to London, where he furthered his education at several hospitals. Upon his return to the US in 1883, he earned a degree from the Homeopathic Hospital College in Cleveland, Ohio. Life soon took him to New York, where, in 1885, he graduated as an ear-and-eye specialist and met his first wife, Charlotte Jane Bell, whom he married in December 1887.[10]

The couple had a son, Hawley Otto, two years later. The family moved around before winding up in Salt Lake City, Utah, with thirty-three-year-old Charlotte expecting another child. It never arrived. Charlotte died suddenly of a stroke in January 1892. Crippen sent his son to Los Angeles, where Crippen's parents now lived, before returning to New York. It proved a fateful decision; for it was there Crippen met and married seventeen-year-old Cora Turner.[11]

The daughter of a Russian Pole, Cora Mackamotzki (her family name) was mature beyond her years. The mistress of another man – one who paid her keep and financed her singing lessons – when she met Crippen, she saw something in the short, large-eyed doctor that convinced her he was marriage material. Crippen happily catered to his young wife's every whim and indulged her theatrical ambitions, picking up the tab for her vocal training.

She believed she was destined for stardom on the opera stage, a belief 'which afterwards did not turn out to have been justified.' The couple lived briefly in St. Louis and then returned to New York, where 'a serious medical problem' resulted in Cora having a hysterectomy. The procedure would ultimately have dire consequences for her husband.[12]

In April 1897, Crippen moved to London to advance his career in homeopathic medicine. Cora joined him in August and was now intent, having given up on opera, to pursue music hall stardom under the name 'Belle Elmore.' 'The humblest English music hall has its standards,' notes one case history, 'and "Belle Elmore", in spite of her personal attractions and pretty clothes, could not attain to them.' Even as Cora's theatrical ambitions floundered, Crippen continued to support her increasingly faded dreams. He eventually set up office in Albion House, partnering with a dentist named Gilbert Rylance to start the Yale Tooth Specialist Company. He also sold snake-oil remedies through the mail 'and marketed himself a specialist of the eye, throat and nose.'[13]

Crippen's salary kept the 'increasingly stout' Cora in jewels and furs. They moved in bohemian circles and socialized with the theatre set for Cora's benefit. Crippen, by all accounts, was a kind, polite and timid man dominated by a wife who could often 'be a sharp-tongued shrew.' Recalled a mutual friend: 'He was not a man's man . . . His wife purchased his ties and decided on the pattern of his clothing. She would discuss the colour of his trousers with the tailor, while he stood aside looking on, without venturing to give an opinion.'[14]

In September 1905, the Crippens moved into 39, Hilldrop Crescent. He had by now met Ethel Le Neve, having hired the twenty-year-old as his private secretary two years prior. Born Ethel Neave, she 'changed her surname to make it sound more middle class.' She was, like Crippen, quiet, gentle and prone to loneliness. The two found solace in one another with Ethel becoming Crippen's safe harbour 'from the strain and storm of existence at home.' When Cora visited Crippen at his office, Ethel witnessed first-hand the woman's domineering nature. In December 1906, Crippen and Ethel's relationship made its way into the bedroom. It remained a passionate but carefree affair until September 1908, when Ethel suffered a miscarriage. The tragedy 'changed the tenor of Ethel's relationship with Crippen' and she now wanted a deeper commitment.[15]

The roles were thus cast by the start of 1910 and the stage set for a drama worthy of any opera.

On Wednesday, 8 July, Dew and Detective Sergeant Arthur Mitch-ell paid a visit to Dr Crippen's home. 'The house was rather a large semi-detached dwelling of the old type standing well back from the road,' noted Dew, 'and partially screened from the street by overgrown trees.'[16]

The detectives introduced themselves to the French maid who opened the door and followed her into the hall. The maid excused herself, and soon a young woman – somewhere between the ages of twenty-five and thirty – appeared. It was Ethel Le Neve. 'She was not pretty, but there was something quite attractive about her,' Dew wrote. '. . . One thing I spotted at once, she was wearing a diamond brooch, which from the description I had been given, I suspected had once been the property of Mrs Cora Crippen.'[17]

Dew asked to speak with the doctor. Ethel said he was at work but would be home later that evening if the detectives wished to come back. Dew wished no such thing and asked Ethel to escort them to Crippen's office. They took a horse-drawn omnibus to Tottenham Court Road and walked the rest of the way to Albion House ('a big block of flats'), where Crippen had an office on the third floor. Dew was underwhelmed by Crippen's appearance; 'an insignificant little man,' he wrote, with 'short-sighted eyes'. If Dew's arrival perturbed the doctor, Crippen showed no outward sign of anxiety. 'He was as calm as I was,' Dew remembered.[18]

'I am Chief Inspector Dew of Scotland Yard. This is a colleague of mine, Sergeant Mitchell,' Dew said. 'We have called to have a word with you about the death of your wife. Some of your wife's friends have been to us concerning the stories you have told them about her death, with which they are not satisfied. I have made exhaustive inquiries, and I am not satisfied so I have come to see you to ask if you care to offer an explanation.'[19]

Crippen readily admitted to lying about Cora's death. He told Dew that Cora – a woman who, by all accounts, could be overbearing – had moved to Chicago to be with her lover. He said he was ashamed of his wife's tawdry behaviour and had fabricated her death to avoid embarrassment.

'Whatever I have said to other people in regard to her death is absolutely wrong,' Crippen said, 'and I am giving this as the explanation.' He said Cora, before her departure, had long held him in contempt and considered him unworthy of her affection. 'She frequently threatened to leave me,' he continued, 'and said that if she did, she would go right out of my life and I should never see or hear from her again.' He admitted to writing her resignation letters from the Guild and running the obituary in *The Era* to try and put an end to her friends' constant questions. He readily admitted to being in love with Ethel and said she now lived with him as his wife.[20]

Ethel also provided a statement, saying she and Crippen had been intimately involved 'for between two and three years' though they had known each other for ten. She said she knew Mrs Crippen, who had treated her like a friend. 'In the early part of February, I received a note from Mr Crippen saying Mrs Crippen had gone to America,' Ethel said. Not long thereafter, Crippen told her Cora had caught a chill on the boat and developed pneumonia. Ethel accompanied Crippen to France and moved into Hilldrop Crescent upon their return. 'The same night or the night after, he told me Belle was dead,' she said. 'I was very much astonished, but I don't think I said anything to him about it.'[21]

It was early evening when Crippen and Ethel reviewed and signed their statements. The couple and the two detectives left Albion House together and took a cab back to Hilldrop Crescent. Crippen and Ethel sat side by side. 'Neither made any attempt to disguise the affectionate relationship which existed between them,' Dew observed. At the house, Dew and Mitchell – with Crippen's consent – went through all eight rooms, 'searching the wardrobes, dressing-tables, cupboards, and every other likely place.' They found nothing. Nor did the cellar suggest anything unusual.[22]

The hour was late by the time Dew and Mitchell left the house. 'It had been a gruelling day for both of us,' Dew recalled. '. . . I was dog tired, yet I could not sleep. The events of the day kept cropping up.'

The next day, Saturday, 9 July, Dew circulated a missing persons notice with a description of Cora Crippen to every police station in London. On the morning of Monday, 11 July, he returned to Albion House to ask Crippen some follow-up questions.[23]

'Then came the bombshell,' Dew wrote. Crippen and Le Neve 'had flown.'[24]

Dew learned the news from Dr Gilbert Rylance, Crippen's business partner, who had received a letter from Crippen on Saturday evening. 'Dear Dr Rylance,' it read, 'I now find that in order to escape trouble I shall be obliged to absent myself for a time.' William Long, a 'dental mechanic' who worked for Rylance and Crippen, told Dew he was surprised to find Crippen in the office early Saturday morning. Asked if anything was the matter, Crippen had replied, 'Only a little scandal.' He provided no further explanation but asked Long to run out and purchase some boy's clothing: a brown tweed suit and matching felt hat, two shirts and two collars, a tie and a pair of boots.[25]

Over the next two days, Dew circulated a description of Cora to police departments throughout the country and searched the now vacant house in Hilldrop Crescent. Although Crippen's sudden departure suggested something foul, there was still no evidence a crime had been committed. 'During this time Mitchell and I returned to the house again and again,' Dew said. 'We searched the building from top to bottom, combing every room and examining every nook and cranny of the garden.'[26]

Dew began searching the cellar on Wednesday, 13 July. Scattered pieces of coal, some tree trimmings, a discarded chandelier and random rubbish covered the brick floor. Dew got on his hands and knees and jabbed at the floor with a poker he took from the kitchen. 'I found that the poker went in somewhat easily between the crevices of the bricks,' he said, 'and I managed to get one or two up, and then several came up pretty easily. I then produced a spade from the garden and dug the clay that was immediately underneath the bricks. After digging down to a depth of about four spadefuls I came across what appeared to be human remains.'[27]

With the help of two constables from the Kentish Town Police Station, the excavation continued late into the night under the watchful eye of Divisional Police Surgeon Thomas Marshall. The smell was awful and prompted the men to fortify themselves 'with a long drink of brandy' in the garden. 'Who can imagine the horror and thrill that went through me?' Dew later recalled. 'At length I had discovered a clue to the poor creature who had vanished many months before as though the earth had opened and swallowed her, as, indeed, it had.'[28]

What lay in the hole in the middle of the cellar was a large, gooey clump: a decomposed trunk, minus the arms, legs, head and 'those particular organs which would have determined the sex of the body'. In the dirt next to it, Dew and his colleagues found strands of fair hair wrapped up in a man's handkerchief, some dark brown hair in a curler, a torn strip of a woman's vest with six buttons attached and a lace collar, two small reddish-brown pieces of cloth, a sizeable chunk of skin, fat, and muscle from the thigh and lower buttock, and other bits of flesh. Also found was a pyjama jacket with its clothing label still attached that read: 'Shirtmakers, Jones Brothers, Holloway, Limited, Holloway, N.' The grave's contents were left in place overnight, under police guard, and transferred to a coffin the next morning. The two constables tasked with the unenviable job lifted the putrid mass with their bare hands.[29]

Another search of the house turned up 'a large quantity' of ladies' clothes, including a number of furs, in a wardrobe and chest of drawers. No doubt Cora would have packed such items for a prolonged trip to America. And if they belonged to Ethel, their presence suggested she left in a hurry. A pair of pyjama bottoms found in Crippen's room matched the pyjama jacket found with the remains. As Dew continued to scour the house, the remains were transported to the Islington mortuary under the supervision of Marshall and the renowned Dr Augustus Joseph Pepper, consulting surgeon at St Mary's Hospital and Home Office pathologist.[30]

Marshall and Pepper conducted the post-mortem in tandem with Inspector Dew and Sergeant Mitchell in attendance. Their examination revealed all the bones had been removed, but the internal organs – 'the heart, lungs, the lower 2½ inches of the windpipe, the gullet, the liver, the kidney, spleen, stomach, pancreas' – appeared healthy and offered no clue as to the cause of death. 'From the remains that I examined,' Pepper said, 'I would say that the person was stout when in life.'[31]

The surgeons estimated the body had been in the ground no more than a few months – eight at the very most – based on the fatty tissues having putrefied 'into a kind of soap, the technical name of which is adipocere.' Also known as 'grave wax', adipocere can help preserve the internal organs and is produced by the decomposition of fat in a wet climate; in this case, the damp clay of the cellar floor.[32]

The amount of time the body spent in the ground was significant, as the Crippens lived at Hilldrop Crescent from 21 September
1905, up to 1 February 1910. Given the couple's five-year occu-
pancy and the fact the remains had been buried no longer than
eight months, it stood to reason the gruesome find in the cellar
had to be Cora Crippen. If it wasn't her, who was it? And what had
happened to her head, bones, arms and legs?[33]

'Even to this day we do not know how or where other parts
of the body were disposed of,' Dew wrote. The inspector believed
Crippen either 'burned them in the kitchen grate' or tossed them
into the Channel on his trip to France. The hair found clamped in
the curler underscored the likelihood that the filleted, gelatinous
mass on the metal gurney was indeed Cora. Dark brown in colour
and up to eight inches long, it showed signs of bleaching. The
length of hair and lack of grey strands told Pepper it belonged to
a woman not yet past middle age. Cora was thirty-six when she
vanished. 'A man often dyes his grey hair black,' Pepper said, 'but
does not bleach it.'[34]

Of considerable interest was a piece of skin measuring seven
inches by six inches. It was evident, from pubic hair on the flesh,
that it came from the lower front part of the abdomen. A four-
inch mark on the skin caught Pepper's attention. 'I afterwards
examined it with particularity. I spent several hours examining it,'
Pepper said. 'It was the mark of a scar.' Having performed abdominal surgery 'many times,' Pepper was confident he knew a surgical
scar when he saw one – and it was known Cora had undergone a
hysterectomy in 1892. He nevertheless sought a second opinion
and turned to a junior colleague at St Mary's, a young pathologist
named Bernard Spilsbury.[35]

A senior CID officer would later recall working his first case
with Spilsbury. 'It was a particularly unpleasant corpse,' he said,
'an exhumation case. I walked into the room and there it was all
laid out ready for examination. I was terribly afraid I should make

a fool of myself, which would never do for a CID officer, so I put on a cigarette and tried to think of something else. After a while Sir Bernard came in. He sniffed twice, looked around the room and said: "You mustn't smoke, please, Johnson. I can't smell the smells I want to smell." He then bent down over the corpse and sniffed away as if it was a rose garden.'[36]

In 1910, the man *Time Magazine* would call 'successor to the mythical Sherlock Holmes', was thirty-three years old and in the infancy of his career. Science had fascinated Spilsbury since childhood – the result of growing up the son of a chemist. The boyhood pursuits of outdoor adventures and rough-and-tumble play paled in comparison to the hours he spent in his father's research lab surrounded by 'slides, test tubes, Bunsen burners and pipettes'. James Spilsbury, frustrated by an unfulfilled dream of being a doctor, pressured his son to pursue a career in medicine. Bernard did as he was told and, though not a stellar student, did just well enough to get accepted into Magdalen College, Oxford in 1896. He spent his three years at Oxford as he spent his childhood, primarily to himself, and made no lasting impression. 'I regarded him as a nice, very ordinary individual,' recalled one Oxford colleague, 'and certainly never expected him to do anything brilliant.'[37]

In the fall of 1899, with a bachelor's degree in hand, he moved to London and began his studies at St Mary's Medical School. He was twenty-three and soon came under the mentorship of Pepper, Dr William Wilcox and Dr A. P. Luff, pioneers in the fledgling and 'beastly science' of pathology. Working with the dead suited Spilsbury's quiet and solitary nature, and he flourished in his studies. He earned his full medical degree in October 1905 and was named St Mary's resident assistant pathologist under Pepper.[38]

Pepper had the utmost confidence in his young protégé when he turned the piece of scar tissue over to Spilsbury for further examination. As it so happened, only two years prior and at Pepper's suggestion, Spilsbury had published the results of a 'special

study of scars and scar tissue formation'. A microscopic examination of the tissue found glands at each end of the mark but none
in its centre, proving it was indeed a scar.[39]

It proved further confirmation of Cora's identity, as did some of
the clothing found buried alongside the remains. 'The undergarments we discovered were shown to friends of Belle,' Dew wrote,
'and they were able to say that they were such as she was in the
habit of wearing.'[40]

All this proved useful, but the body – in its dismembered and
goo-like condition – offered no clue as to the cause of death. It was
Dr Wilcox in his laboratory at St Mary's who, conducting chemical
tests on the internal organs, established the presence of 'a mydri-
atic vegetable alkaloid, of which there are only three – atropine,
hyoscyamin and hyoscin [sic]'. Additional tests narrowed it down
to hyoscine, 'a powerful narcotic poison'. Used rarely as a 'sedative
for cases of delirium, mania and meningitis', a quarter of a grain
can be fatal. Wilcox found two-sevenths of a grain in the stomach,
kidney, intestines and liver.[41]

'This was a toxicology first,' notes one account, as no one had
used the poison to kill before.[42]

Throughout July, while the pathologists sought clues from the
dead, Dew struggled to answer the most pressing question of all:
where were Crippen and Le Neve? 'They might have gone anywhere,' Dew said, 'providing they had sufficient money to pay their
passages.' Indeed, a check of bank records showed Crippen had
withdrawn £37 from a joint account he shared with Cora on the
day he vanished. Further inquiries revealed the doctor had busied
himself two days after Cora was last seen alive by pawning his
wife's jewels for £80.[43]

Dew believed Crippen would attempt to escape the country.
The Yard kept an eye on hotels, shipping offices, railway stations,
ports, and ships bound for distant shores and urged foreign police

departments to be on the alert. 'The French search for the fugitive has taken an original turn,' *The New York Times* reported. 'The police here believe that Crippen is masquerading as a woman, and the descriptions sent out include this probable disguise.' Closer to home, the press coverage resulted in a flood of Crippen sightings. 'I dare not think of the scores of false alarms,' Dew wrote. 'Not a day passed without Crippen and Miss Le Neve being reported to have been seen in some part of the country. Sometimes they were alleged to have been in a dozen places at the same time.'[44]

On 13 July, officers from the Thames River Police boarded the Canadian steamer *Montrose* at Millwall Dock in east London and passed along detailed descriptions of Crippen and Le Neve. It was a long shot, but one worth playing.[45]

Three days later, Scotland Yard released a wanted poster featuring pictures and descriptions of Crippen and Le Neve beneath the all-capital heading MURDER AND MUTILATION. *The Daily Telegraph* called the manhunt 'the most systematic and comprehensive search that has marked any police investigation of recent years.' The Yard, the paper noted, was 'working at high pressure in the elucidation of the mystery.'[46] That same day, Dew applied for a warrant against the couple at Bow Street police court:

> . . . for having on or about the 2nd day of February 1910, at 39 Hilldrop Crescent, Camden Road, in the said County and District, wilfully murdered one Cora Crippen, otherwise Belle Elmore, supposed to be the wife of Hawley Harvey Crippen and that they did mutilate and bury some of the remains in the coal cellar at the above address.[47]

'The first week was completely without result so far as the missing man and woman were concerned,' Dew noted. 'More days went by. Still no clue. I began to get a little nervous.'

'CRIPPEN BAFFLES THE WORLD'S POLICE, WHO ARE ALL ON ALERT' *The Dundee Evening Telegraph* declared on 20 July, announcing Scotland Yard was now offering a £250 reward for any information leading to the fugitive couple's arrest. The second week dragged on with no news; each passing day benefitting 'the first internationally known fugitive from justice.' On the evening of 22 July, Dew, very much feeling the strain, was in his office when someone handed him a telegram from the Liverpool Police. They had received a wireless Marconi communication that day from Captain Henry Kendall on board the *Montrose*.[48] It read:

> Have strong suspicion that Crippen London Cellar Murderer and accomplice are amongst saloon passengers. Moustache shaved off, growing beard. Accomplice dressed as boy, voice, manner and build undoubtedly a girl.[49]

Dew felt 'a wave of optimism' wash over him. 'My fatigue,' he said, 'instantly vanished.'[50]

The couple boarded the *Montrose* in Antwerp on Wednesday, 20 July, having booked their passage in Brussels as Mr John Robinson, fifty-five, and his sixteen-year-old son, John George Robinson, originally from Detroit. Dressed in brown jacket suits, grey felt hats and white canvas shoes, their only luggage was a small handbag. Kendall initially thought nothing of the pair until he noticed a private moment on deck. 'When I saw the boy squeeze the man's hand, I thought it strange and unusual,' Kendall said. 'It occurred to me at once that they might be Crippen and Le Neve.'

The captain shared his suspicions with his chief officer and kept the pair under observation. On the morning of Friday, 22 July, Kendall engaged Mr Robinson in conversation and discussed seasickness amongst the passengers.

'In answer to my observations,' Kendall said, 'he used some medical terms for certain remedies. I was then fully convinced that he was a medical man. I also noticed that Mr Robinson was flat on the bridge of the nose as described in the Police Circulation, and

that there was a deep mark on the nose as if caused by spectacles
. . . I was then positively convinced that it was Crippen and Le
Neve.'

In his cabin, Kendall summoned the ship's Marconi officer and
dictated his message to police for immediate sending.[51]

With authorization from his superiors, Dew made arrangements
through the Liverpool Police to chase Crippen across the Atlantic
in a ship faster than the *Montrose*. His passage was booked on the
White Star liner *Laurentic* under the name Dewhurst to throw off
reporters. Dew arrived in Liverpool on the afternoon of Saturday,
23 July and was 'smuggled' aboard the *Laurentic*, which set sail that
evening for Canada.[52]

The press was not fooled. The high-seas drama dominated Britain's front pages in the days that followed under such headlines as
'INSPECTOR DEW IS ON CRIPPEN'S BACK' and 'CHASE ACROSS
THE ATLANTIC.' 'The annals of crime present no more dramatic
situation than that which has now developed in the pursuit of
Crippen and his typist,' *The London Observer* reported. At least one
paper drew a comparison to another famous case from Scotland
Yard's past. 'A parallel to this Transatlantic chase comes to one's
mind,' noted *The Dundee Evening Telegraph*. 'That was the flight
and pursuit of Franz Müller, the German who slew Mr Briggs in a
railway carriage nearly half a century ago.'[53]

The new-fangled technology of wireless telegraphy between sea
and land lent immediacy to the story, allowing papers to track the
position of each ship in almost real time. On 26 July, *The Ottawa
Free Press* reported the *Laurentic* was only 250 miles behind the
Montrose. 'Interest in the case is still at fever heat,' the paper's
London correspondent responded. 'Not in years has London been
wrought up over a murder mystery. Betting on Crippen's possible
capture is going on in the clubs and on the stock exchange, where

the odds today are 4 to 1 that he would kill himself and 2 to 1 that he and the girl would end their lives. Thousands of dollars have been put up.'[54]

The Daily Telegraph published a chart the following day plotting the position of both steamers. 'Up till now,' the paper said, 'the *Laurentic* has been steadily overhauling her slower rival and wiping out the long start with which the *Montrose* entered upon the race. From the moment the two vessels come abreast, even although many miles apart, the *Laurentic* will continue to draw away gradually from the other.'[55]

On the *Laurentic*, the steamer cutting through the frigid North Atlantic swell, Dew did his utmost to remain incognito by passing himself off as a London businessman. He had a lot weighing on his mind. Was it definitely Crippen and Le Neve onboard the *Montrose*? And if so, would he reach Canada before them? His inability to contact the other ship and coordinate plans fuelled his anxiety. 'I spent hour after hour in the wireless room while attempts were being made to "get through" to the ship on which the suspects were travelling,' Dew recalled. 'It was hopeless. The answering signals simply would not come.'[56]

In the mid-Atlantic darkness on the night of Wednesday, 27 July, the *Laurentic* overtook the *Montrose*, which was heading on a more northerly route. Although the ships never came within sight of one another, they established wireless contact.

'Will board you at Father Point,' Dew telegraphed. 'Please keep any information until I arrive there strictly confidential.'

Captain Kendall on the *Montrose* was terse in his reply. 'What the devil do you think I have been doing?'[57]

On the afternoon of Friday, 29 July, the *Laurentic* reached Father Point, a 'little signal station' in the Gulf of St. Lawrence where river pilots boarded the incoming ships to guide them up the St. Lawrence River to Quebec City. At three o'clock, the 'galaxy of newspaper men and detectives' assembled for the occasion spotted the steamer twelve miles down river. Anticipation had been building for days. 'This little hamlet on the bleak shores of the rapidly widening gulf has never experienced such a week of excitement,' noted the *Montreal Gazette*. 'There are 32 newspaper men here, representing the leading journals of Canada, the United States, and England.'[58]

The tug *Eureka* made its way through the choppy waters and pulled up alongside the steamer at three forty-five. The river pilot boarded the *Laurentic* through the freight hatch, as Dew descended the gangway to the tug, which bobbed and rocked in the cold swell. 'There was no mistaking the Scotland Yard type,' wrote one Canadian reporter, 'a tall, thick-set, broad-shouldered man with grey eyes, a heavy brownish grey moustache, wearing a dark suit, blue tie and black hard-felt hat.'[59]

The reporters on the tug cheered three times for the detective and swarmed him. They unleashed a 'fusillade' of questions, shouting over one another and jostling each other aside to get a photograph. Dew blinked away the rapid-fire flash of camera bulbs and 'merely smiled a slow, thoughtful smile'.

'Why,' he said, 'you fellows are worse than those we have in England.'

The reporters showed no mercy.

'I am sworn to secrecy,' Dew bellowed over their queries. 'I cannot answer any of your questions.'[60]

On shore, Dew found Father Point a rather 'desolate' location with nothing more than the wireless station, a lighthouse and 'a few wooden shacks'. The chief and an inspector from the Quebec City Police welcomed their British counterpart to Canada and escorted him to his accommodations – one of the aforementioned shacks. 'The place was lonely, but it was far from peaceful,' Dew wrote. 'The lighthouse foghorn combined with the vocal and musical efforts of my friends the reporters made sleep impossible.'[61]

A reporter from Boston, having found a piano in one of the huts, entertained his colleagues through the night with show tunes, adapting one – 'Has Anybody Here Seen Kelly?' – into something more suitable for the occasion:

> Has anybody here seen Crippen?
> Crippen from the other side;
> For his hair is black and his eyes are blue,
> And he's going back with Inspector Dew.
> Has anybody here seen Crippen?
> Crippen from the other side.[62]

The next day, Saturday, some newspapermen tried to arrange a baseball match and play the first game in what they dubbed the 'Crippen League', but their efforts fell flat when they couldn't muster enough players. Spirits were beginning to sag when, at six o'clock that evening, the wireless operator passed along word that the *Montrose* was expected early the next morning. Reported the *Montreal Gazette*, 'The little village of Father Point soon dropped into sleep without anything to give a sign of life save the twinkling eye of the giant lighthouse, which blinks all night to the sea.'[63]

Dr Hawley Harvey Crippen and Ethel Le Neve believed they had passed the voyage in perfect anonymity. Unaware their cover was blown, they spent their days strolling the deck as father and son, enjoying their meals in the saloon and reading; one book favoured by Crippen being *The Four Just Men* by Edgar Wallace, about a group of vigilantes who punish criminals beyond the law's reach.

Captain Kendall kept a discreet eye on the pair and sometimes engaged Crippen in conversation. 'I have discussed various parts of the world with him,' Kendall said. 'He knows Toronto, Detroit and California well, and says he is going to take his boy to California for his health [meaning Miss Le Neve].' Ethel, always nearby, kept to herself. As Kendall noted: 'She doesn't speak much but always wears a pleasant smile . . . and he will not leave her for a moment.' Her happy demeanour was commendable under the circumstances. 'Her suit is anything but a good fit. Her trousers are very tight about the hips, and are split a bit down the back and secured with large safety pins.'

Crippen monitored the ship's progress on the tracking board in the saloon. He seemed most curious about what would happen when the ship reached Canadian waters and how passengers would disembark upon reaching their destination. He would sometimes lose himself, staring up at the ship's wireless aerial 'and listen to the cracking electric spark messages being sent by the Marconi operator.' One afternoon, he caught Kendall watching him.

'What a wonderful invention it is!' Crippen exclaimed.[64]

At four-thirty on the morning of Sunday, 31 July, the shrill cry of the *Montrose*'s whistle drifted across Father Point. The sound, signalling the ship's approach, drew bleary-eyed reporters and an anxious Dew from their shacks into a cold, pre-dawn rain to await the steamer's arrival. 'The minutes and hours,' wrote *The New York Times* correspondent, 'passed with tantalizing slowness.' For Dew, the eyes of the world's press on him, it must have been torture. The day dawned bleak and grey with mist clinging to the river.[65]

At about seven-thirty, the ship emerged from the teeming murk. 'A thrill of excitement ran through me as the big ship hove into view,' Dew wrote. He had already coordinated his plans with Captain Kendall via wireless. Disguised as a river pilot, he would be rowed out to the *Montrose* and board the ship mid-stream to make the arrest. With the steamer now in view, the shoreline exploded with activity. 'The rain continued to fall,' reported *The New York Times*, 'and the more ambitious residents, not to be denied the scene of capture, began fitting out their rowboats and variegated sailing craft, ready to hasten to the liner's side immediately she arrived.'[66]

Reporters scrambled into the tug *Eureka* and crammed its small deck to capacity. Dew, wearing a cap and 'a blue uniform with brass buttons' he borrowed from an old pilot, climbed aboard the *Eureka*'s tender with the real pilot and two Quebec detectives. 'My boat swung into mid-stream,' he said. 'The *Montrose* seemed to grow rapidly in bulk as we approached her. Presently we could distinguish forms moving about her decks.' Dew pulled his cap down low to conceal his features.[67]

Crippen and Le Neve were up that morning at six-thirty, as was their custom, and went to breakfast in the saloon. When finished, Le Neve returned to their cabin to read; Crippen took a stroll on deck. The ship's surgeon, Dr C. H. Stewart, joined him. They were standing 'on the portside promenade deck forward, near the companionway leading to the saloon' when they saw the tender drawing near.[68]

'What a lot of men in that small boat,' Crippen said. 'Are they all pilots?'

'There is only one pilot for the ship,' Stewart said. 'Perhaps the others are his friends, who are going to take a little excursion as far as Quebec.'

Crippen appeared to grow uneasy as he watched the boat draw closer. He wondered aloud 'if the men in it could be medical officers.' Dr Stewart said he thought that unlikely.[69]

Dew and the Canadian detectives, once onboard, headed to the bridge and the waiting Captain Kendall. As he and Kendall exchanged greetings, Dew's attention settled 'on a little man who had emerged unconcernedly from behind a funnel on the deck below.' Kendall said nothing as Dew stared intently at the man then hurried from the bridge to have a closer look. He descended to the deck and got within a few feet of the gentleman known to those onboard as Mr Robinson. The man looked like Crippen, yet he wore no spectacles and didn't have the doctor's sandy moustache – but the eyes, those bulging eyes. Dew recognized them instantly and felt 'a sense of triumph and achievement' unequal to any other time in his career.[70]

'Good morning, Dr Crippen,' Dew said.

Crippen, recognizing the man in the pilot's uniform, appeared momentarily stunned but quickly regained his composure. 'Good morning, Mr Dew.'

'You will be arrested for the murder and mutilation of your wife, Cora Crippen, in London, on or about February 1st last.'

'Thank God,' Crippen said. 'The suspense is over.'

One of the Canadian officers handcuffed the doctor and took him away to vacant cabin No. 8.[71]

Kendall now led Dew to cabin No. 5, where the detective found Le Neve sitting on the lower berth. She was still dressed as a boy and, in Dew's words, 'looked the part reasonably well.' Perhaps expecting it to be Crippen, she got to her feet as Dew entered. 'I am Chief-Inspector Dew,' he said. Le Neve shrieked in surprise and collapsed in a dead faint. Dew caught her before she hit the floor.[72]

Brought to with restoratives and provided women's clothing by a kindly stewardess, Le Neve voiced her gratitude for no longer having to wear the uncomfortable disguise, but she made no reply when Dew informed her she was under arrest for murder. He left her in the cabin under the supervision of the stewardess and went to check on Crippen.

'How is Miss Le Neve?' Crippen asked.

'Agitated, but I am doing all I can for her.'

'It is only fair to say that she knows nothing about it,' Crippen said. 'I never told her anything.'

'Whatever may be said and thought about Crippen,' Dew later

wrote, 'one can only admire his attitude towards the girl who had shared his great adventure.'[73]

News of the arrest was transmitted to England via wireless.

'Not only the circumstances of the crime make it of extraordinary interest,' proclaimed *The New York Times*, 'but also the remarkable detective chase across the Atlantic with wireless telegraphy contributing for the first time as a decisive factor in detection, and with the people of Europe and America eagerly intent upon the quest.'[74]

The (London) *Times* couldn't help but note the irony that while the world tracked Crippen and Le Neve's escape, the couple themselves remained oblivious to their global audience. From the moment they fled by boat 'until the moment of their arrest, "Dr" Crippen and Miss Le Neve have been encased in waves of wireless telegraphy as securely as if they had been within the four walls of a prison, for they were, of course, in ignorance of the toils which were being woven around them.' Not all credit, however, was due to science. 'Scotland Yard,' the paper continued, 'took the whole world into its confidence with unprecedented thoroughness. It enlisted not only the services of the official police of other countries, but also the formidable though unofficial detective service supplied by the extensive publicity afforded by the Press.'[75]

The legal paperwork and international red tape cleared, Dew – and Sergeant Mitchell, who had recently arrived from London to assist – boarded the steamer *Magentic* with Crippen and Le Neve and set sail from Quebec on 20 August.

At sea, Crippen's primary concern remained Le Neve's well-being. 'Dr Crippen's love for the girl, for whom he had risked so much, was the biggest thing in his whole life,' Dew wrote. '. . . I admit I was touched.' Crippen, it turned out, was a likeable and fascinating man. 'I found him a good conversationalist, able to talk on almost any subject,' the detective said. He and Mitchell, not totally unsympathetic to the couple's predicament, treated their prisoners well – so much so that Le Neve began referring to Dew, teasingly, as 'Father'.[76]

Dew allowed Crippen and Le Neve to see each other once during the voyage. He arranged one evening for both to be brought to their respective cabin doors at the same time, but they were not allowed to speak. Crippen stood in his doorway; Le Neve stood in hers about thirty feet away. They smiled and raised their hands to one another, and that was it. Dew, watching the strangely touching interaction, felt like an 'interloper'.[77]

With the world's attention turned to the Atlantic, Scotland Yard had continued the investigation at home. Detectives traced the sale of hyoscine to a chemist – Lewis & Burrows – in New Oxford Street. There, employee Charles Hetherington told detectives Crippen purchased five grains of hyoscine hydrobromide on either 17 or 18 January.

'I asked him what it was for, and as far as I remember he stated it was for homeopathic purposes,' Hetherington said. 'We did not have any of it in stock in the form he ordered. We only had it mixed with another substance – in this case, sugar of milk. I told him so, and he told me to order it for him.'

Hetherington said in the four years he had worked at the chemist's, they had never kept five grains of hyoscine in stock. He knew Crippen well as a customer. The doctor purchased 'cocaine, sometimes morphia, sometimes mercury and other drugs,' but never hyoscine. The doctor returned to the shop on 19 January to pick up his order and signed the chemist's sales-of-poison register.[78]

The pyjamas found at Hilldrop Crescent also proved significant. An employee from Jones Brothers, the store that sold them, told detectives the fabric and pattern were not available until December 1908. Furthermore, store records showed a pair had been purchased and delivered to 39, Hilldrop Crescent on 5 January

1909. The Crippens had lived at Hilldrop Crescent from September 1905 to February 1910, bolstering the likelihood that the remains found buried with the pyjama jacket were indeed those of Cora Crippen.[79]

Dr Crippen went on trial at the Old Bailey on 18 October 1910. Admission was by ticket only, with the government receiving 4,000 applications. If the chase across the Atlantic highlighted the new technological frontier achieved by wireless, the court proceedings introduced to the public the grim science of forensic pathology. Of pivotal importance was the piece of skin with the hysterectomy scar. The defence and its medical experts argued it wasn't a scar at all but merely a fold in the skin. Casting doubt on the scar would cast doubt on the identity of the remains.[80]

Testifying in his first capital case, Bernard Spilsbury presented an impressive figure on the stand: 'tall, handsome, well-dressed, a red carnation in his buttonhole'. He spoke in a cold, authoritative tone, emotionally detached from the drama. The disputed mark, Spilsbury testified, lacked glands – a characteristic of scars. While the skin showed evidence of a fold, 'it was not along the line of the scar at all, but formed a kind of crescent around the upper end of the skin quite distinct from the scar'. When defence lawyers argued the skin was not from the navel at all, but most likely a buttock, Spilsbury noted the presence of pubic hair and abdominal muscle.[81]

Crippen's lawyers tried to portray the unshakable Spilsbury as beholden to Pepper and merely parroting his boss's theory. 'I have an independent position of my own,' Spilsbury said, 'and I am responsible for my own opinion, which has been formed on my own scientific knowledge, and not in any way influenced by any supposed connection with Mr Pepper. I have absolute no doubt in my mind as regards the scar . . . I have my microscopic slides here, and I shall send for a microscope in case it should be wanted.'[82]

Spilsbury, in his cool and no-nonsense manner, had asserted his medico-legal dominance – and the jurors took notice. They adjourned on 23 October at 2:15 p.m. and returned twenty-seven minutes later with a guilty verdict. Asked if he had anything to say before the mandatory sentence of death was passed, Crippen replied, 'I am innocent.' He maintained his impenetrable façade of calm even as guards led him from the dock. Ethel went on trial two days later and left the courthouse a free woman.[83]

There was no reprieve for Crippen. On 20 November, the *Daily Mail* published a statement from the doctor. 'In this farewell letter to the world, written as I face eternity,' he wrote, 'I say that Ethel Le Neve has loved me as few women love men, and that her innocence of any crime, save that of yielding to the dictates of the heart, is absolute. To her I pay this last tribute. It is of her that my last thoughts have been. My last prayer will be that God will protect her and keep her safe from harm and allow her to join me in eternity.'[84]

In a letter to Ethel, before she made her farewell visit to the prison, he wrote: 'How am I to endure to take my last look at your dear face? What agony must I go through at the last when you disappear for ever from my eyes! God help us to be brave then.'[85]

Crippen met his end at nine o'clock on the morning of 23 November. By all accounts, he went bravely to his fate, maintaining his placid demeanour to the very end. 'In a trice he was on the trap-doors with his legs strapped together and a rope around his neck,' hangman John Ellis said. 'One swift glance round to be assured that all was right, and my hand shot to the lever. Thud! The fatal doors fell. The slack rope tightened, and in an instant was still. Dr Crippen was dead.'[86]

Two days later, Madame Tussauds advertised its new 'Lifelike Portrait Model of Hawley Harvey Crippen'.[87]

Walter Dew retired from Scotland Yard on 5 December 1910. Not everyone was thrilled with his handling of the investigation. Some in the press questioned why Dew had not kept a better eye on Crippen once the doctor fell under suspicion. At least one MP had wanted to broach the subject in Parliament while Dew was mid-Atlantic, but Home Secretary Winston Churchill rejected the idea. There was an argument to be made that had Crippen not made a run for it, the remains in the cellar might not have been discovered.[88]

Murder and mutilation bookended Dew's career, starting as it did with the Jack the Ripper investigation. In retirement, Dew worked as a private investigator and eventually moved to the coastal town of Worthing in West Sussex. There, he wrote his memoirs, *I Caught Crippen*, published in 1938. He died on 16 December 1947.

Ethel Le Neve slipped into a life of anonymity as Ethel Harvey (Crippen's middle name). She lived in Canada briefly before returning to England and marrying a clerk named Stanley Smith in 1915. They raised two children. Her family never knew her true identity while she was alive.* She died in 1 August967 at the age of eight-four, taking whatever dark secrets she harboured with her.[89]

If the Crippen case marked the end of Dew's career, it very much launched Spilsbury's. His testimony during the trial made him a household name and a darling of the press. Over the next three decades, he would perform 20,000 autopsies and testify for the prosecution in 200 trials. He would become a leading figure in 'the heyday of the Great English Murder, when lurid details of sensational court cases filled the newspapers.'[90]

---

* According to one account, Ethel's children found out two decades after her death. 'It's unbelievable that Mum would have dressed up as a boy,' her daughter, Nina, reportedly said at the time. 'She was rather strait-laced.' (See 'The secret life of Victorian killer Dr Crippen's mistress revealed 107 years after wife's murder.' *The Mirror*, 13 2 October017.)

The piece of scarred tissue introduced the fledgling science of pathology to the mainstream. It fascinated the public all the more because, like some strange, new language, it 'could be interpreted only by the extraordinary skills of an expert' – much like fingerprints. Spilsbury established himself as a keen interpreter of the dead. He would, in the years that followed, become a towering figure; his mere arrival at a crime scene generated headlines. His ability to communicate complex medico-legal matters in simple, everyday language earned him the public's unquestioning trust. 'He called a bruise a bruise . . .' remembered London coroner and barrister Sir William Bentley Purchase. 'He put forensic science into the witness-box on its own separate importance, and not as being ancillary to anything else.'[91]

Compared in his day to Sherlock Holmes and dubbed 'the father of modern forensics', Spilsbury has no modern-day equivalent. His word in the courtroom was sacrosanct and sealed the fate of many a defendant. His self-confidence broached arrogance, and his obstinate belief in the infallibility of his findings would later stir controversy. 'Spilsbury, like the rest of us, could make mistakes,' one contemporary recalled. 'He was unique, I think, in that he never admitted making a mistake. Once he had committed himself to an opinion he would never change it.'[92]

Regardless, Spilsbury's star proved ascendant – and, with it, the legitimacy of forensic pathology.

15

The Brides in the Bath

Forensic pathology points to murder.

On the evening of Friday, 12 December 1913, Margaret Crossley, having tea with her daughter Alice and husband Joseph, noticed a water stain on her kitchen ceiling. Even as she watched, it blossomed like a dark flower, its sinister petals blooming against the white plaster. It stretched across the ceiling and began a slow, wet descent down the wall. Rivulets of water bled through the wallpaper and dampened several pictures. The widowed Margaret ran a boarding house at 16, Regent Street in Blackpool. Two days earlier, a couple from Portsmouth identifying themselves as Mr and Mrs Smith had appeared on her doorstep and inquired about a room. The husband had made a point of making sure the Crossleys had a bath on the premises.

Margaret presently remarked how strange it was that water should be seeping through the wall and ceiling. It had never happened before. She knew Mrs Smith was bathing, for Alice had run the bath, and she now wondered out loud if she should go upstairs and say something. Alice put her teacup down and urged her mother against it. 'Oh, Mother, they will think we are grumbling,' Alice said. 'Do not let us say anything now.'

As Margaret cast her eyes once more to the stain above, Mr Smith entered the kitchen with two eggs he had just purchased. He asked if Margaret might cook them the next morning for breakfast. 'I wondered what was the matter with him,' Margaret later said. 'He looked so wild and agitated.'

He hung about for several minutes and discussed his plans to view the city's fire engine the next day before heading upstairs. From the floor above, Margaret and her family heard him call to his wife through the bathroom door. Alice at first thought Mr Smith was summoning her, as she had the same name as his wife. When he called out a second time, Margaret got up to see if everything was all right. Climbing the stairs, she looked up and saw Mr Smith 'on the bathroom landing; he was standing on the mat in the bathroom doorway'.

'Oh, what's the matter?' Margaret asked.

'My wife cannot speak to me,' Mr Smith cried. 'Fetch Dr Billing; she knows him.'

Dr George Billing lived close by and had treated Mrs Smith three days prior for a headache. It was about eight-thirty when Billing arrived at the Regent Street address and went upstairs to the bathroom. Mrs Smith lay in the bath, her wet skin reflecting the pale light of the room's gas lamp. Mr Smith was kneeling beside the tub and supporting his wife's head with his left arm.

The soapy water, about an inch and a half from the top of the wooden tub, came up to Mrs Smith's breasts. 'Her back was about a foot from the taps,' Billing recalled, 'but her head was raised . . . I put my hands in the water. It was quite hot.'

'Why didn't you pull the plug?' Billing asked.

'I didn't think of it,' Smith replied.

The two men lifted Mrs Smith out of the bath. 'I took hold of her left arm and right leg, and he took the shoulders and right arm,' Billing said. 'The body was quite limp.'

Billing quickly determined the woman was dead, though he couldn't say for how long. The news seemed not to upset Mr Smith, who took the tragedy in cold stride.

Margaret Crossley watched the drama unfold from the stairs.

'What is wrong?' she asked.

'Oh, she is drowned,' Billing said, emerging from the bathroom. 'She is dead.'

Mr Smith called the police and joined Margaret in the kitchen shortly after Billing left.

'How dreadful,' she said. 'What an awful thing this is.'

Smith shrugged off Margaret's concern. His 'hard-hearted' manner soured the landlady's opinion, and now she wanted him gone.

'Now, Smith,' she said, 'you cannot sleep here tonight.'

The news seemed to upset him more than his wife's passing. He insisted he could still sleep in the bedroom he was paying for and where his wife's body now lay beneath a sheet.

'I take care that you do not,' Margaret said, standing her ground.

'When they are dead, they are dead,' Smith replied, but ultimately acquiesced.

Shortly before ten o'clock, Sergeant Robert Valiant of the Black-pool Borough Police Force arrived at the house. He went upstairs, viewed the body and took a statement from Smith, who identified himself as 'a gentleman of independent means.'

Smith's full name was George Joseph Smith. He was forty-one; his wife of only six weeks, Alice, was twenty-five. The two of them had gone for a half-hour walk that evening. Shortly after they returned at 7:45 p.m., Alice decided to have a bath. It was the last thing she ever said to Smith. He stepped out briefly to get some eggs for breakfast and came back twenty minutes later to find her fully submerged in the tub.

'I lifted her head up out of the water and held it until the doctor came,' Smith said. 'We then lifted her out of the bath. The doctor examined her and pronounced life extinct.'

Smith showed no emotion when detailing the evening's tragedy – a point not lost on Valiant, who found the man 'callous and in no way disturbed.'

'Are you going to take your wife home to bury her, or are you going to bury her here?' Valiant asked.

'I will bury her here,' Smith said, 'as my means are limited.'

The body of Alice Smith spent the night in Margaret Crossley's boarding house, while Smith slept next door. He was back the following day, however, with a bottle of whisky in hand. Having taken care of the funeral arrangements that morning, he spent much of the afternoon playing the piano in Margaret's parlour. He told Joseph Crossley he made a point of ordering a cheap coffin.

'I wouldn't bury my wife like that,' Joseph said, 'even if I had not a penny in the world.'

'When they are dead,' Smith said, 'they are done with.'

He finished the whisky by early evening, just in time for the 6:30 p.m. inquest into his wife's demise. It proved to be a short, to-the-point affair lasting no more than half an hour. Smith testified and managed to shed a few whisky-infused tears on the stand. He said he had met his wife, a nurse, three months ago. Dr Billing also presented his findings. Having autopsied the deceased that morning, he determined she suffered from heart disease, evident from a thickening of the valves. He theorized the warm water in the bath increased blood flow through the already overstressed heart, causing Alice to pass out in the tub and drown. It was good enough for the assembled jurors, who found that Alice drowned 'probably through being seized by a fit or a faint. The cause of death was accidental.'

Smith stuck around long enough to see Alice buried in a budget coffin beneath slate-coloured skies on Monday, 15 December. 'Put her in a public grave,' he ordered the undertaker, 'but don't tell her mother.'

More than a year passed before the Crossleys heard any more of George Joseph Smith.

On the afternoon of Sunday, 3 January 1915, the following article appeared in the *News of the World*:

FOUND DEAD IN BATH
Bride's Tragic Fate on Day After Wedding

Particularly sad circumstances under which a bride of a day met her death were investigated at an Islington inquest on

Margaret Elizabeth Lloyd, thirty-eight, wife of a land agent of Holloway. The husband said he was married to the deceased at Bath. After travelling to London she complained of headache and giddiness, and he took her to a medical man, who prescribed for her. The following morning she said she felt much better, and during the day she went out shopping. At 7:30 she said she would have a bath, and she then appeared cheerful. A quarter of an hour later, witness went out, and returned at quarter past eight, expecting to see her in the sitting room. As she was not there he inquired of the landlady, and they went to the bathroom, which was in darkness. He lit the gas, and then found his wife under the water, the bath being three parts full. The next day witness found a letter amongst deceased's clothing, but there was nothing in it to suggest that she was likely to take her life.[1]

Reading the paper over a cup of tea, the story struck a jarring chord with Joseph Crossley. The article did not identify the husband, but surely it was the very man whose wife had drowned in the Crossleys' upstairs bathroom thirteen months earlier. Reading of Margaret Lloyd's death in Islington, more than 200 miles away, one may have very well been reading of Alice Smith's drowning in Blackpool. The circumstances were far too alike to be mere coincidence.

So discomfiting were the similarities, Crossley felt compelled to write a letter to Scotland Yard. He detailed the facts surrounding Alice's drowning and said he feared, in light of Margaret Lloyd's death, that George Joseph Smith was responsible. He included with the letter the *News of the World* clipping as well as one he'd saved from the local Blackpool paper about the inquest into Alice Smith's death. He addressed the envelope to Scotland Yard's Criminal Investigation Department and put it in the post. As it so happened, Charles Burnham, Alice Smith's father, did likewise after reading the same article.

Their letters would launch one of the most 'elaborate investigations' in Britain up to that time, spanning more than forty towns and resulting in statements from 150 witnesses.[2]

The letters landed on the desk of Superintendent John McCarthy of the Yard's CID. McCarthy, detecting something sinister in the two drownings, passed the letters on to the senior officer at Kentish Town Police Station, forty-seven-year-old Detective Inspector Arthur Neil of Y (Highgate) Division. It was in Highgate, at a boarding house run by Louisa Blatch at 14, Bismarck Road, that Margaret Lloyd had died. Known as 'Drooper Neil' because of his slumped shoulders, the detective 'wore a permanently lugubrious expression' and 'was almost unknown to smile'. There was little to smile about in his line of work.[3]

'In years of service I am one of the senior living detectives of the Criminal Investigation Department,' Neil, a twenty-seven-year veteran of the force in 1915, wrote when contemplating his career. 'But at the Yard we have always counted not so much by years as by cases.' Neil's casebook catalogued crimes and investigations of all types. He was a man who identified solely with his work. 'I have learned to know the underworld more thoroughly than I know the road in which I live,' he boasted. 'The methods of its master minds are more familiar to me than the way of life of my nearby neighbours.' He enjoyed his reputation in the press as 'a man-hunter' and believed in harsh justice. 'Those I have hunted down so relentlessly were the enemies of society,' he said. 'And the evidence that delivers a murderer into the hands of the public executioner may well be the means of saving innocent lives. For, in my long experience, I have learned that the man who kills and gets away with it will kill again.'[4]

Now, on this January evening in 1915, a motor car from headquarters delivered the dispatch bag with word of two possibly related deaths. 'I was up to my eyes in work,' Neil said. 'The war was at its height, and I was in the thick of interning aliens and other exhaustive and complicated inquiries that needed my attention.'[5]

Indeed, Britain's declaration of war against Germany the previous August had put greater responsibilities on the Yard. 'The whole of the Criminal Investigation Department found its work become [sic] much wider and in a way more complex,' remembered one Yard official. '. . . If I had believed everything I heard in those days I should have had half the foreigners I met – German or not – put under arrest as spies.'[6]

In the opening months of the conflict, the Special Branch (the 'Irish' having been dropped from its title in 1888) conducted roughly 120,000 background checks into suspected spies and saboteurs. The paranoia proved to be just that, as the Yard and British security services arrested no more than thirty German operatives between 1914 and 1918. The scant numbers hardly mattered. In the minds of suspicious officials, 'it only proved how good the saboteurs' cover was.'[7]

Despite the war-mandated workload, Neil thought the story of the drowned brides was too intriguing to hand off to someone else. He would get on it the following day.

Neil started his inquiries at Bismarck Road and questioned Mrs Blatch. She said in the early-evening hours of 7 December 1914, a couple named Mr and Mrs John Lloyd showed up at her place and asked if she had a room to let. 'I had a room to let on the second floor, furnished as a bedroom,' Blatch said. 'I took them up to see it. The price of the room was seven shillings a week with the use of the sitting room.' Deeming the accommodations satisfactory, the Lloyds agreed to the terms.

'Have you got a bath?' Mr Lloyd asked Blatch. The landlady answered in the affirmative and pointed to the bathroom. The couple paid seven shillings for the first week and made partial payment for the week after that. The following morning, Mr Lloyd took breakfast in the sitting room. He told Blatch his wife was not feeling well. When Mrs Lloyd made an appearance later that morning,

Blatch asked her if she felt better. Mr Lloyd spoke for his wife: 'She is very well now except for a little headache.' The couple lunched together in the sitting room and then went out for the afternoon. 'Mrs Lloyd, before she went out,' Blatch recalled, 'asked me if she could have a bath.'

It was dark when the couple returned. 'I provided tea for them,' Blatch said. 'They stayed in for the evening. About half past seven I went to the sitting room and told Mrs Lloyd her bath was ready. I had got the water hot and put towels and soap in the bathroom. I heated the water on the kitchen stove.'

Blatch went into the kitchen to do some ironing and heard someone she assumed to be Mrs Lloyd going up the stairs. 'After that,' she said, 'I heard a sound from the bathroom. It was a sound of splashing. Then there was a noise as of someone putting wet hands or arms on the side of the bath, and then a sigh. The splashing and the hands on the bath occurred at the same time. The sigh was the last I heard.'

'And what happened next?' Neil asked.

'The next sound I heard was someone playing the organ in the sitting room,' she said. 'It was only a few minutes after I heard the last sound in the bathroom that I heard the organ playing.'

Blatch said she recognized the music. It was the hymn 'Nearer My God to Thee'. The mournful tones of the organ droned on for ten minutes and then stopped. The sound of the front door slamming, followed shortly thereafter by the clang of the doorbell, punctuated the silence. Blatch opened the door to find Mr Lloyd on the stoop. 'I forgot I had a key,' he said, holding up a paper bag. 'I have been for some tomatoes for Mrs Lloyd's supper. Is she down yet?'[8]

'I haven't seen her,' Blatch said.

'I'll go up and ask if she would like them.'

Lloyd walked up the stairs, called out his wife's name and received no reply. He stood outside the bathroom door and called again – only to be met with silence. 'My God,' he said, 'there's no answer.'

He opened the bathroom door and cried out in surprise that his wife was unconscious in the bath.

'When I got into the bathroom,' she told Neil, '[he] had Mrs Lloyd in his arms. He was holding her up over the bath. Her legs were in the bath still. I felt her arm, and it was cold.'

Blatch ran from the house and found, no more than fifty yards from her front door, a police constable on patrol in Archway Road. When Blatch and the constable returned to the house, Mr Lloyd was kneeling beside the naked body of his wife in the bathroom doorway. The constable grabbed a dressing gown hanging from the door, covered the woman, and applied chest compressions until the local doctor arrived and pronounced Mrs Lloyd dead.

Neil asked to see the bathtub. Blatch led him upstairs. The bath presented nothing out of the ordinary. In fact, he thought it would be 'a marvel' for someone to drown in it. 'The more I studied it,' he wrote, 'the more I was convinced it was a physical impossibility.'[9]

Neil thanked the landlady for her time and went to the Highgate Police Station. There, he reviewed the station's ledger – also known as 'The Occurrence Book' – and found the name of the constable who went to 14, Bismarck Road on the evening of 18 December: Stanley Heath.[10]

The constable recalled his horror at seeing the poor woman sprawled naked on the floor. 'I turned to the husband,' he told Neil, 'and said, "Get something and cover the poor creature – don't leave her lying like this."'[11]

Heath said the body was cold by the time he arrived; the six inches of water still in the bath was warm. The husband identified the deceased as thirty-eight-year-old Margaret Elizabeth Lloyd. Lloyd himself was described as 'a man about 40, height 5 feet 9½, complexion and build medium, full dark moustache.'[12]

'At once,' reported Neil, 'I tried to get hold of the doctor who had been called, but he was out on his rounds, so I went in search of the undertaker.' Frederick Beckett told Neil the 'bereaved' husband showed no interest in the funeral details and wished to bury his wife in the cheapest way possible. He even haggled 'over the details of brass fixtures' on the budget coffin. 'When they're dead, they're dead!' Lloyd snapped. 'I don't believe in making a fuss over things of this nature.'[13]

Something, in addition to Lloyd's callousness, struck Neil in this early line of inquiry. The description he had of Lloyd matched the description of George Joseph Smith provided by Mr Burnham – Alice Smith's father – in his letter to police: '5 feet 10 inches in height, brown eyes, walks with knees slightly bent together and feet out.' No one who saw Lloyd, however, could 'say whether there was any peculiarity about his legs or feet.' 'The principal point to establish,' Neil wrote in a report dated 19 January 1915, 'is whether or not Lloyd is identical with Smith.' The case, the detective wrote, 'is not without an element of suspicion, having regard to the similarity of the two cases, though both may have been accidental deaths and simply a remarkable coincidence.'[14]

Both drownings, nevertheless, shared enough similarities to arouse suspicion. Those suspicions flared bright when Neil 'started to check back on the date of marriage.' He discovered John Lloyd and Margaret Elizabeth Lofty wed on 17 December 1914, in Bath, meaning 'this bride was found drowned in her bath on the evening of the next day.' Neil passed the word along to other detectives in Y Division, 'requesting if by some chance any of them knew or had come to hear anything about the matter.' He was 'singularly fortunate' that a sergeant named Dennison had information.[15]

Neil learned the day the couple married they took the train from Bath to London and arrived 'with no luggage beyond a hold-all and a Gladstone bag' at a boarding house at 16, Orchard Road, Highgate. Mr Lloyd had booked a room the previous week and made a specific point of inspecting the bath.

'This is a rather small tub,' he told the landlady, Emma Heiss, 'but I dare say it is large enough for someone to lie in.' Satisfied, he paid a six-shilling deposit and said he'd be back in a few days' time. Lloyd left 'so bad an impression' on Heiss that she decided, in the intervening period, not to rent him a room. When Lloyd turned up at six on the evening of 17 December with his new bride, it was Detective Sergeant Dennison who met him at the door. Dennison had helped Heiss deal with 'undesirable lodgers' in the past. The sergeant informed a highly agitated Lloyd he couldn't take a room without a reference.[16]

'Who are you?' Lloyd demanded.

'I'm acting on behalf of the landlady,' Dennison said and returned Lloyd's deposit.

'They don't want us,' Lloyd said to his wife.

The couple, Dennison told Neil, 'departed in a passion.'[17]

The times Dennison provided coincided with the Lloyds' arrival at the house in Bismarck Road, where Margaret died the following night. From Mrs Blatch's boarding house, Neil traced Margaret's movements to the office of a local solicitor, where she drew up a will bequeathing everything to her husband and appointed him sole executor. She also withdrew nearly £20 – all she had – from her savings account at the Muswell Hill Post Office. 'In a space of a few hours,' Neil wrote, 'I found out that all this had happened in one day, 18 December 1914, for at about eight-thirty that evening the constable had been called to her dead body at Bismarck Road.'[18]

Did Margaret take these actions of her own accord, or did her husband put her up to it? From the doctor who tended to Margaret after she was found in the bath, Neil learned the victim had life insurance. This new detail took the investigation to Bristol and the offices of the Yorkshire Insurance Company from which Margaret had secured a £700 policy on 25 November. The company's manager, Thomas Cooper, said a solicitor from London contacted them on 4 January to 'obtain probate of the will' and secure payment on the policy. The solicitor was Walter Davies of 60, Uxbridge Road, Shepherd's Bush.

'I pondered the thing over pretty deeply,' Neil wrote. 'I concentrated upon all the details in my possession. The inquest had been held, and a verdict of accidental death returned. The husband had cleared out of the neighbourhood – where? Also, was this man identical with Smith at Blackpool? If so, how was I to find out? All these things ran through my mind – yet, irrespective of it all, I was convinced he was a murderer. The onus was upon me to prove it.'[19]

He paid a visit to Charles Burnham, Alice's father, in Buckinghamshire. Burnham told the detective Alice was twenty-five when she died and 'had some training as a nurse.' She was working in Southsea, caring for an older gentleman, when she wrote home in October 1913 to say she'd fallen in love with a man named George Smith and planned to marry. The Burnhams invited the couple to spend a weekend at their home, but the visit only fostered a strong dislike between Charles and his daughter's beau. Burnham said Smith was arrogant, claimed to be a man of independent means, and made a point of emphasizing his lack of desire to work. Parrying questions from the family, Smith revealed very little about himself and was a strange, enigmatic presence in their house.

Despite her family's misgivings, Alice married Smith on 13 November 1913, at the Portsmouth Registry Office. Almost immediately, Smith began harassing the Burnhams, asking them to hand over £100 in savings they had in her name. Charles Burnham refused, prompting ever-more threatening letters from his new son-in-law. 'The views and actions which you have been pleased to take towards our marriage are both inconsistent and contemptible,' read one letter. '. . . I remind you that by causing friction broadcast as you have is the greatest mistake in your lifetime.'[20]

Alice was dead less than a month later. It did not surprise Neil to learn that on the day Alice got married, she took out a £500 life-insurance policy and named her new husband the beneficiary.[21]

There was another sinister postscript. On 13 December, Smith sent a letter to Alice's parents detailing his wife's death the day before. He said the inquest would be held early the following week – when, in fact, it was held the day he wrote the letter. Neil briefed

CID superiors and Sir Charles Matthews, director of public prosecutions, on the investigation thus far. Matthews listened with an incredulous expression as Neil detailed Alice's drowning in Blackpool, Margaret's fatal bath in London, and the similarities between John Lloyd and George Joseph Smith.

'But, Neil,' Matthews exclaimed, 'the idea's preposterous. A verdict of accidental death returned at Blackpool, and the same thing in London. Why, in the face of it, the thing – legally – is impossible.'

'Nevertheless, sir, with all due respect, I'm convinced it's planned, deliberate murder,' Neil said. 'If I can get Smith, or George Joseph Smith, identified as John Lloyd, I'll hold him for perjury.'

The whole thing to Matthews bordered on insanity.

'I cannot for the moment associate myself with your views that he is to be identified as one and the same man,' he told the detective. 'It's incredible to me that a man could murder two women by drowning them in a bath. I have never heard of such a thing during the whole of my lifelong experience.'[22]

The prosecutor nevertheless authorized Neil to investigate further.

Neil had to lure Lloyd into the open. He asked the Yorkshire Insurance Company to approve payout on Margaret's life insurance policy and approached Lloyd's solicitor, Walter Davies, for help. This was not without risk, lest Davies tell Lloyd – but the solicitor agreed to help and provided Lloyd's address at 14, Richmond Road, Shepherd's Bush.

'The address,' Neil subsequently noted, 'is merely an accommodation one as Lloyd has only slept there a few nights.' No one in the building could tell Neil anything worthwhile. Indeed, Lloyd was an enigma. 'Nothing is known of who or what he is,' Neil wrote in a case report. '. . . To my mind this man has no regular employment and I am of the opinion that he has been obtaining his living by victimizing women.'[23]

With no other options available, Neil took a room above The Telegraph pub in January 1915, opposite Davies's office in Uxbridge

Road, and waited for Lloyd to claim his insurance check. Among the stakeout team was Constable Stanley Heath, who knew Lloyd by sight. It was a bitterly cold month, even by London standards, with temperatures dropping as low as ten degrees. 'My chaps used to take it in relays,' Neil wrote, 'two watching from the outside, and two from the warmth of the room by the window.' It proved very much an endurance test, a struggle against the biting cold and the monotony of the wait. Lloyd would appear to collect his spoils at some point; of this, Neil had no doubt.[24]

It happened on 1 February. It was 12:30 p.m. when Neil spotted, through the window, a man approaching the office – 'a man who, although I had never put eyes on him before, I knew to be the murderer from the description I had obtained.' In the street outside the pub, Constable Heath and Sergeant Harold Reed dabbed at their noses with handkerchiefs, the pre-arranged signal to confirm it was indeed Lloyd. Neil hurried down to the street with Sergeant Frank Page at his side. He ordered Page to stay close and warned the others to be ready in the event Lloyd was armed. 'It was wartime, and all sorts of funny things were happening in regard to firearms,' Neil wrote. 'Besides, I was taking no risks.'[25]

Lloyd went into the solicitor's office and emerged an hour later. He raised his collar against the cold and lit a cigarette in the doorway. Neil and Page crossed the street and approached him. It struck Neil that his quarry 'was not dressed in mourning.'[26]

'I am Detective-Inspector Neil, London Metropolitan Police. Are you John Lloyd?'

'Yes,' said Lloyd, exhaling a lungful of smoke, 'I am.'

'The same John Lloyd whose wife drowned in a bath on the night of December eighteenth last, at Bismarck Road, Highgate?'

'Yes, that's me!'

'From my investigations, I have reason to believe you are identical to George Smith, whose wife was found drowned in a bath three weeks after marriage in 1913, at Blackpool. You married Miss Lofty, your last bride, at Bath, Bristol in the name of Lloyd.'

'Yes,' said Lloyd, growing impatient, 'that is so, but that does not prove that my name is Smith. Smith! I don't know the name Smith – my name's not Smith.'[27]

'I shall detain you and send for witnesses,' Neil said. 'If you are identified you will be charged with causing a false entry to be made in the marriage register at Bath.'

At this, the threat of witnesses, Lloyd confessed to being George Smith.

'The entry in the register is not correct,' he said, 'but that is the only charge you can put against me.'

When Neil said other charges might be pending, Smith's guard slipped again.

'Well,' he said, 'I must admit the two deaths form a phenomenal coincidence, but that is my hard luck.'[28]

Smith was taken to Kentish Town Police Station and put in a line-up. Charles Burnham, when called in to review the identity parade, seemed unsure of himself. He stopped in front of Smith and stared at him for several moments. Smith's patience collapsed under Burnham's quizzical gaze.

'I am Smith. He knows me,' he shouted. 'What is the good of fooling about?'[29]

The challenge now lay in securing a murder charge. 'It was not before the 23rd March that my job was completed,' Neil wrote, 'a period during which I and my officers were practically kept on the go night and day all over the country.' Neil had already brought Bernard Spilsbury 'the great pathologist' into the case.[30]

Since the Crippen investigation, Spilsbury had maintained an ongoing presence in the headlines thanks to a high-profile caseload and his appointment as Home Office Pathologist – 'an association that would survive two world wars and last almost four decades.' In 1912, his trial testimony helped send infamous landlord Frederick Seddon to the gallows for the fatal arsenic poisoning of a financially flushed tenant.[31]

Spilsbury's no-nonsense persona held the public under a spell.

'The personality and good looks of the young pathologist,' notes one biography, 'his precise and extremely lucid manner of giving evidence, and his refusal to be awed by anybody captured the popular fancy.'[32]

The Brides investigation only enhanced his prestige.

On the day of Smith's arrest, Spilsbury and an excavation crew arrived at Finchley Cemetery to exhume Margaret Lofty's body. It was taken by hearse to 'a quiet little spot in Summer's Lane, Friern Barnet,' to escape publicity, as the press had started picking up on the story. Spilsbury's examination revealed nothing out of the ordinary. Margaret appeared to have been 'a well-nourished, spare woman.' She had three small bruises on the back of her left arm. 'I formed the opinion,' Spilsbury said, 'that they had been caused before death.' Internally, the organs showed no signs of distress or disease. There was nothing to indicate that Margaret had died from anything other than natural causes.[33]

Eight nights later, in the glow of lanterns, Neil and Spilsbury stood alongside Alice Burnham's open grave in Blackpool as labourers hauled the coffin up. Reporters by now smelled something tantalizing. 'THE DROWNED BRIDES: EXHUMATION OF A BODY AT BLACKPOOL,' screamed a headline in London's *The Evening Mail* on 12 February. *The Globe* ran with 'SECOND EXHUMATION: FIRST OF BRIDES FOUND DEAD IN BATH.' Similar declarations occupied real estate in papers across the country. All the press knew at present was that two women, married to one George Joseph Smith, had drowned in the bath. Beyond that dark coincidence they had nothing to report. Neil took it in stride. 'I admire the English Press reporter, if for nothing else but his tenacity of purpose,' he wrote. 'Many of them, to my way of thinking, are, in experience, as good as the next best Yard man any time, in regard to getting down to rock-bottom facts.'[34]

If Neil hoped Alice Burnham's body might provide rock-bottom facts relevant to a murder charge, he was disappointed. The remains, 'in an advanced stage of decomposition,' offered

Spilsbury little to work with. 'Dirty foul smelling water' had seeped into the coffin. Bits of flesh from Alice's legs and feet floated in the filthy muck. Her face had rotted beyond recognition. Alice, in life, had been a large and pretty woman. 'She was big bodied from the shoulders and around the hips,' Spilsbury noted, 'and the hips were tightly wedged in the coffin.' Most of the internal organs had liquefied into gloop. 'The brain was very decomposed,' Spilsbury observed. 'I do not think there was any haemorrhage. The heart was also decomposed. I was able to discover and examine some of the arteries. They appeared healthy. I was not able to distinguish the lungs.' In short, the pathologist found nothing to indicate a malevolent cause of death.[35]

While in Blackpool, Neil received word of another possible victim. Superintendent Heard of the Kent Constabulary reached out to Scotland Yard for a description of George Smith. The newspaper stories of drowned brides and exhumations brought to Heard's mind an incident that occurred in Herne Bay on 13 July 1912. On that day, a woman named Beatrice 'Bessie' Williams, nee Mundy, drowned in the bathtub of a home she rented with her husband Henry. Something about the case – perhaps Henry Williams's callous response to his wife's death – always struck the superintendent as odd. 'I should be glad if you would forward me a photo of "Lloyd" so that I may make enquiries,' Heard wrote.[36]

The Yard sent Heard a photo. Henry Williams had been clean-shaven, unlike the moustachioed Smith, a.k.a. Lloyd, but Heard thought the two men shared a passing resemblance. He shared the picture with Williams's solicitor and the couple who had lived next door to Henry and Bessie. All agreed it could be the same man. On 15 February 1915, they travelled to London at the Yard's request to view a line-up and identified Smith as the man they knew as Henry Williams. 'This bit of news,' Neil wrote, 'was like a tonic.'[37]

Never before had he encountered a killer of such cunning. 'This man's methods were entirely unknown to any records of authentic criminology,' Neil wrote. 'Neither European nor American police archives could point to such a crime.' And so the investigation now pulled Herne Bay into its ever-expanding orbit. Neil arrived in the seaside town at nightfall on 18 February 1915, to oversee the exhumation of Bessie Mundy. 'It was war time,' he wrote, 'and all around the place was barbed wire and fortifications of every description, and our journey to the particular shed where the examination was to take place was made extremely difficult in the dark . . . The military officials were very touchy at this period about lights of any description owing to the hostile enemy aircraft that visited London via the mouth of the Thames.'[38]

The exhumation was already underway in darkness when Neil arrived at the gravesite:

By the time we came on the scene they had reached the coffin. Unfortunately the grave had become waterlogged, and when near the top, all our united efforts at the webbings seemed to make no difference in getting the coffin from the grave. At last it was decided to pull the coffin out from the tight embrace of its narrow top, a fact due to miscalculation by the broad end, I standing straddle-legged across the grave and pulling with my whole might. Suddenly it came out, almost up-end, and had the coffin not struck me to the side in its sudden release, I should have been precipitated into that fifteen foot dark water-filled grave.[39]

Spilsbury studied the remains the next day. Although the body was in an advanced state of decay, it did – unlike the others – yield one interesting clue. 'About the thighs and abdomen,' Spilsbury noted, 'there was a condition of the skin known as goose skin. That condition occurs in some cases of sudden death, and perhaps more frequently in sudden death from drowning. It is a sort of

corrugating of the surface, a roughness of the surface.' Known sci-
entifically as *cutis anserina*, goose skin 'is caused by rigor mortis
in the erector pilae muscles of the dermis with the skin adopting a
pimpled appearance similar to that of goose bumps'.[40]

The Herne Bay investigation revealed Bessie was thirty-three
when she married Henry Williams – 'a picture restorer' – on
26 1 August910, after only several days of courting. She came into
the marriage with a nice nest egg, having inherited £2,500 (about
£355,000 or $452,000 today) when her father passed away. This
was paid out to her in a monthly allowance.[41] Not long after they
married, Williams stole Bessie's accumulated savings, accused her
of passing along a venereal disease and abandoned her. He left in
his wake a detestable letter:

> Dearest – I fear you have blighted all my bright hopes of a
> happy future. I have caught from you a disease, which is called
> the bad disorder. For you to be in such a state proves you
> could not keep yourself morally clean . . . I don't wish to say
> you have had connections with another man and caught it
> from him. But it is either that or through not keeping yourself
> clean.

From baseless accusation, the letter transitioned into blackmail. He said he was going to London to seek a cure; something
that might take years and 'cost me a great deal of money'. And
he had no intention of covering the cost himself. He told Bessie
to inform her family that the money she received from the trust
established by her father had been kept in a leather bag, which
had recently been stolen. 'If you will not carry out every word of
my advice,' he wrote, 'you will cause a lot of trouble and the whole
affair will be in the Police Court and you will bring disgrace on
yourself and relations.'[42]

Despite this scorched-earth approach, the couple unbeliev-
ably reconciled eighteen months later when Bessie, holidaying in

Weston-super-Mare, spotted Williams on the beach 'looking over the sea'. From such an ill-advised reunion, Bessie blazed the dark path soon to be followed by Alice Burnham and Margaret Lofty. The couple moved into a house at 80, High Street, Herne Bay. On 8 July 1913, Williams had Bessie make out a will that named him the sole beneficiary. The next day, he purchased a bath.[43]

Adolphus Hill, an ironmonger who sold his wares in a shop, said Williams came into his store to inquire about a second-hand bath. 'He asked me the price, and I said it was £2,' Hill told detectives. 'His wife came in a day or two later and offered 37s. 6d., which I accepted. The bath was delivered about 9 July.' Police took possession of the bath, as they had done with the tubs in Blackpool and Highgate, and had it shipped to London.

In the days leading up to Bessie's death, Williams took her to a local doctor named French and said his wife had recently suffered a 'fit'. Bessie didn't argue the point, and French saw no reason to doubt Williams's story. The doctor prescribed a sedative. On Thursday, 12 July, Williams summoned French to the house in High Street. The doctor found Bessie in bed, seemingly in perfect health. Williams said she'd suffered another seizure. Again, Bessie did not refute the claim. French prescribed another sedative and bid them good day. That night, Bessie wrote her uncle a letter:

Last Tuesday night I had a bad fit, and one again on Thursday night. It has left me weak and suffering from nerves and headache, and has evidently shaken my whole system. My husband has been extremely kind and done all he could for me. He has provided me with the attention of the best medical men here, who are constantly giving me medical treatment, and visiting me day and night.[44]

The letter had the air of forced dictation with its effusive praise for Williams and exaggerations about medical treatment. Background checks on the dozen doctors practising in Herne Bay in July

1913 revealed French 'was the most recently qualified'. The next day, Saturday, 13 July, Bessie died while taking a bath.[45]

French received an urgent summons from Williams at eight o'clock that morning: 'Can you come at once? I'm afraid my wife is dead.' The doctor hurried to the house and let himself in. Upstairs, he found Bessie submerged in the tub. 'The face was upwards,' he said, 'the trunk at the sloping end, the feet out of the water resting on the side of the bath a little below the edge. The position of the body kept the legs from slipping down. The head was submerged and the trunk partially so. The mouth was underwater; her arms rested by her side. The right hand contained a piece of soap. The bath was just over three parts full.'[46]

French confirmed Bessie was dead, helped move the body into a bedroom and notified the police. Constable Jonathan Kitchingham arrived at ten-thirty. He observed the body and 'found no indications of violence at all'. Williams told the officer he and Bessie 'got up together at 7:30 a.m. that morning, and he went out to get some fish. He returned about eight o'clock, unlocked the door, went into the dining room and called to his wife.' Met with only silence, he checked several rooms before heading to the upstairs bedroom where they kept the tub and found Bessie underwater.

Nothing about the story aroused suspicion. The coroner, seeing no reason for investigation, held the inquest Monday afternoon with French and Williams as the only witnesses to testify. The jury returned a verdict of 'misadventure by a fit in the bath'. Bessie's family thought otherwise and requested a full post-mortem. No such examination took place. She was buried on the afternoon of Tuesday, 16 July. That same morning, Williams visited his landlord's office to cancel his lease. He put on quite a show and sobbed over his loss. 'Was it not a jolly good job,' he said, 'I got her to make a will?'[47]

*

Back in London, at the Kentish Town Police Station, Neil reviewed an ever-growing mountain of evidence. Every case report and finding had to cross Neil's desk before it could be sent to the director of public prosecutions. Wrote the detective:

> When I add that over two thousand statements were taken, the most ever known to any criminal case in this country, it will give you an idea of the stupendous task I had on hand. I had over one hundred and fifty witnesses ready . . . The banks I went to in tracing the three money transactions taken from Miss Mundy, Miss Burnham and Miss Lofty, alone entailed a tremendous task. I could fill a book on that part of my investigation alone.[48]

There was no doubt Smith killed his three brides, yet – short of a stunning series of coincidences – Neil lacked definitive proof. In every case, Smith had been the last one to see the victim alive, was conveniently out on some errand at the time of their death and always discovered the body when he returned. Without exception, the families of all three victims immediately disliked Smith upon meeting him. The inquests in all three cases had occurred quickly and prevented grieving loved ones from attending. And yet the investigation had more surprises in store. Press coverage of the drowned brides and a picture of Smith published in the papers brought forward two more women. Alice Reavil said she'd married Smith on 17 September 1914 after a ten-day courtship. Edith Pegler said she was Smith's current wife and had been married to him for seven years.[49]

Alice described her marriage as short and disastrous. Five days after exchanging vows, Smith plundered Alice's bank account and left her with nothing. 'I was left with only a few shillings and the clothes I was actually wearing,' she said. 'What he had taken consisted of the whole of my life's savings.'[50]

This raised more questions, for Smith married Alice Reavil nine months after Alice Burnham's death and three months before

Margaret Lofty's fatal bath. Why did Reavil not share the same fate? Just as mystifying was Smith's marriage to Edith, whom he wed in July 1908 after she started working for him as a housekeeper. She believed him to be an antiques dealer who frequently travelled on business. He always returned from these supposed trips flushed with cash – and he made sure Edith never asked too many questions. 'He remarked to me,' she said, 'that if I interfered with his business I should never have another happy day, as the world was wide and he would forfeit it all.'[51]

She last saw him just before Christmas 1914. 'We were living in apartments at 10, Kennington Avenue, Bristol, and I said I was going to have a bath,' she recalled. 'He said, "In that bath there?" – pointing to the bathroom – "I should advise you to be careful of those things, as it is known that women often lose their lives through weak hearts and fainting in a bath."' He left shortly thereafter on another business trip but never returned. Now, horrified, she knew why.[52]

Investigating the jumbled and twisted pieces of Smith's background, Neil made another alarming discovery. In January 1898, under the alias George Oliver Love, Smith married Caroline Thornhill. Police traced Caroline to Canada, where they convinced her to return to England and help the Yard with its inquiry. Her story revealed George Joseph Smith in his depraved totality.[53]

The son of an insurance agent, Smith was born in January 1872 and showed a criminal bent from an early age. He frequently got in trouble as a child and wound up in a reformatory at the age of nine. Seven years of fierce discipline and frequent lashings with 'the birch and the cane' did nothing to set the boy straight. Upon his release, he reverted back to his old ways and was soon doing six months hard labour for stealing a bicycle. He later told Caroline that he joined the army after serving his sentence and did three years in the Northamptonshire Regiment, but Neil attached 'little importance to this supposed devotion to [duty]'. Following another stint in prison in 1896, this time for larceny, Smith opened a bakery in Leicester. It was there in December 1897 that he and Caroline met. He was twenty-six and she was eighteen when they married several weeks later.[54]

The bakery soon went under, leaving the couple desperate for money. He convinced her to find work as a housekeeper and steal from her employers, one of whom was a clergyman. The couple bounced around, living off stolen money and jewels, until Caroline was arrested in Hastings for theft and sent away for three months. Smith didn't stick around and made a quick getaway.[55]

On 5 November 1900, a year after her release, Caroline spotted Smith window-shopping on Oxford Street. 'I called to a policeman and gave him into custody,' she said. 'He abused me very much and said he would punch my head off if he could only get at me.' She took some satisfaction in his two-year prison sentence but fled to Canada to be free of him once and for all.[56]

While the police navigated the complex maze of Smith's personal life, Spilsbury sought the definitive cause of death for Bessie Mundy, Alice Burnham and Margaret Lofty. All three tubs now sat in a storage room at the Kentish Town Police Station, and it was here Spilsbury pondered the mystery. He focused his efforts on Bessie's demise, as the coroner's inquest had ruled epilepsy played a role – something Spilsbury thought unlikely. There was no history of epilepsy in Bessie's family, nor had she ever had a seizure up until the day she died. The pathologist, however, despite his doubts, was not yet ready to rule out the possibility of a fit.[57]

Spilsbury told Neil an epileptic seizure fell into three distinct phases. 'Firstly, the state of complete rigidity of the body, which is called the tonic stage, and which lasts for only a few seconds,' he said. 'Secondly, the stage where there are movements of the . . . face and the trunk. That is called the clonic stage, and usually lasts perhaps for one or two minutes; and thirdly, the last stage of exhaustion, generally accompanied by unconsciousness . . . the complete effects of which may not pass off for several hours.'[58]

Five-feet-seven-inches-tall Bessie had died in a tub five feet long. 'The head end of this bath is sloping,' Spilsbury pointed out, 'and if her feet were against the narrow end when the body was rigid, it would tend to thrust the head up out of the bath.'

During the clonic stage, the legs and arms contract towards the body and then extend rapidly.

'I do not think such a woman would get her head submerged during the second stage of an epileptic seizure, because the trunk, especially the lower part, would be resting on the bottom of the bath, and the body would therefore not be likely to move as a whole down towards the foot end.'

If Bessie did have a seizure, she would have lapsed afterwards into unconsciousness. 'Bearing in mind the length of the body and the size of the bath,' Spilsbury said, 'I do not think she would be likely to be immersed during the stage of relaxation.' The bottom of the tub and its sloping end 'would support the upper part of the trunk and head.'

Even if Bessie had fainted in the tub, it's unlikely she would have drowned.

'In the case of a person taking a bath sitting in the ordinary position and having a faint, the body, becoming limp, would fall back against the sloping back of the bath,' Spilsbury explained. 'If water were then taken in through the mouth or nose it would have a marked stimulating effect and would probably recover the person.'

The pathologist, exploring all angles, took it one step further.

'There is no position in which a person could easily become submerged in fainting,' he said. 'A person standing or kneeling while taking a bath might fall forward on the face and then might easily be drowned. Then the body would be lying face downwards in the water.'

Bessie was lying face-up. The soap found clutched in her right hand was indicative of sudden death – but what had happened? Dr French, who saw Bessie's body in the tub, told investigators both her legs were extended straight out with her feet resting against the end of the bath just below the edge.

'I cannot give any explanation,' Spilsbury said, 'of how a woman – assuming she had an epileptic seizure – could get into that position by herself.'[59]

And, maybe, therein lay the answer. She didn't end up in that position by herself. Supposing someone grabbed her by the ankles without warning, yanked them upwards and pulled her head underwater? Would that cause sudden death?

There was one way to find out. Inspector Neil tells the story:

I obtained the assistance of a very fine lady swimmer, and one used to diving, plunging and swimming from early girl-hood. The baths were filled and in each one demonstrations were given by this young lady in a swimming costume in many positions.

Two demonstrations took place with the young lady swimmer, one in the bath at full length, pressed down by the forehead. In this position, although helpless, the arms can be thrown out to clutch the sides of the bath. Nevertheless, a strong pressure on the forehead would occasion suffocation and insensibility within a few seconds. On the other hand, a demonstration by myself and sergeants on her, nearly proved fatal.

It was decided to test sudden immersion, so, from the ankle, I lifted up her legs very suddenly. She slipped under easily, but to me, who was closely watching, she seemed to make no movement.

Suddenly I gripped her arm, it was limp. With a shout I tugged at her arm-pit and raised her head above the water. It fell over to one side. She was unconscious. For nearly half an hour my detectives and I worked away at her with artificial respiration and restoratives. Things began to look serious, then a quick change began to take place, and her pretty face began to take on the natural bloom of young, healthy womanhood. It had all given us a turn, so practical demonstrations in baths were from that moment promptly discontinued. She told us afterwards that immediately she went under the water with her legs up in the air, the water just rushed into her mouth and up her nostrils. That was all she knew, as she remembered no more until she came to and saw all our anxious faces bending over her.[60]

On Tuesday, 23 March 1915, George Joseph Smith appeared in Bow Street Police Court to have the charge against him amended. 'With every fresh hearing of the case,' reported *The London Weekly Dispatch*, 'some new startling development takes place. The latest is that Smith, originally charged with making a false entry of his marriage at Bath, is now accused of the murder of Beatrice Constance Mundy, Alice Burnham and Margaret Elizabeth Lofty, all of whom were drowned in baths.'[61]

Archibald Bodkin appeared on behalf of the director of public prosecutions. Noted the *Dispatch*:

> 'Remarkable!'
> That was the word which Mr Bodkin, least emotional and most judicially severe of counsel was restrained to use again and again during his opening statement at the latest hearing at Bow-street of the 'Brides in the Bath' case. It was the mildest word applicable to the story he told of the alleged doings of George Joseph Smith, up again on remand.[62]

It took Bodkin nearly three and a half hours to summarize the case. 'He is estimated to have spoken 11,600 words,' according to one reporter's tally, 'and even then not all the alleged marriages were dealt with.' He detailed for the court 'the skill with which sudden and silent death was dealt out to the three women'. He characterized Smith as a brazen, daring killer willing to face a coroner's inquest and the risk of exposure after each drowning. He had made nearly £3,000 off Alice Burnham and Bessie Mundy, and would have made £700 from Margaret Lofty had he not been arrested.

The case, Bodkin stated, was many things, including a crass violation against the character and modesty of women. 'In each of the three cases the woman is going to have a bath, she undresses, is naked, and leaves the door unfastened,' he said. 'Anyone who knows anything about the character of a woman would indeed require to be satisfied that that was accidental; that three wives, in three houses, are going to take three baths and each die in that bath and the door unfastened.'[63]

Neil watched with rightful satisfaction as Smith listened to the case against him. 'I studied him for a moment,' Neil later wrote. 'To this day it has always been a poser to me what women could see in a man of this type. Sallow complexion, bad features, a big sensual mouth, in fact, the sort of fellow a decent man would at once shun as unlikeable.'[64]

Even under such circumstances, Smith maintained his powerful and inexplicable hold over women, as *The Dispatch* observed:

There have been few cases in recent years which have made such an appeal to neurotic, morbid women as this triple murder charge. Every time Smith has been brought up the court has been crowded by women who have not minded from eight o'clock in the morning in a queue formed just like a first night queue at a theatre in order to obtain admittance.

Some of the women never missed a single sitting, and it is to be presumed that they will make desperate efforts to be present at the Old Bailey, assuming the grand jury finds a true bill.[65]

The jury indeed returned a true bill against Smith, and he was committed to trial at the Central Criminal Court for the murder of Bessie Mundy. The proceedings there began on 22 June 1915. The eight-day trial set a record for 264 exhibits and the testimony of 112 witnesses. [66]

Spilsbury, over the course of two days, detailed for the riveted jury the findings of his medical investigation. The soap found in Bessie Mundy's hand underscored his sudden-death theory. Had she suffered a fit, as the defence argued, Bessie would have let go of the soap 'in the third or exhaustion phase'; if she'd merely fainted and slid under the water, her muscles would have relaxed and released the soap. Instead, Spilsbury testified, she had most likely been pulled under. The sudden immersion and violent intake of water into her nose and lungs caused near-immediate death. Her muscles, shocked into contraction, could possibly 'pass instantaneously to the death-stiffening and the [soap] might be retained after death.'[67]

Spilsbury's work on the case bestowed upon him a god-like reverence in matters of science. As Jane Robins writes in her case history, '... his pronouncements were treated as though they came from a great height. Due deference was paid to the medical man, to the scientist, and the public was delighted by the ingeniousness of his Holmesian deductions.'[68]

The case went to the jury on 1 July. During Justice Scrutton's summation, Smith vented his disgust with the legal proceedings. 'This is a disgrace to a Christian nation, this,' he blurted. The judge, ignoring the outburst, continued addressing the jury, which only stoked Smith's outrage. 'You may as well hang me at once, the way you're going on,' he said, leaping from his chair. 'Sentence me and have done with it. You can go on forever,' he said in a petulant tone. 'You cannot make me into a murderer. I've done no murder. You are telling the jury I murdered the woman.'[69]

The jury deliberated for twenty minutes before returning the guilty verdict. 'A murmur expressive of intense relief, almost of applause,' noted one observer, 'ran round the court.'[70]

Asked if he had anything to say, Smith – standing between two warders – mustered a weak rebuttal. 'I can only say I am not guilty.'

The court chaplain placed the dreaded black cap upon the judge's head. 'George Joseph Smith,' Scrutton said, 'the jury, after a careful and patient hearing, have found you guilty of the murder of Bessie Constance Annie Mundy. In doing so, they must have taken an unfavourable view of your relations to Alice Burnham and to Margaret Lofty. They have found you guilty of a cold-blooded and heartless murder, and in that verdict I entirely agree.'

Smith stood motionless, his hands gripping the railing of the dock, as Scrutton formally sentenced him to be 'hanged by the neck until you are dead'.[71]

'Thus, with a pitiful display of bravado and venomous glances directed at the detectives engaged in the case, Smith received the last dread sentence of the law,' the *Daily Mirror* reported. 'The scene was a terrible one, and everyone sighed with relief when it was all over and that sinister figure had disappeared from the dock.'[72]

Three days after the verdict, Madame Tussauds placed the following advertisement in London's papers:

MADAME TUSSAUDS EXHIBITION.
The Brides' Case
Lifelike Portrait Model of
GEORGE JOSEPH SMITH[73]

Smith, unrepentant to the end, went to the gallows at Maidstone Gaol on the morning of Friday, 13 August 1915. 'I am innocent of this crime!' he yelled as hangman John Ellis pulled him onto the trapdoor. The executioner, ignoring the protestations, went about his grim business and pulled the white hood over Smith's head.

'I am innocent!' Smith cried through the fabric. Ellis pulled the lever and dispatched Smith on his fatal plunge. 'Forty-six seconds after leaving his cell,' Ellis later wrote, 'Smith, the Brides Bath Murderer, was dead.'[74]

The body hanged for the requisite hour before being cut down. Detective Inspector Arthur Neil signed the death certificate.

News of Smith's hanging shared column space in one paper with the following announcement: 'It is suggested that all men whose teeth are defective, but who refuse dental treatment, to be passed as "fit" for service with the Expeditionary Force, provided they are not suffering from malnutrition or digestive trouble, and are otherwise medically fit.'[75]

There was, after all, a war on.

16

War Crimes

Air raids and murder. The Flying Squad.

Wartime demands put a strain on Scotland Yard. Although, in the words of one detective, 'large numbers of the criminal classes were drawn into the fighting services,' the same could be said for police officers. The war pulled 3,000 men – 'the equivalent of several divisions' – into its bloody maw. To make up the shortfall, the Yard relied on Special Constables. Enabled under the Special Constables Act of 1831, these volunteer officers supported the regular uniformed police in times of emergency. Special Constables had been a 'temporary improvization' in times of unrest. The outbreak of war and the resulting Metropolitan Special Constabulary, however, made them a permanent fixture. 'After returning from work,' notes one Yard history, 'scores of public spirited men leave their homes again to do voluntary duty as policemen, wearing uniforms scarcely indistinguishable from that of the regular force, except that all ranks wear a peaked cap instead of a helmet.'[1]

Women also played a pivotal role, much to the shock 'of those who were elderly when the war began.' They initially volunteered to help process the flood of refugees from the continent but had no official police powers. From these efforts emerged the non-uniformed Women Police Special Patrols, comprised of members from several philanthropic groups – the primary one being the National Council of Women (NCW). Although not officially tied to Scotland Yard, it served a moral mandate by patrolling streets, parks and areas around military camps to combat public drunkenness, prostitution and to prevent sexual escapades between soldiers and impressionable girls.[2]

Its efforts earned a clause in the Police Act of 1916, allowing 'women to be employed on policing duties'. Granted, they still had no official powers and were not employed by the Yard. On patrol they worked in pairs with a policeman following close behind in case an arrest had to be made. Their duties soon included patrolling underground stations during air raids – but not until 1919 would female officers be 'directly employed by and directly under the orders of Scotland Yard'.[3]

Incendiaries and high explosives battered British cities throughout the war, first by Zeppelins and then long-range heavy bombers called Gothas. The deadliest attack on London occurred on 13 June 1917, killing 162 people and injuring more than 400. 'Some of the bodies had been mutilated beyond recognition,' noted one city coroner, 'and in many cases it was only by marks on handkerchiefs or other articles of clothing that relatives were able to identify hesitatingly their loved ones.' One bomb fell through the roof of the Upper North Street School in Poplar and killed eighteen children. 'It really is murder,' a coroner declared. One London paper described the horror as 'little children being sacrificed here to the Kaiser's hatred of England.' Scotland Yard suffered its own loss in the death of Constable Alfred Smith, killed by a blast as he tried to usher to safety a crowd of factory workers – mostly women and girls – who had come outside to watch the raid.[4]

German bombs killed 1,413 Britons and injured more than 3,000 during the war – small numbers when compared to the Blitz, but nevertheless shocking in their time. Amid this carnage, Londoners 'had their minds taken off more wholesale slaughter by the murder' of a woman, whose death came to light in the smouldering wake of an incendiary raid.[5]

*

Thomas Henry, an inventory clerk, left for work at eight-thirty on the morning of Friday, 2 November 1917. He lived in one of the 'dingy' four-storey houses in Bloomsbury's Regent Square. The houses surrounded a small rectangular garden with 'a few tall plane trees and a shrubbery border' enclosed in a wrought-iron fence about five feet high. As Henry strolled along the footpath on the garden's south side, he noticed a 'bulky parcel' lying in the bushes just beyond the fence, 'as though it had been lifted over and dropped'.[6]

Henry knelt down, reached through the bars and jostled the package. It had considerable heft. 'I thought, at first impression, it was half of a sheep,' Henry said. He jumped the fence for a closer look. The outer layer of wrapping, a sack, was tied with string. He cut through the binding, peered inside the sack and saw something swaddled in bed sheets. Moving the sheets aside, he 'saw the shoulders of a human body'. Horrified, he just had time to register the missing arms, legs and head, and the chemise draped across the chest. He staggered backwards and saw, about a yard away, another sack-wrapped parcel. Compelled by ghoulish curiosity, he opened this second bundle and discovered the missing legs.[7]

Police converged on the scene within half an hour. Divisional police surgeon Dr John Rees Gabe, with a local detective inspector watching over his shoulder, was the first to examine the chopped-up anatomy. 'The remains were those of a woman about thirty years of age, well-nourished, some 4ft 11in in height,' Gabe said. 'There was no sign of disease. She had apparently been dead about twenty-four hours.' The killer dumped the remains in the darkest part of the square away from the streetlamps. It had rained heavily until 4:30 that morning. The wrappings were damp, but not wet, meaning the parcels had been left after the rain stopped. Residents in the surrounding houses told police the square was generally deserted between midnight and six in the morning.[8]

The lack of blood at the scene indicated the murder had happened elsewhere – most likely in a nearby home. 'It would be impossible,' Gabe theorized, 'even on a dark, wet night to carry such a burden far without detection.' The killer had dismembered the body 'with a sharp instrument, possibly a butcher's knife'. Gabe motioned the detective in to have a closer look. The cuts looked clean with no jagged edges, suggesting a strong and skilled hand. Gabe speculated the killer was most likely a butcher or a doctor. The knees had been severed 'through the middle of the joint', cutting through the ligament to avoid the bone. The wrists had been removed in a similar fashion, the blade skilfully 'passing through the place where it was easiest for one who was used to disjointing limbs.' That the sack used to wrap the trunk bore the unfortunate label 'La Plata Cold Storage, Argentina' lent additional credence to the butcher theory.[9]

In addition to the chemise, fringed in lace, the torso was draped in a vest. Beneath it, Gabe found a brown paper bag, folded across the middle, resting on the woman's abdomen. Unfolding it revealed, in angular handwriting, the message: 'BLODIE BELGIM', a misspelling of 'Bloody Belgium'. Since the war's outbreak, more than 200,000 Belgians had fled their shattered homeland and settled in Britain, 'the largest single influx' of refugees in British history. Many of the houses in Regent Square, sub-leased as flats, were home to displaced Belgians. Was this a xenophobic crime? The sheet wrapped around the torso bore the laundry mark '11 H' stitched in red cotton and underlined. Commercial laundries used such markings to specify how an article of clothing or linen should be cleaned and handled. Specific to the laundry they came from, such markings proved 'an invaluable source of identification for police forces'.[10]

Although Regent Square lay within the boundaries of E (Holborn) Division, the murder could have occurred outside the division's territory. For this reason, Senior Chief Inspector Fred Wensley of the CID assumed overall charge of the investigation. An officer of vast experience, Wensley joined the Metropolitan Police in 1888. Like many of his contemporaries, he worked a tough apprenticeship patrolling the night-time slums of Whitechapel during the Ripper killings. It was, in Wensley's words, 'the finest training ground imaginable' for a young policeman: 'Men and women ripe for any crime were to be found in its crowded slums and innumerable common lodging houses,' he wrote '. . . Organized gangs of desperate men and lads, armed with lethal weapons, infested the streets, terrorizing whole areas . . . carrying out more or less open robbery in any direction that offered.' Murder was not uncommon, with bodies 'frequently found in the streets, often near disreputable houses'. Such conditions allowed Wensley the opportunity to watch detectives ply their trade. He joined their ranks in October 1895 with his appointment to the CID.[11]

'The more I saw of detective work, the more it fascinated me,' he recalled in later years. 'There was about it an infinite variety that attracted me more than any sport or entertainment. Brain and body were constantly on alert. I was out at all hours of the night and day, winter and summer alike.' A one-time teetotaller, he took up drinking, 'as no informant would trust a policeman who refused a drink with them.' He received the King's Police Medal in 1909 for 'distinguished service'. Two years later, he won praise for carrying a seriously wounded colleague to safety under fire during the Siege of Sidney Street. Another exploit found him wrestling 'with an armed murderer on a housetop. He brought his man to the ground – and to the gallows.'[12]

He made Chief Inspector in 1912. In September 1916, the CID's Senior Chief Inspector Alfred Ward died in a Zeppelin raid. Wensley, appointed Ward's replacement, would serve until his retirement in 1929 'as effective operational head of the Met's detectives'.[13]

The papers carried news of the laundry mark on Saturday, 3 November, the day after the discovery. A Mrs Thomas, the owner of a laundry on Charlotte Street about a mile from Regent Square, came forward that morning. She said she used the mark on items belonging to a customer named Emilienne Gerard, who hadn't been seen in several days. She provided police Emilienne's address at 50, Munster Square, where the missing woman rented a small flat. Wensley dispatched his men there that afternoon.

The landlady, Mary Rouse, told detectives she last saw 'Madame Gerard' two days prior on the evening of Wednesday, 31 October. Emilienne and her husband, Paul, had moved in on 3 April. A photo of Emilienne showed a woman about thirty years old, 'with a rather full face crowned by light curly hair'. The paperwork the couple completed when they took up tenancy showed she was born in Rouen in 1886. The couple didn't live in the building long before Paul, a chef at an Oxford Street hotel, shipped off to fight in the French Army.[14]

Her husband gone, Emilienne started spending time with a man she claimed to be her brother-in-law. 'Of course,' Rouse was quick to clarify, 'that did not suggest anything improper – and I never saw anything between them which was inconsistent with the ordinary relationship you expect between people with family ties.' Indeed, on one occasion when Emilienne was visiting her husband in France, the brother-in-law paid Emilienne's rent. Just the other day, in fact, he had again visited to let Mary know Emilienne would be out of town for the next couple of weeks and was expecting a sack of potatoes to be delivered in her absence.[15]

Neighbour Adelaide Chester suggested the relationship went beyond the familial.

'Once,' she said, 'when they passed me at the corner of Munster Square, they were quarrelling violently, speaking in French. I last saw her a week before she disappeared. I asked her how she was. "I am all right," she replied, "but I feel so unhappy." "What is the matter?" I asked, but the only reply I got was a shrug of the shoulders.'[16]

Of particular interest to detectives was learning Emilienne had, at one point, scarred her right hand to the point of disfigurement in a cooking accident involving boiling fat. This clarified why the killer chose to sever his victim's hands. The scarring would have helped police identify the remains. Detectives searched Emilienne's flat and found several splotches of blood in the kitchen, 'a piece of butcher's long cloth and two corn sacks'. On the kitchen table was an IOU showing that, on 15 August, Emilienne loaned £50 to a gentleman named Louis Voisin. A bucket filled with reddish water sat on the washstand. In a cupboard, they found six bed sheets with the same laundry mark as the sheet used to wrap the Regent Square torso. A portrait of the man neighbours believed to be Emilienne's brother-in-law sat atop the mantle.[17]

The evidence in the flat, although compelling, did not prove beyond all doubt the dismembered corpse was Emilienne. Yard detectives tracked Voisin down before the end of the day to a basement flat at 101, Charlotte Street, 'less than half a mile from Munster Square, and twice that distance from Regent Square'. The building's landlord said Voisin worked for a sausage-maker in Smithfield Market and kept horses in a stable out back. He said he often saw Voisin 'in possession of sheeps' heads and calves' feet, and pieces of meat were sometimes hung up'. Wensley and two other detectives entered Voisin's flat and found him sitting in a blood-spattered kitchen with a woman named Berthe Roche. Voisin was the man in the portrait Emilienne kept on her mantle. When asked to account for the gore-smeared floor, Voisin – speaking in thick, French-accented English – said he'd recently killed a calf and brought the head home.[18]

Officers knocked on doors in the building and learned neighbours had heard 'the high voices of women' coming from Voisin's flat on the night of 31 October. One neighbour said she saw Roche using the water tap in the back courtyard early the following morning. Asked what she was doing up earlier than normal, Roche, also French, said in her broken English, 'Mr Voisin has just killed a calf and is full of blood. I have been washing his underclothes.' That provided Wensley more than enough justification to bring Voisin and Roche to Bow Street Police Station for questioning.[19]

'Voisin was a short, thick-set man, heavy-jawed and exceedingly powerful in frame,' Wensley noted, 'and he faced me with a sort of aggressive determination.' Wensley summoned a detective-sergeant he knew spoke fluent French so Voisin could provide a statement in his native tongue. The butcher said he knew nothing of Emilienne's disappearance. He said he and Emilienne had been on friendly terms for the past eighteen months and that he sometimes employed her as his housekeeper.[20]

Wensley showed Voisin the framed portrait found in Emilienne's flat and asked why she would have such a thing. 'This is my photograph,' the butcher conceded. 'I have given several away to my friends.'[21]

'When did you see her last?'

'At Munster Square on Wednesday at her house, when she told me she was going to Southampton to see her friend off. Her name is Margueritte. I do not know her other name,' Voisin said. 'Madame Gerard said she might stay a few days. I don't know where she is staying in Southampton. She said she might stay eight or ten days and asked me to pay her rent.'

'What time did Madame Gerard go with Margueritte?'

'Between two and three in the afternoon.'

When Wensley said Emilienne's landlord saw her at home that evening, Voisin made no reply.[22]

Berthe Roche, for her part, said she'd known Voisin for about a year and had lived with him for the past month. She didn't know anyone who lived in Munster Square and was unaware of Voisin ever visiting the address. On the night of 31 October, she said, Voisin went to bed at 10:30, and she followed shortly thereafter. Sometime around midnight, the building's concierge knocked on their door and alerted them to the air raid.

'I got up frightened, but Voisin remained in bed,' she said. 'He is not afraid. I went out into the passage and remained there until about three o'clock, when the concierge returned. I then warmed some coffee in her room and returned to bed.'

She was adamant that no one had called on them that evening.[23]

Wensley detained Voisin and Roche overnight while his men built the case. They tracked down an acquaintance of Emilienne's who said he'd dined with her at an Italian restaurant in Soho Square the night of 31 October. At no point during the meal, did Emilienne mention plans to travel.[24]

Wensley resumed the interrogation Sunday morning and studied the man across from him. He was not pleasant looking, Voisin, with his 'heavy jaw, eyes sunken in his fleshy face, and dark upturned mustaches.' The butcher returned the detective's gaze with a look of smug satisfaction. 'I carefully considered the position,' Wensley recalled. 'There was one test that might be applied to Voisin which would either go far to clearing him or to show that he had a guilty knowledge of the crime. Could I justify myself in applying it?'[25]

Wensley had to consider Judges' Rules, a recently established cornerstone in British law to protect criminal suspects against self-incrimination. It required police officers to inform suspects they were under no obligation to answer questions and anything they said could be used against them in court. Failure to do so could render anything said during an interrogation as inadmissible. The detective picked his words carefully.

'Ask him,' Wensley told the translator, 'if he has any objection to writing the words "Bloody Belgian".'

Voisin answered in French. 'No. Not at all.'[26]

Wensley produced some paper and a pencil and slid them across the table. Voisin, 'an illiterate man,' scrawled the phrase in a shaky hand across the page. The handwriting was similar but smaller compared to that found on the body, but the spelling was the same: 'Blodie Belgim'.[27]

Wensley showed no reaction. 'Perhaps you're not feeling quite yourself,' he said. 'Would you like to try again?'

Voisin wrote the phrase five times, spelling it the same way each time.

'The final copy bore a very close resemblance in every particular to that of the original,' Wensley reported. 'I knew then that it was only a question of time before the other points in the case would be cleared up.'[28]

It didn't take long. A detective sergeant named Collins used a set of keys found on Voisin when they searched him at the station to now access the cellar at 101, Charlotte Street. The place smelled of rot and decomposition. In the dank basement light, Collins observed bloody butcher blocks and gore-stained saws and knives. He found the head of a hammer lying among the ashes in a grate, a stone knife sharpener with blood on it and two brown paper bags similar to the one found on the body. He saw 'a hearth rug, which appeared to be moist with blood, and a sack with moist blood on it'. Hanging up was 'a man's shirt very wet with water and bearing bloodstains, and a woman's flannel dressing jacket, also very wet and stained with blood'. Collins found an earring sticking to a blood-stiffened towel hanging nearby. A wooden barrel filled with sawdust sat in one darkened corner. In it, he found a woman's severed head and hands.[29]

Collins summoned Dr Bernard Spilsbury.

The pathologist performed a cursory examination at the scene. 'The mark of a severe scalding' covered the back of the right hand in its entirety and extended up most of the middle finger. There were no scars on the left hand, but the ring finger bore the indentation left by a band. Blood and sawdust covered some of the lifeless face between Spilsbury's hands and matted a thick crown of 'light-coloured hair'. He saw an abrasion on the tip and right side of the nose and 'a good deal of bruising' on the right side of the face. A wound, about an inch long, stood out in dark red on the right side of the head. A deep gash ran from the front of the right ear 'and opened into a cavity in the cheek'. The head had been removed by a clean chop through the middle of the neck, slicing the larynx. An earring in the right ear matched the one found stuck to the towel.

At St Pancras Mortuary, Spilsbury found 'the vertebrae attached to the head completed the series of those attached to the trunk.'[30]

Once cleaned, the head revealed more signs of damage. Spilsbury noted large wounds that exposed bone on the top and back of the skull. 'Death ensued sometime after the injuries to the head,' he concluded, 'about half-hour or perhaps longer. The injuries, which could have been caused by severe blows, and could not have been caused accidentally, would have caused unconsciousness immediately. Death was due to shock and loss of blood following the injuries to the head.' Emilienne's husband, Paul, recalled from France, identified the body. He told Wensley he started receiving fewer letters from Emilienne after she met Voisin. In the letters she did send, she sometimes mentioned Voisin and 'how good he was to her.'[31]

Wensley and Spilsbury now faced the challenge of reconstructing the crime. Benzidine is a crystalline compound once used in the manufacturing of dyes. When applied to a bloodstain, it creates a chemical reaction and results in a blue discoloration. The splotches in Emilienne's flat and the water in the washstand bucket tested positive for blood – but the amount evident, in Spilsbury's opinion, 'was not such as was to be expected if murder had been done there.' Spilsbury believed Emilienne had lost at least two pints of blood. The heavy splatter and smears found throughout Voisin's basement dwelling also tested positive – but was it human or, as Voisin claimed, that of a butchered calf?[32]

Applying science not available to Inspector Richard Tanner during the 1866 Duddlewick investigation, Spilsbury identified both animal and human blood in the dried, rust-coloured muck. Not until 1901 had German scientist Paul Uhlenhuth developed a test for differentiating the two. He did this by injecting proteins from a chicken egg into a rabbit and then extracting the rabbit's blood and mixing it with egg whites. The egg proteins separated from the liquid in the resulting concoction to create a cloudy substance he called precipitin. Additional tests with other animals revealed 'the blood of each . . . had its own distinct protein.' Injecting a rabbit with human cells, he discovered the same held true for human blood. In the resulting paper titled 'A Method for Investigation of Different Types of Blood, Especially for the Differential Diagnosis of Human Blood', Uhlenhuth noted his findings 'should be of particular importance for forensic medicine.'[33]

Using Uhlenhuth's serum, Spilsbury found 'human blood everywhere' in Voisin's basement – on the walls, floors and ceiling, particularly around the back door leading into the courtyard behind the building. 'Bit by bit,' Wensley noted, 'we filled in the gaps until we gained a fairly coherent idea of the whole grim and dramatic episode, although some of the details were a matter of inference.'[34]

Spilsbury, no stranger to human butchery, was nevertheless disturbed by the murder. The image of Emilienne's 'shattered and dismembered fragments' pieced together in the morgue lingered in his mind for days, but those fragments told an interesting story. The wounds to the head, although they cut to the bone, did not actually fracture the skull. A blunt instrument wielded by someone of Voisin's size and strength would have caused much more damage, which prompted Spilsbury to believe it more likely Roche had delivered the fatal blows. Wensley harboured no doubt Emilienne and Voisin were lovers. 'Whether she knew that he was living with Berthe Roche or not, she had certainly never met the other woman,' the detective wrote. 'I am inclined to think that she did not know of her existence.' And therein lay the root cause of the tragedy.[35]

It was Wensley's theory that on the night of Wednesday, 31 October 1915, as the German Gothas passed over London, dropping their deadly cargo, Emilienne 'was seized with the idea of spending the night in the refuge of her lover's room in the basement of 101 Charlotte Street.' She ran the short distance from her home to Voisin's flat and let herself in. There, she found not Voisin's comforting embrace, but the jarring sight of another woman 'sitting with strained nerves in a lighted room'. Voisin, being 'of a more phlegmatic temperament', was most likely in bed asleep.[36]

A confrontation ensued, each woman surprised by the other. Neighbours heard their angry recriminations over the drone of German engines and the rumbling of bombs. Roche, in a rage, grabbed some heavy instrument close at hand and sprang 'like a wild cat at her rival'. Bruising on Emilienne's right hand showed she made some attempt to defend herself. She screamed as she staggered towards the door leading into the courtyard. The commotion woke Voisin, who emerged from his room to find – in Wensley's words – 'two half-hysterical Frenchwomen' fighting for his affection. Worried the noise might prompt the neighbours to call the police, he grabbed a towel, approached Emilienne from behind and wrapped it around her face to stifle her cries. Roche closed in and delivered one blow after the other, slicing skin down to the bone. Emilienne put up a fierce struggle. She tossed her head from side to side in the towel; her left earring catching on the fabric and tearing free of her lobe.[37]

According to Spilsbury, either Roche or Voisin – most likely the former – attempted to choke Emilienne to death, as evident by the blood found on the dead woman's heart during the post-mortem. Instead, she succumbed from shock and bleeding. 'Whether the murder was carried out exactly in this way or not,' Wensley said, 'it was in the highest degree probable that Berthe Roche must have struck the numerous early blows, for they had been dealt by a person of no great physical strength.' Voisin, built from years of skinning, cutting and hoisting carcasses, would have delivered the fatal blow in a far more efficient manner. Now, they faced the challenge of dumping the body.[38]

Voisin dragged Emilienne's corpse into the cellar and put his expertise and the tools of his trade to vile use. 'They must have been in some perplexity as to what should be done with the head and hands,' Wensley wrote, 'and a clumsy expedient seems to have been determined upon.' The need to cover their tracks and divert attention elsewhere prompted Voisin to visit Munster Square on 1 November to inform the landlady about Emilienne being out of town and the expectant potato delivery. He then let himself into the flat with a key, leaving noticeable traces of blood around the place, and took one of the sheets, which he used to wrap the body. His intent was to trick the police into believing that after killing Emilienne here, the culprit fled the apartment and took 'some parts of the body with him'. It was, Wensley pointed out, a ludicrous plan. 'How Voisin could have failed to see that, if the head and hands were sent there disguised as a sack of potatoes, the land-lord would have inevitably recalled enough of the conversation to betray him . . . is difficult to understand.'[39]

On 6 November, Wensley told Voisin and Roche they were being charged with murder and presented his theory of the crime. Roche exploded. '*Salaud, tu m'as trompé, salaud, salaud!*' ('Bastard, you cheated on me, bastard, bastard!'), she screamed at Voisin, who merely shrugged his shoulders. 'It is unfortunate,' he said.[40] When confronted with the discoveries in his cellar, Voisin stressed Roche had nothing to do with any of it and made a ridiculous effort to clear himself:

> I went to Madame Gerard's place last Thursday at 11 a.m., and when I arrived the door was closed but not locked. The floor and the carpet were full of blood. The head and hands were wrapped in a flannel jacket, which is at my place now. They were on the kitchen table. That is all I could see. The rest of the body was not there. I was so astonished at such an affair that I did not know what to do. I go to Madame Gerard's every day. I remained five minutes stupefied. I did not know what to do. I thought a trap had been laid for me.

Fearing such a trap, he didn't bother going to the police, but 'commenced to clear up the blood'. He searched the flat and found a pail 'full of blood and water, and there were blood-stained finger-marks on the handle of the jug'. He rolled the head and hands up in Emilienne's bedroom rug. 'I then went back into my house and had luncheon,' he said, 'and later returned to Madame Gerard's and took the packet to my place. I was still thinking that this was a trap.' He said it made no sense for him to kill Emilienne. Why would he do such a thing? He'd paid her a visit that day out of concern. 'I knew Madame Gerard was beginning mixing up [sic] with bad associates and had taken people to her flat,' he said. 'I know she took someone there that night.'[41]

Wensley found the story almost laughable in its absurdity. Voisin's relationship with the victim, the blood in his flat, the precision with which the body had been dismembered, and the 'BLODIE BELGIM' handwriting sample betrayed the butcher's attempt at explanation. Two weeks later, on 20 November, despite Voisin's effort to clear Roche of any wrongdoing, a coroner's jury returned a verdict of 'wilful murder' against the pair. 'We must give the ruffian one credit,' noted a detective with grudging respect. 'He tried to exonerate his paramour.'[42]

When the case went to trial in January 1918, the defence tried to exclude the 'BLODIE BELGIM' evidence on the grounds that Voisin's handwriting sample was self-incriminating. The judge, Mr Justice Darling, disagreed. 'It was quite proper for the police to ascertain who wrote "Blodie Belgium" [sic],' he said. 'It would be greatly in favour of Voisin if his handwriting did not resemble the writing on the paper. What was done was not setting a trap for the man: it was a legitimate attempt to assist the police.'[43]

The jury found Voisin guilty. It acquitted Roche on the murder charge due to a lack of evidence but convicted her of being an accessory after the fact. Darling sentenced her to seven years in prison.[44]

Voisin went to the gallows at Pentonville Prison on the morning of 2 March 1918, for what the press called 'the first air-raid murder'. 'So ends one of the most remarkable dramas in crime,' observed the *Weekly Dispatch*, 'a drama which in all probability would never have eventuated had not an air raid on the night of Wednesday, 31 October 1917, caused Mme. Gerard to seek cover at 101 Charlotte-street'.[45]

But the drama had not entirely run its course. Shortly into her prison sentence, Berthe Roche went insane and was transferred to an asylum. She died there the following year.[46]

The Yard won plaudits in the States for its quick work on the Voisin case. 'The ability of Scotland Yard to solve swiftly grewsome [sic] and baffling mysteries . . . was no sudden acquired ability,' reported the *Chicago Tribune*. 'It was the ability evolved from a century of experimentation, hope, and despair.' Closer to home, Wensley's star proved ever ascendant as the press seemingly mentioned his name in connection with every major case that played out in the papers. It's alleged his reputation among criminals evolved to such an extent that the words 'Mr Wensley will see you' became the most dreaded words in the London underground.[47]

Police work meant everything to Wensley. In 1918, his younger son, Harold, serving at the front with the Lincolnshire Regiment, caught influenza and died four days after the armistice. Wensley's eldest son, Frederick, serving in the same regiment, had died three years prior in a training exercise. 'These were the boys whom I showed how to live,' he wrote, 'and who showed me how to die.' He buried his grief in his work and, in doing so, proved instrumental in modernizing the Yard's operations.[48]

In 1919, he was promoted to Superintendent. He proposed dividing the Metropolitan Police District (MPD) into four distinct areas and assigning each one to a senior Yard officer. The intent was to eliminate rivalry between the divisions. Divisional detectives were basically confined to the division in which they worked. Encroaching on another division's 'territory' was considered poor form. Under Wensley's plan, each of the four senior officers over-seeing the MPD would coordinate 'the activities of the divisions under his jurisdiction and [liaison] closely with each other.' Sir Nevil Macready, the new police commissioner appointed follow-ing Edward Henry's retirement in August 1918, gave the idea his stamp of approval and appointed 'four area superintendents': Francis Carlin, Albert Hawkins, Arthur Neil and Wensley. The press dubbed them 'The Big Four.'[49]

That same year, Wensley put forward the idea of establishing a group of detectives with a roving brief to 'travel around London in a tarpaulin-covered wagon, following up crimes and hunting down criminals wherever they might hear of them.' In 1920, 'the Mobile Patrol Experiment' – as the squad was called – made the transition from wagons to motorized vehicles. Scotland Yard acquired two large Crossley tenders – personnel carriers – from the demobil-ized Royal Flying Corps to patrol the north and south side of the Thames. This updated mode of transportation gave rise to a new name: The Flying Squad. The post-war increase in automobile pro-duction and availability fuelled a new type of crime called 'smash and grab', with criminals speeding away in cars faster than the sluggish Crossleys. To meet these new challenges, the squad was amalgamated with the CID and equipped with the more powerful Lea-Francis motor car, its 14 hp engine capable of 75 mph. Noted an internal Police Order issued in 1920:[50]

> In the event of an officer receiving information or seeing anything that leads him to believe that persons with a motor car or other vehicle have committed or are suspected to be committing crimes and have decamped, he should at once communicate the available information to C.1. giving the nature of the crime or suspected crime, description of persons and car and direction in which they are proceeding . . . It will be appreciated that the object of the information so sent to C.1. is to have the officers patrolling in motor cars warned by wireless.[51]

Time Magazine offered its readers a glimpse of 'the Wensley method' for solving perplexing mysteries. 'Slumping into a big arm chair in his second-story room at Scotland Yard, he would light his pipe, stare out at the muddy Thames, sit for hours like a stone.' His 'prestige throughout the force was enormous'.[52]

On the night of 4 October 1922, Percy Thompson was fatally stabbed while walking home from the theatre with his wife, Edith. She said the killer, dressed in a hat and overcoat, rushed them in the darkness of Belgrave Road near the Kensington Gardens inter- section, pushed her to the ground and left her momentarily dazed. When she came to, she found Percy still upright but bleeding from the mouth before he collapsed to the pavement and drowned in his own blood. Wensley oversaw the investigation and found Edith intriguing. 'There was no doubt that her distress was genuine,' he wrote. 'She could scarcely have been called a pretty woman, but she had a distinctly attractive personality. She carried herself well, was dressed tastefully – she still wore the evening gown in which she had gone to the theatre and spoke with an air of culture. In moments of animation she must have been a woman of consider- able fascination.'[53]

Wensley and his men initially believed the murder to be a random act of violence. 'Of course, it was not many years after the war,' he wrote, 'and during that time there had been a few cases of people doing extraordinarily motiveless things.' But questioning the couple's friends and relatives in the cold, wet hours imme- diately after the killing, detectives learned twenty-nine-year-old Edith had a lover nine years her junior – a merchant seaman named Frederick Bywaters. Wensley put the Flying Squad to use and had it racing around the city in search of Bywaters at his known haunts. He was arrested less than twenty-four hours later.[54]

In Bywaters' bedroom, detectives found sixty love letters from Edith. 'I am feeling very blue today darlint [sic], you haven't talked to me for a fortnite . . .' she wrote in one typical missive. 'I fear that we, you & I, will never reap our reward, in fact, I just feel today dar-lint, that our love will be in vain. He talked to me again last night a lot, darlint . . . He said he began to think that both of us would be happier if we had a baby, I sad [sic] "No, a thousand times No" & he began . . . to plead with me.'[55]

Edith was brought in again the next day for questioning and caught a glimpse of Bywaters waiting to be interrogated. 'Oh, God!' she cried. 'Oh, God, what can I do? Why did he do it? I did not want him to do it . . . I must tell the truth.' Warned whatever she said could be used against her in court, she confessed to know-ing Bywaters killed her husband. Police charged the couple with murder. 'Why her?' Bywaters protested when told. 'Mrs Thompson was not aware of my movements.' The discovery of more letters suggested Edith had perhaps tried once to poison her husband and, on another occasion, hid pieces of broken glass in one of his meals. 'I used the "light bulb" three times,' she wrote, 'but the third time he found a piece – so I have give it un fill [sic] you come home.' Police exhumed Percy's body 'one moonlight night' but no trace of poison was found in his system.[56]

A jury found the pair guilty and sentenced them to death. No doubt existed as to Bywaters' guilt. He freely admitted to the crime and said, repeatedly, Edith had nothing to do with it. The jury, however, convicted Edith on the grounds she goaded Bywaters into the killing – an older woman manipulating the affections of a younger man. Condemned to hang, she broke down in the courtroom. Edith's death sentence shocked the public. Indeed, 'few people thought it would actually be carried out.' There would be no reprieve. Both went to the gallows simultaneously, Edith at Holloway Prison and Bywaters at Pentonville just half a mile away, on the morning of 9 January 1923.[57]

Some reports said she was dragged screaming to her fate; others said she was stupefied by a sedative, could hardly walk, and fell through the trapdoor tied to a chair. However she met her end, it proved unpopular. 'They hanged her,' her lawyer said, 'for her immorality.'[58]

A large crowd gathered outside Holloway to hear word of Edith's execution. 'The influence of what was passing behind those walls,' noted one person in attendance, 'came out to us and lay like an invisible shadow upon the throng.' Edith's hanging was far from clean. The sudden, fatal jolt of the rope produced a vaginal haemorrhage, causing some speculation she may have been pregnant. The prison chaplain who witnessed the execution suffered a nervous breakdown and had to retire. Hangman John Ellis eventually lost himself to the bottle and committed suicide.[59]

Wensley had no qualms about the case. Edith, as far as he was concerned, shared equal guilt with Bywaters. 'Whichever of them first thought of murder,' he wrote, 'there is no question that she had such power over him that he was prepared to do her bidding, even at the cost of his own life.'[60]

Beyond such matters, Wensley focused his efforts 'on the encouragement of forensic scientific investigation'. The pre-war years of the early twentieth century had seen 'the level of crime [remain] more or less constant'. For Scotland Yard, it had been a period of evolution with the adoption of fingerprinting and the simultaneous establishment of its Photographic Branch, the use of telegraphy and wireless communications, and the efficiency of motor transport – all of which would take on greater significance in a more violent, post-war world and a decade dominated by 'headline-making murder cases'.[61]

17

The Crumbles

A House of Horrors. The reason police wear rubber gloves.

Thursday, 1 May 1924. John Beard, a one-time Scotland Yard detective turned private investigator, led Mrs Jessie Mahon into his living room. Neither could know the suspicions that brought her here would forever change police work. He offered the nervous woman a chair and asked her how he could be of service. It was, she replied, a matter involving her husband. Beard nodded, prepared to hear a story he had heard countless times before.

'Patrick has been absent from home on numerous occasions,' she said. 'I had trouble with him some years before regarding a woman, but that had all blown over.'

Fearing another betrayal, she had searched his clothing the previous night for evidence of infidelity and found, in one of his coat pockets, a claim ticket for a bag at Waterloo Station. She pulled it from her purse and passed it to Beard: ticket no. 2413, dated Monday, 28 April.

It seemed scant proof of any wrongdoing.

'And where's your husband now?' Beard asked.

'Travelling,' she replied, adding that no luggage appeared to be missing from the couple's home. 'He's sent a series of telegrams from Eastbourne, Hastings and Bexhill. Each contains an excuse for not returning home. He even phoned to say he couldn't attend a bowling tournament, which he had promoted in Richmond.'

Beard wondered why a man would take a trip without luggage.

Jessie went on to explain she and Patrick were supposed to meet with a solicitor earlier in the week to sign some papers related to the pending closure of Consols Automatic Aerated. She worked at the soda fountain company as a secretary; Patrick as a sales manager.

'He failed to put in an appearance,' she said. 'I had to inscribe his signature on the documents.'

Having returned home from the solicitor's office in a despondent mood, she had searched the house for some clue as to Patrick's recent activities. In doing so, she found a rental agreement for a bungalow, which her husband had booked from 5 April to 11 June at three and a half guineas a week. This she found particularly disturbing, not merely because of what it implied, but because she was due to enter the hospital soon for an operation.

Beard's suspicions, until now on a low simmer, flared bright and hot. As he later remembered: 'The query that flashed through my mind was – Why should a man whose wife was about to enter hospital in London want to take another place for eight weeks?'

But Jessie had more to tell.

'He returned home after the Easter holiday and looked bronzed,' she said. 'From a number of blisters on his right hand, I concluded he had been at the seaside and had been rowing.'

'Did he have blisters on both hands?' Beard asked.

Jessie couldn't recall.

Beard's instincts told him there was more than infidelity happening here.

'I decided that Mahon was involved with something serious,' he recalled, 'and I determined to investigate the matter. It was clear that Mrs Mahon did not share my suspicion. We both agreed that the bag at Waterloo held the key to the mystery of Mahon's secret comings and goings.'

The two drove to Waterloo Station, a central London terminus for the national railway. He told Jessie to wait amidst the bustling travellers and made his way to the cloakroom, where he presented the claim ticket to the attendant.

The mystery piece of luggage was a Gladstone bag, a small suitcase built over a frame that can separate into two sections. It was locked, but Beard managed to pry one side open just enough to peer inside.

'When I did this,' he said, 'I saw a silk garment on which there were bloodstains, and also a large knife. Disinfectant powder fell out on my trousers while I was examining the bag.'

Beard closed the side of the bag, returned it to the attendant and asked for the claim ticket. He told Jessie, as they walked to his car, there was nothing wrong and instructed her to put the ticket back in her husband's coat pocket.

That evening, after Beard and Jessie parted ways, he called an old friend and one-time work colleague Fred Wensley.[1]

'It was conceivable,' Wensley wrote, 'that all this might have an innocent – or, at any rate, a non-criminal – explanation. One of the possibilities that flitted across my mind was that the owner of the bag might have had associations with some woman and used the bag when marketing for temporary housekeeping with her.'[2]

All the same, a knife and bloody garment seemed to warrant a bit of further inquiry, so Wensley asked Chief Inspector Percy Savage to investigate.

Born into policing in 1878 above the holding cells of the Acton Police Station, where his father was Station Sergeant, Savage spent his youth 'cradled in the Metropolitan Police'. The policeman's tools of the trade were young Savage's toys of choice. 'I played with a pair of steel handcuffs,' he wrote in his lively memoirs, 'and made the dickens of a noise with a police whistle.'[3]

Savage had seen police work evolve in his twenty-four-year career.

'When I joined in 1900, there was not a single telephone at Scotland Yard or at any of the stations,' he wrote. 'If the public wanted the police, they had to fetch them. There were no motor cars . . . A horsed dispatch van took a whole day to convey important papers from Scotland Yard to the outside stations. Fingerprints were unknown and old criminals were identified by unreliable photographs or personal recognition. Policemen carried heavy oil lamps on their belts. Oil lamps and even candles were the illuminants at many police stations.'[4]

The case he was now handling would see police work take another evolutionary step forward.

Savage dispatched two plainclothes sergeants to stake out the cloakroom at Waterloo Station. Shortly after 6:30 p.m., on Friday, 2 May, Patrick Mahon – using the name 'Waller' – claimed the bag. He looked sharp in a tailor-made brown suit, matching tie and hat, tanned leather gloves, brown leather shoes, and a folded umbrella under his arm. The two detectives approached as he turned to leave.

'We are police officers,' one said. 'Is that your bag?'

Mahon smiled. 'I believe it is.'

'You'll have to come with us to Kennington Police Station.'

Mahon's smile faded. 'Rubbish!'

He nevertheless obeyed without further objection.

Savage received word at Scotland Yard that Mahon had been brought in. He retrieved his car from the motor pool and drove with Detective Inspector Thomas Hall to Kennington Police Station. When Savage entered the interrogation room and introduced himself, Mahon stood up to greet him. The time was 8:30 p.m.

'Chief Inspector Savage?' he said, his smile having returned. 'I've heard about you, but this is the first time we've met.'[5]

The man, Savage thought, presented an impressive façade: athletic in build, brown curly hair that showed the first hints of grey, 'an intellectual forehead', and a face that radiated good health. Savage informed Mahon he would be taken to Scotland Yard for questioning. 'As we drove there,' Savage later wrote, 'he remained silent but apparently cool and indifferent.'[6]

They arrived at 9 p.m. at the gothic pile of red and stone brick on Victoria Embankment. Savage and Hall escorted Mahon to a private room furnished with several chairs and a table. He politely declined when offered a drink and sandwich. With that pleasantry out of the way, Savage got down to business and placed the bag on the table.

'Now look at this carefully,' he said. 'Is this your bag?'

'Yes,' Mahon replied.

'Do you have the key?' Savage asked.

'No. I lost it.'

Savage forced the lock and opened the case. 'I took out the contents,' he recalled, 'and placed them on the table – a torn pair of silk bloomers, two pieces of new white silk, a blue silk scarf – all stained with blood and grease – and a large cook's knife. There was also a brown canvas racket bag, with the initials "E.B.K." Disinfectant powder coated everything.'

Mahon watched in silence, his face a blank slate.

'How do you account for possession of these things?' Savage asked.

'I'm fond of dogs,' Mahon said. 'I suppose I have carried home meat for dogs in it.'

Savage was incredulous. 'You don't wrap dog's meat in silk,' he said. 'Your explanation does not satisfy me.'

Mahon stared off into space. 'Dog's meat,' he said, almost whispering to himself. 'Dog's meat.'

'I'll have to detain you while we make further inquiries,' Savage said, breaking the man's reverie.

The detective found himself in a delicate situation. He couldn't outright accuse Mahon of wrongdoing, for he had no confirmation a crime had been committed – yet something unbecoming had obviously occurred. Savage knew from experience it was best to wait out such situations and let the suspect stew in their own discomfort.

Mahon shifted in his chair under Savage's relentless gaze. A clock on the wall ticked away the long, agonizing minutes, emphasizing the room's heavy silence.

'You seem to know all about it,' Mahon said.

'I cannot tell you what I know,' Savage said. 'It is for you to tell me what you know, and how these things came into your possession.'

The silent standoff resumed.

As the long minutes dragged, Mahon appeared to consider his options. He leaned forward in his chair and rested his chin in his right hand. Savage eyed him patiently, wondering at the man's mental machinations. It was 11 p.m. when Mahon finally spoke.

'I wonder,' he said, 'if you can realize how terrible a thing it is for one's body to be active, and one's mind fail to act.'[7]

The words reminded Savage of a passage from Shakespeare's *King Lear*: 'We are not ourselves when nature, being oppressed, commands the mind to suffer with the body.'[8]

Mahon fell silent for another half-hour, declining the offer of a snack, before speaking again.

'I am considering my position,' he said.

Another fifteen minutes crawled by before Mahon finally cracked. 'I suppose you know everything,' he said. 'I'll tell you the truth.'

Savage cautioned Mahon of his rights, as Detective Inspector Hall poised his pen at the ready. Slowly, as if weighing each word, Mahon began telling his story. It was two-thirty in the morning when he finished and, bone-white in appearance and trembling, asked for a glass of whisky to calm his nerves. Savage complied, awestruck and horrified by the tale.

It was, the detective admitted, 'the most amazing statement I have ever heard in my long career'.[9]

The Crumbles is a wild and desolate two-mile stretch of shingled beach lapped by the cold grey waters between Eastbourne and Wallsend on England's south coast in Sussex.

'It is a lonely life on the Crumbles,' remembered one resident. 'At dark, the lights of Eastbourne in the distance remind one of a great necklace of jewels cast down at the edge of the sea with a few diamonds and rubies dropped behind it where the lights twinkle. Crossing the Crumbles after dark is a sinister experience, for you seem to be dogged by a follower a few feet behind as soft shingle falls into the holes made by your feet; then a rabbit will start away in the silence, and you start and turn and realize that human companionship is miles away, over there where the lights are.'[10]

It was four o'clock in the morning of Saturday, 3 May, when Savage, Hall and a police photographer left Scotland Yard and sped south in a police car. They stopped at the East Sussex Constabulary to alert the local superintendent of their presence and purpose, then proceeded to a holiday cottage on the Crumbles. They reached their destination at 8:30 a.m. The seaside gloom, coupled with the grim anticipation of what lay in wait, lent a haunting quality to the sound of the crashing surf.

The whitewashed cottage, surrounded by a stone wall, appeared quaint from the outside: gabled windows and a low-slung roof with four brick chimneys. A small gate in the wall gave access to a flagstone path that led to a porch ablaze with climbing roses. Dubbed 'Officer's House', it was one of several similar bungalows in a row that had once housed coastguard personnel. Now, they served as holiday rentals.

Savage, Hall and Inspector William McBride, the photographer, followed the path up to the porch. The smell of salt and seaweed hung heavy in the cold morning air but soured to something foul as they drew closer to the bungalow. Savage pulled from his pocket a house key found on Mahon and opened the front door. 'The sickly stench that assailed our nostrils as soon as we stepped inside,' he wrote, 'convinced us of the gruesome character of the secret about to be revealed.'[11]

The men worked their way through the house, lighting oil lamps to dispel the darkness, revealing a nightmare scene of human wreckage. If Mahon's statement had been hard to believe, the visual proof was even more so.

The house had 'four bedrooms, a dining-room, a sitting-room, kitchen, and scullery' – all of which stank of decomposition. From the sitting room, the detectives followed a thick smear of blood across the hallway, through one of the bedrooms and into the scullery. There, they found a bloodied axe with a broken handle and what appeared to be pieces of boiled human flesh in a sauce-pan and tub. In another bedroom they discovered a saw, its teeth clotted with blood and flesh 'similar to the kind used by butchers for sawing up meat'.[12]

In the sitting room, Savage noted charred bones in the fire-place. He made a similar discovery in the dining room's hearth. In a coal bucket beside the fireplace they found a severed leg, bent in half at the knee. Also in the dining room was a two-gallon tureen half filled with blood. A layer of congealed fat and a boiled piece of flesh floated on top.[13]

Savage and his men catalogued the horrors, all the while strug-gling against the cloying odour. They followed the smell down the hallway to a closed bedroom door. The carpet at the door's base appeared to have been recently cleaned. Kneeling down for a closer inspection, Savage saw blood on the bottom edge of the door. 'These stains,' the detective theorized, 'must have been caused by the door swinging over a pool of blood sitting on top of the carpet before the carpet had been scrubbed.'[14]

Savage pulled hard at the spotless carpet to reveal a layer of bloodstained felt underneath. Lifting up the felt, he saw 'a further stain on the floorboards, almost exactly the same shape and size as that on the felt.' Someone had bled through the carpet onto the floorboards, but only the carpet had been cleaned.[15]

Inside the bedroom, the stench hit them like a physical force. The point of origin was a trunk with the initials 'E.B.K.' on the side. They opened the lid to a horrendous sight. '[We] found four portions of the trunk of a woman's body,' Savage noted. 'Two portions [were] wrapped in women's garments and brown paper tied with string. One portion [was] in a woman's garment and sacking. The fourth portion was in a woman's garment only.' Next to the body, or what remained of it, was a large, square, blood-smeared biscuit tin 'containing the intestines, liver, lungs, heart, and other parts or organs.' Crammed into a hatbox also found in the bedroom they found thirty-seven boiled pieces of human anatomy – five of which had pubic hair.[16]

The detectives hauled all the butchered body parts into the garden, photographed them and then put them back the way they'd been found. 'The search of the house and the unpacking of the boiled and unboiled portions of her body was a gruesome and sickening task,' Savage wrote in his report. 'The stench was appalling, and we did not complete the work until a later hour in the afternoon.'[17]

The men retreated from the cottage and drove to Eastbourne Police Station. There, Savage called Lt Colonel Omerod, the chief constable of East Sussex, to report their findings. Omerod, upon hearing the extent of the crime, formally requested that Scotland Yard handle the investigation. Savage ordered a uniformed officer from the station to guard the cottage. The crime scene now secure, the detectives began the long drive back to London.

As they sped through the Sussex countryside, the mercury-coloured sea falling away behind them, Savage pondered Mahon's story – one of fatal attraction: *'The woman's name was Emily Beilby Kaye'* . . . *'we quarrelled over certain things'* . . . *'her head fell on an iron coalscuttle'* . . . *'I had to get rid of the body'* . . . *'I had to cut up the trunk'* . . . *'burnt the head'* . . . *'the ghastly smell* . . .'[18]

The detectives pulled into Scotland Yard at midnight. A constable retrieved Mahon from a holding cell. Even after all these hours, he maintained a façade of dapper respectability – a fact that only annoyed the worn-out Savage. The hour was late, and he had little patience for this 'inordinately vain man who possibly thought that his studied phrases would favourably impress me.'[19]

'You must consider yourself in custody,' Savage said, 'and you will be charged with murder. You will be held for a time in a cell at Cannon Row Police Station.'[20]

Mahon seemed unbothered by the news, perhaps convinced his erudition would set him free – yet his upper-class appearance and mannerisms could not conceal his criminal and lecherous past. Indeed, while Savage and his team uncovered the horrors inside the bungalow, Detective Inspector Thomas Frew at Scotland Yard had pieced together Mahon's backstory.

Patrick Mahon was born in 1889 in Liverpool, 'one of a large family of struggling middleclass folk' and devout Irish stock. He attended church every Sunday as a child and stayed clear of trouble. His quick wit, good looks and fondness for sports – particularly football – ensured an active social life and popularity with the ladies, which would ultimately prove his undoing. His roving eye favoured a dark-haired girl two years his junior at school. They were still teenagers when he first proposed to Jessie Hannah, but both families opposed the marriage. It was not until two years later, in April 1910, that the twenty-year-old Mahon married eighteen-year-old Jessie at the West Derby Office in Liverpool.[21]

He felt confined by marriage almost immediately, but it was Jessie who suffered. He took a mistress to the Isle of Man the following year for a romantic getaway and financed the trip with forged checks. He subsequently served a twelve-month sentence for embezzlement – and so began a long, downward spiral with Jessie steadfast at his side, always willing to forgive. He found work at a dairy upon his release and became a father with the birth of his daughter, but not even parenthood set him straight. Before his child's first birthday, he embezzled £60 from his employer and returned to prison for a year. He again found Jessie waiting when he got out, but her loyalty meant little to him.

Mahon's constant womanizing proved a detriment to steady employment. In 1916, to finance his affairs, he broke into a bank and bashed a cleaning lady over the head with a hammer. Plagued by a bizarre combination of guilt and infatuation, he stayed with the woman until she regained consciousness, kissing her and begging for her forgiveness. A five-year prison sentence followed, during which Jessie gave birth to their second child, a son, who passed away from an illness without ever meeting his father. Jessie, in her husband's absence, found a job as a clerk at Consols Automatic Aerators Ltd, a soda fountain manufacturer. When Mahon emerged yet again from prison, Jessie helped him land a £12-a-week job at the company as a salesman.[22]

A grateful Mahon promised Jessie he would turn his life around. A Scotland Yard assessment of Mahon makes the following observation: 'He was keenly disposed to "philandering" or having "affairs" with this or that woman casually, as they attracted him. But he never wished to sever his connection with the domestic hearth. He felt in his own mind that the woman he had married was his anchor: that, if he cast off from her, he would be adrift.'[23]

Mahon, with his easy smile and ebullient charm, excelled at his job. His inner demons – at least for the moment – seemed pacified by this newfound stability. And then, in the summer of 1923, Consols Automatic went into receivership. The firm of chartered accountants hired to sort through the company's financial records kept Jessie and Patrick on the payroll. This required Patrick to sometimes visit the company's headquarters in London, where he met a thirty-eight-year-old typist named Emily Beilby Kaye.[24]

Mahon dressed like a dandy, spoke fluent French and was prone to quote classics in their original Latin. Emily was tall, slender and a passionate athlete. The attraction proved mutual and immediate. 'Miss Kaye, of course, was aware of the fact that I was married, knew my wife by sight and had spoken to her on many occasions on the phone,' Mahon said in his statement to Savage.[25]

Carnage soon followed.

Knowing there was little sleep in his immediate future, Savage picked up the phone on his desk. 'I telephoned to Sir Bernard Spilsbury,' he recalled, 'that prince of pathologists whose uncanny skill has sent scores of murderers to their just doom.' The two men arranged to meet at the bungalow in a few hours' time.[26]

News of the grim findings in the cottage had leaked by early morning Sunday, 4 May, prompting a crowd of morbid spectators to gather on the shingled beach outside Officer's House.

Daybreak was no more than a thin, slate-coloured ribbon on the horizon when Spilsbury arrived with his new assistant, Hilda Bainbridge, bundled up in a fur coat and a hat pulled low over her brow. She worked in the pathology department as a records keeper at St Bartholomew's Hospital, where Spilsbury maintained his laboratory. Her work ignited a fascination with post-mortems, which soon led to the 'unusual privilege' of her watching Spilsbury work in his sanctum. Impressed by her natural curiosity and strong stomach, Spilsbury hired her to transcribe his notes and accompany him on cases. This was her first murder. The presence of a woman at such a ghastly scene caused a murmur to ripple through the crowd, as she and Spilsbury passed through the gate in the stone wall and disappeared inside the house.[27]

Someone had drawn the curtains across the windows to deny the crowd outside the show it craved. Spilsbury, with his desensitized nose impervious to the rancid smell, worked his way through each room, running his magnifying glass over every surface, studying the putrid remains. Hilda followed, taking notes, her nerves ironclad and demeanour unruffled. The pathologist paid particular attention to the cauldron-shaped coalscuttle in the sitting room, as it was on this – Mahon claimed – Emily hit her head when she fell during an argument.

It was, in Savage's words, 'a flimsy thing'. Other than a bent leg, it showed no signs of heavy impact – let alone violent contact with a human head. Spilsbury saw no trace evidence of hair or skin; only two tiny specs of blood. In the bedroom with the trunk, biscuit tin and hatbox, Spilsbury was startled to see Savage scooping up 'chunks of putrid flesh' with his bare hands 'like fish on a quayside' and placing them in a bucket.[28]

'Are there no rubber gloves?' the pathologist asked.[29]

The detective looked nonplussed and told Spilsbury he never wore gloves. This was how things had always been done. As he would later write in his memoirs, 'If we wanted to preserve human hair on clothing or soil or dust on boots, we had to pick it up with our fingers and put it in a piece of paper.'[30]

'You run a grave risk of septic poisoning,' Spilsbury said, pointing to Savage's gore-covered hands. 'No medical man outside a lunatic asylum would dream of doing such a thing.'[31]

Spilsbury made a note to consult with authorities back in London and educate them on the risks of infection. The results would have implications for policing around the world.

Ready to begin his grim task, he donned his white surgical apron and black, elbow-length rubber gloves. In the cottage's wall-enclosed garden – free of the horrific odour inside – he set up a worktable. Officers carried out the chopped and severed remains. Spilsbury began by cataloguing the contents of the hatbox with its thirty-seven pieces of what had once been Emily Kaye. One piece of flesh had been cut away from the right shoulder and included the shoulder blade, part of the collarbone and a fragment of bone from the upper-right arm. Another piece of meat contained skin, fat and muscle from the region of the navel. Flesh, fat and muscle

– all of which had been boiled – made up the remaining thirty-five pieces of human detritus.[32]

As the surf rumbled beyond the garden wall, Spilsbury reached into the trunk and pulled out 'four large pieces of human body'. One piece, which included a small section of vaginal wall, lower part of the spine and upper thighbone, had been carved from the left side of the pelvis. The second piece, attached to a portion of thighbone, formed 'the lower part of the right half of the trunk'.

The right half of the chest 'with the spinal column from the level of the sixth vertical bone from the neck to a point at which the pelvis had been sawn off' comprised the third segment, which also included the breastbone, the right breast and 'most of the left ribs'. Spilsbury applied pressure to the breast and noted 'milky fluid escaped from the nipple'. The left half of the chest – also with an attached milk-filled breast – completed the grim puzzle. The back of the left shoulder blade appeared heavily bruised.

The four pieces, when put together on Spilsbury's worktable, made up 'almost the whole' trunk of a woman. The biscuit tin presented the final trove of horrors, containing as it did an eight-inch long portion of large intestine and a piece of bowel 'with the lower end or neck of the womb or uterus'. Spilsbury, his gloves glistening with body fluids and his white apron bloodied, noted the tin contained 'organs of the chest and abdomen with the exception of those fragments which I found attached to the wall of the chest and with the exception of the bulk of the uterus and one ovary, which was missing.'[33]

Further examination would be necessary back in London. The dismembered Emily Kaye was returned to the trunk for transport, her internal organs consigned once more to the biscuit tin.

On Tuesday, 6 May, Patrick Mahon appeared in Police Court in the village of Hailsham, eight miles from the bungalow, and was formally charged with murder. Hundreds of people lined the street outside. When the doors to the court opened at 3:45 p.m., the crowd surged forward. 'Coats were torn and hats were smashed in the melee,' noted one reporter. 'Within a few moments over 200 persons had managed to squeeze into the space normally accommodating between 40 and 50.'[34]

Mahon entered the dock in a green-striped fawn coat, his unshaven face twitching nervously as he looked about the courtroom, and struck an indignant tone when the charge of wilful murder was read aloud. 'I have already made a statement,' he said, 'and it was not murder, as my statement clearly shows.' He was remanded into custody.[35]

The next day, Spilsbury summoned Savage to Westminster Mortuary. In a tiled room that stank of formaldehyde, the remains of Emily Kaye – pieced together like a grotesque jigsaw puzzle – lay on a metal gurney with a circular hole drilled at the bottom to drain blood. The grim reconstruction had taken Spilsbury three sleep-deprived days.

The organs found in the biscuit tin, along with those attached to the dismembered pieces of trunk, formed a near-complete set of human organs. Although police had collected nearly a thousand bone fragments from the cottage, there was, according to the pathologist, 'no sign of any skull bone . . . or neck bone.' There was nothing to suggest any of the dismemberment had occurred while Emily was still alive. The only sign of trauma before death was bruising on the left shoulder.[36]

The organs appeared healthy; adhesions on the right lung being the only evidence of prior illness. The partial corpse did surrender one vital secret. An ovary was missing, and the uterus had been 'separated from its neck by a clean cut.' The remaining ovary, however, provided a possible motive.

'When I cut into the ovary, I found a large yellow body which is characteristic of a condition of pregnancy,' Spilsbury said. 'This is also confirmed by microscopical examination . . . There was no indication of any previous pregnancy or of pregnancy that had run its full term. No disease was found to account for natural death and there's no condition that accounts for an unnatural death.'

'Meaning?' asked Savage.

'Meaning with the head and neck missing, there's no evidence the cause of death was unnatural.'[37]

Without the neck, Spilsbury could not look for pressure marks left by fingers or examine the small hyoid bone, which often breaks in cases of strangulation. Likewise, without the head, he couldn't check for the haemorrhaging in the eyes or lining of the mouth that's common in choking deaths.

Savage studied the human remains in front of him. Was this the result of an accidental death and Mahon's panicked response to it, as he told Savage – or was the whole thing premeditated?

On the night of his arrest, Mahon had confessed to decapitating Emily's lifeless body and incinerating her head. He said the moment he placed it on the hearth, Emily's dead eyes opened as flames of red and blue filled her sockets. A crash of thunder sent him fleeing outside into a sudden storm. He took a moment in the rain to collect himself before going back inside to finish the job. 'I burned the head in an ordinary fire. It was finished in three hours. The poker went through the head when I poked it. The next day I broke the skull and put the pieces in the dust-bin. The thigh bone I burned. It is surprising what a room fire will burn.'[38]

Neither Savage nor Spilsbury believed it. Savage had already made a return visit to the bungalow with a severed sheep's head supplied by a butcher. It took four hours to burn the head down in the sitting-room grate. Even then, it left behind a considerable amount of debris. It was, the detective noted, 'a gruesome but interesting and necessary experiment.'[39]

In an effort to locate the head, local residents were presently helping police search 'the Crumbles from dawn to dark with the aid of cocker spaniels and Labradors.' Police boats were dredging rivers, while volunteers scoured area landfills.[40]

Outside the mortuary, Savage took a deep breath and cleared

away the stench of chemicals and decomposition. Mahon's statement – the story of a one-sided love affair gone terribly wrong – was all he had to go on as he launched his investigation.

'It is in the interrogation of witnesses and the taking of statements that the Scotland Yard officer proves the value of his long experience,' Savage wrote. 'He must preserve a spirit of absolute impartiality and fairness, and not strike until he is convinced that there is a *prima facie* case to answer.'[41]

The detective found himself in a peculiar situation. A murder usually resulted in the arrest of a suspect; in this case, the suspect had been arrested before the discovery of a crime. It was, in essence, a murder investigation in reverse. Savage had to determine the validity of Mahon's story. He felt the pressure. This was his first murder case since being promoted to Chief Inspector the month before.

'I confess that I entered upon my new duties with some amount of trepidation,' he later wrote. 'I had now been in the service for twenty-four years and had gone about my work without any idea of personal glorification, but as a member of a hardworking team of good fellows with only one object in view – the subjugation of crime.'[42]

Having worked beyond the limelight for so many years, Savage now found himself very much the centre of attention. It seemed every newspaper in the country was reporting on the findings in 'the Crumbles bungalow'.

And so Savage, with his 'allotted squad of . . . inspectors, sergeants and constables', immersed himself in Mahon's sordid tale to uncover what really happened. 'The inquiries I made,' he would later write, 'revealed Mahon as a cunning, atrocious and vainglorious murderer.'[43]

Savage began his lines of inquiry gathering background on the victim.

Thirty-eight-year-old Emily Beilby Kaye had worked as a typist and shorthand writer for Robertson, Hill and Co., a London accounting firm in Copthall Avenue. Originally from Manchester, she moved to London a year and a half before the murder and lived at the Green Cross Residential Club for Women at 68, Guildford Street, Bloomsbury.

She was, one acquaintance told the detective, 'a bright and cheerful girl and took a great interest in outdoor sports'. In the winter, she played hockey and – during the summer – proved a fierce opponent on the tennis court. 'In everything she did she was thorough and delighted to excel in work or play'. Indeed, it seemed she pursued her career and financial wellbeing with equal vigour. Tragic circumstances fuelled her ambition. Her parents died when she was seventeen, leaving her to fend for herself. She had already accrued £600 in investments by the time she arrived in London and took up her secretarial work at the accounting firm.[44]

In June 1923, one of the firm's partners, a Mr Hobbins, was appointed receiver of Consols Automatic Aerators – where Patrick and Jessie Mahon worked – and decided to keep Patrick on as a sales manager. It was through Hobbins that Mahon met Emily. Here, Savage could only rely on what Mahon told him: that the dalliance began in September 1923 when he and Emily spent an afternoon by the Thames in the left-bank town of Staines. 'As a result,' Mahon said, 'I realized she was a woman of the world, which knowledge came rather as a surprise to me.'[45]

Whether this is true or not, Savage believed Emily's feelings for Mahon intensified as the days stretched into weeks and then months. 'She certainly was infatuated with her lover and trusted him implicitly,' Savage noted in his case report. He based this theory on a review of Emily's bank records that showed she began selling her investments in February 1924, much to Mahon's benefit.[46]

On 16 February, she withdrew four £100 notes from the bank and gave them to Mahon – something to which he admitted. He cashed two of the notes at the Bank of England prior to Emily's death and one in the wake of her murder, using a false name and address each time. Savage was unable to trace the fourth, as it remained in circulation.

Having cashed in her savings, Emily began demanding more of Mahon's attention. 'She wished me to see her more frequently, which I was unwilling to do for several reasons,' Mahon said in his statement. 'She reproached me on several occasions as being cold, and told me quite plainly that she wished my affection and was determined to win it if possible.' He said he ultimately relented 'in the hope of gaining time, but from that moment I felt more or less at the mercy of a strong-minded woman, whom, though I liked her in many ways, I did not tremendously care for.'[47]

Most likely, by this point, Emily knew she was pregnant.

'She became thoroughly unsettled and begged me to give up everything and go abroad with her,' Mahon told Savage. 'I plainly told her that I could not agree to such a course.'[48]

To buy time, Mahon took her on holiday to Southampton, where – in March – they stayed at a hotel under the names 'Mr and Mrs P. H. Mahon'. Ada Smith, secretary of the Green Cross Club, where Emily lived, told Savage that Emily returned to London at the end of the month with a diamond-and-sapphire engagement ring on her finger.

'She came bounding into my room exclaiming, "It's fixed, my dear,"' Ada said. 'I asked to what she referred, and, pointing to an engagement ring, she replied, "The date." She was radiantly happy, but would say no more about the event beyond saying she was leaving the next week. She left in a taxicab during the first week of April. No fiancé was ever seen or known at the club.' Emily told her closest friend at Green Cross, Edith Warren, that she and her fiancé planned to move to South Africa and settle in Cape Town. Edith only recalled hearing Emily mention her beau's name, "Pat", once.[49]

In Mahon, Savage saw a man of 'diabolical trickery.'[50]

'He never intended to take her abroad,' the detective wrote in his case summary. 'His sole idea was to get rid of her. He was in a hopeless predicament. He had fleeced the woman who reposed every confidence in him, and he knew that when her child was born his own villainy would be exposed. He therefore decided to murder her in such circumstances as he hoped would lead friends to suppose that she had gone to South Africa.'[51]

Mahon, for his part, never admitted to buying Emily a ring, proposing marriage or knowing she was pregnant. He told Savage Emily purchased the ring in secret and forced him into 'a love experiment', whereby the two of them could spend a prolonged period of time together. 'It was essential from her point of view,' Mahon said, 'that she had a chance of acting as wife in every sense of the word to me. Her idea was that by having a holiday for some time together alone, she doing everything, she could convince me by her attention and devotion that I could be happy with her.' When Mahon refused, Emily became irate.[52]

Emily, notes one case document, 'could not be easily thrown aside'. Mahon enjoyed a comfortable life. His wife kept him around despite his rampant infidelity, he was father to a doting daughter, he excelled at his job and he'd recently been made captain of his lawn bowling team. Emily posed a threat to the natural order of things and had to be eliminated. The answer to Mahon's growing problem appeared on Friday, 4 April, in a newspaper advertisement for a furnished holiday cottage on the Crumbles in Pevensey Bay. There, according to Mahon, Emily hoped 'she would convince me with her love that I could be perfectly happy with her'.[53]

He telephoned the landlord, George Muir, and rented the cottage under the name Waller for three weeks starting on 11 April, explaining its desolate location would suit his ill wife's need for peace and quiet.

'Pat, old boy,' Emily supposedly told Mahon after he booked the cottage, 'you will never regret it. I can make up fully for all you have to give up.'

Mahon told Savage that using the name 'Waller' had been Emily's idea to avoid a scandal, lest anyone discover she was shacking up with a married man. 'I felt in myself very depressed and miserable,' he said, 'and did not wish to spend the three or four days together as she desired, but as I had given my word and as I felt that I could definitely prove how foolish the hope was on her part to expect to keep my affection, even could she gain it, I thought I had better go through with it.'[54]

Mahon took Emily out for drinks on the evening of the fourth. He told her to move out of the Green Cross Club and into the Kenilworth Court Hotel in Eastbourne until the cottage was move-in ready. Still adamant about eloping abroad, Emily penned a letter to her sister Elizabeth on 5 April and announced her plans.

'I knew from her she was going abroad because she was engaged to a man named Pat who had a good post in South Africa – Cape Town – who wanted her to go with him,' Elizabeth told Savage. 'She said they would be off in ten days' time. I understood they were to be married when they had been out there a little while.' Beyond that, Elizabeth knew nothing more about her sister's suitor.[55]

On 7 April, two days after writing the letter, Emily packed all she owned into a hatbox and a trunk emblazoned with her initials, 'E.B.K.', and left the club for good. She travelled to the Eastbourne hotel, where, according to Savage, 'she waited alone for her lover.'[56]

Piecing together what transpired and the timeline of events proved tricky, as Savage's primary source of information was an unreliable narrator. For those who knew Emily, Mahon was nothing more than a scrawled name in a letter or a mysterious figure mentioned in conversation but never really discussed. Mahon himself offered conflicting dates in multiple statements to Scotland Yard. He first said Emily died in the bungalow on the night of 16 April and then revised it to 15 April – his reason being he had a date in London on the sixteenth with another woman, a Miss Ethel Duncan. It was, to say the least, a shocking admission.

Savage found Ethel living with her sister on Primrose Avenue in Richmond. Traumatized by the news coverage of Mahon's misdeeds, Ethel told Savage how she met the man, her story punctuated by huge gasping sobs.

She said she was hurrying home from work in the rain on the night of Thursday, 10 April. As she crossed Richmond Bridge, its streetlamps haloed in the downpour, she became aware of a man walking alongside her. He introduced himself as 'Pat' and let it be known, in the course of their conversation, he was unhappily married. He described his home life as a 'tragedy'.

'I'm sorry,' Ethel said.

'Oh,' Mahon replied, 'we agreed to go our ways.'

Not wasting time, he asked Ethel to dine with him. She agreed. Mahon, rain dripping from the brim of his hat, made plans for the following Wednesday. Ethel gave him her address before they parted ways.[57]

'The episode gives a clue to the psychology of the man,' notes one contemporary account. 'Murder must have been very close to his mind at that time, and yet he could philander with still another woman.'[58]

'There are tricks in every trade and in particular that of a detective,' Fred Wensley liked to remind his men. '. . . Pure reasoning is all very well, but the blood and bones of all practical detective work is information.' Indeed, it was a random piece of information – a casual remark – that shed a glaring light on Mahon's dark intentions.[59]

Mahon's interaction with George Muir, the bungalow's landlord, had been brief and transactional – nothing more than a phone call and a quick meeting at the cottage to retrieve the keys and pay the first week's rent. Savage interviewed Muir as a matter of course to ensure all available avenues had been explored. Muir confirmed Mahon's story. He said he received a call on 4 April from a man named Waller and the two met a week later to walk through the cottage and agree to the rental terms. Almost as an afterthought, Muir mentioned he saw the man known to him as Waller in London the next day, 12 April, at the junction of Victoria Street and Vauxhall Bridge, carrying a shopping bag.[60]

In his statement to Savage on the night of his arrest, Mahon said Emily died in the cottage on the night of 15 April. Panicked and needing to rid himself of the body to avoid his affair coming to light, Mahon said he travelled to London on 17 April and purchased a meat saw and carving knife from a kitchen supply store in Victoria Street. He returned to the cottage that night.

'When I got back to the bungalow,' Mahon said, 'I was still so upset and worried that I could not then carry out my intentions to decapitate the body.'[61]

The shop on Victoria Street was Staines Kitchen Equipment Co. The sales clerk identified Mahon from a photograph and confirmed he'd sold Mahon 'a ten-inch cook's knife and a meat saw' just after 1 p.m. on 12 April – not the seventeenth, as Mahon claimed. Savage now had evidence of premeditation. 'Two days after making his new acquaintance [Ethel],' Savage wrote, Mahon 'intended to cut up the body of the girl who was then waiting at the hotel at Eastbourne for him to escort her to the bungalow on the Crumbles.'[62]

Savage had, to the best of his abilities, established the chain of events leading up to the slaughter in the bungalow. Certainly, there was some truth in Mahon's version of events – specifically, Emily's infatuation as evident from the letters she wrote and the statements provided by her friends. But as to the happenings in that cottage on the beach, he had only Mahon's word. It's known that Emily was alive on 13 April, as someone staying in a neighbouring bungalow spotted her through a window. On 14 April, a milkman making his rounds also saw her.

After that, she was never seen alive again.

Only two people know for sure what happened in the bungalow – but the one who lived to tell the story was a compulsive liar. Here then, based on Mahon's statement, is what transpired.

Patrick Mahon took the evening train to Eastbourne on Saturday, 12 April, and dined with Emily at the Kenilworth Court Hotel. After dinner, they summoned a taxicab and reached the bungalow at ten-thirty. No sooner had they settled in the sitting room, with its cheery yellow wallpaper dotted with blue flowers, than tempers flared. Emily, expecting the two of them to soon leave for Paris and then travel on to South Africa, became angry when she learned Mahon did not have a passport. She demanded they travel to London together so he could get one. He agreed, and the two of them made the trip by train on Tuesday, 15 April. At Victoria Station, they went their separate ways – Emily to go shopping and Mahon to get his passport. It's worth noting there is no independent corroboration this trip actually happened.

Mahon met Emily at the station an hour later and told her he'd secured the proper documentation. On the journey back to Eastbourne, however, he came clean and said he'd done no such thing. The couple argued, with Emily demanding he get a passport and Mahon refusing. It was evening when they reached Eastbourne and returned to the bungalow. The seaside air was cold and sharp; the chill between the couple even more so. Mahon busied himself lighting a fire in the sitting room's small hearth. Emily approached as he broke up pieces of coal with the small axe kept by the fireplace.

'Pat, I am determined to settle this matter one way or the other tonight,' she said. 'My actions mean I have burned my boats.'

By this, Mahon assumed Emily was referring to her moving out of the residential club.

'For me, there's no turning back,' Emily said. 'Can't you realize,

Pat, how much I love you and that you mean everything to me and that I can never share you with another?'

Mahon stood up and placed the coal axe on a nearby coffee table. Very much aware that 'a crisis was coming', he tried to de-escalate the situation by going to bed. He heard Emily mutter something behind him as he walked towards the bedroom. He turned his head just in time to see her grab the axe and hurl it at him. 'I barely had time to avoid it striking me on the right shoulder,' he told Savage. 'It hit over the framework of the door. I was astounded by the suddenness of the attack. She leapt across the room clutching at my face.'

If Mahon's story is to be believed, the two of them fought a desperate struggle. They staggered across the sitting room, locked in a violent embrace, and tumbled over an easy chair to the left of the fireplace. Emily smacked her head on the iron coalscuttle. 'It appeared to stun her,' Mahon said. 'This happened about twelve o'clock, midnight. I attempted to revive her, but found I could not. The reaction after the struggle having set in, the consequences to me came home with stunning force.'

Mahon said he stumbled into the garden and sat there for a while 'in a state bordering on madness'. He lingered in the garden for hours before his senses returned – and, with them, the courage to re-enter the bungalow. It was nearing daybreak when he did so. Back inside the cottage, he dragged the body into one of the bedrooms and covered it with a fur coat. He placed some of Emily's clothing beneath her head to staunch the flow from the still bleeding wound. The sun was up by now and flooding the bungalow in the cold light of day. Hungry, Mahon took a taxi into Eastbourne to find some breakfast.[63]

It's at this point in Mahon's narrative that Ethel Duncan, the woman he met on that rainy night in Richmond, makes another appearance. On the afternoon of 15 April – the day Emily died – Ethel received a telegram from Mahon. 'Charing Cross, 7 tomorrow. Sure. – Pat'. Although Mahon was supposedly in London that day with Emily to get a passport, the telegram was wired from Hastings at 3:49 p.m., less than twenty miles from Eastbourne. The telegram, coupled with the purchase of the saw and carving knife three days prior, was further evidence 'Mahon was not expecting to be encumbered by the presence of Emily Kaye.'[64]

Ethel and Mahon met on the evening of the sixteenth at the Victoria Station Restaurant. He showed up with his right wrist wrapped in a bandage and told a concerned Ethel he'd hurt himself preventing an old lady from falling off a bus. Over dinner, he said he lived in a bungalow – 'a rather charming place belonging to a pal' – near Eastbourne and suggested Ethel join him there for the upcoming Easter weekend. She agreed and received a telegram the next day from Mahon – but signed in the name 'Waller' – with money to cover her travel expenses.[65]

Thursday, 17 April, was a day of horrors in the cottage. It's here that Mahon's statement veers towards the truth. Armed with his meat saw and carving knife, Mahon went to work. 'I severed the legs from the hips, the head, and left the arms on,' he said. 'I then put the various parts in a trunk in the bedroom and locked the door.'[66]

Ethel took the 11:15 a.m. train to Eastbourne on Good Friday, 18 April, and was met by Mahon – sharply attired in 'a fawn-coloured suit' – at the station. They lunched at the Sussex Hotel, took a driving tour through the Sussex countryside and dined that evening at the Royal Hotel in Eastbourne before taking a taxi to the bungalow. All seemed normal when they reached the house, although it was clear Mahon had recently played host to another woman. In the bedroom where she put her bag, Ethel noticed a hairbrush with a tortoiseshell handle, some cosmetics and a pair of buckled shoes. Mahon said his wife had recently visited and left the items behind. There was no reason for Ethel not to believe the man she was about to share a bed with.[67]

'On that Good Friday night,' Savage noted, 'they had occupied the same bedroom that had been shared . . . by Miss Kaye, whose dismembered corpse now lay in a trunk in an adjoining room. Miss Duncan had not the faintest suspicion of the tragic character of the atmosphere into which she had been lured.' Indeed, Mahon's demeanour, Ethel told Savage, suggested nothing out of the ordinary. 'He appeared to be quite normal,' she said, 'and in good spirits.'[68]

She went shopping by herself in Eastbourne on Saturday. Mahon dropped her at the train station that morning before heading to the local racetrack, where, Savage theorized, 'I believe he changed the fourth of the £100 notes Miss Kaye had received from the sales of her securities.' By now, Savage believed, Mahon was eager to be rid of Ethel. He had more grisly work to do. It was time to send her packing, so he arranged to have a telegram sent to himself.[69]

On Easter Sunday, Mahon cut his hand while trying to put a lock on one of the bedroom doors. He told Ethel a friend of his was storing some valuable books in the room and he wanted to make sure they were adequately protected. Ethel didn't see any books through the partly opened door, but she did glimpse a large trunk. She thought nothing of it. Later that day, he showed her a telegram: 'Important see you Tuesday morning. Lee.' Mahon apologized. 'We'll have to go up to London tomorrow,' he told her. 'I have to be in town at nine o'clock tomorrow morning.'[70]

The couple returned to London on the afternoon of Monday, 21 April, and caught a show at the Palladium Theatre after dinner. It was nearly midnight when Mahon dropped Ethel off at her house on Worple Avenue. He would be in touch, he said. The next time Ethel saw Patrick Mahon, it would be in a courtroom.

'I should have gone stark raving mad if I had not had Miss Duncan with me,' Mahon told Savage. 'It was ghastly. The damn place was haunted. I needed human companionship.'[71]

After dropping off Ethel, he returned to his home on Pagoda Avenue and spent the night alongside Jessie in his marital bed, cocooned – if only briefly – in a sense of normalcy. As far as Jessie was concerned, her husband had been travelling on business. He ventured back to the murder house on Tuesday morning, a cold rain falling dark and slow. The sound of thunder punctuated his grim work. 'On that day,' he said, 'I burnt the head in the sitting room grate. I next burnt the feet and legs in the same grate.'[72]

Later that night, he fled the cottage back to London and this time stayed away until Saturday morning. 'I had to cut up the trunk,' he said. 'I also cut off the arms. I burned portions of them. The smell was appalling, and I had to think of some method of disposing of the portions. I then boiled some portions in a large pot in the bungalow, cut the portions up small, packed them in the brown bag, and I threw them out of the train while travelling between Waterloo and Richmond. These portions were not wrapped up in anything. This was about ten o'clock on Sunday night.'

Mahon had intended to spend that Sunday night, 27 April, at home – but seeing as he had not been able to dispose of all the flesh, he checked into a hotel and resumed his morbid task the next day, aimlessly riding the train and tossing bloody chunks of Emily away along the route. On Monday, 28 April, he deposited the bag at the Waterloo Station cloakroom and returned home to Jessie. 'The bloodstained cloth that was in the bag was a pair of bloomers that I got out of the girl's trunk,' he said. 'I tore them up and used them to wrap up some of the flesh.'[73]

Jessie suffered years of indignity as Mahon's wife, yet always managed to forgive. It was nice to have Patrick home, but his recent absences and stories of business travel aroused old fears. And so she went through his coat pockets on the evening of 30 April and discovered the baggage claim ticket. In the end, a suspicious wife proved Mahon's downfall. Had Jessie not voiced her concerns to a private investigator, the crime may not have come to light. Mahon himself would later concede the only reason he retrieved the bag from Waterloo Station 'was because I was returning to the bungalow to get more flesh.' His use of the name 'Waller' left no connection between the cottage and anyone named Patrick Mahon. If not for Jessie, Savage wrote in his case report, 'Miss Kaye would never have been reported missing because her friends would have assumed that she had sailed for South Africa.'[74]

Of course, one question remained: How was Emily Kaye actually killed?

'If the head had been found, there would have been definitive evidence to show the nature of the wounds received,' Savage wrote. 'However, from the position of various articles in the bungalow and the trail of blood in the rooms, there is little doubt that Miss Kaye was struck on the head with an axe as she was passing through the doorway of the sitting-room to the bedroom.'[75]

Mahon claimed their physical confrontation began when Emily threw the coal axe at him. He said it barely missed him and struck the doorframe to the bedroom – yet the doorframe showed no signs of damage when Savage and his team visited the bungalow the night of Mahon's arrest.

The crime made headlines on both sides of the Atlantic. '"The Bungalow Murder" at Which "Crimeless England" Stands Aghast' cried the *St. Louis Post-Dispatch* in a full-page story on Sunday, 13 July 1924.

The trial commenced two days later. Mahon – a 'wolf in sheep's clothing', according to Savage – appeared in a blue lounge suit ordered from his tailor for this very occasion. Four days of gruesome testimony followed, with Mahon himself taking the stand in his own defence. He hardly did himself any favours, as he detailed how he dismembered Emily's corpse.[76]

His appearance throughout spanned the spectrum of bronzed and confident to pale and terrified. At one point – seemingly overcome with emotion – 'Mahon collapsed and cried bitterly.' The act failed to impress. The jury took forty-five minutes in their deliberations on 19 July and found him guilty. Asked by the judge why sentence of death should not be pronounced, Mahon replied: 'I feel too conscious of the bitterness and unfairness of the summing-up which you have just uttered to say anything except that I am not guilty.'[77]

Guards led him away as he sobbed.

The Crumbles murder had a lasting impact on how police investigate and process crime scenes. It exposed law enforcement's 'poor understanding or even acknowledgement of the concept of contamination and trace evidence . . . and the lack of understanding of proper crime scene practice'. Prior to the butchery in the bungalow, detectives processed crime scenes with their bare hands.[78] Notes Savage:

> We police officers not only had no rubber gloves, but we lacked many other things which were essential to the efficient performance of our duties . . . We had no tapes to measure distances, no compass to determine direction, no apparatus to take fingerprints, no first-aid outfit, no instrument to find the depth of water, no magnifying glass. In fact, we had no appliances available for immediate use on the scene of a crime.[79]

In 1912, French criminologist Edmond Locard theorized that 'every contact leaves a trace'. He applied his theory that same year in the Lyon Strangler case. The victim, Marie Latelle, was found murdered in her parents' home. Police suspected Marie's boyfriend, a local bank clerk named Emile Gourbin, who said he spent the night of Marie's murder out on the town with friends. Locard analysed grime swabbed from Gourbin's fingernails and discovered it contained traces of the same cosmetic powder worn by Marie. Gourbin, when confronted with the evidence, ultimately confessed. Locard's 'Exchange Principle', as it became known, established the foundation for modern forensic science.[80]

The principle also extends to the concept of evidence contamination, specifically 'when two objects come into contact

Detectives escort Patrick Mahon, his face covered, from the house of horrors on the Crumbles.

with one another they may also damage or deform one another,' and underscores the importance of proper evidence collection. Indeed, Locard's use of swabs to collect the filth beneath Gourbin's fingernails illustrated the necessity of so-called 'murder kits.' Although Locard's findings were well established by the time of the Crumbles murder, it was not until Spilsbury saw Savage scooping up Emily's flesh with his bare hands that such kits came into existence.[81]

In the wake of the investigation, Spilsbury reviewed Scotland Yard's procedures and discovered 'police officers were hopelessly ill-equipped' to handle crime scene evidence. In consultation with a London doctor and Detective Superintendent William Brown of Scotland Yard, Spilsbury created the Murder Bag for investigators in the field. This crime-scene processing kit, the first of its kind, was stored in a cowhide case and included 'rubber gloves, a hand lens, a tape measure, a straightedge ruler, swabs, sample bags, forceps, scissors, a scalpel, and other instruments that might be called for'. Indeed, it is because of the Crumbles murder that donning rubber gloves became a standard procedure at crime scenes around the world.[82]

Nine Murder Bags would eventually occupy a shelf in the CID office, their contents evolving alongside methods of investigation and evidence gathering. One detective kept a flask of whisky in his case for those occasions that necessitated going out on bitter winter evenings.

It wasn't whisky Patrick Mahon drank on the morning of 3 September 1924 in the condemned cell at Wandsworth Prison, but the customary shot of brandy offered by the warden to soothe the nerves. Guards pinioned Mahon's hands behind his back and marched him through a door concealed behind the cell's bookcase and into the adjoining death chamber. He was led straight to the trapdoor with its large white 'T' drawn in chalk, showing the prisoner where to stand. The noose dangled at chest level.

Two warders on either side of the trap made sure Mahon stood in the right place. Their task done, the hangman pulled a white execution hood over Mahon's head and fastened his ankles with a leather strap. The noose was placed around his neck, its brass eyelet held firm by a stopper beneath the left angle of Mahon's jaw. Without any hesitation or grim ceremony, the hangman yanked the safety pin from the base of the trapdoor-release mechanism and pulled the lever. Mahon tried to avoid the plunge by jumping off the trapdoor as it opened. His attempt failed. He fell backwards, slamming his back against the edge of the trap.

Seconds later, the fatal drop of 7 ft 8 in snapped his neck.[83]

18

In the Trunk

Embracing the press. Blood will tell.

Norman Thorne, a Sunday school teacher and chicken farmer, followed the Crumbles murder with much interest, clipping articles from his local newspaper. Detectives found the yellowed cuttings in his dresser. He lived in the town of Crowborough, not far from Mahon's infamous murder bungalow, and quickly came under suspicion when his fiancé, twenty-six-year-old Elsie Cameron, vanished on Friday, 5 December 1924.[1]

Elsie lived with her parents in Kensal Rise, northwest London, and left home suddenly that afternoon to visit Norman, with whom she had a tempestuous relationship. She departed with little money and without having arranged any accommodations for her weekend away. Her parents contacted police six days later after Elsie failed to return home or send word. Sussex authorities investigated the matter for several weeks, questioning the co-operative Thorne several times, before contacting Scotland Yard for assistance. Yard detectives dug up Thorne's farm on 15 January 1925 and found Elsie's travel case. Confronted with the evidence, Thorne said he didn't kill Elsie but knew where she was.[2]

He said Elsie had unexpectedly shown up at the farm in a combative mood on the evening of 5 December and badgered him over his philandering ways and reluctance to marry. He left mid-argument to pick his neighbours up from the train station. When he returned home, he found Elsie hanging from a ceiling beam with a clothesline wrapped around her neck. He took her body down and laid her across a table. He was scared to alert the police, believing they'd accuse him of murder. 'I got my hacksaw,' he said, 'and sawed off her head, and the legs, by the glow of the fire.'[3]

He wrapped her limbs in sacking and placed her head in a biscuit tin before burying her quartered body in his chicken run. When police finally recovered the remains, they found the head packed so tightly in the tin 'that it was extracted with difficulty.' Sir Bernard Spilsbury found no evidence of hanging – despite Thorne's insistence to the contrary. 'I made a thorough search of the neck,' Spilsbury said. '. . . After I had turned the skin back I cut across the creases and in between fifteen and twenty such cuts I found no single area which suggested haemorrhage or which suggested crushing of the tissues, and no thickening or reddening of the skin itself resulting from pressure by a rope.'[4]

Spilsbury's word, as expected, proved sacrosanct in court. Thorne was hanged at Wandsworth Prison on 22 April 1925. The minister who tended to Thorne in his final moments believed the man to be innocent, as those sentenced to die often confessed in hopes of leniency. Acquaintances of Thorne also refused to believe the man capable of murder. Questions about his guilt lingered long after his fatal drop. In the end, none of it mattered. 'The crimes of Patrick Mahon and Norman Thorne,' notes one account, 'are linked by time, place and circumstance, and perhaps by the sincerest form of flattery.'[5]

'My own view,' noted Frederick Wensley, 'is that this was a crime of imitation. Had Mahon never murdered Emily Kaye, Elsie Cameron might still be alive.' He elaborated:

> Thorne, although unlike Mahon, a man without criminal antecedents and whose life had hitherto been without reproach, was confronted with much the same problem – a woman who had become a nuisance to him. Mahon's methods suggested a way out to him and he adopted them, avoiding it should be said, many of the mistakes made by the other.[6]

If Thorne was copycatting Mahon, Mahon was copycatting two other killers. In 1904, bigamist George Albert Crossman murdered one of his eight wives and cemented her corpse in 'a large heavy tin box'. The following year, Arthur Devereux murdered his wife and two-year-old twins, stashed their bodies in a trunk and put the trunk in storage.[7]

Crossman, Devereux, Mahon and Thorne followed the same modus operandi of murder and concealment, hiding the bodies of their victims to eradicate evidence of a crime. In doing so, they established 'a fashion in trunk murders' and set the stage for another infamous crime of this type.[8]

Tuesday, 10 May 1927. London's grey skies and persistent spring drizzle had surrendered to unseasonably warm weather. 'Basking or perspiring in the sunshine of today,' noted one cheery weather report, 'few will worry whether Spring has gone a-borrowing from summer's store or whether, as meteorological experts assert, a friendly atmospheric pressure is responsible for the recent smiling days.' One observer with an eye for fashion noted that many 'Society Women' out and about had not ordered 'enough summer frocks to take advantage of mid-summer weather in early May.' Dresses of black and navy blue seemed to outnumber the more appropriate style of 'floral chiffon and crepe de chine frocks.'[9]

On that sultry Monday morning, Albert Glass, the clerk in the Charing Cross Station cloakroom, busied himself tracing the source of a putrid and sickly sweet odour. The cloakroom usually smelled of old leather and musty suitcases, but the pleasant scent, reminiscent of miles travelled and adventures elsewhere, lingered now beneath the stench of rot. It was 9 a.m. Albert traced the smell to a trunk made of black American leather, fastened shut by two iron fittings and bound in a thick leather strap.[10]

He pulled the trunk clear of the other luggage and pried it open. 'It was a revolting sight,' remarked one clerk, who had the misfortune to peer over Albert's shoulder. 'We saw a number of brown paper parcels and realized at once that they contained human remains.' Another clerk, overwhelmed by it all, collapsed in a dead faint. The horror sent Albert scrambling for a railway constable, who, in turn, called the Bow Street Police Station.[11]

Divisional Detective Inspector William Steele took the call and arrived at the station at 9:30 a.m. Glass showed him the offending trunk. Steele noticed 'the unpleasant smell' at once and knelt down for a closer inspection. On the handle was a cardboard label with the words 'F. Austin to St Lenards', a misspelling of St Leonards, a resort town on England's south coast. The initials 'I.F.A.' had been painted in white on the lid; one side of the trunk bore a large, white 'A'. The detective lifted the lid and peered inside. 'I saw four parcels, a lady's black bag and a pair of shoes,' he said. 'I lifted two small parcels on the top and saw underneath human remains wrapped in paper, and clothing protruded through the brown paper. Under these wrappings I saw a woman's head.' No one, when queried, could remember who dropped the trunk off or when.[12]

Steele, with his car windows down, transported the trunk and its grim contents back to Bow Street, where Divisional Police Surgeon Dr Thomas Rose examined the remains. Present was Fred Wensley, recently appointed Chief Constable of the CID, 'to decide what steps should be taken.'* The case posed immediate challenges: detectives had no clue as to the woman's identity, the time or place of death, and had no viable suspect or witnesses. 'We felt,' wrote Wensley, 'that this was one of those murder cases that might have happened anywhere.' Consequently, the investigation

---

* The office of Chief Constable of the CID was 'created more as a means of recognition for [Wensley's] remarkable service than as a permanent police post.' (*The New York Times*, 'Crime Expert Quits at Scotland Yard', 26 June 1929.)

transferred out of division to the CID with Chief Inspector George Cornish taking the lead.[13]

Cornish joined Scotland Yard in February 1895 as a twenty-one-year-old recruit from the Wiltshire countryside. 'It was the first time I had been in London,' he recalled, 'or indeed far from my father's farm.' The capital overwhelmed him. 'During the three weeks' training which was the rule in those days, I lived with the other recruits in a Section House in Kennington,' he wrote. 'There were a number of other country lads there, and we spent our spare time in exploring London. We were stolidly determined not to be bewildered by anything or anybody, but I think that we were all inwardly astonished at the crowded pavements, the endless stream of hansom cabs, horse buses and carriages.'[14]

Having completed three weeks of drills, he was sworn in by the assistant commissioner, given his uniform and sent off to Whitechapel. 'More than a little of the bad old days of Fagin and Bill Sikes still remained in the stews of the East End,' he said. 'Wireless had not been thought of, motor-cars were unknown, and the science of crime detection was still in its infancy.' Young constables learned on the job and had to pass a number of examinations. 'There were good libraries in the reading-rooms of the police stations where we could get all the textbooks we wanted on law and police procedure,' Cornish remembered, 'but general education and general knowledge which form an important part of these examinations was another matter.' He and the other forty men in his housing unit paid a shilling a week for a schoolmaster to provide lessons in the evenings.[15]

His studious ways paid off. He joined the CID in 1902, made Detective Sergeant three years later, and was transferred to headquarters in 1909. His upward trajectory saw him assist in the hunt for Crippen and work other high-profile cases that spanned the gamut from arson to gangland violence. He became head of Criminal Investigations for D (Marylebone) Division in 1919 and returned to Central Office as Chief Inspector in 1925.[16]

After his cursory examination at Bow Street, Dr Rose brought the trunk to Westminster Mortuary in Horseferry Road for a more thorough study alongside Dr Henry Bright Weir. Cornish and his detective sergeant, Leonard Burt, met the doctors at the mortuary. The rotten-vegetable smell of decomposition filled the room when Rose opened the trunk. 'It was ghastly enough to be unforgettable,' Burt said. The first items pulled from the trunk were a pair of black women's shoes with rubber heels, size five, and a handbag, emptied of everything except five pieces of spearmint chewing gum.[17]

Packed tightly beneath these items lay the quartered remains of a woman's body, each bloody portion wrapped in an item of women's clothing and brown paper, and bound in string. 'It was my job,' Burt wrote, 'to remove them parcel by parcel, take off the wrappings, and preserve all the terrible exhibits.'[18]

Burt unwrapped the first bundle. He gently pulled away two towels and a pair of blue cotton underpants with the name 'P. Holt' written on the label to reveal the victim's arms. They'd been severed at the shoulders and ripped from the sockets. The next parcel, wrapped in a coat, proved to be the right leg. The left leg was bound in a white underskirt with a lace border. Both appendages had been severed in similar fashion to the arms. Next, Burt retrieved from the trunk a large, ball-shaped object wrapped in a bloody duster. He braced himself as he carefully removed the rag from around the woman's head. Her tongue protruded between clenched teeth. Last was the torso, swathed in 'a pale blue jumper and other garments'. Also in the trunk was a white merino undervest with two laundry marks: numbers 447 stitched in black cotton and 581 in black ink.[19]

Burt struggled to keep his composure. 'I succeeded in not being sick,' he recalled with pride, 'but my face was wet with sweat.' The woman's appearance, the doctors said, 'indicated that she was of the working class.' They noted nine teeth missing from her upper jaw and seven from the lower. Heavy bruising was evident

above her left eye and on the right side of her head. She had similar contusions on the left shoulder blade, the upper-right arm, the
right elbow and forearm, the left forearm and the right side of the
abdomen.[20]

'All these bruises,' Rose told the detectives, 'were caused shortly
before death. The bruises on the right temple and the left eye were
caused by a direct blow – also the one on the abdomen. The other
bruises were made by pressure.'[21]

The woman had blue, but well-manicured, fingernails; her left
hand was clenched in a fist around her thumb. When cobbled
together, the various body parts made up a woman of stocky build,
about thirty-five years old and five feet three inches in height, with
brown bobbed hair. Rose told Cornish he believed the woman 'had
received a severe blow on the forehead, and that when unconscious someone had put a hand over her mouth and nose, causing
death by suffocation.' Judging from the jagged wounds to the neck,
the head had been hacked off. She'd been dead, Rose estimated,
for roughly three weeks.[22]

Rose now applied scalpel to flesh and dissected the torso with
incisions extending from the shoulders, down the chest and to the
navel in a large Y. Skin and muscle gave way, then he applied saw
to bone. The lungs appeared congested and the heart was empty
of blood. 'With these exceptions,' he noted, 'the woman's internal
organs are healthy.' He found traces of chocolate in her stomach.[23]

Throughout his long career, Cornish had worked murders of
all kinds. Regardless of motive, regardless of the circumstances –
whether it be a crime of passion or a random act of violence – the
killer's 'first reaction is to usually get away from the body' and
dispose of 'anything that he thinks might incriminate him.' The
killer who keeps his nerve will ditch the weapon, burn bloodstained clothing, establish his alibi and 'get rid of everything that
can connect him to the murder.' If questioned by authorities,
he will deny ever being in the vicinity of the crime. But Cornish

believed there to be an exception to this rule, as he wrote in his 1935 memoir:

> Murders of the 'trunk' type, with their several variations, are different. Here the murder is almost always premeditated. The murderer does not try to hide himself, he attempts to hide the body of his victim. His hope is that either the crime will never be discovered at all, or if it is, that time will have destroyed the clues . . . So far no crime of the 'trunk' type has gone unpunished in this country, although they have provided us with some of the most difficult as well as the most interesting cases.[*][24]

Cornish studied the trunk and the gore-smeared clothing. 'There were several clues to work on,' he later recalled. He would put detectives on the trail of 'P. Holt' and the origins of the laundry marks. 'The people at Charing Cross Station such as the cloak-room attendants, porters and taxi drivers had to be seen and questioned at once,' Cornish wrote. 'There was plenty of hard work ahead.' As Cornish pondered his strategy, an inspector from the Yard's Photographic Branch captured the grim items on film. The Yard's Press Bureau would send pictures to the newspapers for publication in the evening's early editions.[25]

Historically, relations between Scotland Yard and the press had been less than harmonious. Much ink had been flung over the years, criticizing the force – but Yard officials, even if begrudgingly, recognized the important role newspapers played in assisting investigations. In the early 1880s, Howard Vincent, first head of the CID, 'used press advertisements in the hunt for fugitives.' It earned him a rap on the knuckles from his Home Office superiors, who viewed the practice as bad form – but attitudes slowly changed.

---

* This may have been the case when Cornish was writing his memoir – but in June 1934, a woman's severed torso was found in two trunks in Brighton and King's Cross railway stations. The crime was never solved.

In 1919, the Yard introduced press briefings and, that same year, established its Press Bureau to better control the circulation of information. The Charing Cross case helped illustrate how news coverage could put a police inquiry on the right track.[26]

With no crime scene to investigate, queries began that afternoon at Charing Cross. Albert Glass, the luggage attendant who made the discovery, supplied the first link in the chain of evidence. He produced for detectives a crumpled yellow cloakroom ticket – No. 04190 – and said, as far as he could tell, the trunk had been left at the station at about 1:30 p.m. on Friday, 6 May. An attendant named Haystead received the trunk when it was dropped off, but remembered nothing of the owner's appearance. 'He asked what time the cloakroom was closed,' Haystead said. 'Then he said he had an appointment to keep and left.'[27]

If not for the quick actions of a shoe-shiner that Friday afternoon, the ticket may have been lost forever. William Davis, having just finished with a customer, saw a man in his mid- to late-thirties emerge from the station and hail a taxi. Such a thing would normally go unnoticed, Davis told Inspector Steele, but he saw the man quite deliberately throw a piece of paper – 'rolled up into a tight ball' – onto the ground as he got into the cab. Davis recognized the yellow paper as a cloakroom ticket and returned it to Glass, who kept it on his desk in the event the trunk's owner returned for his property.[28]

As the skies darkened on that first day of investigation, the evening papers went to press with a plea from Scotland Yard for information, accompanied by the pictures taken at Westminster Mortuary of the trunk and its contents. Some reporters couldn't help but notice similarities between the Charing Cross mystery and the happenings 'in a lonely bungalow on the Crumbles Beach.' Noted the (London) *Daily Herald*:

Circumstances attaching to the two cases are similar in certain respects. In both instances, the remains of the victims were left in railway cloakrooms; but while Mahon absent-mindedly left the ticket for the bag in a pocket for his wife to find, the supposed perpetrator of this new crime flung the document, untorn, through the window of his taxi-cab, to be rescued by a hanger-on at the station.[29]

One man who read that evening's papers with considerable interest was G. H. Ward, owner of Brixton Trunk Stores in Brixton Road, south London. He was startled to see, beneath the screaming headline announcing the discovery of a dismembered woman, a photograph of a trunk that until recently had sat on his sales floor. Realizing he might have information of interest, he went to Scotland Yard that evening and asked to speak with Chief Inspector Cornish.

'On seeing the photograph,' Ward said, 'I immediately recollected a man purchasing a similar trunk early last week.'

'How can you be sure it's the same trunk?' Cornish asked.

'It is an antique, somewhat obsolete sort of trunk and that enabled me to identify it,' Ward said. 'The purchaser had on a dark suit. He paid less than a pound for the trunk, and I helped it onto his shoulder.'[30]

Cornish pressed Ward for more details. Ward couldn't be sure of the date, but said the man entered his store 'between ten and eleven o'clock in the morning' on the Monday, Tuesday or Wednesday of the previous week.[31]

'He said he wanted a cheap one,' Ward said. 'Finally, he selected one. It had the letter "A" painted on it, and it was bound round with a strap. I offered to send the trunk, but the man replied that he was not going very far with it and would carry it himself.'

'What happened next?' asked Cornish.

'Well,' Ward replied, 'he put the trunk on his shoulder, walked out of the shop, turned to the left, and disappeared.'

Further questioning by Cornish elicited a vague description of the mystery customer: mid- to late-thirties with a neatly trimmed moustache, sharply attired in a dark suit and just under six feet tall.[32]

And with that, Cornish wrote, 'so ended the first day's hunt.'[33]

What the press called 'the keenest brains of Scotland Yard' pursued their lines of inquiry through the night, resulting in an early morning break on Wednesday, 11 May. Cornish began his day with news that detectives had traced laundry mark number 447 to a cleaner's in Shepherd's Bush. 'We hurried down to see the manageress who told us that the number was the mark used on the linen of a Mrs Holt of South Kensington,' Cornish wrote. 'Holt' was the name written on the pair of women's underwear found in the trunk. The manageress told Cornish the underwear most likely belonged to someone in Mrs Holt's employ, as the number was written in black ink. 'The customers' linens are marked in red,' the manageress explained, 'and their servants in black.'[34]

Mary Holt lived in a white terraced house at 3, Tregunter Road in Chelsea. She was unaccustomed to detectives showing up on her doorstep in possession of her knickers, but she invited Cornish in and sat for his questions. She identified the undergarments as having belonged to her daughter, but they'd gone missing several months prior when a cook she employed left her service. Cornish asked Mrs Holt what the cook looked like. She described the woman as somewhat stout, about five feet tall, with brown hair worn in a bobbed fashion. 'When Mrs Holt described the cook to me,' Cornish wrote, 'I hoped that we had identified the murdered woman, the description of the two were very much alike.'[35]

And the woman's name? Cornish asked.

'Mrs Roles,' replied Holt. 'Mrs Elsie Roles.'[36]

Holt said she'd hired Elsie the previous summer, sometime in June or July, through a servants' agency in Chelsea. She lived on and off in the Holt household until she left for good in November. Mrs Holt said a former maid, Frances Askey, had planned to rent a room with Elsie – beyond that, she knew nothing more. Cornish thanked Mrs Holt and arranged for a formal statement to be taken that evening at the Chelsea Police Station. 'I now had to try to trace Mrs Roles if she was alive,' Cornish noted, 'or if she was dead to find someone to identify her.'[37]

The servants' agency had no forwarding address for Elsie Roles, but they had one for Frances Askey. 'What she told us,' Cornish wrote, 'took us a stride further on in our inquiries.' Askey told Cornish that she and Elsie had grown quite close, bonded in their servitude to the Holts. In between polishing the china and making the Yorkshire puddings, Askey said, Elsie 'revealed a great deal about her private life.'[38]

Elsie Roles was, in actuality, thirty-six-year-old Minnie Alice Bonati. She was married to Bianco Bonati, an Italian waiter at Canuto's restaurant in Baker Street. The two had been separated for several years. Recently, Askey said, Minnie 'had been associated with a man named Roles.' The two had lived together for some months in a boarding house in New King's Road. Minnie often used Roles's name to 'stifle gossip' or went by her maiden name, Budd. The pair had since separated, and Roles now rented a room in Lambeth Road.[39]

'Mr Roles, when we found him, showed no surprise at our visit,' Cornish reported. 'In fact, he seemed to have been expecting us, a fact which rather astonished me, for so far no clue to the dead woman's identity had appeared in the newspapers.' Frederick Roles, a road worker, spoke freely of his romantic entanglement with Minnie – a volatile affair that often spiralled into violence. The two had lived together sporadically for three years but went their separate ways in July 1926 when Minnie's drink-fuelled temper proved too much to bear. And that wasn't all.[40]

'She's been promiscuous in her relations with men,' Roles said. 'If you expect to locate and question all the men who have known

Minnie within recent months, you'll have a major job on your hands – and quite a lot of suspects.'[41]

'What makes you so sure a crime's been committed?' Cornish asked.

Roles balked at the question. 'When I read the description of the murdered woman in the papers, I was sure it was Minnie,' he said, 'and I was certain that you would come and see me about it in due course.'[42]

Thursday, 12 May. The dismembered body of Minnie Bonati still lay in the morgue at Westminster Mortuary. The remains had been cleansed of all gore and assembled on a gurney. Bianco Bonati stood in pained silence as an attendant wheeled the gurney out of the cold-storage room. Cornish, lingering nearby, nodded at the attendant, who pulled back a white sheet to expose the human wreckage. Bonati took a tentative step forward and studied what remained of his ex-wife.

'It's her,' he said.

'You're sure?' Cornish asked.

Bianco nodded and said Minnie had a crooked index finger on the right hand, very small ears and, he added – staring at the dead woman's lips pulled back in a rigor-mortis sneer – four 'thick' teeth in the front.[43]

'We had found the identity of the dead woman,' Cornish wrote, 'but we were still without a clue as to her murderer.' Prior to visiting the mortuary, Bianco had shared with Cornish the details of his marriage. He said he and Minnie married on 27 April 1913, moved into a house in Balcombe Street and settled down for the long haul. And there the story might have ended, but – in the late summer of 1923 – Bianco took Frederick Roles in as a lodger. Several weeks later, Bianco kicked Roles and Minnie, then lovers, out of the house.[44]

'Did you see her again after that?' Cornish asked.

'Oh, I have seen her a good many times,' Bianco said, 'but the only times on which I have seen her have been when she called for money.'

'And you gave her money?' Cornish asked.

'Yes. Several times. I could not see her on the street.'[45]

Bianco said he never asked Minnie about her relationship with Roles, and the two of them soon fell into a pattern. She'd turn up on Bianco's doorstep asking for a handout, Bianco would oblige, and Minnie would vanish until her purse once more grew light. Then, one day, she simply stopped showing up.[46]

It seemed to be another dead end. Neither Bianco nor Frederick Roles matched the description of the man who purchased the trunk from Henry Ward. 'Mrs Bonati's husband,' Cornish wrote, 'satisfied us that he was quite innocent of any connection with the murder.' Bianco directed Cornish to Minnie's mother and a sister. They vouched for Bianco's character ('He is a fine chap') and confirmed Minnie's promiscuity. More than a month had passed since their last contact with Minnie. They 'thought nothing of not seeing her recently, because she was of a roving disposition and changed her address frequently'. Although Minnie liked to run around with other men, her mother said, she 'had been living alone lately in a room in Limerston Street, Chelsea.'[47]

Cornish questioned Minnie's neighbours, one of whom reported seeing her on the street outside the building at about two o'clock in the morning of Wednesday, 4 May, six days before the discovery at Charing Cross. There was no doubt it was Minnie because the two of them had exchanged greetings. 'No one seemed to have seen her since,' Cornish said, 'and we therefore concluded that she had been murdered either on or just after this date . . . All our possible suspects had cleared themselves. We had found out the identity of the dead woman, but we were still without a clue as to her murderer.'[48]

*

Detectives slogged forward on multiple fronts. While Cornish tracked down Minnie Bonati's family and associates, Detective Sergeant Leonard Burt tried to trace the trunk's movements. Press coverage, meanwhile, brought to Scotland Yard a taxi driver named Edward Sharpington with an interesting story.

The cabbie told Burt he picked two men up outside the Royal Automotive Club on 6 May and drove them to Westminster Police Court to pay a traffic summons. No sooner had the two paid their fare than a gentleman emerged from an office block across the street at 86, Rochester Row and hailed a ride. Sharpington pulled up and helped the man carry a trunk from the building's doorway.[49]

'It's heavy,' Sharpington said. 'Is it full of money?'

'No, it's certainly not money,' the man said, laughing. 'It's books.'

The two men wrestled the trunk into the taxi.

'Charing Cross Station, please,' the man said.[50]

Sharpington told Burt all this happened at around 1:30 p.m. The timing fit, as the trunk had been left at Charing Cross – less than two miles away – between half past one and quarter to two.

Cornish dispatched Burt and Inspector Steele to 86, Rochester Row, a four-storey building with a shop on the ground floor and office space above. The second and third floors were leased by Geoffrey Gush, a solicitor, who told the detectives he had sublet two furnished rooms on 22 March to a man named John Robinson, 'who carried on a business there under the name of Edwards & Co., Business Transfer Agents'. He paid a month's rent in advance and did so again in April before vanishing from the premises on 9 May, leaving in his wake a brief note to his landlord:[51]

Dear Sir:

I am sorry to inform you that I have gone broke, so cannot use your office further. Let the people who supplied the typewriter take it away. My rent is paid.

J. Robinson[52]

Why had Robinson vacated his office when he'd paid rent through to 22 May? The detectives questioned everyone in the building. The solicitor's clerk recalled having to step around a large trunk when entering the building at 1:30 p.m. on Friday, 6 May. When he walked past the doorway again fifteen minutes later, the trunk was gone. No one had a forwarding address for Robinson, but the solicitor had one for Robinson's typist. She told Burt and Steele the last time she saw Robinson was the afternoon of 4 May, when he stumbled into the office drunk. Disgusted, she left and never returned.[53]

The detectives returned to Scotland Yard and reported their findings. 'Chief Inspector Cornish,' Burt wrote, 'listened with an intentness and a respect never shown by Lestrade or Gregson to Sherlock Holmes.' The inspector at last had a possible suspect. Through Robinson's bank, information gleaned from the rent he paid for the office space, Cornish obtained the address of a boarding house in north London. The landlady told Cornish that Robinson had only been a tenant for six weeks before disappearing on 9 May.[54]

Detectives searched Robinson's room, its furnishings sparse with a bed against one wall and a bureau and small desk against another. In a waste bin beneath the desk, they found a crumpled piece of paper. It was a return notice from the Post Office, saying a telegram addressed to '"Robinson, the Greyhound Hotel, Hammersmith" could not be delivered, as the addressee was unknown there.'[55]

Queries at the Greyhound Hotel revealed the Robinson in question was John Robinson's estranged wife. 'She had not received the telegram,' Cornish later noted, 'owing to a curious mischance which assisted me considerably, but which if written in a detective story would probably be dismissed as being too "convenient".' The telegram had initially been delivered into the hands of a newly hired barmaid, who, not recognizing the name Robinson, passed it back to the messenger boy and said no one by that name worked at the hotel. The boy shrugged, stuffed the telegram back in his pouch and returned it to the Post Office. Cornish now learned John Robinson was living in De Laune Street, Kennington and had plans that evening – it was by now 19 May – to grab a drink at the Elephant & Castle pub in Walworth.[56]

When Robinson – a thirty-six-year-old 'fair-haired man of medium height and good build' – arrived at the pub, he found two detectives waiting. 'He was quite willing to come back to Scotland Yard with us to be questioned, and to all intents and purposes his statement was satisfactory,' Cornish noted in his report. 'He told us a good deal about himself, his army career and the various jobs which he had done since then. The business which he had started in Rochester Row failed because he had not had sufficient money to advertise it properly.'[57]

Robinson detailed his movements of May fourth through to the sixth, painting a routine story of days in the office and nights at the pub. He knew nothing of a trunk or Minnie Bonati. He agreed to stand in a line-up, but neither Edward Sharpington the cabbie, Henry Ward the trunk dealer, nor a porter from Charing Cross Station recognized him. Cornish had no choice but to let Robinson go.[58]

The investigation had thus far been a massive enterprise. 'Hundreds of persons were interviewed, no less than thirty of Mrs Bonati's friends were traced, hundreds of anonymous letters poured into Scotland Yard, garages all over London were visited, and house-to-house searches were made in some districts.' And now the most promising lead in the investigation had fizzled. 'Robinson strolled out of Scotland Yard,' Cornish said, 'and it looked very much as though I had been following a false clue, as yet another suspect had cleared himself . . . Twelve days had now passed, and we seemed to have exhausted every possible source of information without getting any nearer finding the murderer.'[59]

*

In the early morning hours of Saturday, 21 May, Cornish held a
conference at Scotland Yard to review the evidence with his detectives and Chief Constable Wensley. The men once more examined
the clothing from the trunk. One item that stuck out was the duster
used to wrap Minnie's head in. It was covered in blood and dirt. 'It
was just possible that there might be some name or laundry mark
on it, so I took it away and washed it out,' Cornish wrote. As he
held it under a tap and scrubbed away the grime, his eyes widened.
There, beneath the film of muck, was one word: 'Greyhound.'[60]

Wensley ordered detectives back to Robinson's one-time office
at Rochester Road to conduct a more thorough search. Its furnishings were typical: a few chairs, a safe and a roll-top desk. Recalled
Burt, 'It was amazing, I thought to myself, that there shouldn't be a
blood-stain anywhere, for surely this was where Minnie Bonati had
been murdered, and her body cut up into pieces and crammed
into the trunk.' Burt and another detective sergeant named Clarke
dropped to their hands and knees, magnifying glasses at the ready,
and went over the carpet. They found nothing. Clarke picked up a
wastebasket beneath the desk and dumped its contents onto the
floor.

'My lord!' he exclaimed.[61]

Amongst the scattering of discarded papers was a bloodstained
matchstick. 'We stared at it without a word, wondering what it's
history had been,' Burt said. 'Surely, Robinson, after he had murdered and dismembered his victim, had sat in the very chair where
I was sitting, had lit a cigarette and thrown the match into the
waste-paper basket as he had done a thousand times before.' More
startling was the possibility a murder had occurred in a room 'less
than 100 yards from the Westminster Police Court, and within half
a mile of Scotland Yard.'[62]

At the Greyhound Hotel, meanwhile, a barmaid recognized the
duster as one of hers. Cornish asked how she could be so sure. The
hotel supplied its thirty-seven employees with dusters that looked
identical.

The barmaid said she washed it one evening at home in the sink after having soaked a yellow rag. The rag's dye discoloured the water and stained the duster, giving it a yellowish tint. In explaining this, she mentioned she shared a room with the former Mrs Robinson. 'When I heard this,' Cornish noted, 'I was sure that my hunt was nearing its end.'[63]

Scotland Yard detectives arrested John Robinson in the early morning hours of Monday, 23 May, at his rented room in De Laune Street, a long street of terraced houses running parallel to London's theatre district. Robinson was asleep in bed when detectives entered the room. 'The arrest was carried out swiftly and silently,' reported one paper. 'Robinson was in a taxi-cab speeding to Scotland Yard before the other occupants of the house were aware of what had taken place in the bedroom on the upper floor.'[64]

Robinson, perhaps sensing Cornish was primed with new evidence, abandoned all pretence.

'I realize this is serious,' Robinson said. 'I met that woman at Victoria. I took her up to my offices and want to tell you all about it. I done it and cut her up.'

Cornish held up a hand and cautioned Robinson of his rights.

'All right,' Robinson said. 'I'll tell you.'[65]

Robinson said he met Minnie Bonati near Victoria Station around four o'clock on the afternoon of 4 May. She seemed the forward type, so he invited her back to his office at Rochester Row. Once there, she asked him for money and flew into a temper when he said he had none to spare. She became violent and tried to hit him. Robinson said he pushed Minnie backwards and lashed out with his fist, causing her to fall and hit her head on a chair. He left her there and returned to his room.

'I returned to my office about ten o'clock the following morning,' he said. 'I was surprised to find that she was still there. She was dead. I was in a hopeless position then. I didn't know what to do. I sat down and decided to cut the body up in pieces and cart it away in parcels.'

Robinson said he went to a stationery store in Victoria Street and purchased 'six sheets of brown paper and a ball of string.' He then paid a visit to Staines Kitchen Equipment Co., the very store Patrick Mahon purchased the blade he used to carve up Emily Kaye, and bought a large kitchen knife.[66]

'I then went back to my office and I cut off her arms and legs,' he said. 'I made it up into four parcels and tied them up in the brown paper and string. I finished the job quickly as I could before dinner. I put the three smaller parcels in the cupboard, and the trunk in a corner of the room. I then went to a public-house and had a drink, and later I went home. I afterwards met my wife.'

On the morning of Friday, 6 May, Robinson purchased the trunk from Henry Ward's shop in Brixton. He caught a bus back to his office and packed Minnie's limbs and torso into the trunk. He did the same with the head after wrapping it in the duster from the Greyhound Hotel. It was thirsty work. When done, he headed out for a late-morning drink. At the pub, Robinson saw a man he often chatted with over pints and said he needed help carrying a heavy trunk down from his office. The man agreed to lend a hand. With the trunk downstairs, Robinson went into the street and hailed the taxi that took him to Charing Cross Station.

'I returned to my office, and later I met my wife,' he said. 'I buried the knife under a tree on Clapham Common. There was very little blood from the body when I cut it up.'

Robinson's statement was verified that same day. His former typist identified the yellow 'Greyhound' duster as being a rag he kept in his office. Police even tracked down the man who helped Robinson carry the trunk downstairs. Shortly after 1 p.m., Cornish – along with Chief Constable Wensley and Sergeant Clarke – accompanied Robinson to Clapham Common and retrieved the buried knife. At five-thirty that evening, Cornish officially charged Robinson with murder.[67]

*

John Robinson's trial at the Old Bailey began on Monday, 11 July 1927. A long line of people, including 'many women fashionably dressed in summer frocks', waited outside the courtroom in hopes of a seat. Robinson entered the dock in a grey suit, white shirt and a blue bow tie with white polka dots. 'The accused man,' noted a reporter, 'walked firmly to the front of the dock, and stood with hands in front of him on the dock rail, the sun shining down on his upturned faced. In clear, distinct tones he pleaded not guilty to the charge.'[68]

The trial lasted two days. Robinson testified in his own defence, repeating the story he'd told Cornish. He said he acted in self-defence and had no clue Minnie was dead when she hit the floor. 'When she fell to the ground she sort of got into a sitting position and then fell on her right side with her right arm underneath her,' he said. 'I picked up my hat and I said, "Now then, you can get out of it as quick as you like. I am off."'[69]

Asked why he never called police when it became apparent the woman was dead, Robinson said, 'I was in a blue funk. I did not know what to do. If I had gone to the police they would have been sure to have arrested me.'[70]

His story didn't help him – nor did the testimony of Sir Bernard Spilsbury, who had been asked in the course of the investigation to examine the body. 'A stir went through the courtroom when the famous pathologist stepped into the witness box,' *The Coventry Evening Telegraph* reported. 'Sir Bernard gave his evidence in clear, deliberate tones, which could be heard without difficulty in every corner of the court.'[71]

'In my opinion,' Spilsbury said, 'death was caused by asphyxia or suffocation brought about by covering over the mouth and nostrils, and after the woman had been violently assaulted.'[72]

That was all the jury needed to hear. It adjourned at 4 p.m. on Wednesday, 13 July and returned at 5:36 p.m. Robinson eyed the jurors as they filed in and took their seats, shifting his gaze only when the clerk asked for the verdict.

'We find him guilty.'[73]

Asked by the judge if he had anything to say before sentencing, Robinson replied, 'No, my Lord,' and visibly braced himself. 'He looked directly at his lordship as the death sentence was being delivered,' one reporter wrote, 'but, as the words "The sentence of the Court is that you be taken from hence to the place whence you came and then to a place of execution and there hanged by the neck" were uttered, Robinson's face flushed. This grew more perceptible when the words "and your body will afterwards be buried in the precincts of the prison" were spoken by the judge.'[74]

John Robinson was hanged on Friday, 12 August 1927.

'The careful chopping up of a body already dead always seems to be unforgivable to juries . . .' Detective Sergeant Burt wrote in hindsight. 'The Crippen case proved how a jury's sympathy is eternally forfeit when a killer (for whom possibly excuses can be found) is callous enough to dismember his victim. The Robinson case rubbed in the lesson.'[75]

Across the Atlantic, *The New York Times* cheered the Yard's handling of the investigation. 'When clue after clue had failed to lead to an arrest,' the paper marvelled, 'it appeared that Scotland Yard had to do with a master criminal.' That might have been slight exaggeration, but the case indeed proved a good showing for 'Scotland Yard's famous detectives'.[76]

Unlike the case of Patrick Mahon, who was turned in by his wife and arrested as he retrieved his bloody luggage, the Charing Cross murder provided no such advantage. The Yard started on a trail already cold. Even Cornish worried 'whether we should ever be able to clear it up'. Cooperation with the press proved vital in cracking the mystery. Without it, taxi driver Edward Sharpington may never have come forward to inform detectives 'he had picked up a man with a trunk on the 6th of May from the doorway of 86, Rochester Row'.[77]

That piece of information revealed the scene of the crime, uncovered the bloody matchstick and put detectives on Robinson's trail. Cornish called out Sharpington's contribution in a case summary dated 28 July 1927. 'His assistance to us was of great value,' Cornish wrote, 'and I beg to recommend that he be granted a suitable reward from the Informant's Fund.'[78]

He also acknowledged the stubborn determination of the men under his command, who – working 'long periods each day investigating every clue and piece of available information' – took 260 statements over the thirteen-day manhunt. 'All officers,' Cornish wrote, 'displayed indefatigable energy and I submit that the result of the case reflects great credit upon all concerned.'[79]

The gruesome details of the Charing Cross murder had not long faded from the papers when another high-profile slaying thrust the Yard's famed sleuths once more into the headlines. The killing occurred not in London but fifty miles to the northeast along a quiet country road. The victim this time was not a woman who'd run afoul of her lover, but a police officer slaughtered execution-style. His death would introduce to the British public the 'fingerprints' of guns.

19

Point-Blank

Bullet holes for eyes. 'Gun finger-prints'.

Postman William Ward made his usual rounds between the towns of Romford and Abridge on the morning of Tuesday, 27 September 1927. On this particular day he was running behind schedule, his progress hampered by a thick fog that veiled the trees on either side of the road and obscured the blacktop ahead. He had just left the post office in Havering and was driving down a wooded stretch of lane in Essex when he spotted an object on the grassy shoulder. It was, he realized as he drew closer, a man.

'I am accustomed to seeing tramps sitting on the side of the road early in the morning, and I didn't pay much attention,' Ward said. 'The fact, however, that he had his legs stretched out towards the centre of the road attracted me just as I was passing.'[1]

Ward pulled over and got out of his van to investigate. As he approached the man on foot, he realized it was local police constable George Gutteridge, who he knew well. The two often crossed paths in the morning, as the constable walked home from his nightly rounds.

'Hello, George!' Ward said. 'What's the matter?'

Gutteridge made no reply. He was sitting with his back against a row of hedges. Ward could see a pencil clutched in the constable's right hand and a notebook lying open on his lap. His helmet lay next to him.

'His left hand was clenched stiff,' Ward said, 'as though he had been clawing the air in a futile attempt to grasp something to pull himself up. I spoke to him again, and still there was no answer.'[2]

Ward touched Gutteridge's left hand; the skin was cold. 'I bent down and saw that his face was covered with blood,' he said. 'I did not know exactly if he was dead or not. At first I thought that he might have been knocked down by a car. Anyhow, I knew I had to get help.'[3]

It was about 6 a.m. He ran to the nearby cottage of Alfred Perrit, an insurance salesman, and told him of the 'gruesome find'. Perrit followed Ward back to the scene and 'realized Gutteridge was dead'. The body 'was still warm' and surrounded by 'a great pool' of congealed blood.[4]

A small crowd gathered as news spread. A farmer who lived nearby showed up with bandages, hot water bottles and brandy 'in case they were needed'. 'We thought from his appearance,' the farmer said, 'that he had been bludgeoned on the head. We did not know until afterwards that he had been shot.'[5]

Realizing nothing could be done, the farmer dragged a rug from his car and used it to cover the body until police arrived. Ward returned to his van and drove to the next town of Abbotts Tawney, where he telephoned the local police. 'The hue and cry was raised to all police stations,' states one report, 'and in a short space of time a large force of police was on the scene.'[6]

Detective Inspector John Crockford of the Romford Police arrived in a taxi at quarter to eight. He noticed the grass near the body had been 'marked by something like a motor car wheel being driven firmly against it'. A trail of blood smeared across the roadway suggested the constable had been attacked on the opposite side 'and struggled to the place where his body was found'. Two .455 calibre bullets near the fallen officer gave hint to the cause of death. Blood obscured the dead man's features and matted his hair in a grotesque tangle, making it impossible to inspect the wounds. Crockford sent the taxi that brought him to retrieve Dr Robert Woodhouse, the local physician.[7]

Trinity Mirror/Mirrorpix/Alamy

The scene of PC Gutteridge's murder.

An hour later, just shy of nine, Woodhouse worked his way through the onlookers and ranks of uniformed constables, knelt beside the fallen officer and made the official pronouncement of death. He found the positioning of the body, with its legs outstretched, peculiar. 'A shot person usually sags at the knees and falls in a heap,' Woodhouse noted. 'I am convinced, therefore, that he had been taken to the side of the road and there laid down.' Based on body rigidity, Woodhouse estimated Gutteridge had been dead no more than five hours. The body was carried to the nearby Royal Oak pub, only a short distance from the Gutteridge family home, and placed in the cart shed.[8]

When Captain John Unett, the chief constable of Essex, 'received a report from his officers on the spot, he telephoned Scotland Yard asking for the co-operation of the Metropolitan Police.'[9]

At the Royal Oak, with Inspector Crockford in attendance, Woodhouse cleaned Gutteridge's face and head to reveal 'two holes which appeared consistent with the entry of two large bullets' about two inches in front of Gutteridge's left ear. The base of the skull was 'practically blown away'.[10] Woodhouse detailed the devastation:

> There were four wounds from shots in the head and neck. Two of them, apparently the first two, had been fired at him from the side. One of these passed through his head from cheekbone to cheekbone, and the other through the upper part of the neck below the jawbones. These two shots had apparently not killed him, and he reached there and was laid down near the far side of the road, two more shots had been fired into his head. One pierced each eye, both emerging at the back, practically at the same place.[11]

Woodhouse described the revolver used as 'a Service weapon of heavy calibre'. The skin around both eye sockets was blackened and burned, evidence the killer had placed the muzzle against the constable's face. The first two shots to the side of the head had been fired from some distance. The two bullets found at the crime scene were accounted for. The other two, Woodhouse told Crockford, 'are embedded in his skull. The post-mortem by the surgeons will prove that.'[12]

Crockford, appalled by the overkill, ordered the body moved to the Romford Mortuary for autopsy. He stepped from the shed into the bucolic surroundings of Stapleford Abbotts, trying to reconcile the morning's savagery with such a pastoral setting: the wooded lanes and timbered buildings, the rolling farmland awash in the light of an autumn afternoon. The men from Scotland Yard would no doubt be arriving by nightfall. He would do what he could before then. He got to work and ascertained certain facts.

Thirty-eight-year-old Police Constable George William Gutteridge was a seventeen-year veteran of the Essex County

Constabulary, having joined the police service in April 1910. He did a ten-month stint in the Army, starting in April 1918, and re-joined the constabulary in February the following year. He transferred to the Epping Division in March 1922 'and was assigned a beat that included Stapleford Abbotts, Kelvedon Hatch, Lambourne End and Stamford Rivers'. Tall in height and broad in width, he cut a formidable figure, which could often be found at the bar in the Royal Oak. Outgoing and good-humoured, he enjoyed the camaraderie found over a pint or two – or several. 'On more than one occasion,' according to one account, 'he was discovered drunk in a hedge after last orders.' Well liked on the beat, Gutteridge lived in Stapleford Abbotts at 2, Townley Cottages – 300 yards from the murder scene – with his wife Rose, his daughter Muriel, aged twelve, and four-year-old son Alfred.[13]

Crockford walked the short distance to the Gutteridge home. A shocked and grief-stricken Rose told Crockford her husband had come home at six o'clock the previous evening and spent time with the family. At 11 p.m., she went upstairs to bed, leaving her husband to ready himself for that night's patrol. It was the last time she saw him alive.

Gutteridge left home each night at 3 a.m. and rendezvoused for a quick chat with PC Sydney Taylor at nearby Howe Green, a quarter-mile from the murder site. 'We talked for a few minutes and then parted some time about 3:15 a.m.,' said Taylor, who walked the neighbouring beat. 'Everything was quiet. The night was still and clear then. I went back towards Passingford Bridge, and then turned off towards Lambourne. I passed nothing on the road. I heard nothing. At the time when, presumably, Gutteridge was shot, I should have been nearly a mile away and rather in a hollow. No sound reached me.'[14]

Although newspapers would describe the murder scene as isolated, a number of farms and cottages dotted the surrounding area. Police fanned out to knock on doors. Their efforts paid off at the farmhouse of Montague Martin, 300 yards from Howe Green across a grass field.

'Some time after three o'clock, near to the half-hour, I think I was awakened,' Martin said. 'As I lay in bed, I heard a single report, but nothing after that. I was drowsy and I went to sleep again without wondering much what the report was.' Gertrud Decies, whose cottage sat just off the lane a mile from where Gutteridge died, told a similar story. 'I was lying awake, for I have an invalid in the house,' she said. 'I am certain that I heard several reports as though a gun or something had been fired, and after that there was the sound of a motor-car passing up the hill at a fast speed.' From the noise of its engine, she 'judged that it was a heavy car'.[15]

'Murder investigations, so far as Scotland Yard is concerned, happen much more frequently in books than in real life,' Chief Constable Fred Wensley wrote. 'From a detective point of view, these homicide crimes are either very simple or very difficult to handle. In the great majority of cases, people are killed in some emotional crisis, and the guilt of a particular person is palpable immediately. Once in a while, however, there happens a crime that taxes the energy and resource of those who have to deal with it.'[16]

The Gutteridge investigation, stretching over four long months, proved such a case and fell to CID Chief Inspector James Berrett.

Berrett was already well known when he and Sergeant John Harris arrived in Essex that Tuesday afternoon in one of Scotland Yard's new Lea-Francis motor cars. 'Inspector Berrett is one of the few Yard chiefs who wears a beard,' reported the *Sunday Post*, 'and has often been referred to as "King Edward's double".' Another newspaper claimed he was 'the only bearded detective in the country.' He had joined Scotland Yard in 1893 and spent most of his career 'in our great CID' where he rose to his present rank. In being a detective, he revelled in 'the age-old thrill of the hunters and the hunted! He believed nothing short of destiny had guided him to police work and 'enjoyed every day of every year' on the job.[17]

Berrett at once felt the weight of the investigation. 'From the time I was put in charge of the case, I was no longer Berrett,' he wrote. 'I was ten, twenty, thirty thousand police officers in every corner of the kingdom – if necessary, in every civilized country in the world.'[18]

He established his base of operations at Romford Police Station and familiarized himself with the particulars of the case before driving out to the scene. The lane, fifteen feet across, still bore grisly scars from the pre-dawn's violence. 'A small company of police and detectives searched the roadside and the adjourning fields all day in the hope of finding a weapon or something which would give them a clue to the murderer.' No such clue was found. Blood stained the grass shoulder where Gutteridge had been found, while 'the stains of blood on the road told a clear tale.'[19]

Berrett theorized Gutteridge was six feet from the grass shoulder on the right, most likely as he stood looking towards Stapleford Abbotts 'in the direction of his home'. The six feet 'would have been just the space occupied by a car, drawn up by the roadside and facing towards the way from which Gutteridge was walking.' The constable was most likely questioning the driver when the first shots were fired. After being shot twice, Gutteridge, based on the crimson blotches on the roadway, 'must have staggered a rolling course to the left side of the road and collapsed flat on his back', dropping his notebook in the process but holding firm to his pencil. His helmet most likely came off when he hit the ground.[20]

Berrett surmised that Gutteridge may have come across a vehicle with its lights out, something that would have undoubtedly aroused the suspicions of a constable patrolling 'the lonely high road in the frosty darkness before dawn'. The fact Gutteridge had his notebook out indicated 'some technical offence had been committed, which required the constable to write in his book the name and address of the driver and the number of the car, in case the issue of summons should afterwards be contemplated.' Even if all seemed normal with the vehicle, any worthwhile officer would have questioned the driver as to why they were out at such an hour. And yet, beyond these deductions built on a vague foundation of dried blood, the crime scene offered nothing more.[21]

A possible break, however, came later in the afternoon when Berrett learned a local doctor had reported his car stolen that morning. The blue 1927 Morris Cowley four-seater, registration number TW 6120 and upholstered in imitation blue leather, had vanished from Edward Lovell's garage sometime in the pre-dawn hours. Berrett and Harris sped to the doctor's bungalow in the village of Billericay, some twenty miles from the murder site.[22]

The house on London Road sat in the shadow of a large oak tree. Passing through a white picket fence set in a thick hedgerow, Berrett and Harris saw a detached garage to the right of the house with its double barn doors wide open. Dr Lovell told the detectives he discovered his car missing at nine o'clock that morning when he left the house for work. 'I went to the garage, which is near the bedroom window,' he said. 'The lock had been cleverly picked and the car stolen.' Neither he nor his wife heard anything during the night that aroused their suspicions. 'I believe it was pushed to the road and pushed along some distance before it was started.'[23]

Two neighbours told Berrett and Harris they heard the heavy rumble of a motor car sometime between two and three in the morning. Neither thought anything of it, as they often heard Lovell driving off on late-night calls. They said the sound of the engine faded in the direction of Mount Nessing, 'along the by-road, which could be taken by anyone wishing to reach the scene of the murder without touching the main road.'[24]

Forty-two miles away in the south London district of Brixton, a brewery clerk named A. J. McDougal arrived home from work shortly before six that evening. He lived at 21, Foxley Road, a small cul-de-sac 'little known even to local residents'. He had left the house at seven-thirty that morning, the day cold and wet with mist, and couldn't help but notice the car parked in the alley behind his home. 'It was so close to my back door,' he said, 'that I almost fell over it as I came out.' It was a blue Morris Cowley, much like the one his neighbour owned. He had thought nothing of it that morning, but now it piqued his curiosity.[25]

While at work, he had read about the murder of Constable Gutteridge. The gruesome nature of the killing proved irresistible fodder for the press, which speculated the killer 'himself was a superstitious crook who fancied that a murdered person's eyes held in their death gaze the photo of the slayer, and that believing this he deliberately fired into the wounded man's eyes'. With details of the killing fresh in his mind, McDougal, a car enthusiast, noticed the vehicle parked near his back door had an Essex registration number. He hurried inside and called the police.[26]

Detective Sergeant Charles Hearns arrived in the alley behind McDougal's house at 6:45 p.m. and drove the car back to Brixton Police Station. In the station's courtyard, Hearns and Detective Constable Harold Hawkyard examined the vehicle by torchlight. On the windshield, they observed what appeared to be 'the blood-stained impression of a hand' and bloodstains on the driver's side running board. The detectives noted that 'appearances pointed to a struggle having taken place'. The 'front left wing' of the car bore the impact wounds of a collision. Inside the car, on the driver's side floor mat, they found two spent .455 calibre shell casings. The scene at the station 'became one of suppressed excitement' as detectives realized they had found the possible murder car. Brought down from Essex the following day, Dr Lovell positively identified the vehicle as his.[27]

News of the car's recovery brought Berrett back to London. The cul-de-sac in which it was found ran 'to the rear of only a few houses' in Foxley Road and would be of little use to non-residents. Berrett believed the car had been abandoned by someone 'thoroughly acquainted with the district'. Detectives, assisted by Scotland Yard's Flying Squad, fanned out 'in search of men believed to be lying low in south London and Paddington districts'. Many officers on the hunt, mindful of the killer's savagery, armed themselves – a rarity for British police.[28]

Ballistics, although still a fledgling science in the 1920s, had been applied to criminal investigations in the past. In January 1784, John Toms shot and killed a Lancashire carpenter named Edward Culshaw and 'then robbed him of his watch and some pence'. A piece of wadding retrieved from the fatal wound was matched to a torn corner of a ballad sheet found in Toms's pocket. Modern ballistics, however, took stronger root more than fifty years later.[29]

In January 1835, a Bow Street Runner named Henry Goddard was sent to Southampton to investigate an attempted burglary at the Hamilton Place home of wealthy Mrs Maxwell. According to initial reports, butler Joseph Randall 'had been most courageous in his efforts to protect the property of his mistress' and exchanged gunfire with the would-be crooks. He told Goddard he 'had narrowly escaped being shot by a pistol ball, discharged through the window in the pantry' where he slept. A sceptical Goddard asked to see Randall's guns and ammunition. His inspection under magnifying glass 'found an identical pimple on all the bullets, including the one that had allegedly been fired at Randall'. When Goddard checked Randall's ammunition mould, he found in it 'a corresponding pinhead-sized hole', meaning all the bullets – including the one supposedly fired by the crooks – came from Randall's arsenal. Exposed, the butler confessed to staging the gunfight in hopes of currying favour with his employer.[30]

Primitive ballistics again came into practice on 24 October 1860, when a suspected poacher shot and killed Police Constable Alexander McBrian in a Lincolnshire churchyard. Wadding – 'charred at the edges and having a smell of gunpowder, or Sulphur'

- recovered at the crime scene matched the wadding found in the un-discharged barrel of suspect Thomas Richardson's shotgun. Reported *The Times*, 'The pieces of paper found in the church-yard, and also those that came from the left barrel of the gun, had formed part of *The Times* newspaper of the 27th March [1854].' Richardson was convicted and sentenced to death, but a subsequent confession saved him from the hangman.[31]

What is 'probably the earliest recorded use of ballistics evidence' by Scotland Yard stemmed from the murder of Police Constable George Cole on the foggy night of 1 December 1882. Cole was shot and killed when he came across a thief attempting to break into a church in the East End. The case languished for nearly two years before an informant pointed detectives in the direction of one Thomas Orrock, who enjoyed shooting his gun on Tottenham Marshes. Police canvassed the wetlands in north London and dug a bullet from a tree trunk. The bullet was an exact match, in terms of weight and type, to the bullet removed from Cole's body. It was enough to charge Orrock - in prison for another offence - with the constable's murder. Whitechapel gunmaker James Squires matched the bullets from the tree, the victim, and one found in Cole's truncheon to a gun Orrock once owned. Orrock went to the gallows on 6 October 1884.[32]

Four years later, French physician and criminologist Alexandre Lacassagne, a professor of forensic medicine at the Institute of Legal Medicine in Lyon, suggested that bullets - when fired from a gun - were scarred by grooves known as 'rifling marks'. He stumbled across this theory while autopsying the body of seventy-eight-year-old Claude Moiroud, who had been shot to death. One bullet had cut a path through Moiroud's abdomen, passed through his kidney and lodged in his spine. Another round buried itself in a shoulder bone, while a third was found in the soft tissue of the larynx. A microscopic inspection of all three bullets revealed each one bore identical markings despite having passed through different parts of the body.[33]

'It was extraordinary,' Lacassagne wrote. 'The bullet found in the larynx, which had not collided with anything hard, was creased along its access with the same kind of furrow as the bullet that was lodged in the shoulder . . . It seemed to be a kind of marking or identity of the revolver.'[34]

Police suspected a young man named Echallier of the killing and found a gun hidden beneath the floorboards of his girlfriend's house. They turned the weapon over to Lacassagne, who contacted the manufacturer, Maison Verney-Cassons. Lacassagne learned 'that gunmakers cut helical grooves' in the barrel, imparting a spin on the bullet to steady its trajectory. Much like a finger leaves a print, these grooves leave markings on the bullet. Intrigued, Lacassagne acquired the corpse of an eighty-year-old man from the local hospital and shot it twice – once in the abdomen and once in the shoulder – with Echallier's gun. An examination of the bullets revealed markings identical to those found on the bullets recovered from the murdered Moiroud.

'The formations are so identical,' Lacassagne wrote, 'that they must have come out of the same revolver.' Echallier was subsequently convicted and sentenced to life in prison, while Lacassagne went on to publish his findings in 1889 in the *Archives of Criminal Anthropology*.[35]

In 1912, back in England, Scotland Yard tackled 'a landmark case involving firearms' that put Lacassagne's theory to the test. Responding to a burglar alarm on the night of 9 October at the home of Countess Flora Sztaray at 6, South Cliff Avenue, Detective Inspector Arthur Wells of the Eastbourne Borough Police was shot through the heart and killed. The countess, out to dinner at the time, returned home to find the fallen officer sprawled 'on the porch over the front door.' The killer, in his haste, had left a trilby hat near the body. At the request of local authorities, the Yard put Chief Inspector Eli Bower on the case. Bower had barely arrived in town when 'a man who gave the name of Doctor Power informed me that he knew the murderer to be one . . . John Williams.'[36]

The doctor was actually a one-time medical student named Edgar Power, who told the chief inspector he had plans to meet Williams at Moorgate Street Station in central London. When Williams showed up to meet his friend at the station's restaurant, Bowers approached from behind and arrested him on suspicion of murder.

Williams appeared in Eastbourne Police Court on 12 October with an apron over his head to thwart newspaper photographers. The press delighted in the disguise and bestowed upon Williams the villainous sobriquet 'The Hooded Man'. In the act of 'consoling' Williams's distraught wife, Power learned the murder weapon had been disassembled and buried on the beach in Eastbourne. Power convinced her the gun would be found and should be hidden somewhere else. When she took him to the oceanfront to retrieve it, the informed Inspector Bower lay in wait.[37]

Scotland Yard took possession of 'the revolver in two parts, minus the hammer and two screws' and turned to twenty-five-year-old Robert Churchill, a firearms expert who owned a gun shop in Leicester Square, for help. Since 1910, Churchill had applied his expertise in a number of criminal cases for Scotland Yard and the Director of Public Prosecutions. Intrigued 'by guns – and by murder – since his early childhood', Churchill – miserable in his marriage – devoted most of his time to 'cataloguing the rifling of various kinds of guns'. He replaced the .25 automatic's missing hammer and screws, test-fired a round in his shop and matched it to the bullet retrieved from the murdered Inspector Wells.[38]

To better highlight the match for jurors, Sergeant William McBride from the Yard's Photograph Branch took close-up shots 'to illustrate the pattern of grooves on the bullets'. He also took close-up pictures of dental-wax impressions Churchill made of the gun barrel's interior, showing the rifling that etched the pattern when the bullet was fired from the gun. Williams was sentenced to death and Churchill became known as 'the Spilsbury of ballistics'.[39]

'It is known that a pistol or revolver barrel is rifled to impart spin to the bullet,' Churchill would later write. 'It is therefore easy to examine a bullet, count the number of grooves, measure their width and angle of twist, and to state the make of weapon used. What is not generally known is that every bullet groove differs even from its next-door neighbour in its peculiar markings. Under the microscope, no two blades of grass are alike, and under the microscope each groove has its own set of minute lines and striations.'[40]

Churchill's knowledge and expertise would prove vital in the Gutteridge investigation.

The Gutteridge case languished for three months, as police followed leads and anonymous tips into nowhere. At one point, Berrett and Sergeant Harris worked 130 out of 160 consecutive hours, knocking on doors and reviewing criminal records, trying to match elements of the crime with known ruffians and car thieves. On 15 January 1928, Gutteridge's mother published a plea in the *News of the World*, begging anyone with information to come forward. And then fate intervened. On the night of Friday, 20 January, police tracked a car stolen the previous November to an automotive shop in Clapham Junction owned by a known car thief named Frederick Guy Browne.[41]

Broad of beam, powerfully built and nearly six feet tall, Browne was not someone to trifle with. 'His good qualities and physical gifts,' notes one contemporary account, 'would have suited him for service in, say, a mounted police force or for frontier work. As it was, he grew up a desperado and an outlaw, his powers being degraded into ferocities.' His good qualities, as they were, included abstinence from smoking and drinking, and being faithful to his wife.[42]

His criminal career began – or, came to the attention of authorities – in 1909 when he was twenty-eight and arrested for stealing a bicycle. He served twelve months hard labour. The following year he did time for larceny and, the year after that, a stretch for burglary. In 1913, police nabbed him for stealing stolen property. He married his wife, Caroline, in 1915 and served in the Royal Engineers from March 1917 to November 1918. Following a dishonourable discharge for burglary, he found work as a mechanic. Around this time, he also discovered a knack for 'stealing and altering motor cars,' a crime for which he was convicted in 1924 and sentenced to four years in prison.[43]

He wasted little time establishing a name for himself at Parkhurst Prison by 'the violence of his conduct, assaulting warders, breaking up his cell, and being generally riotous'. He proved too fierce for prison officials, who transferred him to Dartmoor asylum 'to be tamed'. And there he remained until his release on 30 March 1927. Shortly thereafter, he opened a garage and repair yard near Clapham Junction and launched 'a wild career of burglary and car stealing', with his auto shop providing the perfect front.[44]

On the night of 12 November, Browne and William Kennedy, who at the time managed Browne's garage, stole a Vauxhall from a home in the London borough of Tooting and sold it for £100 to a butcher named Benjamin Stow in Sheffield. In January, Stow was involved in an auto accident. When police matched his car's registration number – YE 8722 – with the Vauxhall stolen two months prior, Stow gave up Browne and Kennedy. Sheffield authorities passed the information along to W (Clapham) Division of Scotland Yard.

Detective Inspector William Barker and ten other officers staked out Browne's garage at 7a, Northcote Road. They saw him drive up in an Angus-Sanderson car and enter the premises at 7:50 p.m. Moments later, with Barker and Detective Sergeant John Miller in the lead, the officers stormed the garage and took Browne by surprise.

'I am going to charge you with stealing a Vauxhall car,' Barker announced.

'What do I know about stealing a car?' Browne replied.

Barker was struck by Browne's imposing physicality. 'He seemed to be boiling inwardly, holding himself in,' Barker recalled. 'He went pale and gripped his hands tightly together as though trying to master his feelings.'[45]

He searched Browne and found in the man's possession a skeleton key, 'a stockingette mask to cover the head completely, and also twelve rounds of .455 revolver ammunition.' The garage itself had several cars, previously reported stolen, that Browne had obviously been working on to change their appearances. Outside, Detective Constable Beavis searched the Angus-Sanderson and found more skeleton keys and 'a Webley Mark VI revolver no. 351931 fully loaded.' Beavis brought the articles inside and showed Browne. 'Ah. You've found that, have you?' Browne said. 'I'm done for now.'[46]

No mention was made of the Gutteridge murder. Browne was taken to the Tooting Police Station. 'They were quite decent,' Browne later said. 'They put me in a big room with a big table, and they were laughing about something . . . there was a lot of chatter.' With Browne in custody, police searched the garage and Browne's home at 33a, Sisters Avenue. Their efforts turned up three more guns: a 'fully loaded Webley revolver no. 299341 . . . a small-plated .22 six-chambered revolver no. 16769 . . . a Smith & Wesson no. 61900 fully loaded in six chambers' and more than fifty rounds of ammunition.[47]

At 12:46 a.m., Berrett and Harris entered the holding room and arranged Browne's guns on the table in front him. Berrett introduced himself and said he'd 'been making inquiries' regarding the murder of PC Gutteridge the previous September in Stapleford Abbotts, Essex. 'Will you account for me your movements on the night of the 26th September and the early morning of 27th September and for your possession of the Webley revolver and ammunition? I caution you that anything you say will be taken down and may be given in evidence.'[48]

'Why should I tell you anything?' Browne grumbled but relented under Berrett's glare. He said he was at home with his wife on the night in question and had never been to Stapleford Abbotts. 'I heard most about it when the murder took place,' he said. He claimed his guns were for protection against possible thieves when delivering cars to clients and that none of them had been fired. 'I have no connection to the murder of PC Gutteridge,' he said. 'Personally, I am not interested in it because it does not interest me.'[49]

At 1:45 p.m. on Monday, 23 January, Detective Inspector Barker charged Browne with stealing the Vauxhall. The case suffered an early setback when Bridget Hulton, the car's rightful owner, was unable to positively identify the vehicle as hers. The police, nevertheless, kept Browne in custody as he was now their prime suspect in the Gutteridge killing. William Kennedy, however, remained elusive.[50]

The forty-two-year-old William Kennedy had a lengthy criminal record of non-violent offences, ranging from indecent exposure to public drunkenness, loitering, house-breaking and larceny. He'd been in and out of the army and served in South Africa before being dishonourably discharged for desertion. He had recently returned to Liverpool after a short time in London working for Browne. On the same day Browne was charged with stealing the Vauxhall, Kennedy went for a pint at the Ye Cracke pub in Rice Street, where he knew landlord Joseph Thomas. On a previous visit to the pub, Kennedy had pulled Thomas aside and asked a favour.[51]

'He showed me an automatic revolver,' Thomas said. 'It [was] a Savage. He asked me if I could get him some ammunition . . . The revolver was loaded when he showed it to me. He asked me to get him some similar ammunition, fifty or a hundred rounds.'[52]

Now, on the evening of 23 January, Kennedy was back to see if Thomas had made good on the request. Thomas told him he 'had no intention' of doing any such thing. Unnerved by the episode and 'tired and afraid of Kennedy,' he informed the Liverpool Police. He told them Kennedy was living in a room at 119, Copperas Hill. Liverpool detectives relayed the information to Scotland Yard, who dispatched Inspector Albert Kirschner to help bring Kennedy in.[53]

Detectives made their move shortly before midnight on 25 January. They pulled up near the Copperas Hill address in a cab but lost the element of surprise. Kennedy heard them arrive. 'While I was in the house,' he said, 'I heard the taxi man being told to drive to the next street. That gave me the tip.'[54]

Kirschner, along with Liverpool Detective William Mattinson and three other officers, had just taken positions undercover when they spotted a man walking away from the house. He moved quickly 'with his overcoat turned up, and the front of the brim of his trilby hat turned down with his left hand over his face.'

Mattinson emerged from his hiding place and followed. 'When I got close to him,' Mattinson said, 'I recognized him to be . . . William Henry Kennedy.' The two had crossed paths before.

Mattinson approached Kennedy on his left side.

'Come on, Bill,' he said. 'Now, then, come on, Bill.'

Kennedy spun around. He pulled a pistol from the right pocket of his overcoat and jabbed the muzzle beneath Mattinson's ribs. 'Stand back, Bill,' Kennedy said, 'or I'll shoot you.'

The gun clicked when he pulled the trigger but failed to discharge.

Mattinson grabbed Kennedy's gun hand and twisted his arm up in the air. He punched Kennedy in the left side of the neck. The blow knocked Kennedy off balance and loosened his grip on the gun. Mattinson wrenched the revolver away, seized Kennedy by the back of his coat collar, and shoved him into the arms of Kirschner and the other men before sinking to his knees. 'I went sick,' he said. He quickly regained his composure and helped bundle Kennedy into the waiting taxi. [55]

'Yes,' Kennedy said, as they drove to the Dale Street Police Station, 'I had a premonition something was going to happen to me today, and I intended going. You are lucky to get me.' [56]

At the station, he apologized to Mattinson. 'I am sorry,' he said. 'I have no grudge against the police – but you should have been in heaven now, and there was one for me.'

'I did not expect that from you,' Mattinson said. [57]

The gun never discharged because the safety was still on. A bullet was stuck halfway up the barrel. 'If ever a miracle happened,' remarked one detective, 'it was that night.' [58]

Detectives brought Kennedy to Scotland Yard the next day and allowed his wife, Pat, to accompany him. The two had only married eight days prior. Berrett entered the room, introduced himself and got down to business.

'You are being detained on a charge of stealing a Vauxhall motor car,' Berrett said. 'I have been making inquiries for some time past regarding the murder of PC Gutteridge. Can you give me any information about that occurrence?'

Kennedy pondered his situation. He leaned his elbows on the table and buried his head in his hands. 'I may be able to tell you something. Let me consider. Can I see my wife?'

Berrett agreed and summoned Pat Kennedy into the room. She sat next to Kennedy and grasped his hand.

'You know, my dear,' he said, 'when I was arrested at Liverpool yesterday, I told you I thought it was something more serious than stealing a car. These officers are inquiring about that policeman murdered in Essex.'

Pat appraised Kennedy with wet eyes. 'You didn't murder him, did you?'

'No, I didn't – but I was there and know who did,' he said. 'If I am charged with murder and found guilty, I shall be hanged and you will be a widow. On the other hand, if I am charged and found guilty of being an accessory after the fact, I shall receive a long sentence of penal servitude and I shall be a long time away from you. Will you wait for me?'

'Yes,' Pat replied, her voice thick with emotion.

'What shall I do, then?'

'Tell these gentlemen the truth.'

'All right,' Kennedy said, and turned to Berrett. 'You can take down what I want to say, and I will sign it.'[59]

And with his wife by his side and Berrett listening, Kennedy – over the next three hours – gave up what he knew.

Kennedy and Browne met as inmates at Dartmoor and reconnected in June or July 1927 upon Kennedy's release. Kennedy was working as a farm labourer when he received a letter from Browne. 'He told me he was starting a garage in Battersea and invited me to come down and act as manager,' Kennedy said. 'He said he could not offer me much money at first – but it would cost me nothing for board and lodgings, as I could live at his garage.' Kennedy took Browne up on the offer, and the two were soon partners in crime.

'I well remember the day of twenty-sixth September,' Kennedy said. 'He suggested that I should accompany him to Billericay to assist him in stealing a car.' They travelled that afternoon to Billericay and scoped the village, spotting the car parked in Dr Lovell's garage. They hid in a field across the street and waited for nightfall, but the lights in the doctor's house stayed on well past midnight. It was roughly 12:30 when the windows went dark.

Kennedy and Browne emerged from their cover and approached the house. Lovell had closed and locked the garage before going to bed. Browne pried the doors open with a tyre iron, and the two men rolled the car down to the street. They pushed it another 100 yards away from the house before starting the engine and driving off with Kennedy in the passenger seat.

'We went for a long run around country lanes at a great pace,' Kennedy said. 'We got to several crossroads and corners, where it was necessary for us to examine sign-posts – but, eventually, we got to a kind of main road on the way to Ongar. When we got some distance upon this road, we saw someone who stood on the bank and flashed his lamp as a signal to stop.'

Browne sped past the dark figure and only stopped at Kennedy's urging when both men heard the shrill cry of a police whistle. They watched in the car's mirrors as the individual approached, the lamplight growing ever brighter. 'When the person came up,' Kennedy said, 'we saw it was a policeman.'

The constable walked up to the driver's window and leaned down to ask Browne where he was going and where he was coming from. Browne said they'd come from a local garage, where they'd had some repairs done.

'Do you have a driver's licence?' the constable asked.

'No,' Browne replied.

The policeman asked once more where they were coming from. Browne stammered in his response.

'Is the car yours?' the policeman asked.

'No,' Kennedy said. 'It's mine.'

The policeman shone his light into the car to get a good look at their faces and asked if they knew the registration number.

'You'll see it in the front of the car,' Kennedy said, squinting against the light.

'I know the number,' the policeman countered, 'but do you?'

Kennedy, who just happened to see it when pushing the car out of Lovell's garage, recited it from memory: 'TW 6120.'

'All right,' the policeman said, pulling his notebook from a pocket. 'I'll take some particulars.'

The car's interior took the full, deafening brunt of the gun report; another followed in quick succession. Kennedy blinked away the dazzle of the muzzle flash and saw the policeman stumbling backwards, tracing an unsteady path to the side of the road, where he collapsed on the grass embankment. Browne had 'a large Webley revolver in his hand.'

'What have you done?' Kennedy said.

The two men got out of the car and walked over to the policeman, who lay on his back, groaning loudly. The fallen officer stared up at his two assailants with eyes open wide.

'I'll finish the bugger,' Browne said.

'For God's sake,' Kennedy cried, 'don't shoot anymore. The man's dying.'

Browne stared into the policeman's eyes. 'What are you looking at me like that for?' he said, bending low with the Webley. He placed the barrel under each eye. The gunfire echoed down the dark lane.

They got in the car and hurtled towards London. Browne passed the Webley to Kennedy and asked him to reload it.

'In my excitement,' Kennedy told Berrett, 'I dropped an empty shell in the car. The other three I threw away into the roads.'

They passed through sleeping villages, the names of which Kennedy couldn't recall, and into a thickening fog. It obscured the roadway ahead and the dark silhouettes of trees and hedgerows that loomed on either side. Unable to fully see where he was going, Browne side-swiped a tree at a bend in the road and damaged the 'near side front wing.' They reached Brixton, abandoned the car in Foxley Court and returned to Browne's garage by six that morning.

Tension between the two men immediately began to fester. The constant news coverage of Gutteridge's death panicked Kennedy. 'I suggested to Browne that we should go right away from London, as I knew enquiries were sure to be made,' he said. 'Browne said there was no danger, and induced me to stop, and said if I made up my mind to leave him he would blow my brains out. He had the Webley revolver in his hand when he said this, and, as I knew it was loaded, I thought he would.'

By December, however, Kennedy was free to leave and returned to Liverpool by train on the seventeenth. He came back to London with Pat on 13 January but fled once more after Browne's arrest.[60]

Berrett did not believe Kennedy's story. 'I am convinced that they were equally guilty,' he said:

> In my reconstruction of the murder I place Kennedy as the man who shot first, for I have difficulty visualizing how the driver of the car – admittedly Browne – could have shot from the driving seat not only so that the bullets entered where they did but could have shot unseen by Gutteridge. Any movement of the driver's hands towards the pocket, and particularly any sudden presentation of a revolver, would have been seen by the man bending over the side of the car, and he had only to withdraw his head to avoid the shot.

While Berrett had no doubt Browne fired the fatal shots on the side of the road, he believed Kennedy 'shot the officer from the seat beside the driver'.[61]

Berrett charged Browne and Kennedy on 6 February with the murder of PC George Gutteridge. Kennedy said nothing, but Browne balked at the accusation. 'You are charging me with murder? It's absurd,' he said. 'I know nothing about it.' He maintained his ignorance throughout the trial, which began at the Old Bailey on Monday, 23 April 1928.[62]

The trial was the first in the UK – and one of the earliest overall – to feature ballistics evidence. Robert Churchill, in his workshop, identified the spent shell casings found in the stolen car as having been manufactured by the Royal Laboratory Arsenal in Woolwich during the First World War and shot from a Webley Mark IV, revolver. He subsequently matched the casings to the Webley revolver found in Browne's garage, having test-fired fifty other Webleys 'into a pigskin target at close range' to eliminate all doubt. He did this using the recently developed comparison microscope, which allowed shell casings to be examined side by side. '. . . Conceivably two grooves in different weapons might be almost alike,' he explained to Berrett, 'but that all the minute lines and striations in two weapons could resemble one another in strict sequence would be too remote a coincidence to dwell upon.'[63]

Churchill educated the jury on rifling patterns. He explained how 'the cap of the cartridge case takes the imprint of the breach shield of the revolver' – not unlike someone leaving behind a bloody fingerprint – making it possible to identify from what gun a bullet was fired. Furthermore, the bullet fired through Gutteridge's left eye was of a type no longer in production. The bullet shot into the officer's right eye was 'from a cartridge loaded with black powder'. The Webley retrieved from Browne's car at his garage was 'loaded in two chambers with ammunition bearing all the characteristics and of the make and loaded with the very powder associated with the bullets which inflicted two of the four wounds to the dead constable's head.'[64]

Churchill's testimony and Kennedy's statement to police proved damning. Browne insisted he was home the night of the murder. He at first refused, on such a basis, to take the oath before testifying. 'It says here, "The whole truth",' he said, reading the oath card. 'I shall never know the whole truth about this; how can I swear to the whole truth?' His performance, in the eyes of the jury, lacked conviction.[65] Browne and Kennedy hanged on 31 May.

The science that convicted the two men remained something of a mystery to the public. Playwright George Bernard Shaw questioned its reliability. In a letter to Browne's family, he ignored the complexity of rifling patterns to dismiss the evidence as wholly fabricated:

We were assured that the Bertillon measurements were infallible until the finger-print method was substituted. There was this to be said for both of them. No persons anxious to secure a conviction could tamper with the dimensions of skin markings of the accused. But anyone with access to a discharged cartridge case and to a revolver can tamper with the revolver, so that by simply putting the cartridge case into one of the chambers and snapping the hammer on it a mark made on the hammer or cylinder can be reproduced on the cartridge case, and a jury deeply impressed by a manufactured coincidence.[66]

The press was more intrigued with the *Weekly Dispatch* proclaiming Browne and Kennedy to have been 'Hanged by a Microscope'. The *Yorkshire Evening Post*, on the day of the execution, ran an article headlined 'THE "PERSONALITY" OF FIREARMS: GUN "FINGER-PRINTS".' It read, in part:

> That 'personality' exists in rifles, revolvers and pistols . . . has, of course, long been known. But the Gutteridge murder trial was the first occasion in this country when this 'personality' has been given such enormous value . . . The new silence of 'gun finger-prints' may be said to depend on the old truth – no two things in the world are alike.[67]

Despite the Gutteridge case, it took another two years and the 1929 St Valentine's Day Massacre in Chicago to anchor ballistics in the mainstream. The killers who gunned down seven members of George 'Bugs' Moran's gang in a garage on the city's North Side were dressed as police officers. Ballistics expert Calvin Goddard, a former US Army colonel and medical officer who co-developed the comparison microscope in 1925, was able to prove rounds fired from machine guns used by the Chicago Police Department did not match the casings found at the scene. His work resulted in the 'opening of the first private scientific crime detection laboratory in America' and 'brought legitimacy to the fledgling science of forensic ballistics'.[68]

It made no difference to Chief Inspector Berrett, who retired in 1931. 'Since the [Gutteridge] case, there have been many articles in the press dealing with the "finger-prints" of revolvers, but I do not propose to dwell on the subject.'[69]

What he did dwell on, after nearly four decades at Scotland Yard, was the nature of crime.

'At the end of 38½ years' experience I have learned something of the world and those who live in it,' he wrote. 'I am no nearer finding an explanation for crime than I was when I started . . . Crime, from start to finish, is a dirty game played by dirty players.'[70]

Epilogue

Fingerprints from Yesteryear

An Enduring Legacy.

In 1936, Scotland Yard opened 'the world's first specialized training programme for detectives', where officers learned the finer aspects of detection and evidence gathering. While would-be detectives learned the tricks of the trade, detectives in the field put new investigative breakthroughs to use.[1]

On the morning of 12 April 1937, railway worker Frank Cox took a quiet footpath to work. It cut through a thick wood in the Bedfordshire town of Leighton Buzzard, about fifty miles north of London, and often served as a lovers' lane for young couples. Roughly ten yards from the main road, he saw the body of a woman strewn across the path. 'All she was wearing was a short coat, black kid gloves and silk stockings,' Cox recalled. 'Her other clothing was at her side. A scarf was tied tightly around her neck, and the flesh round the scarf was all swollen.'[2]

He draped his raincoat over the body and ran to fetch the police. 'The girl had extensive injuries,' notes one report. 'They were so bad that it was thought perhaps she might have been knocked down by a motor car and dumped at the spot.' That theory didn't last long, as it became apparent she had been raped and murdered. 'GIRL FOUND STRANGLED ON LONELY PATH', declared that day's *Evening Standard* in a front-page headline. 'Scotland Yard has been called in'.[3]

Police identified the victim at the scene as twenty-three-year-old Ruby Keen. She lived with her widowed mother in a house thirty yards from where she was found. The killing caused immediate anxiety for the Bedfordshire Constabulary, as Keen was engaged to one of its constables while simultaneously dating another. Scotland Yard's Inspector William Barker, who arrested Frederick Browne in the PC Gutteridge case, handled the investigation. He arrived at the murder spot that afternoon.[4]

Local police, not wanting to disturb the scene, had left Ruby as she'd been found. Barker noticed numerous but indistinguishable footprints around the body, suggesting a struggle. There was, however, a clear impression left by a knee. A plaster cast was made and sent to the Yard's forensic laboratory, which had opened the year before. 'The impression was so clear,' reported *The Evening Standard*, 'that the cast has revealed certain peculiarities, which may prove of vital help.' Specifically, an examination of the cast revealed a trouser crease and the pattern of the fabric.[5]

Barker canvassed clothing stores in Leighton Buzzard. He found a merchant who identified the pattern in the plaster as being similar to 'a blue suit with white pin stripes, which he had sold to a young man the previous week.' Consulting his sales receipts, the merchant identified the customer as Leslie George Stone.[6]

Witnesses told Barker they saw Stone, a twenty-four-year-old soldier recently discharged from the Royal Artillery, with Ruby at three local pubs the night of the murder. The two had been an item prior to Stone entering the service and shipping off to Hong Kong. Upon his return home, Stone was perturbed to learn of Ruby's engagement to another man and invested much time in trying to win her back. A forensic analysis of the suit Stone was wearing that night revealed the fabric's pattern matched that found in the cast of the knee print.

Soil samples removed from the print also matched those found on Stone's trouser leg. This, however, was not enough. Barker took the suit to London, where Home Office analyst Dr Rhode Lynch put it under the microscope. His examination of Stone's coat turned up 'a tiny silk thread, one inch in length and containing thirty-eight to forty filaments'. The thread matched those in a beige slip Ruby had been wearing when she was killed.[7]

Fibre analysis was a relatively new field of forensics, having developed through the early 1900s. The evidence, coupled with an eventual confession at trial, landed Stone a death sentence. 'When that sentence is carried out,' reported the *St. Louis Post-Dispatch*, fascinated by the science, 'it may be truly said that here was a man hanged by a thread.' Stone went to the gallows on 13 August 1937.[8]

Scotland Yard and science made headlines again two years later. 'For the first time in the history of English justice,' the *Guardian* reported on 13 October 1939, 'evidence of saliva was offered yesterday as a clue to a man's identity.' In May that year, a wealthy sixty-four-year-old widower named Walter Dinnivan was found beaten to death in his home. The killer had snatched the rings from Dinnivan's fingers, rifled through his desk and – using a key Dinnivan always kept in his pocket – stolen money from a safe. Several cigarette butts were found lying about the place. When the local constabulary called Scotland Yard for help, the case fell to Chief Inspector Leonard Burt, who, as a detective sergeant, had assisted Chief Inspector George Cornish in the Charing Cross Trunk mystery.[9]

Burt's investigation led him to sixty-nine-year-old fishmonger Joseph Williams, who local ladies claimed had started flashing a lot of money around shortly after the killing. While Burt worked the case, the Yard's forensics laboratory got to work. In 1930, scientists discovered that a segment of the population secretes blood group antigens in their saliva. The Yard's forensics team was therefore able to determine the killer's blood type from saliva found on the cigarette butts. 'The smoker,' Burt noted, 'was of a blood group found in only three per cent of the population.'[10]

A Yard detective managed to snatch a few of Williams's discarded cigarette butts from an ashtray at a pub. Saliva from the stubs matched that found on the butts left in Dinnivan's home.

It was enough to arrest Williams and get his fingerprints, which matched those lifted at the scene. As officers escorted Williams into the police station, he held his cuffed wrists up for the waiting press. 'Take a pretty picture, lads!' he said.[11]

Williams went on trial in October and routinely interrupted the proceedings by insisting – very loudly – that he was innocent. His protestations, coupled with the jury's inability to understand the saliva evidence and dismiss the fingerprints, resulted in a verdict of not guilty. The verdict stunned Scotland Yard. 'I know at least one presumably innocent person,' recalled a Yard superintendent, 'having been found so by a jury, who actually *did* commit murder.' Immediately following the trial, Norman Rae – a crime reporter with the *News of the World* – took Williams out for a drink. 'To the hangman,' Williams said, hoisting a double whisky, 'who has been cheated of his victim.'[12]

Williams died in March 1951. Shortly thereafter, Rae published a sensational story, relating how Williams had called him in the middle of the night following his acquittal.

'I couldn't sleep,' a sobbing Williams said. 'Christ, I couldn't get to sleep at all. I've got to tell somebody. You see – the jury were wrong. The jury were wrong. It was me!'[13]

Scotland Yard is more than the metonym and headquarters of the London Metropolitan Police. It's something woven into our cultural fabric, a conduit between history and pop culture. We can trace today's true crime obsession, in large part, to the Yard's early cases with their sensational news coverage, in-depth narratives of criminal trials and the celebration of detectives. The Victorian era in particular saw the press revel in gory descriptions of crime scenes and murder. There was nothing subjective or detached in such coverage: the intent was to shock, play up the drama and stoke the public appetite for more. News as bloody entertainment gave rise to our enduring fascination with crime and investigation.

Murder scenes, such as the dilapidated house where the London Burkers killed 'The Italian Boy' or the site off Edgware Road where James Greenacre dumped Hannah Brown's severed corpse, became tourist attractions and fertile ground for souvenir hunters. The stables where Daniel Good disembowelled and incinerated his common-law wife attracted the morbidly curious from across London. Times haven't changed. Tourists from around the world still descend on Whitechapel to see where Jack the Ripper committed his barbaric deeds.

Murder plays no favourites, inflicting the rich (alas, the unfortunate Lord Russell slaughtered in his bed) and the poor, and generating macabre interest across all demographics. Murder culture thrived as Scotland Yard learned its grim trade from one blood-spattered crime scene to the next. Into the early twentieth century, the Yard's investigations played out in the press like great dramas with a well-defined cast, the crimes dripping in intrigue and suspense. And sifting through the clues, assembling the scattered pieces of puzzle, was a new kind of policeman.

The detective, in the words of author Kate Summerscale, was 'as magical and scientific as the other marvels of the 1840s and 1850s – the camera, the electric telegraph and the railway train. Like the telegraph and train, a detective seemed able to jump time and place; like a camera, he seemed able to freeze them.'[14]

Dickens, as we've seen, imbued the Yard's detectives with an almost mythic quality and, through Inspector Bucket in *Bleak House*, helped introduce the detective archetype with his powers of observation, deductive reasoning and dedication to the profession of crime-solving. He's not a detective by hobby. It's his job. Indeed, Bucket is the first Scotland Yard detective 'to play a significant part in an English novel' and help stoke the 'growing popular romance around the figure of the detective'. It's no stretch to say Bucket might not exist on the page if not for his flesh-and-blood inspiration, Scotland Yard detective Charles Frederick Field.[15]

In 1868, Dickens's friend Wilkie Collins published *The Moonstone*. T. S. Eliot called it 'the first, the longest, and the best of modern English detective novels'. The protagonist, Sergeant Cuff, was inspired by Inspector Jonathan Whicher (both had a passion for gardening), while the story borrowed elements from the murder at Road Hill House, including the country manor setting and the missing nightdress. Cuff fails to solve the case, much as Whicher was perceived to have failed when he accused Constance Kent of murder. The book, with its complex mystery, multiple narrative threads, and myriad clues laid out for the reader to discover in real time with the detective, is – according to Dorothy Sayers – 'impeccable . . . *The Moonstone* set the standard.'[16]

Bucket and Cuff, working their respective mysteries, represent 'the insistent rise of the modern professional police force in England'. The Yard's been providing great fodder for writers ever since. Through its macabre catalogue of cases, Scotland Yard has built into the collective imagination an everlasting iconography – one of foggy, lamplit streets and cobblestones, of gentleman detectives armed with magnifying glasses and pursuing shadowy killers. 'When it comes to international branding for law enforcement,' observed the *Los Angeles Times*, 'it's hard to beat Scotland Yard.'[17]

Over time, the imagery we associate with the Yard has transcended national boundaries. Like the red telephone box, double-decker bus and country pub, the Yard – through its blue call boxes and the 'Bobby' on the beat – has come to represent a romantic view of England. And yet, such quaintness aside, the Yard from its inception has been a modern, ground-breaking force. Like any large law-enforcement agency, it's faced its fair share of criticism over the years, but its historical importance and contributions to modern-day policing are without dispute.

It's not hard to find Scotland Yard's fingerprints from yesteryear on more recent investigations. Between 1940 and 1956, a serial bomber detonated twenty-two explosives throughout New York

City, targeting subway stations, theatres, Radio City Music Hall and other public places. The blasts injured fifteen and prompted the *New York Journal-American* to declare the culprit to be 'the greatest individual menace New York City ever faced'. Police, desperate for some sort of break, consulted psychiatrist Dr James Brussel in 1956 to 'draw a profile of the bomber's inner self – an emotional portrait'.[18]

Brussel got to work by examining the neat, handwritten and taunting letters the bomber had sent to the press over the years. He theorized the bomber was 'probably very neat, tidy, and clean shaven. He goes out of his way to seem perfectly normal . . .' The profile helped lead the NYPD to George Metesky, a disgruntled former employee of Consolidated Edison. Some accounts claim this to be the first criminal profile, but Scotland Yard police surgeon Dr Thomas Bond's 1888 profile of Jack the Ripper is the forerunner of modern-day 'mind hunting'.[19]

Today, nearly every police department and law enforcement agency employs canines to track suspects, search for missing people, sniff out drugs and detect explosives. While the Yard's novel attempt in 1888 to use dogs to hunt Jack the Ripper never developed beyond the experimental stage, it nevertheless 'constituted an important historical moment, demonstrating . . . the utilization of dogs to follow scents for the primary purpose of urban policing and forensic investigation.'[20]

Watch any true crime documentary, and you'll see a detective or crime scene investigator pull on a pair of rubber gloves and gather evidence with tweezers, eyedroppers and cotton swabs. The collection and handling of evidence is vital to any investigation – and we have Scotland Yard to thank for cementing the foundation for such techniques. 'The Crumbles case' set the standard for reducing the risks of 'contamination and cross-transference of evidence'.[21]

The establishment of Scotland Yard's Fingerprint Branch in 1901 and its use of the Henry Classification System revolutionized criminal identification. It formed the basis for the modern-day Automated Fingerprint Identification System, which used a computer to match prints against a large database and remained in place until the 1990s.

Throughout Scotland Yard's long history, we see cases involving early bloodstain analysis and breakthroughs in serology – evolutionary steps that would eventually culminate in the first murder solved by DNA evidence. In 1983 and 1986, two teenage girls were raped and murdered in the English county of Leicestershire. DNA profiling of semen found in both victims pointed to a single killer. The police profiled the blood and saliva specimens of all adult males living in the vicinity of the slayings. Their efforts eventually resulted in identifying twenty-six-year-old Colin Pitchfork as the killer and clearing another man who falsely admitted to the crimes. Pitchfork is serving a life sentence.

Through techniques it introduced or advanced, including the creation of the world's first plainclothes Detective Branch, Scotland Yard transformed police work on a global scale. As the world's first modern, professional and centrally organized police force, the Yard established the model for such departments elsewhere with its rank-and-command structure.

The intent of Scotland Yard upon its creation was the prevention of crime, not merely responding to it – a novel concept for its time. American cities took notice with Boston establishing the first 'publicly funded, organized' police department in the US in 1838. New York City followed suit in 1845, and Philadelphia did likewise in 1854. All three departments modelled themselves on Scotland Yard, adopted its methods, and began setting up their own detective branches in the late 1850s.[22]

Scotland Yard built a name for itself on a foundation of hard lessons and public failures, evolving from a fledgling force into a world-renowned organization – 'the most famous brand name in policing and . . . the most respected.' 'The Bermondsey Horror', 'The Murder at Road Hill House', Jack the Ripper, Dr Cream, Dr.

Crippen, 'The Brides in the Bath' . . . These crimes – just to name a few – and the many grisly waypoints in between, defined modern detective work and still resonate today. Sometimes, they provide a startling postscript.[23]

On 22 October 2010, workers adding an extension onto the Richmond home of broadcaster Sir David Attenborough made a grim discovery. Using a mini-digger to clear away earth in the back garden, they came across 'a dark round object' lying on top of some Victorian tiles. Closer examination revealed the find to be a skull. Scotland Yard was summoned and soon confirmed the morbid relic was human.

Forensic analysis revealed it to be that of a white woman with missing teeth who died at 'roughly menopausal age'. Carbon testing carried out at the University of Edinburgh indicated the skull belonged to someone who had lived between 1650 and 1880, 'partly because the bones had a marine dating, meaning the person would have eaten a lot of fish consistent with Londoners at the time'. The skull was fractured, an injury indicative of 'a fall down the stairs' and had 'low collagen levels consistent with it being boiled'.

The garden where the skull was found occupies the former site of the Hole in the Wall pub, which sat 100 yards from the house where maid Kate Webster murdered, dismembered and boiled Julia Thomas to sludge in March 1879.

Thomas was fifty-five when she died and known to wear false teeth. Based on the evidence and location – plus a review of census records and the original case files and trial transcript – Scotland Yard provided the West London Coroner's Court in October 2011 with 'clear, convincing and compelling evidence' the skull was indeed Julia's despite being unable to trace any living descendants for DNA testing.

More than 130 years after the killing, the coroner ruled the cause of death to be 'asphyxiation by strangulation and a head injury'.[24]

It was, noted one Yard official, a prime example of what happens when 'good old-fashioned detective work, historical records and technological advances' come together.[25]

A fitting summary, perhaps, of what the Yard has done best since 1829.

Acknowledgements

Writing is a solitary pursuit, yet no one writes a book alone. *Scotland Yard* would not have happened without agent extraordinaire Jonathan Lyons, who saw the project's potential from the get-go, added considerable polish to the proposal, provided rock-solid guidance, and helped keep my writer nerves in check. Across the Atlantic, the wonderful Kate Walsh championed the book in Britain. I'm thankful to both for their kindness and their representation.

After you've completed a manuscript, you nervously pass it into the care of others. Heartfelt thanks go to the amazing people at Welbeck Publishing in the UK and Pegasus Books in the US. At Welbeck, Oliver Holden-Rea graced the pages with a keen eye for story, sharing my enthusiasm for dark and twisted history. Copy-editor Nicky Gyopari put her eagle eyes to excellent use and saved me on the page. Obviously, any mistakes in the book are mine alone. At Pegasus, Claiborne Hancock and Jessica Case welcomed Scotland Yard's bloodiest and most infamous cases Stateside and gave them a good American home.

The vast majority of this book was written during the pandemic. As such – other than a few days in London – much of the research was done online. Many thanks to the staff at the British National Archives in Kew, who helped locate and digitize needed documents. Elsewhere, the online British Newspaper Archive is another priceless resource when it comes to digging into the past. Alan Moss, retired Chief Superintendent of the Metropolitan Police, was more than patient with questions I sent his way. He also dug up the records of my paternal grandfather, who was a detective-inspector with the Yard during the war years.

Since our paths first crossed seven years ago, fellow scribe and bestselling biographer Brian Jay Jones (*Washington Irving, Jim Henson, George Lucas*, and *Becoming Dr. Seuss*) has become a great friend in the truest sense of the word. He shares my passion for strong, cold martinis (yes, we text each other pictures of the drinks we make) and loudly cheered this project on from the sidelines. When writing a book, it's great to have another writer you can vent to - especially if cocktails are involved! In the run-up to this project, Lissa Warren provided wise counsel and helped get things rolling. A seasoned publishing professional, it was Lissa who suggested I scrap my original title (I was trying to be clever) for something more straightforward. *Scotland Yard* is about as straightforward as it gets!

I've been fortunate over the years to have unwavering love and support from my parents, Bill and Susan; my sister, Sarah; and my nephew, Ben, an absolute book fanatic. *Scotland Yard* is dedicated to my parents, as I have them to thank (blame) for my fascination with crime. It might have something to do with them having sat me down when I was seven or eight to watch *Dirty Harry*. It obviously made an impact.

It's always difficult trying to find words to adequately thank my wife, Katie, and my sons, Spencer and Cameron, for their love, humour, and patience. Katie is my first reader and toughest critic, my best friend, and the world's best partner. My sons give me something to be proud of every day. I love you guys.

References

Prologue: The Yard

1 James and Critchley, p. 8; 'of unbridled vice . . .' Phillips, p. 19.
2 'the usual place . . .' Stowe, p. 157; 'the Regent Street . . .' Thornbury, p. 134.
3 James and Critchley, pp. 9, 11.
4 *The Evening Mail*, 'The Murders in Ratcliffe Highway,' 11 December, 1811.
5 *The Morning Chronicle*, 'Horrid and Unparalleled Murders!' 9 December, 1811; 'I also heard . . .' *The Evening Mail*, 'The Murders in Ratcliffe Highway,' 11 December, 1811.
6 *The Evening Mail*, 'The Murders in Ratcliffe Highway,' 11 December, 1811.
7 *The Morning Chronicle*, 'Horrid and Unparalleled Murders!' 9 December, 1811.
8 *The* (London) *Star*, 'The Murders in Ratcliffe Highway,' 11 December, 1881.
9 James and Critchley, p. 15.
10 *The Evening Mail*, 'The Murders in Ratcliffe Highway,' 11 December, 1881.
11 Ibid.
12 'for driving the . . .' *The* (London) *Star*, 'Murder of Mr Marr and Family,' 10 December, 1811; *The London Courier and Evening Gazette*, 'Horrible Murders,' 9 December, 1811.
13 *The* (London) *Globe*, 'Interment of Mr and Mrs Marr, and Infant Son,' 16 December, 1811.
14 *The London Chronicle*, 'More Murders at Ratcliffe,' 20 December, 1811.
15 'who collected . . .' *The* (London) *News*, 'More Murders,' 22 December, 1811; 'characters highly respected . . . inhumanely massacred.' *The* (London) *National Register*, 'Another Murder!' 22 December, 1811; *The London Chronicle*, 'Coroner's Inquest,' 23 December, 1811.
16 *The Public Ledger and Daily Advertiser*, 'Coroner's Inquest,' 23 December, 1811.
17 Ibid.
18 'a large piece of waste ground . . .' *The Stamford Mercury*, 'More Horrid Murders!' 27 December, 1811.
19 'the most superb of the century . . .' De Quincey, p. 76; 'the Ripper was hunted . . .' Hurd, p. 101.
20 'London's cluttered cobblestone . . .' Read, pp. 95–96; 'the night constable . . .' *The Englishman*, 'The New Police,' 4 October, 1829.
21 'up to a dozen . . . two shillings a night.' Hurd, p. 102; 'The frequent instances . . .' *The London Chronicle*, 'Coroner's Inquest,' 23 December, 1811.
22 Read, pp. 93–95; 'dingy, fetid . . .' *The Illustrated London News*, 'The Police Offices of London,' 22 August, 1846.
23 *The Illustrated London News*, 'The Police Offices of London,' 22 August, 1846.
24 'swarms of poverty-stricken . . .' *The Illustrated London News*, 'The Police Offices of London,' 22 August, 1846; 'the first Englishman . . .' Begg and Skinner, p. 7; 'actively sought to . . .' Fido and Skinner, p. 28.

25 Read, p. 96.

26 Ibid., p. 98.

27 Ibid., pp. 96, 99.

28 'more than 3,000 criminals . . .' Ibid., pp. 100–101; 'Treasury parsimony . . .' Fido and Skinner, p. 28.

29 Hurd, p. 103.

30 Browne, p. 54.

31 Ibid., pp. 60–61.

32 *The* (London) *Star*, 'The Late Murders,' 28 December, 1811.

33 Cunningham, p. 692.

34 'thoughtful section . . .' Browne, p. 53; 'who remained blinkered . . .' Begg and Skinner, p. 14.

35 'of as perfect . . .' Hurd, p. 71; 'forerunners to the Royal Irish . . .' Fido and Skinner, p. 193.

36 'difficult to reconcile . . . detection in crime'. Hurd, p. 71.

37 Begg and Skinner, p. 16.

38 Introductory text to the Metropolitan Police Act 1829. Online at https://www. legislation.gov.uk/ukpga/Geo4/10/44/introduction.

39 Begg and Skinner, p. 16.

40 '17 Divisions . . .' Fido and Skinner, p. 12; Browne, p. 81; Hurd, p. 103.

41 Fido and Skinner, p. 12; Hurd, p. 103; 'really had any idea . . .' Begg and Skinner, p. 18.

42 Moss and Skinner, pp. 13–15; 'borrowed the organizational structure . . .' Walker and Katz, p. 25.

43 Fido and Skinner, pp. 15–16.

44 'a forerunner of the modern . . .' Fido and Skinner, p. 15; 'I had to put on . . .' Begg and Skinner, pp. 18–19.

45 'faced a small street . . .' Begg and Skinner, p. 17; origins of the Scotland Yard name. See Fido and Skinner, p. 234, and Moss and Skinner, p. 17.

46 'from the still-unfinished . . . "proceeded" on duty'. Browne, p. 87.

47 *The Birmingham* (UK) *Journal*, 'The New Police London,' 3 October, 1829.

48 'Since the new police . . .' Letter to the Editor in *The Times*, 7 October, 1829.

49 'verbal and physical . . .' Begg and Skinner, p. 19; 'crowds of drunken . . . *gens-de-harms*.' *The Times*, 'The New Police,' 14 October, 1829.

50 *The Times*, 'The New Police,' 14 October, 1829.

51 'a practical example'. *The Times*, 'The New Police,' 14 October, 1829; Fido and Skinner, p. 106; Begg and Skinner, pp. 19–20.

1: The Unhallowed

1 *Drakard's Stamford News*, 'Resurrectionists,' 26 November, 1830.

2 Shelley, pp. 37–38, 40.

3 All information cited and quoted in this paragraph comes from 'The study of

anatomy in England from 1700 to the early 20th century,' *Journal of Anatomy*, 20 August11 (vol. 19, issue 2), published online 18 April, 2011.

4 Text from the Murder Act, 1751, can be found at The Statues Project, 1751: 25 George 2 c.37: The Murder Act.

5 'the absolute necessity . . .' Bailey, p. 44.

6 'the most desperate and abandoned . . .' 16 guineas for a corpse, Bailey, pp. 45, 47; method employed to steal a corpse. Pietila, Antero (October 2018), 'In Need of Cadavers, 19th Century Medical Students Raided Baltimore's Graves,' *Smithsonian Magazine*, (online at https://www.smithsonianmag.com/history/in-need-cadavers-19th-century-medical-students-raided-baltimores-graves-180970629/); 'dreadful crime . . .' *The Berkshire Chronicle*, 'A Knowledge of Anatomy obtained without the assistance of Burkers or Resurrectionists,' 31 December, 1831.

7 'high walls topped . . .' and families maintaining vigil, Jackson, p. 108.

8 *The Northampton Mercury*, 'Preservation of the Dead,' 27 February, 1830.

9 BBC (20 June, 2014), 'The macabre world of books bound in human skin'; *The Scotsman*, 'Dressed to Kill: Burke Trial Gown Found After 200 Years'. 6 August, 2012; 'William Burke,' The University of Edinburgh Anatomical Museum website.

10 *The Trial, Sentence, and Confessions of Bishop, Williams, and May at the Old Bailey on Friday, December 2, 1831* (will be referenced as TSC), p. 14; *The Evening Mail*, 'Inquest on the Italian Boy,' 9 November, 1831

11 'a good one' and 'particularly fresh' and 'It appeared . . .' TSC, p. 14; cut on the forehead. *The Evening Mail*, 'Inquest on the Italian Boy,' 9 November, 1831

12 *The Berkshire Chronicle*, 'The Italian Boy,' 12 November, 1831.

13 TSC, pp. 15, 19.

14 The exchange between Thomas and prisoners is based on TSC, p. 19; *The Evening Mail*, 'An Inquest on the Italian Boy,' 9 November, 1831.

15 TSC, p. 11.

16 *The Times*, under the section heading 'POLICE,' 7 November, 1831.

17 Ibid.

18 TSC, p. 17.

19 'aged 13 . . . deaf and dumb.' *The Evening Mail*, 'An Inquest on the Italian Boy,' 9 November, 1831.

20 TSC, p. 25.

21 *The Evening Mail*, 'An Inquest on the Italian Boy,' Wednesday, 9 November, 1831; TSC, pp. 16, 17.

22 TSC, pp. 17–18.

23 Ibid., p. 23.

24 Ibid.

25 'The room . . .' *The Globe*, 'Inquest on the Italian Boy,' 9 November, 1831; 'The reason I don't like to say . . .' *The Public Ledger and Daily Advertiser*, 'The Italian Boy-Adjourned Inquest,' 11 November, 1831.

26 *The Public Ledger and Daily Advertiser*, 'The Italian Boy-Adjourned Inquest,' 11 November, 1831.

27 'where, on benches . . .' Notes and Queries, p. 223.

28 TSC, pp. 19–20.

29 Ibid., p. 21.

30 TSC, p. 22; 'You know I can't . . .' *Bell's Weekly Messenger*, 'Alleged Case of Horrid Murder by Burking an Italian Boy', 13 November, 1831.

31 Burial and *Times* extract from Wise (Kindle Edition).

32 *The Morning Advertiser*, 'The Murder of the Italian Boy', 12 November, 1831.

33 'were used for opening . . . punching out teeth'. *Bell's Weekly Messenger*, 'Alleged Case of Horrid Murder by Burking an Italian Boy', 14 November, 1831; *The Public Ledger and Advertiser*, 'Alleged Murder of the Italian Boy', 12 November, 1831.

34 'in the expectation that . . .' flesh and scalp, *The Times*, 'The Murdered Italian Boy', 21 November, 1831; 'a jacket . . . in cinders and ash'. TSC, p. 27.

35 'an elderly Birmingham-based padrone . . . for a fee'. Wise (Kindle Edition); *The Times*, 'The Murdered Italian Boy', 21 November, 1831; 'The face . . .' TSC, p. 24.

36 'was of such a character . . .' *The London Courier and Evening Gazette*, 'The Murdered Italian Boy', 21 November, 1831; 'wilful murder . . .' *The Times*, 'Trial of Bishop, Williams, and May of the Italian Boy', 3 December, 1831; 'declared that all . . .' *The* (London) *Morning Herald*, 'Final Examination of the Parties Charged with the Murder of the Italian Boy', 26 November, 1831.

37 *The Public Ledger and Daily Advertiser*, 'Trial of the Three Resurrection Men for the Murder of the Italian Boy', 3 December, 1831.

38 Details of boy's death. See TSC, pp. 36–37.

39 Bishop statement. See TSC, pp. 37–38.

40 Ibid., pp. 40, 42.

41 'In less than two minutes . . .' *The Preston Chronicle*, 'The Trial of Bishop, May, and Williams for the Murder of the Italian Boy', 10 December, 1863.

42 Wise (Kindle Edition).

43 Ibid.

44 Anatomy Act of 1832. Ibid.; 'the removal, storage, use . . .' Human Tissue Authority website; BBC News, 'Q&A: Human Tissue Act', 30 August, 2006.

2: Severed

1 'was only a small step away . . .' Begg and Skinner, p. 22; 'subversive . . . House of Correction'. Browne, p. 104.

2 Browne, pp. 104–105; 'in military order . . . breathed his last'. *The London Courier and Evening Gazette*, 'The Meeting of the National Union', 14 May, 1833.

3 'justifiable homicide . . . spirit of the constitution'. Browne, pp. 105, 106; 'the Popay incident discouraged . . .' Melville, pp. 310–11.

4 'obligated to investigate . . .' Begg and Skinner, p. 19.

5 'something dark behind it'. *The Morning Post*, 'A Mutilated Human Body Found', 30 December, 1836.

6 Ibid.; 'I at first thought . . . tied down'. *The Public Ledger and Daily Advertiser*, 'The Mysterious Affair in the Edgware Road', 2 January, 1837; *The Times*, 'Suspected Murder', 30 December, 1836.

7 *The Public Ledger and Daily Advertiser*, 'The Mysterious Affair in the Edgware Road', 2 January, 1837.

8 Ibid.

9 'engaged in housework'. ibid; 'It might have lain . . .' *The Times*, 'Suspected Murder', 30 December, 1836.

10 *The Morning Post*, 'A Mutilated Human Body Found', 30 December, 1836.

11 Ibid.

12 'No discovery had been made . . .' *The Times*, 'Suspected Murder', 30 December, 1836.

13 Ibid.

14 'numerous applications . . .' *The Morning Post*, 'A Mutilated Human Body Found', 30 December, 1836; 'obtain any trace . . .' *The Morning Post*, 'The Late Mysterious Murder in the Edgware Road', 12 January, 1837; *The Chelmsford Chronicle*, 'The Edgware Road Murder', 13 January, 1837.

15 *The Chelmsford Chronicle*, 'The Edgware Road Murder', 13 January, 1837.

16 *The Weekly True Sun*, 'The Edgware Road Murder', 14 January, 1837.

17 Ibid.

18 *The Times*, 'Discovery of the Head of a Female', 8 January, 1837; 'The Late Mysterious Murder in the Edgware Road', 10 January, 1837.

19 'because the smell . . .' *The Weekly True Sun*, 'The Edgware Road Murder', 15 January, 1837; 'The eyebrows are . . .' *The Times*, 'The Late Mysterious Murder in the Edgware Road', 10 January, 1837.

20 *The Evening Standard*, 'The Edgware-Road Murder', 13 February, 1837.

21 *Bell's Weekly Messenger*, 'Discovery of the Legs of the Woman', 5 February, 1837.

22 'so that a portion . . . not much decayed'. Ibid; 'Altogether in its general character . . .' *The Morning Post*, 'The Edgware Road Murder', 6 February, 1837.

23 *The Northampton Mercury*, 'The Edgware Road Murder', 18 March, 1837.

24 see William Gay's inquest testimony in *The Morning Herald*, 'The Edgeware Road Tragedy', 28 March, 1837; and Gay's trial testimony in Huish, p. 325.

25 'Oh God . . . not swear positively'. *The Evening Standard*, 'The Edgware Road Murders – Examination of Two Persons and Extraordinary Confession of One of Them', 28 March, 1837.

26 Ibid.

27 *The Morning Herald*, 'The Edgeware Road Tragedy', 28 March, 1837.

28 Ibid.

29 *The Evening Standard*, 'The Edgware Road Murders – Examination of Two Persons and Extraordinary Confession of One of Them', 28 March, 1837.

30 *The Morning Herald*, 'The Edgeware Road Tragedy', 28 March, 1837.

31 Ibid.

32 Huish, p. 365.

33 Gale sentence. Ibid., p. 439; Greenacre sentence. Ibid., p. 435

34 *The Morning Post*, 'Greenacre,' 4 May, 1837; *English Chronicle and Whitehall Evening Post*, 'The Execution of Greenacre,' 2 May, 1847; 'The Trial of J. Greenacre and Sarah Gale,' p. 30.

35 *The Windsor and Eton Express*, 'Diabolical Murder.' 25 February, 1837; Moss and Skinner, p. 32.

3: Unsolved

1   *The Morning Chronicle*, 'Another Murder of a Female,' 10 May, 1837.

2   'Eliza is dead!' *The Morning Chronicle*, 'The Late Murder in Laxton-Place, Regents Park,' 12 May, 1837; *Freeman's Journal*, 'Another Murder of a Female,' 10 May, 1837.

3   'a glass half full of ale . . .' *Freeman's Journal*, 'Another Murder of a Female,' 10 May, 1837; 'one of her hands was covered . . .' *The Morning Herald*, 'Another Woman Murdered.' 10 May, 1837.

4   *The Morning Chronicle*, 'The Late Murder in Laxton-Place, Regents Park,' 12 May, 1837.

5   Ibid.

6   'The subject . . .' *The Morning Advertiser*, 'The Frederick Street Murder,' 16 May, 1837; 'it is probable . . .' *Bell's Weekly Messenger*, 'Another Woman Murdered,' 14 May, 1837.

7   'She felt pestered . . .' *The Morning Chronicle*, 'The Late Murder in Laxton-Place, Regents Park,' 12 May, 1837; description comes from *The Weekly True Sun*, 'The Frederick-Street Murder – Additional and Latest Particulars,' 14 May, 1837.

8   'the factories of most . . .' *The Weekly True Sun*, 'The Frederick-Street Murder – Additional and Latest Particulars,' 14 May, 1837; *The Morning Advertiser*, 'The Frederick Street Murder,' 16 May, 1837.

9   Worsley, p. 83; 'a well-dressed man . . .' *The Evening Chronicle*, 'Another Dreadful Murder,' 28 May, 1838.

10 *The Evening Chronicle*, 'Another Dreadful Murder,' 28 May, 1838.

11 'having a higher standard . . .', Lock (*First Cases*), p. 17; 'bars, theaters, prostitues . . .' Honeycombe, p. 42; 'When I saw the poor countess . . .' quoted in 'Three Detective Anecdotes: 1 – The Pair of Gloves.' by Dickens (Reprinted Pieces), p. 163.

12 *The Morning Post*, 'The Murder at Lambeth,' 30 May, 1838.

13 *The Examiner*, 'The Murder of Eliza Grimwood,' 3 June, 1838

14 'inhuman massacre.' *The Morning Post*, 'The Murder at Lambeth,' 30 May, 1838; 'unfortunate Eliza Davies,' *The Cambridge Chronicle and Journal*, 'The Murder of Eliza Davies,' 2 June, 1838; 'Those with retentive memories . . .' quoted in Bondeson (Kindle edition)

15 Death of Nancy in 'Oliver,' Worsley, p. 83.

16 From a lyric sheet by Seven Dials printer James Catnatch published on 5 June,

1839. Reproduced online at 'The Unsolved Murder of Mr Westwood' (see 'General Websites' in Bibliography).

17 *The London Courier and Evening Gazette*, 'The Murder and Arson in Princes Street,' 5 June, 1839.

18 Ibid.

19 Ibid.

20 Ibid.

21 *The Globe*, 'The Murder in Soho,' 11 June, 1839.

22 *Bell's Weekly Messenger*, 'The Dreadful Murder,' 9 June, 1839.

23 Begg and Skinner, p. 28; 'rather peculiar . . . from his violence.' *The Evening Mail*, 'The Murder of Mr Westwood,' 7 June, 1839.

24 'flew into . . . instantly leave the place.' *The Times*, 'Murder of Mr Westwood - Additional Particulars (from the *Observer*),' 10 June, 1839; *The Morning Herald*, (no headline), 13 August, 1839.

25 Begg and Skinnger, pp. 28–29.

26 'a roving commission . . . by the new.' Browne, pp. 84, 144

27 'prototype police force.' Fido and Skinner, pp. 27, 28; 'the police in and near the Metropolis' and expanding Metropolitan Police District, see Metropolitan Police Act 1839 (can be accessed at Legislation.gov.uk).

28 *The Times*, 'Horrible Murder of Lord William Russell, Uncle to Lord John Russell, Secretary for the Colonies,' 7 May, 1840.

29 'Several noblemen . . . lose my character.' Ibid; Harman, p. 24.

30 *The Times*, 'Horrible Murder of Lord William Russell, Uncle to Lord John Russell, Secretary for the Colonies,' 7 May, 1840.

31 'The socket which . . .' Pearce testimony (Courvoisier trial). Old Bailey Proceedings Online.

32 Tedman testimony (Courvoisier trial). Old Bailey Proceedings Online.

33 Pearce and Beresford testimony (Courvoisier trial). Old Bailey Proceedings Online. *The Times*, 'Horrible Murder of Lord William Russell, Uncle to Lord John Russell, Secretary for the Colonies,' 7 May, 1840.

34 Mancer testimony (Courvoisier trial). Old Bailey Proceedings Online.

35 *The Times*, 'Horrible Murder of Lord William Russell, Uncle to Lord John Russell, Secretary for the Colonies,' 7 May, 1840.

36 'silver dressing articles . . . this property behind.' Harman, pp. 23, 24.

37 'The excitement produced . . .' *The Times*, 'Murder of Lord William Russell,' 9 May, 1840; 'This is really too horrid . . .' Harman, p. 4.

38 'besieging . . . course of the day.' *The Times*, 'The Murder of Lord William Russell,' 9 May, 1840.

39 *The Times*, (no headline). 8 May, 1840.

40 'several plumbers . . . stolen property.' *The Times*, 'The Murder of Lord William Russell,' 9 May, 1840; Pearce testimony (Courvoisier trial). Old Bailey Proceedings Online.

41 Pearce and Peolaine testimony (Courvoisier trial). Old Bailey Proceedings Online.

42 'had been doing some private study,' Harman, p. 193; 'It is not generally known . . .' *The Independent*, 'Vital clue ignored for 50 years,' 9 December, 2012.
43 Letter filed away until the 1890s. Harman, p. 194; *The Independent*, 'Vital clue ignored for 50 years,' 9 December, 2012.
44 *The Morning Chronicle*, 'Trial of Courvoisier for the Murder of Lord William Russell,' 19 June, 1840.
45 'persons of distinction.' Ibid.; Pearce testimony (Courvoisier trial). Old Bailey Proceedings Online.
46 Harman, pp. 168–169, 174
47 Ibid., pp. 172, 178.

4: Detective Days

1 *The Times*, 'To The Editor of the Times,' 30 May, 1840.
2 *The Morning Post*, 'Horrible Murder and Mutilation of a Female,' 8 April, 1842.
3 Ibid.
4 Ibid.
5 'utmost apparent coolness . . . and very dark.' Ibid.; Gardiner testimony (Good trial). Old Bailey Proceedings Online.
6 'My God . . . entrails extracted.' *The Morning Post*, 'Horrible Murder and Mutilation of a Female,' 8 April, 1842.
7 'at about the third . . .' Ibid.; Allen testimony (Good trial). Old Bailey Proceedings Online.
8 'I never smelt . . .' Tye testimony (Good trial). Old Bailey Proceedings Online; 'was most overpowering . . . a number of fragments . . . thigh bones.' *The Morning Post*, 'Horrible Murder and Mutilation of a Female,' 8 April, 1842.
9 Tye and Clarke testimony (Good trial). Old Bailey Proceedings Online.
10 'dressed in a blue bonnet . . .' Brown testimony (Good trial). Old Bailey Proceedings Online; 'a murder of the most appalling nature.' *The York Herald*, 'Horrible Murder and Mutilation of a Female,' 16 April, 1842; 'Vehicles of every description . . .' *The Times*, 'The Murder at Roehampton,' 12 April, 1842.
11 'in a fit of ungovernable rage' Browne, p. 116; 'constantly . . . hands of justice.' *The Times*, 'The Roehampton Murder,' 16 April, 1842.
12 Begg and Skinner, p. 35; 'exerting themselves to the utmost . . .' *The Times*, 'Horrible Murder and Mutilation of a Female,' 8 April, 1842; 'the conduct of the metropolitan police . . .' *The Planet*, 'Conduct of the Police,' 17 April, 1842.
13 *The Evening Standard*, 'Apprehension of Good the Murderer,' 18 April, 1842.
14 Browne, pp. 120–21.
15 *The Morning Post*, 'New Police Arrangement,' 12 July, 1842.
16 Begg and Skinner, p. 37
17 Begg and Skinner, p. 38; '£84 more than uniformed officers,' calculating carriage speed, sergeants' salary. Lock (*First Cases*), p. 43.
18 Browne, pp. 122, 124.
19 'with a large scale loss of life.' T. H. Tulchinsky, 'John Snow, Cholera, the Broad

Street Pump; Waterborne Diseases Then and Now. Case Studies in Public Health.' 2018:77–99. doi: 10.1016/B978-0-12-804571-8.00017-2. Epub 2018 Mar 30. PMCID: PMC7150208; 14,000 dead. *The London Gazette*, 'Cholera epidemics in Victorian London'. 1 February, 2016 (https://www.thegazette.co.uk/all-notices/content/100519)

20 *The Morning Chronicle*, 'A Visit to the Cholera Districts of Bermondsey,' 24 September, 1849.
21 'At this time . . .' Worsley, p. 114.
22 *The Morning Post*, 'The Bermondsey Murder,' 20 August, 1849.
23 '11 petticoats . . .' Worsley, p. 114; 'an extremely fine woman . . .' *The Globe*, 'The Bermondsey Murder,' 20 August, 1849.
24 'in the household . . . society of ladies.' *The Globe*, 'The Bermondsey Murder,' 20 August, 1849; *The Bermondsey Murder: A Full Report on the Trial of Frederick George Manning and Maria Manning* (referenced here on out as TBM), pp. 5–6.
25 Worsley, p. 115; 'The Mannings, through their extravagance . . . rear of the house'. *The Evening Standard*, 'The Murder in Bermondsey – Inquest on the Body,' 20 August, 1849.
26 *The Times*, 'Extraordinary Discovery of a Murder,' 18 August, 1849; 'The Bermondsey Murder,' 2 August5, 1849; 'Poor Mr O' Connor . . .' Flynn testimony (Manning trial). Old Bailey Proceedings Online.
27 'The nest was there . . .' Worsley, p. 116. 'I proceeded to remove . . .' Barnes testimony (Manning trial). Old Bailey Proceedings Online.
28 'The fractures were quite sufficient . . .' Lockwood testimony (Manning trial). Old Bailey Proceedings Online.
29 'from its propriety' *The Morning Post*, 'The Bermondsey Murder,' 20 August, 1849; 'Kirk testimony (Manning trial). Old Bailey Proceedings Online.
30 *The Stirling Observer*, 'The Bermondsey Murder,' 30 August, 1849.
31 Ibid.
32 The *Guardian*, 'The world's first hack: the telegraph and the invention of privacy,' 15 July, 2015.
33 'about a third of the railway network.' Lock (*First Cases*), p. 97; 'scarcely arrived at Scotland Yard.' *The Stirling Observer*, 'The Bermondsey Murder,' 30 August, 1849; *The Evening Standard*, 'The Bermondsey Murder,' 24 August, 1849.
34 *The Times*, 'The Bermondsey Murder,' 28 August, 1849.
35 Ibid.
36 *The Stirling Observer*, 'The Bermondsey Murder,' 30 August, 1849; *The Globe*, 'Bermondsey Murder – Arrest of Manning,' 30 August, 1849; 'extensive robberies.' TBM, p. 21; Lock (*First Cases*), p. 101.
37 TBM, p. 25.
38 *The Globe*, 'Bermondsey Murder – Arrest of Manning,' 30 August, 1849.
39 'what part of the head . . . sum of money, £500.' Massey testimony (Manning trial). Old Bailey Online Proceedings; Lock (*First Cases*), p. 101.
40 Maria's lack of emotion. Worsley, pp. 117; 'History teaches us . . .' TBM, p. 50.
41 'There is no law for me . . .' TBM, p. 63

42 'Jezebel' and 'The Lady Macbeth of Bermondsey'. Worsley, p. 117; 'The terrible excitement . . .' *The Evening Mail*, 'The Bermondsey Murder', 29 October, 1849.

43 Worsley, p. 113.

44 'I believe that a sight . . .' *The Times*, 'To the Editor of the Times', 14 November, 1849; 'a fine shape . . .' Worsley, p. 119.

45 Madame Hortense inspired by Maria Manning and Bucket modeled after Field. Worsley, p. 89; 'perform the most difficult . . .' *Household Words*, 'The Modern Science of Thief-Taking,' 13 July, 1850.

46 'As a connoisseur . . .' *Household Words*, 'The Modern Science of Thief-Taking,' 13 July, 1850.

47 Dickens *(Christmas Books)*, 'The Detective Police', pp. 720, 723.

48 Ibid., p. 723.

49 Ibid., p. 720.

50 Ibid., 'On Duty With Inspector Field,' pp. 745, 747.

51 'something of a reserved . . .' Ibid., 'The Detective Police,' p. 721; attacked by the swell mob. Ibid., 'Three Detective Anecdotes,' pp. 741-2.

52 'Commissioner Mayne's favourite officer'. Summerscale, p. 55; 'to search Parisian . . .' Lock *(First Cases)*, p. 99.

53 Summerscale, p. 55; 'the Prince of Detectives'. Fido and Skinner, p. 283.

5: A Murder in the Manor

1   *The Morning Post* (no headline). 10 July, 1860

2   Summerscale, p. 62

3   Ibid., p. 3; 'He was well and happy'. *The Bath Chronicle and Weekly Gazette*, 'Horrid and Mysterious Murder,' 5 July, 1860.

4   *The Bath Chronicle and Weekly Gazette*, 'Horrid and Mysterious Murder,' 5 July, 1860.

5   Ibid.

6   Summerscale, pp. 8, 12-15; *The Bath Chronicle and Weekly Gazette*, 'Horrid and Mysterious Murder,' 5 July, 1860.

7   'I noticed some blood . . . falling lower down'. *The Bath Chronicle and Weekly Gazette*, 'Horrid and Mysterious Murder,' 5 July, 1860.

8   'Blood was splashed all over his face'. Rhode, p. 45; 'When it was lifted up . . . fell off the body'. *The Reading Mercury*, 'The Mysterious Murder Near Frome'. 28 July, 1860; 'I can't describe the horror and amazement . . .' Summerscale, pp. 17-18.

9   Rhode, pp. 47-50.

10 Ibid., pp. 47, 48

11 'My impression is that . . .' *The Wiltshire Times and Trowbridge Advertiser*, 'Horrid and Mysterious Murder,' 7 July, 1860.

12 Summerscale, pp. 196-7.

13 *The Bath Chronicle and Weekly Gazette*, 'Horrid and Mysterious Murder,' 5 July, 1860.

14 Ibid.
15 *The Morning Post,* (no headline), 10 July, 1860
16 *The Bath Chronicle and Weekly Gazette,* 'Horrid and Mysterious Murder,' 5 July, 1860.
17 Summerscale, p. 34.
18 'It seems almost incredible . . .' *The North Devon Gazette,* 'Barbarous and Mysterious Murder,' 10 July, 1860; 'Nothing, absolutely nothing . . .' *The Frome Times,* 'The Murder at Road,' 18 July, 1860.
19 *The Wiltshire Times and Trowbridge Advertiser,* 'Horrid and Mysterious Murder,' 7 July, 1860.
20 'a circuitous one . . .' *The Bath Chronicle and Weekly Gazette,* 'Horrid and Mysterious Murder,' 5 July, 1860; 'surrounded by shrubs . . . six feet of water and soil.' *The Ulverston Mirror and Furness Reflector,* 'The Road Murder.' 28 July, 1860.
21 *The Leeds Times,* 'The Mysterious Frome Murder,' 21 July, 1860.
22 Exchange between Which and Constance is quoted in *The London Express,* 'The Late and Mysterious Murder at Road, Near Frome,' 21 July, 1860.
23 'in consequence . . .' *The London Express,* 'The Late and Mysterious Murder at Road, near Frome,' 21 July, 1860; *The Leeds Times,* 'The Mysterious Frome Murder,' 21 July, 1860; 'make use of expressions . . .' *The Morning Advertiser,* 'The Frome Murder,' 30 July, 1860.
24 *The London Express,* 'The Late and Mysterious Murder at Road, near Frome.' 21 July, 1860
25 *The Frome Times,* (no headline), 1 August, 1860.
26 Ibid., 'The Road Murder.'
27 Ibid.
28 'Better that 99 guilty persons . . .' *The Devizes and Wiltshire Gazette,* 'The Road Murder,' 2 August, 1860; 'The case, as got up . . .' *The Portsmouth Times and Naval Gazette,* 'The Road Murder,' 4 August, 1860; 'With reference to the . . .' *The Frome Times,* 'The Road Murder,' 8 August, 1860.
29 *Bell's Weekly Messenger.* 'House of Commons – Wednesday,' 18 August, 1860.
30 'That Mr Whicher's zeal . . .' *The London Daily News,* 'The Road Murder,' 13 August, 1860.
31 Browne, p. 158.
32 'a house for religious ladies.' *Bell's Weekly Messenger,* 'The Road-Hill Murder,' 1 May, 1865; 'increasingly depressed' and 'mental breakdown.' Fido and Skinner, p. 284; 'congestion of the brain.' Summerscale, p. 225.
33 Rhode, p. 214.
34 *The Times,* (no headline), 27 April, 1865.
35 Rhode, p. 265.
36 Ibid., p. 266.
37 Ibid., pp. 272–3; Summerscale, pp. 258–9.
38 Begg and Skinner, pp. 49–50.
39 *The Times,* (no headline), 27 April, 1865; 'penal servitude for life.' Browne,

p. 161; Constance's life in Australia and death. Summerscale, pp. 289–290, Begg and Skinner, p. 49.

6: A Zealous Effort

1 'a magnificent and stupendous work . . .' *The Scotsman*, 'Opening of the Liverpool and Manchester Railway,' 15 September, 1830; 'Manchester to Liverpool: The First Inter-city Railway.' BBC News, 23 July, 2009.
2 *Journal of Victorian Culture*, vol. 21, issue 1, 1 March, 2016. 'Shattered Minds: Madmen on the Railways, 1860'; 'a scientific commission . . . travellers by rail.' *The Lancet*, 'The Influence of Railway Travelling on Public Health.' See 'Introduction' and p. 43.
3 Ibid., p. 53.
4 Colquhoun, pp. 9–10.
5 *The Saturday Review*, 'Railway Imprisonment,' 16 July, 1864.
6 Vernez and Jones testimony. Knott, pp. 18–19; *The Times*, 'The Murder on the North London Railway,' 12 July, 1864; Colquhoun, pp. 1–2.
7 Vernez, Jones, and Ames testimony. Knott, pp. 18–19
8 Ames testimony (Müller trial). Old Bailey Proceedings Online; 'had been dragged . . .' and 'thick cane with . . .' *The Times*, 'The Murder on the North London Railway,' 12 July, 1864.
9 'on the 6-foot way . . .' Knott, p. xiii.
10 'I found it was the body . . .' Timms testimony (Müller trial). Old Bailey Proceedings Online; *The Times*, 'The Murder on the North London Railway,' 19 July, 1864.
11 'the mutilated body . . .' *The Times*, 'The Murder on the North London Railway,' 12 July, 1864; Dougan testimony (Müller trial). Old Bailey Proceedings Online.
12 'ten shillings . . . a number of letters and papers.' Dougan testimony (Müller trial). Old Bailey Proceedings Online; *The Leeds Mercury*, 'Horrible Murder in a Railway Carriage,' 12 July, 1864; *The Times*, 'Murder in a First-Class Carriage on the North London Railway,' 11 July, 1864.
13 Brereton testimony (Müller trial). Old Bailey Proceedings Online.
14 'the temporal bone . . .' Toulmin testimony (Müller trial). Old Bailey Proceedings Online; *The Leeds Mercury*, 'Horrible Murder in a Railway Carriage,' 12 July, 1864.
15 Colquhoun, p. 24.
16 Kerressey testimony (Müller trial). Old Bailey Proceedings Online; Hatmaker name on label and 'Mr Briggs had been attacked . . .' Knott, pp. xiv, xv.
17 'framework supporting . . .' and 'dropped, as it were, out of the carriage . . .' *The Bradford Review*, 'Horrible Murder in a Railway Carriage,' 14 July, 1864; 'He was then alive . . .' Kerressey testimony (Müller trial). Old Bailey Proceedings Online; Colquhoun, p. 24.
18 'a gold watch . . .' *The York Herald*, 'Horrible Murder in a Railway Carriage,' 16 July, 1864.

19 'a large gold key . . .' and 'a large, old-fashioned . . .' *The Bradford Review*, 'Horrible Murder in a Railway Carriage,' 14 July, 1864; 'S. W. Archer . . .' *The York Herald*, 'Horrible Murder in a Railway Carriage,' 16 July, 1864.

20 *The Times*, 'Murder in a First Class Carriage on the North London Railway,' 11 July, 1864; *The Belfast Morning News*, 'The Murder on the North London Railway,' 15 July, 1864.

21 'of the class generally used . . . flattened and crushed.' *The Belfast Morning News*, 'The Murder on the North London Railway,' 15 July, 1864; 'was a good 'Paris nap'. *The Evening Standard*, 'The Atrocious Murder in a Railway Carriage,' 16 July, 1864.

22 *The* (London) *Morning Herald*, 'Horrible and Atrocious Murder in a First-Class Carriage of a Train on the North London Railway,' 12 July, 1864.

23 *The Evening Standard*, 'The Atrocious Murder in a First-Class Carriage on the North London Railway,' 12 July, 1864.

24 'Our police have a character to keep . . .' *The Daily Telegraph*, (no headline), 13 July, 1864.

25 Browne, p. 166.

26 Colquhoun, pp. 27, 28.

27 Begg and Skinner, p. 50-1.

28 'on the other side of the road'. Begg and Skinner, p. 51; Colquhoun, p. 28.

29 Colquhoun, pp. 30-1.

30 *The Daily Telegraph*, (no headline), 13 July, 1864.

31 'of the most . . .' *The Evening Standard*, 'The Atrocious Murder in a Railway Carriage,' 16 July, 1864; 'At the station at Bow . . .' *The Evening Standard*, 'The Atrocious Murder in a Railway Carriage,' 14 July, 1864.

32 'a gentlemanly foreigner . . . a black hat'. *The Preston Herald*, 'The Railway Murder,' 16 July, 1864; *Reynolds's Newspaper*, 'Latest Particulars of the Atrocious Railway Carriage Murder,' 17 July, 1864.

33 *The Preston Herald*, 'The Railway Murder,' 16 July, 1864.

34 *Reynolds's Newspaper*, 'Latest Particulars of the Atrocious Railway Carriage Murder,' 17 July, 1864; Colquhoun, p. 57.

35 'The police . . .' *The Evening Standard*, 'The Atrocious Murder in a Railway Carriage'. 15 July, 1864; 'Folkestone, Dover, Southampton . . .' *Reynolds's Newspaper*, 'Latest Particulars of the Atrocious Railway Carriage Murder,' 17 July, 1864.

36 'It would seem . . .' *Reynolds's Newspaper*, 'Latest Particulars of the Atrocious Railway Carriage Murder,' 17 July, 1864; 'who answered in certain points . . . unlucky individual'. *The Times*, 'The Murder on the North London Railway,' 18 July, 1864.

37 'a man wearing . . .' *Reynolds's Newspaper*, 'Latest Particulars of the Atrocious Railway Carriage Murder,' 17 July, 1864; 'Fantasy sightings . . .' Colquhoun, p. 63; 'a day or two . . .' *The Times*, 'The Murder on the North London Railway,' 18 July, 1864.

38 For letter arguing against murder, see *The Times*, 'Letter to the Editor,' 18 July,

1864; for Letter from An Occasional Traveller, see *The Evening Standard*, 'To the Editor', 14 July, 1864.

39 'a man of very moderate intelligence . . .' Knott, p. xvi; Matthews testimony (Müller trial). Old Bailey Proceedings Online.

40 Colquhoun, p. 66; *The Globe*, 'The Murder on the North London Railway', 20 July, 1864.

41 *The Globe*, 'The Murder on the North London Railway', 20 July, 1864.

42 *The Times*, 'The Murder on the North London Railway', 21 July, 1864.

43 Ibid.

44 Colquhoun, p. 71; 'I could swear to it'. *The Globe*, 'The Murder on the North London Railway', 20 July, 1864.

45 Blyth testimony (Müller trial). Old Bailey Proceedings Online.

46 Ibid.

47 Ibid.

48 Ibid.

49 Knox, p. xvii; *The Morning Advertiser*, 'The Murder on the North London Railway', 20 July, 1864; 'passports for two witnesses . . .' Colquhoun, p. 85; 'dispatches . . .' *The Morning Post*, 'The Murder on the North London Railway', 21 July, 1864.

50 Colquhoun, p. 85; Begg and Skinner, p. 54.

51 *The Times*, 'The Murder on the North London Railway', 20 July, 1864.

52 'I was twenty days in the Harbour of New York . . .' Begg and Skinner, pp. 54–5; Colquhoun, p. 86; *The London Daily News*, 'The Murder on the North London Railway', 21 July, 1864.

53 'a splendid ship . . . beautiful proportions and graceful lines'. *The Illustrated London News*, 'The "City of Manchester" Screw Steamer', 19 July, 1851; 'I was confined to bed . . .' *The Evening Standard*, 'Müller in Liverpool', 17 September, 1864.

54 'The personal characteristics . . .' *The Globe*, 'The Murder on the North London Railway'. 20 July, 1864; 'The conclusive evidence . . .' *Reynolds's Newspaper*, 'Suspected Discovery of the Murderer of Mr Briggs', 24 July, 1864.

55 Colquhoun, pp. 112-13.

56 'on the north side of Union Square'. Colquhoun, p. 119; *The Evening Standard*, 'Müller in Liverpool', 17 September, 1864.

57 Colqohoun, p. 121; 'The police . . .' *The Evening Standard*, 'Müller in Liverpool', 17 September, 1864.

58 *The New York Times*, 'Great Britain: The Mysterious Murder. Supposed Discovery of the Perpetrator. His Flight to America. Further Particulars', 4 August, 1864.

59 'Here was a case . . .' *The Brooklyn Eagle*, 'Murder Will Out', 6 August, 1864.

60 'In consequence . . .' Tanner's 9 August, 1864, report. MEPO 3/75; *The Evening Standard*, 'Müller in Liverpool', 17 September, 1864.

61 'It was a sad sight . . .' *The New York Times*, 'The Tallahassee', 29 September, 1864.

62 'Up to this date . . .' Tanner's 23 August, 1864, report. MEPO 3/75.

63 'cheerfully' *The New York Daily Herald*, 'The London Railway Murder,' 26 August, 1864. 'make an affidavit . . .' *The Evening Standard*, 'Müller in Liverpool,' 17 September, 1864.
64 'How are you Müller . . .' *The New York Daily Herald*, 'The London Railway Murder,' 26 August, 1864.
65 Clarke testimony (Müller trial). Old Bailey Online Proceedings; Colquhoun, p. 129.
66 Tanner testimony (Müller trial). Ibid.
67 Ibid; 'At this time . . .' *The Evening Standard*, 'Müller in Liverpool,' 17 September, 1864
68 Details and dialogue from Tanner's first hand account. *The Evening Standard*, 'Müller in Liverpool,' 17 September, 1864
69 *The New York Daily Herald*, 'The London Railway Murder,' 26 August, 1864.
70 Knott, pp. 152, 153.
71 Ibid., pp. xviii-xix.
72 Tanner's 28 August, 1864, report. MEPO 3/75.
73 *The New York Daily Herald*, 'Müller, the Alleged Railway Murderer, on his way to England,' September 4, 1864; *The Evening Standard*, 'Müller in Liverpool,' 17 September, 1864; Colquhoun, p. 150.
74 *The Evening Standard*, 'Müller in Liverpool,' 17 September, 1864.
75 Ibid.
76 Ibid.
77 Ibid.
78 Knott, pp. xx-xxi.
79 Ibid., p. 147.
80 Colquhoun, p. 237; 'dissolved in tears.' *The Times*, 'The Murder on the North London Railway,' 3 October1, 1864.
81 'the doom awarded . . .' *The Times* (no headline), 15 November, 1864.
82 'There can only be one thing . . .' *The Times*, 'Müller's Execution,' 15 November, 1864.
83 'In a few minutes . . .' *Western Daily Press*, 'Execution of Müller: His Confession,' 15 November, 1864.
84 *The Times,* (no headline), 15 November, 1864.
85 *The New York Times*, 'The Arrest of Müller, the English Railway Murderer,' 26 August, 1864.

7: A Death in Duddlewick

1 *The Evening Standard*, 'Shocking Murder in Shropshire,' 17 January, 1866.
2 *The Owestry Advertiser*, 'Murder in Shropshire,' 24 January, 1866.
3 Ibid.
4 Ibid.
5 *The Shrewsbury Free Press and Advertiser for Salop*, 'The Shocking Murder at Duddlewick,' 3 February, 1866.

6 Ibid.

7 Ibid.

8 'Of the deceased . . .' *The Morning Advertiser*, 'The Mysterious Murder in Shropshire,' 29 January, 1866

9 'been sleeping off the drink . . .' Lock (CID), p. 19.

10 19 January, 1866, letter from Chief Constable Cureton to Metropolitan Police. MEPO 3/80.

11 Tanner's 31 January, 1866, report. MEPO 3/80.

12 'had very strong . . .' Tanner's 31 January, 1866, report. MEPO 3/80; 'that a youth . . . violent rage.' *The Chelmsford Chronicle*, The Mysterious Murder in Shropshire, 2 February, 1866; 'He sometimes neglected . . .' *The Shrewsbury Chronicle*, 'The Murder at Duddlewick Near Bridgnorth,' 26 January, 1866.

13 Tanner's 31 January, 1866, report. MEPO 3/80.

14 Ibid.

15 Ibid.

16 Ibid.

17 *The Morning Advertiser*, 'The Mysterious Murder in Shropshire,' 29 January.

18 Moss and Skinner, p. 27

19 *The Shrewsbury Free Press and Advertiser for Salop*, 'The Shocking Murder at Duddlewick,' 27 January, 1866.

20 beating rabbits. S. Gupta, 'Criminology: Written in blood,' *Nature* 549, S24–S25 (2017); 'one of the earliest presumptive tests . . .' Bell, p. 276; 'employment of the peroxide of hydrogen . . .' Taylor (paper), *Detecting Blood in Medico-Legal Cases*; 'Comparative tests for occult blood in gastric contents and feces, with especial reference to the Benzedin test,' *Boston Medical and Surgical Journal*, 8 August, 1907, p. 170.

21 Taylor, *Detecting Blood in Medico-Legal Cases*.

22 *The Shrewsbury Free Press and Advertiser for Salop*, 'The Duddlewick Murder,' 24 March, 1866; 'Report of Examination of Articles of Clothing,' MEPO 3/80.

23 *The Shrewsbury Free Press and Advertiser for Salop*, 'The Duddlewick Murder,' 24 March, 1866.

24 'Mystery will long . . .' *The Shrewsbury Chronicle*, 'The Murder at Duddlewick Near Bridgnorth,' 2 February, 1866.

25 'of the London detective squad.' *The Chicago Tribune*, 'Müller, the Fugitive Criminal, Caught,' 28 August, 1864; 'byword for a new breed of detective,' and Tanner's retirement and death. Colquhoun, p. 281; Fido and Skinner, p. 259.

8: Martyr and Monster

1 'separate locked cubicles.' Fido and Skinner, p. 20; the *Guardian*, 'Largely Forgotten: A Manchester Police Officer Who Gave His Life on Duty,' 26 September, 2012.

2 *The Preston Chronicle*, 'The rescue of two Fenian Head-Centres and the Murder of Sgt. Brett,' 21 September, 1867.

3   Ibid.

4   'a miscellaneous lot . . .' Rose, p. 36.

5   *The Preston Chronicle*, 'The rescue of two Fenian Head-Centres and the Murder of Sgt. Brett,' 21 September, 1867.

6   Ibid.

7   Begg and Skinner, p. 60.

8   *The Dundee Courier*, 'Execution of the Murderers of Brett at Manchester,' 25 November, 1867.

9   The *Guardian*, 'Largely Forgotten: A Manchester Police Officer Who Gave His Life on Duty,' 26 September, 2012; Fido and Skinner, p. 45.

10 'my ideal of . . . the Arctic Circle.' *The Irish Examiner*, 'Soldier, Fenian, and Patriot: Recounting the life of Cork's Ricard O'Sullivan,' 27 April, 2018; Begg and Skinner, p. 59.

11 *The Irish Examiner*, 'Soldier, Fenian, and Patriot: Recounting the life of Cork's Ricard O'Sullivan,' 27 April, 2018; *The Evening Standard*, 'Capture of 'Colonel Burke,' 25 November, 1867.

12 Begg and Skinner, pp. 55–57; 'Peg-Leg Dick.' Ibid., p. 58.

13 Details from *The Evening Standard*, 'Capture of 'Colonel Burke,'' 25 November, 1867.

14 Hansard: HC Deb 09 March 1868, vol. 190 cc1215-8.

15 *The Shields Daily New News*, 'The Clerkenwell Fenian Outrage,' 21 December, 1867

16 Hansard: HC Deb 09 March 1868, vol. 190 cc1215-8.

17 *Reynolds's Newspaper*, 'Attempt to blow up Clerkenwell Prison by Alleged Fenians,' December 15, 1867.

18 Ibid.

19 Ibid

20 'created no suspicion . . .' *Saunders's News-Letter*, 'Attempt to blow-up the prison and Clerkenwell,' 14 December, 1867; 'sympathetic to the Irish cause.' *The Irish Times*, '150 years ago today, a Fenian became the last person to be publicly executed in England,' 26 May, 2018; 'women and children . . .' *The New York Times*, 'Affairs in England,' 29 December, 1867; 'against society and humanity . . .' *The Dublin Evening Mail*, 'The Outrage at Clerkenwell,' 14 December, 1867.

21 'The protection which ought . . .' *The Shields Daily News*, 'The Clerkenwell Fenian Outrage,' 21 December, 1867; 'We told Mayne . . .' Begg and Skinner, pp. 62-3.

22 Fitzgerald, p. 315.

23 *Dictionary of Irish Biography*. https://doi.org/10.3318/dib.000415.v1; O'Brien, p. 229.

24 Ibid.

25 *The Morning Post*, (no headline), 28 April, 1868.

26 *Freeman's Journal*, 'The Execution of Barrett,' 27 May, 1868.

27 *Reynolds's Newspaper*, 'Calcraft's Purveyors,' 31 May, 1868.

28 Fido and Skinner, p. 163.

29 'Comptroller-General of Convicts . . .' Begg and Skinner, p. 64; 'grow beards and . . . of government tyranny'. Fido and Skinnger, p. 113.
30 Shipayer-Makov, p. 35; 'In those times . . .' Lansdowne, p. 7.
31 Fido and Skinner, p. 287; Browne, p. 172.
32 'No matter the intricacy . . .' Howe, p. 39; 'The detectives had . . .' Lansdowne, pp. 6–7.
33 Begg and Skinner, pp. 66, 67.
34 *The Morning Advertiser*, (no headline), 19 April, 1871.
35 Ibid.
36 'that the deceased died . . .' *The Evening Standard*, 'Extraordinary Disclosures,' 18 April, 1871; 'the horror-mongling population . . .' *Freeman's Journal*, 'Mrs Davey, Agnes Norman, and Pook,' 17 July, 1871.
37 'wherever something went . . .' The *Daily Telegraph*, (no headline). 18 July, 1871.
38 *The Morning Advertiser*, 'The Charge Against a Girl of Murdering Children,' 19 May, 1871.
39 Ibid.
40 Ibid.
41 Ibid.; 'During the six weeks . . .' Inspector James Pay's 28 April, 1871, report. MEPO 3/102.
42 *The Morning Advertiser*, 'The Charge Against a Girl of Murdering Children,' 19 May, 1871.
43 'sobriety and civility'. Ibid.; 'She was in service . . .' Inspector James Pay's 28 April, 1871, report. MEPO 3/102.
44 *The Bristol Mercury*, 'The Extraordinary Charge of Murdering Children,' 20 May, 1871; Inspector James Pay's 28 April, 1871, report. MEPO 3/102.
45 The *Daily Telegraph*, (no headline), 18 July, 1871.
46 Ibid.
47 *South London Chronicle*, 'Extraordinary Charge of Child Murder,' 6 May, 1871.
48 *The Irish Times*, 'Agnes Norman,' 2 May, 1871.
49 Lock (CID), p. 52.

9: The Trial of the Detectives

1 *The Graphic*, 'Detectives,' 3 July, 1880.
2 Description of Gunn finding woman, their brief conversation, and the extent of her injuries. *The Evening Standard*, 'The Eltham Tragedy,' 5 May, 1871.
3 Gun testimony (Pook trial). Old Bailey Proceedings Online.
4 'I should say . . .' Gun testimony (Pook trial). Old Bailey Proceedings Online; 'marks as though . . .' *The Evening Standard*, 'The Eltham Tragedy,' 5 May, 1871.
5 'the growing din and congestion of the metropolis'. Murphy (Kindle Edition).
6 Harris testimony (Pook trial), Old Bailey Proceedings Online; 'respectable and hard-working . . .' *The* (London) *Daily News*, 'The Mysterious Tragedy at London,' 1 May, 1871.

7 *The* (London) *Daily News*, 'The Mysterious Tragedy at London,' 1 May, 1871.

8 Harris testimony (Pook trial), Old Bailey Proceedings Online.

9 Murphy (Kindle Edition); *The* (London) *Daily News*, 'Marlborough-Street,' 31 July, 1865.

10 *The* (London) *Daily News*, 'The Eltham Murder,' 2 May, 1871; 'It is of so common . . .' Ibid., 'The Mysterious Tragedy at Eltham,' 1 May, 1871.

11 Ibid., 'The Eltham Murder,' 2 May and 3 May, 1871; 'She was . . . ' Trott testimony (Pook trial), Old Bailey Proceedings Online.

12 'remarked that she was going . . .' *The* (London) *Daily News*, 'The Eltham Murder,' 2 May, 1871; 'was on terms of intimacy,' Mulvany testimony (Pook trial), Old Bailey Proceedings Online; Murphy (Kindle Edition).

13 'She was a dirty young woman . . .' *Reynolds's Newspaper*, 'The Murder of a Servant Girl at Eltham,' 7 May, 1871.

14 Exchange between Pook and police. *Reynolds's Newspaper*, 'The Murder of a Servant Girl at Eltham,' 7 May, 1871.

15 Billington testimony (Pook trial), Old Bailey Proceedings Online; *South London Press*, 'Jane was 16, pregnant, and brutally murdered.' 23 April, 2021; 'The announcement was received . . .' *The* (London) *Daily News*, 'The Eltham Murder.' 17 July, 1871.

16 *The Times*, (no headline), 18 July, 1871.

17 'the acumen . . . remains unpunished.' *The Times*, (no headline), 18 July, 1871; details of Squire murder. *The Times*, 'Double Murder at Hoxton,' 11 July, 1872.

18 'horrid spectacle.' *Reynolds's Newspaper*, 'Double Murder at Hoxton,' 14 July, 1872.

19 *Lloyds's Weekly Newspaper*, 'Terrible tragedy in Hoxton,' 14 July, 1872.

20 Ibid.

21 More than 2,000 people. Ibid.; 'The audacity of the criminal . . .' *The Times*, (no headline), 20 July, 1872.

22 'found to be quite dead . . . fist in.' *The Times*, 'Supposed Murder,' 26 December, 1872.

23 'eked out a living.' Ibid., 'The Coram-Street Murder,' 27 December, 1872; daughter spending Christmas with Harriet. *The Ipswich Journal*, 'Horrible Murder in Great Coram Street, London,' 28 December, 1872.

24 'has had . . . caused by pain.' *The Times*, 'The Coram-Street Murder,' 27 December, 1872; 'as if after . . . had been wiped.' *The Manchester Times*, 'Shocking Murder in London,' 28 December, 1872.

25 *The Manchester Times*, 'Shocking Murder in London,' 28 December, 1872.

26 Ibid.

27 *The Times*, 'The Coram-Street Murder,' 27 December, 1872; *The Manchester Times*, 'Shocking Murder in London,' 28 December, 1872; *The Bristol Mercury*, 'The Great Coram-Street Murder.' 25 January, 1873.

28 *The Bristol Mercury*, 'The Great Coram-Street Murder.' 25 January, 1873.

29 Ibid.

30 'The indignation . . .' Ibid.; *The Times*, (no headline), 31 January, 1873.

31 Moss and Skinner, p. 62.

32 Begg and Skinner, p. 69.
33 'ornaments and so forth'. Griffith, p. 254. Begg and Skinner, p. 69.
34 'though small in scale . . .' Browne, p. 185; Begg and Skinner, pp. 71-2; *Ally Sloper's Half Holiday*, 'Harry Benson, Prince of Swindlers', 14 December, 1889.
35 Browne, p. 185; Begg and Skinner, p. 72; *Ally Sloper's Half Holiday*, 'Harry Benson, Prince of Swindlers', 14 December, 1889.
36 'Bank of London'. *Ally Slope's Half Holiday*, 'Harry Benson, Prince of Swindlers', 14 December, 1889; 'complex and elaborate'. Fido and Skinner, p. 270; Begg and Skinner, p. 73.
37 Fido and Skinner, p. 270; 'conspiracy to defeat the ends . . .' *The Globe*, 'The Charge Against Detectives', 19 October, 1877.
38 'The British public . . .' Storey and Hoar, p. 444.
39 'to inquire . . . French detective system'. Browne, p. 190; 'a central detective force . . .' Begg and Skinner, p. 78.
40 'take precedence . . .' Begg and Skinner, pp. 78, 81, 82; 'The head of the new department . . .' Browne, p. 190.
41 Griffiths (vol. 1), pp. 133.
42 Browne, pp. 191-2; Begg and Skinner, pp. 81, 82.

10: Human Wickedness

1   *The London Weekly Dispatch*, 'Justice at Fault', 17 August, 1879.
2   'one of the most sensational . . . ' *The Freeman's Journal*, 'The Barnes Mystery', 31 March, 1879.
3   *The Croydon Times*, 'Extraordinary Discovery', 19 March, 1879.
4   *The Daily Telegraph*, 'Extraordinary Discovery', 10 March, 1879.
5   Wheatley inquest testimony. *The Croydon Times*, 'Extraordinary Discovery', 19 March, 1879.
6   Childs trial testimony. O'Donnell, p. 152.
7   *The Croydon Times*, 'Extraordinary Discovery', 19 March, 1879.
8   Lock (CID), p. 84.
9   *The Croydon Times*, 'Extraordinary Discovery', 19 March, 1879.
10 *The Daily Telegraph*, 'Extraordinary Discovery', 10 March, 1879.
11 'Now that the weather . . .' *The Manchester Evening News*, (no headline), 27 March, 1879; 'a brutal murder . . . Oxford and Cambridge Boat-Race'. *The Penny Illustrated*, 'A Parallel to the Waterloo Bridge Mystery', 15 March, 1879.
12 'soft substance'. *Lloyd's Weekly Newspaper*, 'The Barnes Mystery', 23 March, 1879; 'It had been . . .' George William Court trial testimony. O'Donnell, p. 152.
13 Bond trial testimony. Ibid., p. 168.
14 'the body had been . . .' *The Daily Telegraph*, 'The Barnes Mystery', 26 March, 1879.
15 'a small garden . . .' O'Donnell, p. 13; 'No. 2 is a small . . .' *The Times*, 'The Alleged Murder at Richmond', 31 March, 1879.
16 Elizabeth Ives trial testimony. O'Donnell, pp. 102-103.

17 'a large one . . .' Ibid., p. 103; *The Daily Telegraph,* 'The Barnes Mystery,' 27 March, 1879.

18 Henry Porter trial testimony. O'Donnell, p. 112.

19 Ibid., pp. 112-3.

20 Robert Porter trial testimony. Ibid, pp. 106-7.

21 Henry Porter trial testimony. Ibid., p. 119.

22 Ibid., p. 115

23 O'Donnell, pp. 44-5.

24 Ibid. p. 46.

25 Ibid.

26 Ibid., p. 47; 'light freckled complexion . . .' *The Dublin Evening Telegraph,* 'The Barnes Mystery,' 29 March, 1879.

27 Pearman trial testimony. O'Donnell, p. 157.

28 'quantity of charred bones' is from the opening statement of the Crown. O'Donnell, p. 91; 'fatty substance'. Pearman testimony. Ibid., p. 156; 'The copper had been wiped out . . .' *The Daily Telegraph,* 'The Barnes Mystery,' 29 March, 1879.

29 Pearman testimony. O'Donnell, pp. 155, 156; 'gave Katherine warning . . .' *The Times,* 'The Alleged Murder at Richmond,' 31 March, 1879.

30 'held little intercourse . . .' *The New York Times,* 'A Woman on the Gallows,' 30 July, 1879; 'a genuine lady . . .' O'Donnell, pp. 42; 'as very much . . .' Ibid., p. 13.

31 'connected and lived . . . to two years'. *The New York Times,* 'A Woman on the Gallows,' 30 July, 1879; 'no less than . . .' *The Daily Telegraph,* 'The Barnes Mystery,' 31 March, 1879.

32 'who appears to have engaged . . .' *The Daily Telegraph,* 'The Barnes Mystery,' 31 March, 1879.

33 'such as would be . . . at the time'. *The New York Times,* 'A Woman on the Gallows,' 30 July, 1879; 'the clothes-line being filled . . .' *The Times,* 'The Alleged Murder at Richmond,' 31 March, 1879.

34 *The Daily Telegraph,* 'The Barnes Mystery,' 26 March, 1879.

35 'I recognized pieces . . .' Bond testimony. O'Donnell, p. 169.

36 'Though it would be hardly . . .' *The Times,* 'The Supposed Murder at Richmond,' 29 March, 1879.

37 *The Dublin Evening Telegraph,* 'The Barnes Murder,' 29 March, 1879.

38 See Dowdell testimony. O'Donnell, pp. 155-7.

39 Ibid., p. 156.

40 See Webster's first statement. O'Donnell, pp. 175-7.

41 *The Daily Telegraph,* 'The Barnes Mystery,' 31 March, 1879.

42 'I never laid a hand . . . up until now' Webster's first statement reproduced in O'Donnell, p. 177; 'The lying woman . . .' Dowdell trial testimony. Ibid., p. 156.

43 *The Times.* 'The Murder at Richmond,' 1 April, 1879.

44 'all members . . .' *The Times,* 'The Richmond Murder,' 2 April, 1879; O'Donnell, pp. 51-2.

45 *The Wolverhampton Express and Star,* 'The Richmond Murder,' 3 July, 1879.

46 *The Dundee Evening Telegraph*, (no headline), 9 July, 1879.
47 See closing speech for the defense reproduced in O'Donnell, pp. 183–90.
48 'I am not guilty . . . ' O'Donnell, p. 212; 'inquire into the truth'. Ibid., p. 213.
49 *The Dundee Evening Telegraph*, (no headline), 9 July, 1879.
50 'untimely end'. Webster's confession in O'Donnell, p. 67; 'a crime of rare atrocity'. *The Pall Mall Gazette*, 'The Richmond Murder', 9 July, 1879.
51 See Webster's confession reproduced in O'Donnell, pp. 67–8.

11: 'From Hell'

1 'conversant with Irish . . . entirely with Fenianism'. Begg and Skinnger, pp. 89, 90; 'intelligence on Irish . . .' Fido and Skinner, p. 246; 'Williamson off his . . .' Ibid., p. 234.
2 *The Times*, 'Dynamite Outrages in London', 31 May, 1884; Sweeney, p. 22.
3 Sweeney, p. 22.
4 *The Daily Telegraph and Courier*, no headline, 26 January, 1885; *The Referee*, no headline, 25 January, 1885.
5 'did much to lower . . .' Fido and Sinner, p. 235.
6 'military man . . . militarise the Force'. Begg and Skinner, p. 112.
7 'During the melee . . .' *The Shields Daily Gazette*, 'The Battle of Trafalgar Square', 14 November, 1887; *The Evening Star*, 'The Trafalgar Square Demonstration', 14 November, 1887; 'A police beyond . . .' *The Northern Echo*, 'Trafalgar-Square', 14 November, 1887; also see Fido and Skinner, pp. 23–4
8 Details of Mary Ann Nichols murder come from CID Chief Inspector Donald Swanson's case summary dated 19 October, 1888, RSB, pp. 31–3; *The Times*, 'The Whitechapel Murder', 3 September, 1888. Details of Annie Chapman's murder come from Swanson's report to the Home Office on 19 October, 1888, RSB, pp. 74–7.
9 'On Saturday morning . . .' *The Morning Post*. 'Another Woman Murdered in Whitechapel', 10 September, 1888; 'noiseless midnight terror'. *The Star*. 'Leather Apron: The Only Name Linked with the Whitechapel Murders', 5 September, 1888.
10 Details of Elizabeth Stride murder taken from Chief Inspector Donald Swan's report dated 19 October, 1888, RSB, p. 136; Details of Catherine Eddowes murder taken from the inquest testimony of surgeon Frederick Gordon Brown, RSB, p. 229; 'The anxiety is intense . . .' *The London Daily News*. 'The Atrocities at the East End'. 3 October, 1888.
11 Ibid.
12 'As a breeder of bloodhounds . . .' *The Times*, 'To the Editor of the Times', 2 October, 1888; 'for the purpose of testing . . .' RSB, p. 331.
13 *The Globe*, 'The East-End Murders', October 9, 1888.
14 first use of sniffer dogs. Neil Pemberton (2013) 'Bloodhounds as Detectives', *Cultural and Social History*, 10:1, 69–91, DOI: 10.2752/147800413X 13515292098197; 'for the immediate . . .' *The Times*, 'The Whitechapel Murder', 13 November, 1888.

15 'ruled with a too iron hand . . .' *The* (London) *Echo,* 'Why Mr Monro Retired,' 31 August, 1888; 'Of course, I complied.' Anderson, p. 135.

16 Anderson, pp. 135–6.

17 'charged with a fluid . . .' Report by Chief Inspector Donald Swanson, dated 6 November, 1888, RSB, p. 209.

18 'a most horrifying spectacle . . .' *The Daily Telegraph,* 'The East-End Tragedies,' 10 November, 1888.

19 'The viscera were found . . .' Dr Thomas Bond's initial post-mortem examination report. RSB, p. 383; 'Sweet Violets,' *The Daily Telegraph,* 'The East-End Tragedies,' 10 November, 1888.

20 *The Daily Telegraph,* 'The East-End Tragedies,' 10 November, 1888.

21 *The Times,* 'The Whitechapel Murder,' 13 November, 1888.

22 *The Evening Standard,* 'Another Arrest,' 18 October, 1888.

23 Douglas, p. 19.

24 *The Pall Mall Gazette,* 'The Whitechapel Tragedies,' 4 November, 1889.

25 Ibid.

26 Letter from Anderson to Bond. RSB, p. 400.

27 Moss and Skinner, p. 94.

28 The profile, dated 10 November, 1888, is reproduced in RSB, pp. 401–2.

29 'Sir Charles Warren . . .' *Lloyd's Weekly Newspaper,* 'The Murders and Sir Charles Warren,' 11 November, 1888.

30 Fido and Skinner, p. 279; *The Morning Post,* 'Resignation of Sir Charles Warren,' 13 November, 1888.

31 'What becomes most apparent . . .' reported by Chief Inspector Donald Swanson, dated 10 September, 1899, RSB, pp. 532–3.

32 'the dissection was performed . . .' *The Evening Standard,* 'The Rainham Mystery,' 13 June, 1887.

33 Begg and Skinner, p. 142; 'The corpse was a mere trunk . . .' *The Daily Telegraph,* 'The Whitehall Murder,' 3 October, 1888; 'in a dark recess . . .' *The Evening Standard,* 'Shocking Discovery in Westminster,' 3 October, 1888.

34 *The Daily Telegraph,* 'The Whitehall Murder,' 3 October, 1888.

35 Ibid.

36 *The London Daily News,* 'The Atrocities at the East End,' 3 October, 1888.

37 *The Times,* 'The Murder in Westminster,' 4 October, 1888.

38 Ibid.

39 'I have an arm that will fit that.' Ibid; 'for if it had been cut off . . .' *The Times,* 'A Thames Mystery,' 12 September, 1888.

40 *The Times,* 'The Murder in Westminster,' 4 October, 1888.

41 Ibid.

42 'Spirits of wine.' Ibid.

43 'We all heard the crashing of timber . . .' *The Evening Standard,* 'The Shocking Discovery in Westminster,' 4 October, 1888.

44 'It was known . . . within two feet of him.' *The Evening Standard,* 'The Shocking Discovery in Westminster,' 4 October, 1888; 'regarded as providential.' *The Times,* 'The Murder in Westminster,' 4 October, 1888.

45 'provided by a gentleman . . .' *The Morning Post*, 'The Whitehall Mystery,' 18 October, 1888; stocking stuck to leg, matches trunk. *Reynolds's Newspaper*, 'The Whitehall Mystery'. 21 October, 1888.

46 *The Evening Standard*, 'Horrible Discovery in the Thames'. 5 June, 1889; *St. James Gazette*, 'The Thames Mystery,' 17 June, 1889; 'There is reason to believe . . .' *The Times*, 'The Thames Mystery,' 11 June, 1889.

47 Inventory of body parts. *The Times*, 'The Thames Mystery,' 11 June, 1889. 'The system of cutting up . . .' *St. James Gazette*, 'The Thames Mystery,' 17 June, 1889.

48 *The Evening News*, 'The Thames Horror,' 26 June, 1889.

49 *The Globe*, 'The Thames Mystery,' 26 July, 1889.

50 Fido and Skinner, p. 135

51 Macnaghten, Melville. *Days of My Years*, London: Edward Arnold, 1914, pp. 55–6.

52 *The New York Times*, 'Dismay in Whitechapel,' 1 October, 1888.

12: Dr Death

1 'appropriately . . . warren of corridors'. Weinreb, et al., p. 583; three-quarters of a mile in length. *The Times*, 'Electric Lighting at New Scotland-Yard,' 6 June, 1891; New Scotland Yard. Begg and Skinner, p. 142.

2 Motor cars on London streets, emergence of fingerprints. Begg and Skinner, p. 141.

3 *The Times*, 'Electric Lighting at New Scotland-Yard,' 6 June, 1891.

4 Ibid.

5 'Someone has given me a drink . . .' McLaren, p. 16; held down by arms and legs. *Lloyd's Weekly Newspaper*. 'Poisoning Mystery in Lambeth'. 18 October, 1891; 'A tall gentleman . . .' dies on way to hospital, strychnine poisoning. Shore, pp. 9, 10.

6 Letter extracts quoted in Honeycombe, p. 41

7 Lock (CID), p. 129.

8 *The Evening Standard*, 'The South London Poisoning Cases,' 23 June, 1892.

9 Ibid.; 'eyes rolled . . . of a twitch'. Rose testimony (Neill trial), Old Bailey Proceedings Online.

10 *The Evening Standard*, 'The South London Poisoning Cases,' 23 June, 1892.

11 'She turned black in the face'. Ibid.; Copping testimony (Neill trial). Old Bailey Proceedings Online.

12 Broadbent testimony (Neill trial). Old Bailey Proceedings Online.

13 Ibid.

14 'With the progress . . .' Browne and Stewart, p. vi; '249 people . . .' Worsley, p. 129.

15 'ghastly, inscrutable smile . . .' Doyle, p. 167; In his book *The Case of the Murderous Dr Cream*, Dean Jobb writes that 'Holmes was the perfect fictional hero for an era when unraveling mysteries became a guilty pleasure'. See pp. 24–7.

16 The details and symptoms of strychnine poisoning are taken from Boys, p. 75;

Details about Emma and Alice. *The Evening Standard,* 'Mysterious Poisoning in South London. Inquest Today,' 13 April, 1892 and 'The South London Poisoning Case,' 14 April, 1892; Eversfield testimony (Neill trial), Old Bailey Proceedings Online.

17 'seemed to . . .' Eversfield testimony (Neill trial), Old Bailey Online Proceedings; Shore, pp. 19–20.

18 'Comley testimony (Neill trial), Old Bailey Proceedings Online.; Shore, pp. 19–20.

19 Conversation quoted in Shore, p. 19.

20 Honeycombe, p. 44.

21 Shore, pp. 3–6; Jobb, pp. 144–6, 152.

22 Shore, p. 6.

23 Honeycombe, p. 42; Shore, p. 17.

24 Honeycombe, pp. 42–3; Shore, pp. 17, 20, 21–4.

25 Ibid.

26 McIntyre testimony (Neill trial). Old Bailey Proceedings Online.

27 Ibid.

28 McIntyre and Tunbridge testimony (Neill trial). Old Bailey Proceedings Online; Jobb, p. 96.

29 Tunbridge testimony (Neill trial), Old Bailey Proceedings Online; 'We have Neill . . .' Jobb, p. 96.

30 'That Neill was the writer . . .' Jobb, p. 99; 'You have the wrong man . . .' Tunbridge testimony (Neill trial). Old Bailey Proceedings Online.

31 Tunbridge testimony (Neill trial). Old Bailey Proceedings Online.

32 Honeycombe, p. 45.

33 'Probably no criminal was ever executed . . .' *The Quebec Morning Chronicle,* 'Thomas Neill Executed,' 16 November, 1892.

34 'I am Jack . . .' and 'I am ejaculating!' Honeycombe, p. 45.

35 'casting guillotined heads.' The *Guardian,* 'Madame Tussaud: the astounding tale of survival behind the woman who made history,' 4 October, 2018; £200 for Cream's clothes. Honeycombe, p. 45.

13: The Murder Squad

1 Read, p. 90; Dalrymple, B.E. (2006), Fingerprints in Mozayani, A., Noziglia, C. (eds), *The Forensic Laboratory Handbook.* Forensic Science and Medicine, Humana Press. https://doi.org/10.1385/1-59259-946-X:117; 'fingermarks of ancient pensioners . . . over the years.' Fido and Skinner, p. 84; 'bloody fingerprints or impressions . . . identification of criminals,' Innes, p. 32.

2 'which used five of . . .' Fido and Skinner, p. 10; 'might apply more or less pressure.' Read, p. 89.

3 'retained their unique details . . .' Loops, whirls, and arches. Fido and Skinner, p. 84; first book on fingerprints to be published. Holder, Robinson, and Laub, pp. 1–13.; Rojas and 'became the first country . . . ' Ibid., pp. 1–14

4 'easily filed, searched . . .' Fido and Skinnger, p. 117; 'numerical values . . . were subdivided'. Cherrill, pp. 22–3; Holder, Robinson, and Laub, pp. 1–14.

5 Quoted in Holder, Robinson, and Laub, pp. 1–14

6 Ibid.

7 Ibid., pp. 1–15; Wilton, G. W., 'Finger-Prints: The Case of Kangali Charan, 1898,' *Judicial Review*, 49:4, pp. 417–27. HeinOnline.

8 Ibid.

9 Henry's demonstration. Fido and Skinner, p. 19; 'in which fingerprint . . . most English-speaking countries'. Holder, Robinson, and Laub, pp. 1–15.

10 'It was housed . . .' Cherrill, p. 26; 29 of 54 pickpockets. Fido and Skinner, p. 85.

11 Read, pp. 10, 14.

12 Read, p. 10; *The Dundee Evening Post*, 'Identified by Finger-Marks'. 15 September, 1902; *The South London Mail*, 'The Recent South London Burglaries,' 20 September, 1902; *The North Devon Gazette*, 'Remarkable Evidence,' 9 September, 1902; 'Scotland Yard, once known as . . .' Honeycombe, p. 130.

13 The *Weekly Dispatch*, 'Finger-Prints,' 21 September, 1902.

14 'a small training school . . .' Begg and Skinner, p. 162; 'I don't know . . .' Tullett, p. 117.

15 'Many of the police chiefs . . .' *St. Louis Post-Dispatch*, 'Impression of Chief Desmond's Finger Tips and the Man Who Took Them,' 12 June, 1904.

16 Ibid.

17 *St. Louis Post-Dispatch*, 'To Identify Crooks By Fingerprints,' 29 October, 1904; *St. Louis Magazine*, 'Were St. Louis Police the first in the U.S. to use fingerprinting?' 16 May, 2019; 'to teach fingerprinting . . . U.S. Government's fingerprint collection'. Holder, Robinson and Laub, pp. 1–17.

18 Read, p. 11; Collins testimony (Stratton trial), Old Bailey Proceedings Online.

19 Collins testimony (Stratton trial). Old Bailey Proceedings Online.

20 Stanton testimony (Stratton trial). Ibid.

21 Collins testimony (Stratton trial). Ibid.

22 'From my experience . . .' Collins testimony (Stratton trial), Ibid.; first use of fingerprints in British murder trial. Holder, Robinson, and.Laub, pp. 1–17.

23 *The Woolwich Gazette*, 'The Deptford Mask Murders,' 12 May, 1905.

24 *The Edinburgh Evening News*, 'Masked Murderers Executed,' 23 May, 1905.

25 Fido and Skinner, pp. 117, 118.

26 700 detectives; 'The County Police . . . compelling them to do so'. Home Office memorandum quoted in Tullett, p. 9.

27 Tullett, pp. 9–10.

28 Dew, pp. 1, 115.

29 Ibid., pp. 115–16.

30 Ibid., pp. 1, 193.

31 Ibid., p. 261.

32 *The Uttoxeter New Era*, 'Murder of a Cripple,' 4 November, 1908.

33 Ibid.

34 'Bands of men . . . without a collar or tie'. Ibid; *The Salisbury Times*, 'The Meadow Road Tragedy,' 11 December, 1908.
35 Ibid.
36 Lock (CID), p. 182; 'obtained sad confirmation . . . disorder in the bedroom'. *The Salisbury Times*, 'The Meadow Road Tragedy,' 6 November, 1908.
37 *The Salisbury Times*, 'The Meadow Road Tragedy,' 6 November, 1908.
38 Lock (CID), pp. 182-3; *The Wiltshire Times and Towbridge Advertiser*, 'Who Killed Teddy Haskell?' 3 April, 1909; *The Salisbury Times*, 'The Meadow Road Tragedy,' 11 December, 1908.
39 *The Wiltshire Times and Towbridge Advertiser*, 'Who Killed Teddy Haskell?' 3 April, 1909; *The Dundee Courier*, 'Jury Finds Mrs Haskell Not Guilty of Murder,' 5 April, 1909; Lock (CID), p. 183.
40 Dew, p. 21.
41 Ramsland (Kindle edition).
42 Dew, p. 3.

14: Chasing Crippen

1 Dew, pp. 38-9.
2 Dew's 6 July, 1910 report. MEPO 3/198.
3 Dew, p. 39
4 Dew's 6 July, 1910 report. MEPO 3/198.
5 Exchange quoted in Dew, p. 39.
6 Dew, p. 40.
7 Melinda's quotes and the text of the supposed letters from Cora are taken from Melida's trial testimony. Young, pp. 23-4.
8 Details of Crippen's interaction with the Martinettis comes from Clara Martinetti's trial testimony. Young, pp. 12-17.
9 Dew's 6 July, 1910, report. MEPO 3/198.
10 'that rare thing . . .' Young, p. xiii.
11 Watson, pp. 11-12.
12 'which afterwards did not . . .' Young, p. xiv; 'a serious medical problem'. Watson, p. 13. Unless otherwise noted, details of Cora's background come from Young, pp. xiv-xv and Watson, pp. 12-16.
13 'The humblest English music hall . . .' Young, xiv; 'marketed himself . . .' Watson, p. 16.
14 'increasingly stout . . . sharp-tongued shrew'. Watson, p. 19; 'He was not a man's man . . .' Young, p. xviii.
15 'changed her surname . . .' Watson, p. 19; 'from the strain and storm . . .' Young, p. xx; 'changed the tenor . . .' Larson, p. 74.
16 Dew, p. 41.
17 Ibid.
18 Ibid., pp. 42-3.
19 Ibid., p. 43.

20 Crippen's statement is reproduced in Young, pp. 34–9.

21 Ethel's statement is reproduced in Young, p. 194.

22 Dew, pp. 50–1.

23 Ibid, p. 53.

24 Ibid.

25 Trial testimony of Rylance and Long. Young, pp. 29–31.

26 Dew, pp. 55–6, 57.

27 Ibid, p. 57.

28 Watson, pp. 35–6; 'long drink of brandy'. Dew, p. 57; 'Who can imagine . . .'
    The Dunstan Times, 'My Race with Crippen,' 7 February, 1927.

29 'those particular organs . . .' Young, p. xxxi; Testimony of Dr Augustus Pepper.
    Ibid., pp. 47–8; Watson, p. 38.

30 'a large quantity'. Dew testimony. Young, p. 41; Watson, p. 40.

31 Pepper trial testimony. Young, pp. 48, 50.

32 'grave wax' Evans (Kindle edition).

33 Years of residency at Hilldrop Crescent. (Crown Counsel's Opening Statement)
    Young, p. 6.

34 'Even to this day . . . burned them in the kitchen grate'. Dew, p. 60; hair details;
    'A man often dyes his grey hair . . .' Watson, pp. 43–4.

35 'I afterwards examined it . . .' Pepper testimony. Young, p. 48; 'many times'.
    The Aberdeen Evening Press, 'Crippen,' September 14, 1910; Pepper seeks
    Spilsbury's opinion. Evans (Kindle edition).

36 Howgrave-Graham, p. 100.

37 'successor to the mythical . . . ' Time Magazine, 'Sherlock Spilsbury,' 2 July,
    1934; 'slides, test tubes . . .' Evans (Kindle edition); 'I regarded him . . .' Tullett
    and Browne, p. 21.

38 'beastly science'. Tullett and Browne, pp. 23, 30; Evans (Kindle edition).

39 'special study of scars . . .' Evans (Kindle edition); Browne and Tullett, p. 53.

40 'The undergarments we discovered . . .' Dew, p. 60

41 Wilcox's trial testimony. Young, p. 60

42 Evans (Kindle edition).

43 Dew, pp. 62–63.

44 'The French search . . .' The New York Times, 'Crippen Dressed as Woman?'
    19 July, 1910; 'Not a day passed . . .' Dew, p. 66.

45 Kendall statement, 4 August, 1910. MEPO 3/198.

46 Watson, pp. 57–8; 'the most systematic . . . the elucidation of the mystery'.
    The Daily Telegraph, 'North London Crime,' 16 July, 1910.

47 Watson, p. 58.

48 'The first week . . .' Dew, p. 66; 'CRIPPEN BAFFLES THE WORLD'S POLICE'
    The Dundee Evening Telegraph, 'STILL AT LARGE'. 20 July, 1910; 'the first
    internationally known . . .' Watson, p. 5; Ibid., pp. 60–1.

49 Kendall statement, 4 August, 1910. MEPO 3/198.

50 Dew, p. 66.

51 Kendall statement, 4 August, 1910. MEPO 3/198.

52 'smuggled'. Dew, p. 69.

53 'INSPECTOR DEW IS ON CRIPPEN'S BACK' and 'A parallel to this Transatlantic chase . . .' *The Dundee Evening Telegraph*, 25 July, 1910; 'CHASE ACROSS THE ATLANTIC' and 'The annals of crime . . .' The *Observer*, 24 July, 1910.

54 *The Ottawa Free Press*, 'Detective is Catching Up with Crippen,' 26 July, 1910.

55 *The Daily Telegraph*, 'Chase of Crippen – Position of the Steamers To-Day,' 27 July, 1910.

56 Dew, p. 70.

57 Ships passing, wireless exchange between Dew and Kendall. Larson, p. 345.

58 *The (Montreal) Gazette*, 'Inspector Dew Arrives in Canada.' 30 July, 1910.

59 Ibid.

60 Ibid.

61 Dew, p. 70.

62 The *Montreal Gazette*, 'Crippen Caught,' 1 August, 1910

63 Ibid.

64 Details of Crippen's time onboard and Ethel's poor-fitting costume come from 'Captain Kendall's Message' printed in the *Daily Mail* on 31 July, 1910, and reprinted in *The* (London) *Times*, 1 August, 1910.

65 *The New York Times*, 'Crippen, I want you.' 1 August, 1910.

66 'A thrill of excitement . . .' Dew, p. 72; 'The rain continued to fall . . .' *The New York Times*. 'Crippen, I want you,' 1 August, 1910.

67 'a blue uniform with brass buttons.' *The New York Times*, 'Crippen Caught Admits Identity Girl Collapses.' 1 August, 1910; 'My boat swung into mid-stream . . .' Dew, p. 72.

68 *The New York Times*, 'Crippen Caught Admits Identity Girl Collapses,' 1 August, 1910.

69 Conversation between Crippen and Stewart. Ibid.

70 Dew, pp. 72-3.

71 *The New York Times*, 'Crippen Caught Admits Identity Girl Collapses,' 1 August, 1910.

72 Ibid; 'Looked the part reasonably well' and 'I am Chief-Inspector Dew,' Dew, p. 74.

73 Dew, pp. 75-76.

74 *The New York Times*, 'The Crime and the Pursuit,' 1 August, 1910.

75 *The* (London) *Times*, 'Crime and Science' and 'The Story of the Flight,' 1 August, 1910.

76 Dew, pp. 76-7, 83, 84; 'Father.' *Lloyd's Weekly Newspaper*, 'Miss Le Neve and the Crippen Case,' 13 November, 1910.

77 Ibid., pp. 84-85.

78 Details of Crippen's purchase comes from Hetherington's trial testimony. Young, pp. 75-76

79 Testimony of William James Chilvers. Young, pp. 144-5.

80 4000 applications. Larson, p. 369.

81 'tall, handsome . . .' Browne and Tullett, p. 53; 'it was not along the line of the scar . . .' presence of pubic hair and abdominal muscle. Watson, pp. 47, 48.

82 Tullett and Browne, p. 54.

83 Spilsbury's early biographers Tullett and Browne write, 'Here was a new, dominating voice in the courts of justice,' p. 54; 'I am innocent'. Young, p. 183. For Ethel Le Neve's trial, see Appendice D in Young, pp. 192–211.

84 Statement reproduced in Young, pp. 188–9.

85 Reproduced in Ibid., p. 190.

86 'In a trice . . .' quoted in Watson, p. 96.

87 See Madame Tussaud's ad on p. 6 of *The Westminster Gazette*, 25 November, 1910.

88 Dew resigns. Watson, p. 99; criticism regarding handling of case, argument to be made for Crippen fleeing. Ibid., p. 63.

89 Ibid., p. 100.

90 The *Guardian*, 'Forensic Science: Secrets of the Case Against Crippen,' 16 August, 2008.

91 'could be interpreted . . .' Robins, pp. 237, 238; 'He called a bruise a bruise . . .' Tullett and Browne, p. 242.

92 Ibid., pp. 237, 239; 'Spilsbury, like the rest of us . . .' Simpson, *Medico-Legal Journal*, 1961;29(4):182–189. soiL10.1177/002581726102900402.

15: The Brides in the Bath

Unless otherwise noted, quoted dialogue and information is derived from the trial transcript in the *Notable British Trials* series edition *The Trial of George Joseph Smith*, edited by Eric Watson.

1 The article is reproduced in Appendix VI of Watson, p. 323.

2 Watson, p. 28.

3 'Drooper Neil . . . unknown to smile'. Tullett, p. 48.

4 Neil, pp. 1–2.

5 Ibid., p. 18.

6 Wensley, p. 241.

7 Begg and Skinner, p. 182.

8 'Nearer My God to Thee'. Honeycombe, p. 125.

9 Neil, p. 19.

10 Ibid.

11 Ibid.

12 'a man . . .' Neil's 19 January, 1915 report. MEPO 3/225B.

13 Neil, p. 19.

14 '5 feet 10 inches . . .' Robins, p. 126; 'say whether there . . . a remarkable coincidence'. Neil's 19 January, 1915 report. MEPO 3/225B.

15 Neil, p. 20.

16 Watson, pp. 24–5.

17 Ibid., p. 25.

18 Ibid., p. 26; 'In a space . . .' Neil, p. 21.

19 Ibid.
20 Letter read during Burnham's trial testimony. Watson, p. 142.
21 Ibid., p. 18.
22 The conversation between Neil and Matthews is quoted in Neil, pp. 21–2.
23 'The address is . . . by victimizing women.' Neil's 2 February, 1915 report. MEPO 3/225B.
24 'My chaps . . .' Neil, p. 23.
25 Ibid., pp. 23–4.
26 'was not dressed in morning.' Neil's report, 5 February, 1915. MEPO 3/225B.
27 Neil, pp. 23–4.
28 Neil testimony. Watson, p. 257.
29 Ibid.
30 Neil, p. 27.
31 Evans (Kindle edition).
32 Browne and Tullett, p. 59.
33 'a quiet little spot . . .' Ibid., p. 27.
34 *The Evening Mail*, 'THE DROWNED BRIDES,' 12 February, 1915; *The Globe*, 'SECOND EXHUMATION,' 10 February, 1915; 'I admire . . .' Neil, p. 29.
35 'dirty foul smelling water,' face decomposed beyond recognition. Robins, p. 140.
36 Ibid., p. 142.
37 Ibid; 'This bit of news . . .' Neil, p. 28.
38 Neil., pp. 29, 31.
39 Ibid., p. 31.
40 'is caused by rigor mortis . . .' Ralebitso-Senior, p. 51.
41 Watson, pp. 64–5.
42 The letter was read into testimony during Smith's trial (see testimony of Maud Crabbe). Ibid., p. 87.
43 'looking over the sea.' Browne and Tullett, p. 89.
44 Letter reproduced in Watson, p. 11.
45 'was the most recently qualified.' Browne and Tullett, p. 91.
46 'Can you come at once . . .' Browne and Tullett, p. 91; 'The face was upwards . . .' French's inquest testimony is reproduced in Watson, p. 39.
47 Browne and Tullett, p. 92; 'misadventure by a fit . . .' letter from Smith to Bessie's family, quoted in Watson, p. 13; 'was it not a jolly good job . . .' Watson, p. 14.
48 Neil, p. 30.
49 Ibid., p. 32; Robins, pp. 143, 148.
50 Reavil statement reproduced in Watson, p. 22.
51 Robins, pp. 144, 149; 'He remarked to me . . .' Pegler statement reproduced in Watson, p. 23.
52 'We were living in apartments . . .' Pegler statement reproduced in ibid., p. 23.
53 Watson, p. 2; Robins, pp. 156–7.
54 'the birch and the cane.' Tullett, p. 49; 'little importance . . .' Watson, pp. 1, 2.
55 Robins, p. 160.

56 'I called to a policeman . . .' Caroline's statement partially reproduced in Watson, p. 315.
57 Evans (Kindle edition).
58 Spilsbury testimony. Watson, p. 207.
59 Spilsbury's analysis is reproduced in Browne and Tullet, pp. 99–100.
60 Neil, pp. 33–4.
61 *The* (London) *Weekly Dispatch*, 'Triple Charge of Wife Murder,' 28 March, 1915.
62 Ibid.
63 Ibid.
64 Neil, p. 24.
65 *The* (London) *Weekly Dispatch*. 'Brides Case Ends at Bow-Street.' 16 May, 1915.
66 Watson, p. 29.
67 Paraphrased summary of Spilsbury's testimony. *The Lancashire Evening Post*, 'Dr Spilsbury's Evidence,' 29 June, 1915.
68 Robins, p. 241.
69 *The Irish Independent*, 'Death Sentence,' 2 July, 1915.
70 *The Daily Mirror*, 'Death Sentence in Brides Case,' 2 July, 1915.
71 *The Irish Independent*, 'Death Sentence,' 2 July, 1915.
72 *The Daily Mirror*, 'Death Sentence in Brides Case,' 2 July, 1915.
73 *The People*. 4 July, 1915.
74 See Ellis's account in Robins, p. 234.
75 See, for example, *The Evening Star*, 13 August, 1915, p. 3.

16: War Crimes

1 'large numbers . . .' Wensley, p. 241; 'the equivalent of . . . instead of a helmet.' Browne, p. 294.
2 Browne, p. 295.
3 See Fido and Skinner, pp. 292–3.
4 *The Globe*, 'Little Victim's of Kaiser's Hatred,' 15 June, 1917.
5 'had their minds . . .' Browne, p. 298.
6 *The Times*, 'Bloomsbury Murder Mystery,' 3 November, 1917.
7 Ibid., 'Bloomsbury Murder Mystery,' 7 November, 1917.
8 'The remains were those . . .' Ibid., 'Bloomsbury Murder Mystery'. 3 November, 1917; 'The Bloomsbury Murder,' ibid., 7 November, 1917.
9 'It would be impossible . . .' *The People*, 'Diabolical Murder in London'. 4 November, 1917; 'with a sharp instrument . . . disjointing limbs'. *The Times*, 'Bloomsbury Murder Mystery,' 3 November, 1917; 'La Plata Cold Storage'. *The Times*, 'Bloomsbury Murder Mystery,' 7 November, 1917.
10 *The Times*, 'Bloomsbury Murder Mystery,' 3 November, 1917; 'the largest single influx . . .' *BBC Magazine*, 'World War One: How 250,000 Belgian refugees didn't leave a trace,' 15 September, 2014; 'an invaluable source . . .' Evans (Kindle edition).

11 'the finest training . . . disreputable houses'. Wensley, pp. 14–15; joined CID, Ibid., p. vi.

12 'The more I saw . . .' Wensley, p. 19; 'as no informant . . .' Fido and Skinner, p. 280; 'distinguished service,' Kirby, p. 131; *The* (London) *Daily News*, 'Wensley the Great Detective is Dead,' 5 December, 1949; 'with an armed murderer . . .' *The Aberdeen Press and Journal*, 'Death of 'Yard' Man Who Knew No Fear'. 5 December, 1949; *The New York Times*, 'Noted Detective Dead,' 26 September, 1916.

13 'effective operational head . . .' Fido and Skinner, p. 281.

14 'with a rather full face . . .' *The Times*, 'Murdered Woman Identified'. 6 November, 1917.

15 *The Daily Mirror*, 'Sack Victim Wife of French Soldier,' 6 November, 1917; 'Of course, that did not . . .' *The Sheffield Independent*, 'Murder Mystery,' 6 November, 1917; *The Birmingham Daily Post*, 'The Bloomsbury Mystery,' 13 November, 1917; Wensley, p. 236.

16 *The Sheffield Independent*, 'Murder Mystery,' 6 November, 1917.

17 'a piece of butcher's long cloth . . .' Décharné, p. 325; Evans (Kindle edition); *The Times*, 'The Murder of Mme. Gerard,' 17 January, 1918; Browne and Tullett, p. 111.

18 'less than half a mile . . .' Browne and Tullett, p. 111; 'in possession of . . .' *The* (London) *Daily News*, 'The Bloomsbury Murder,' 13 November, 1917.

19 'the high voices of women'. Thomson (Kindle edition); 'Mr Voisin has just . . .' *The Scotsman*, 'The London Murder,' 16 November, 1917.

20 Wensley, p. 231.

21 *The Times*, 'Murder Mystery,' 21 November, 1917

22 Ibid.

23 Ibid.

24 Ibid., 'Murder Mystery,' 13 November, 1917.

25 'heavy jaw, eyes sunken . . .' Browne and Tullet, p. 112; 'I carefully considered the position . . .' Wensley, p. 232.

26 *The Times*, 'The Murder of MME. Gerard'. 18 January, 1918.

27 Wensley, p. 232.

28 Ibid, p. 233.

29 *The Western Evening Herald*, 'The London Murder,' 16 November, 1917.

30 *The Times*, 'Bloomsbury Murder Mystery,' 7 November, 1917.

31 Ibid; 'Death ensued sometime after . . .' *The Scotsman*, 'The London Murder Mystery,' 7 November, 1917; 'how good he was to her'. *The Liverpool Echo*, 'The London Crime,' 12 November, 1917.

32 Browne and Tullett, p. 115; two pints of blood lost. Evans (Kindle edition).

33 'the blood of each . . .' Ramsland (Kindle edition); 'should be of particular importance'. Evans (Kindle edition)

34 'human blood everywhere'. Browne and Tullet, p. 115; 'Bit by bit we filled the gaps . . .' Wensley, p. 234.

35 'shattered and dismembered fragments'. Browne and Tullett, p. 114; 'Whether she knew . . .' Wensley, p. 234.

36 Ibid., p. 235.

37 Ibid., p. 235.

38 'Whether the murder . . .' Ibid., p. 235; *The Times*, 'Bloomsbury Murder Mystery,' 7 November, 1917.

39 Wensley, p. 236.

40 '*Salaud, tu m'as . . .*' *The Times*, 'Murder Mystery,' 21 November, 1917.

41 Ibid.

42 Wensley, p. 237; *The Times*, 'Murder Mystery,' 21 November, 1917; 'We must give . . .' Thomson (Kindle edition).

43 Thomson (Kindle edition).

44 Wensley, p. 240.

45 'the first air-raid murder . . . Charlotte-street.' The (London) *Weekly Dispatch*, 'The First Air Raid Murder,' 3 March, 1918.

46 Wensley, p. 240.

47 *The Chicago Tribune*, 'The Mystery of Mme. Gerard,' 24 May, 1936; 'Mr Wensley will see you.' *The* (London) *Daily News*, 'Wensley the Great Detective is Dead,' 5 December, 1949.

48 'These were the boys . . .' Wensley, p. 244. For details on the deaths of his sons, see Wensley, pp. 242–4.

49 Begg and Skinner, pp. 189–90.

50 Fido and Skinner, pp. 92, 281; Begg and Skinner, pp. 192–193; Kirby, p. 218.

51 Begg and Skinner, p. 193.

52 'the Wensley method . . . like a stone.' *Time Magazine*, 'GREAT BRITAIN: Scotland Yardsman,' 8 July, 1929; 'prestige throughout the . . .' Fido and Skinner, pp. 92, 281.

53 Honeycombe, pp. 163–4; 'She could scarcely . . .' Wensley, p. 259.

54 Wensley, p. 261, 263, 272

55 'I am feeling very blue . . .' Honeycombe, pp. 153–4.

56 Wensley, pp. 269–70, 271.

57 'few people believed . . .' Young, p. xxix, xxx.

58 Begg and Skinnger, p. 197

59 'The influence . . .' *The Pall Mall Gazette*, 'Mrs Thompson Executed,' 9 January, 1923; *The Times*, 'Tragic Affair of the Milliner and the Murderer,' 4 November, 2018; Begg and Skinner, p. 197.

60 Wensley, p. 275.

61 'on the encouragement . . .' Fido and Skinner, p. 282; on the assessment of the pre-war years and violent post-war period, see Begg and Skinnger, pp. 198, 206–7.

17: The Crumbles

1 The details and quotes from Jessie Mahon's conversation with John Beard come from *The Dundee Courier*, 'Last Scene in the Crumbles Trial,' 21 July, 1924.

2 Wensley, pp. 317–18.

3 Savage, p. 19.

4 Ibid., p. 14.

5 Details of Mahon's arrest and his exchange with detectives is from Ibid., pp. 183–4.

6 Ibid., p. 184.

7 Mahon's interrogation is detailed in Savage's memoir, pp. 184–6; and Savage's trial testimony in Wallace, pp. 35–7.

8 Savage, p. 185.

9 Ibid., p. 186, 190.

10 *The People*, 'The Horror In Our Midst,' 11 May, 1924.

11 Savage trial testimony. Wallace, p. 42; 'The sickly stench . . .' Savage, p. 190.

12 'four bedrooms . . .' Ibid., p. 190; 'similar to the kind . . .' *The Western Evening Herald*, 'The Crumbles Trial,' 15 July, 1924.

13 *Western Evening Herald*, 'The Opening of the Crumbles Trial at Lewes Assizes,' 15 July, 1924.

14 Burney and Pemberton (Kindle edition).

15 Ibid.

16 '[We] found four . . .' Savage trial testimony. Wallace, p. 44; 'containing the intestines . . .' *Northern Daily Mail*, 'Crumbles Case,' 4 June, 1924; 37 pieces of anatomy. Spilsbury testimony. Wallace, p. 107.

17 Burney and Pemberton (Kindle edition).

18 Quotes are lifted from Mahon's statement reproduced in Wallace, pp. 38–42.

19 Savage, p. 192.

20 Based on a paraphrased statement. Ibid.

21 'one of a large . . .' Wallace, pp. 10–11; Tullett, p. 67.

22 Wallace, pp. 12–14; Honeycombe, p. 169.

23 Wallace, p. 14.

24 Ibid.

25 Emily as tall, athletic, and slender. Honeycombe, p. 170; 'Miss Kaye, of course . . .' Mahon statement reproduced in Wallace, p. 49.

26 Savage, p. 192.

27 'unusual privilege.' Browne and Tullett, p. 174; Evans (Kindle edition).

28 'flimsy thing.' Savage, p. 192; 'chunks of putrid . . . quayside.' Evans (Kindle edition).

29 Tullett, p. 66.

30 Savage, p. 178.

31 Ibid.

32 Spilsbury trial testimony. Wallace, p. 107.

33 Ibid., pp. 108–12.

34 *The Yorkshire Post and Leeds Intelligencer*, 'Before the Magistrates,' 7 May, 1924.

35 Ibid.

36 Spilsbury trial testimony. Wallace, p. 113.

37 Ibid., pp. 111, 114.

38 Flames in Emily's eyes. Wallace, p. 20; 'I burned the head . . .' Mahon statement reproduced in ibid., p. 68.

39 Savage, p. 202.

40 Ibid.

41 Ibid., p. 180.

42 Ibid., p. 173.

43 Ibid., pp. 174, 196.

44 'a bright and cheerful . . . work or play'. *The Yorkshire Post and Leeds Intelligencer*, 'The Bungalow Crime,' 7 May, 1924; £600 in savings. Honeycombe, p. 170.

45 Mahon meets Emily through Hobbins. Honeycombe, pp. 169–170; 'As a result . . . 'Mahon statement reproduced in Wallace, p. 49.

46 Savage, p. 197.

47 Mahon statement reproduced in Wallage, p. 50.

48 Ibid., p. 51.

49 'She came bounding . . .' *The* (London) *Daily Chronicle*, 'London Woman Identified as Bungalow Victim,' 6 May, 1924; beau known as 'Pat'. Edith Warren's trial testimony. Wallace, p. 75.

50 Savage, p. 198.

51 Ibid., p. 197.

52 'love experiment'. Wallace, p. 16; 'It was essential . . .' Mahon's trial testimony reproduced in ibid., p. 187.

53 'could not be easily . . .' Ibid., p. 15; 'she would convince me . . .' Mahon statement reproduced in ibid., p. 51.

54 Mahon statement reproduced in Ibid., p. 53.

55 Elizabeth's trial testimony. Ibid., p. 72.

56 Trunk with initials 'E.B.K.'. Ibid; 'she waited alone . . .' Savage, p. 198.

57 *The Dundee Evening Telegraph*, 'Miss Ethel Duncan's Ordeal at the Bungalow Trial,' 17 July, 1924.

58 Wallace, p. 17.

59 Wensley, p. 19.

60 *The Daily Mirror*, 'Mahon Trial Begins Afresh After the Collapse of a Juror,' 15 July, 1924; Muir trial testimony. Wallace, p. 77.

61 Savage, p. 187.

62 *The Yorkshire Post and Leeds Intelligencer*, 'Bungalow Murder Surprise,' 17 July, 1924; 'ten-inch cook's . . .' Honeycombe, p. 171; 'Two days after . . .' Savage, p. 199.

63 Mahon's account is based on his statements to police and his trial testimony reproduced in Wallace, pp. 49–57, 68–70, 132–73; *The Dundee Evening Telegraph*, 'Patrick Mahon's Amazing Story of Bungalow Tragedy,' 22 May, 1924.

64 'Charing Cross, 7 . . .' *The Western Daily Press*, 'Mahon on Miss Kaye's Fondness for Him,' 18 July, 1924; 'Mahon was not . . .' Evans (Kindle edition).

65 *The Dundee Evening Telegraph*, 'Miss Ethel Duncan's Ordeal at the Bungalow Trial,' 17 July, 1924; Ethel's trial testimony. Wallace, pp. 83–94.

66 Savage, p. 187.

67 Honeycombe, p. 168.

68 Savage, p. 200.

69 Ibid.

70 'Important see you . . .' Ibid., p. 201; 'We'll have to . . .' Honeycombe, p. 169.

71 Mahon statement reproduced in Wallace, p. 70.

72 Ibid., p. 40.

73 Ibid.

74 'was because I . . .' Ibid., p. 68; 'Miss Kaye would . . .' Savage, p. 201.

75 Savage, pp. 201–2.

76 The *Louis Post-Dispatch*, '"The Bungalow Murder" at Which "Crimeless England" Stands Aghast,' 13 July, 1924; 'wolf in sheep's . . .' Savage, p. 202.

77 'Mahon collapsed . . .' *The Coventry Evening Telegraph*, 'The Crumbles Tragedy,' 18 July, 1924; 'I feel too . . .' quoted in Wallace, p. 277.

78 'poor understanding . . .' Williams, p. 171.

79 Savage, p. 178.

80 McCrery, pp. 123–125.

81 'when two objects . . .' Chisum and Turvey, p. 237.

82 'police officers were . . . be called for.' Evans (Kindle edition).

83 Honeycombe, pp. 178–179.

18: In the Trunk

1 Honeycombe, p. 180, 183, 186.

2 Ibid., p. 180, 183–185

3 Ibid., p. 185.

4 Ibid.; 'I made a thorough . . .' Browne and Tullet, p. 192.

5 Honeycombe, p. 187; 'The crimes of . . .' Browne and Tullett, p. 185.

6 Wensley, p. 325.

7 'a large heavy tin box.' *The Witney Gazette*, 'Body in a Cemented Box,' 2 April, 1904.

8 'fashion in trunk murders.' Brown and Tullett, p. 305.

9 'Basking or perspiring . . .' *The Western Daily Press*, 'Warm Days,' 9 May, 1927; 'Society Women . . . frocks.' *The Nottingham Journal*, 'Diary of a Londoner,' 9 May, 1927; flowers out and about. *The Sheffield Daily Telegraph*, 'London Day by Day,' 9 May, 1927.

10 *The Nottingham Evening Post*, 'Midnight Police Talk,' 13 May, 1927.

11 'It was a revolting sight . . .' The (London) *Daily Herald*. 'Woman's Body in a Trunk,' 1 May, 1927; *The Nottingham Evening Post*. 'Midnight Police Talk,' 13 May, 1927.

12 Description of the trunk. The (London) *Daily Herald*. 'Woman's Body in a Trunk,' 1 May, 1927; 'I saw four parcels . . .' *The Nottingham Evening Post*. 'Midnight Police Talk,' 13 May, 1927.

13 Wensley, pp. 288–9.

14 Cornish, p. 3.

15 Ibid., pp. x, 4, 9–10.

16 Ibid., pp. 9, 17, 33, 89, 141.

17 'It was ghastly enough . . .' Burt, p. 175; Cornish, p. 179; Honeycombe, p. 188; *The Hull Daily Mail*, 'Trunk Crime,' 15 June, 1927; *The Shields Daily News*, 'Trunk Mystery: New Clue,' 11 May, 1927.

18 Burt, p. 175.

19 'a pale blue jumper and other garments.' Cornish, p. 171; The (London) *Daily Herald*, 'Woman's Body in a Trunk,' 11 May, 1927; *The Hull Daily Mail*. 'Trunk Crime,' 15 June, 1927; *The Shields Daily News*, 'Trunk Mystery: New Clue,' 1 May, 1927.

20 'I succeeded in not being sick . . .' Burg, p. 175; The (London) *Daily Herald*, 'Woman's Body in a Trunk,' 11 May, 1927; *The Hull Daily Mail*, 'Trunk Crime,' 15 June, 1927.

21 *The Hull Daily Mail*, 'Trunk Crime,' 15 June, 1927.

22 'had received a severe blow . . .' Cornish, p. 171; Honeycombe, p. 188; The (London) *Daily Herald*, 'Woman's Body in a Trunk,' 1 May, 1927; *The Hull Daily Mail*, 'Trunk Crime,' 15 June, 1927; *The Shields Daily News*, 'Trunk Mystery: New Clue,' 11 May, 1927.

23 *The Hull Daily Mail*, 'Trunk Crime,' 15 June, 1927.

24 Cornish, pp. 169–70.

25 Ibid., p. 172.

26 'used press advertisements . . .' Moss and Skinner, p. 70; Press Bureau established in 1919. Fido and Skinner, p. 211.

27 'He asked what time . . .' The *Daily Herald*, 'Woman's Body in a Trunk,' Wednesday, 1 May, 1927; *The Times*. 'Body in Trunk Mystery,' 14 May, 1927.

28 'rolled up into a tight ball.' Cornish, p. 173; The (London) *Daily Herald*, 'Woman's Body in a Trunk,' Wednesday, 1 May, 1927.

29 The *Daily Herald*, 'Woman's Body in a Trunk,' Wednesday, 1 May, 1927.

30 *The Gloucester Citizen*, 'London Trunk Sensation,' 1 May, 1927.

31 Cornish, p. 172.

32 *The Times*, 'Sale of Trunk Traced,' 12 May, 1927.

33 Cornish, p. 173.

34 The phrase 'keenest brains of Scotland Yard' appeared in several British papers on 12 May, 1927; 'The customers' linens . . .' Cornish, p. 173.

35 'When Mrs Holt described . . .' Cornish, p. 174; *The Dundee Evening Telegraph*, 'Police Unraveling Trunk Mystery,' 12 May, 1927.

36 *The Sheffield Daily Telegraph*, 'The Trunk Mystery,' 13 May, 1927.

37 Cornish, p. 174.

38 'What she told us . . .' Ibid., p. 175; 'revealed a great deal . . .' *The New York Daily News*, 'When Justice Triumphed,' 8 May, 1938.

39 'had been associated . . .' *The Daily Herald*, 'Woman in Trunk Identified,' 13 May, 1927; 'stifle gossip.' *The New York Daily News*, 'When Justice Triumphed,' 8 May, 1938.

40 Cornish, p. 175.

41 'She's been promiscuous . . .' *The New York Daily News*, 'When Justice Triumphed,' 8 May, 1938.

42 Cornish, p. 175.

43 *The New York Daily News*, 'When Justice Triumphed,' 8 May, 1938.

44 Cornish, p. 176.

45 *The Nottingham Evening Post*, 'Midnight Police Talk,' 13 May, 1927.

46 Ibid.

47 'Mrs Bonati's husband . . .' Cornish, p. 175; 'thought nothing of not seeing her . . .' *The Sheffield Daily Telegraph*, 'The Trunk Mystery,' 14 May, 1927; 'been living alone lately . . .' *The New York Daily News*, 'When Justice Triumphed,' 8 May, 1938.

48 *The New York Daily News*, 'When Justice Triumphed,' 8 May, 1938; 'No one seemed to have . . .' Cornish, pp. 175, 176.

49 Burt, pp. 176–7.

50 Ibid., p. 177.

51 'who carried on . . .' Cornish, p. 177; *The Belfast Telegraph*, 'The Trunk Murder Arrest,' 24 May, 1927.

52 *The New York Daily News*, 'When Justice Triumphed,' 8 May, 1938.

53 Honeycombe, p. 190.

54 'listened with an intentness . . .' Burt, p. 178; Cornish, p. 178; *The New York Daily News*, 'When Justice Triumphed,' 8 May, 1938.

55 Cornish, p. 179.

56 'She had not received the telegram . . .' Cornish, p. 179; Honeycombe, p. 190.

57 'a fair-haired man . . .' *The Dundee Evening Telegraph*, 'Alleged Confession in Trunk Crime,' 24 May, 1927; 'He was quite willing . . .' Cornish, pp. 179–180;

58 Cornish, p. 180.

59 'Hundreds of persons . . .' *The Belfast Telegraph*, 'Trunk Murder Arrest,' 24 May, 1927; 'Robinson strolled out . . .' Cornish, pp. 180, 182.

60 Cornish, p. 185.

61 Burt, p. 178.

62 'We stared at it . . .' Ibid., pp. 178–9; Browne and Tullett, p. 309; 'less than 100 yards . . .' *The Dundee Evening Telegraph*, 'Alleged Confession in Trunk Crime,' 24 May, 1927.

63 Cornish, pp. 185–186.

64 *The Belfast Telegraph*, 'Trunk Murder Arrest,' 24 May, 1927.

65 Ibid.

66 Robinson and Patrick Mahon purchasing knifes from the same store. Honeycombe, p. 191.

67 Robinson's statement is reproduced in Cornish, pp. 187–8; *The Dundee Evening Telegraph*, 'Alleged Confession in Trunk Crime,' 24 May, 1927.

68 *The Dundee Evening Telegraph*, 'Robinson on Trial at Old Bailey,' 11 July, 1922.

69 *The Coventry Evening Telegraph*, 'Trunk Murder Trial,' 12 July, 1927.

70 *The Daily News*, 'Trunk Trial: Robinson's Story,' 13 July, 1927.

71 *The Coventry Evening Telegraph*, 'Trunk Murder Trial,' 12 July, 1927.

72 Ibid.

73 The *Birmingham Gazette*, 'Robinson to Die,' 14 July, 1927.

74 Ibid.

75 Burt, p. 180.

76 *The New York Times*, 'Trunk Murder Case Solved in London,' 25 May, 1927.

77 'whether we should . . .' Cornish, p. 201; 'he had picked . . .' MEPO 3/1628.

78 MEPO 3/1628.

79 Ibid.

19: Point-Blank

1 The *Londonderry Sentinel*, 'English Murder Mystery,' 29 September, 1927.

2 Ibid.

3 The *Belfast Telegraph*, 'Murder of P.C. Gutteridge,' 28 September, 1927.

4 The *Londonderry Sentinel*, 'English Murder Mystery,' 29 September, 1927.

5 The *Belfast Telegraph*, 'Murder of P.C. Gutteridge,' 28 September, 1927.

6 Ibid.

7 'marked by something . . . ' Moss and Skinner, p. 143; 'and struggled to the place . . .' The *Londonderry Sentinel*, 'English Murder Mystery,' 29 September, 1927; *The Weekly Telegraph*, 'The Murdered Constable,' 8 October, 1927.

8 'A shot person . . .' The *Belfast Telegraph*, 'Murder of P.C. Gutteridge,' 28 September, 1927; Honeycombe, p. 193.

9 'received a report . . .' The *Belfast Telegraph*, 'Murder of P.C. Gutteridge,' 28 September, 1927.

10 Donnelley (Kindle edition).

11 The *Belfast Telegraph*, 'Murder of P.C. Gutteridge,' 28 September, 1927.

12 Ibid.

13 Donnelley (Kindle edition).

14 The *Belfast Telegraph*, 'Murder of P.C. Gutteridge,' 28 September, 1927.

15 Ibid.

16 Wensley, p. 301.

17 'Inspector Berrett is one . . .' *The Sunday Post*, 'Shot Constable Riddle,' 2 October, 1897; 'only bearded detective . . .' *The Birmingham Daily Gazette*, 'Detective Retires,' 28 September, 1931; 'in our great CID'. Berrett, p. ix; 'the age-old thrill . . .' Ibid., p. v; 'enjoyed everyday of . . .' Ibid., p. 3.

18 'From the time . . .' Berrett, p. 6

19 'a small company . . .' The *Belfast Telegraph*, 'Murder of P.C. Gutteridge,' 28 September, 1927; The *Belfast Telegraph*, 'Murder of P.C. Gutteridge,' 28 September, 1927.

20 The *Belfast Telegraph*, 'Murder of P.C. Gutteridge,' 28 September, 1927.

21 Ibid.

22 *The Dundee Courier and Advertiser*, 'Abandoned Motor Car,' 29 September, 1927.

23 The *Belfast Telegraph*, 'Essex Murder Mystery Developments,' 29 September, 1927.

24 Ibid.

25 'little known . . .' *The Westminster Gazette*, 'Net for Men Who Shot Policeman,' 29 September, 1927; 'it was so close . . .' *The Sheffield Daily Telegraph*, 'Murdered Constable,' 29 September, 1927.

26 *The Sunday Post*, 'Shot Constable Riddle,' 2 October, 1927.

27 Ibid.; Honeycombe, p. 194; Donnelley (Kindle edition); 'the bloodstained . . . suppressed excitement.' *The Sheffield Independent*, 'Clues in Shot Policeman Mystery,' 29 September, 1927.

28 'to the rear . . . with the district.' *The Westminster Gazette*, 'Net for Men Who Shot Policeman,' 29 September, 1927; 'in search of men . . .' *The Sheffield Independent*, 'Clues in Shot Policeman Mystery,' 29 September, 1927.

29 'then robbed him . . .' *The Leeds Intelligencer*, 'Leeds, January 27,' 27 January, 1784; Moss and Skinner, p. 133.

30 'had been most . . . in the pantry.' *The Hampshire Advertiser and Salisbury Guardian*, (no headline), 24 January, 1835; 'found an identical . . . pinhead-sized hole.' Moss and Skinner, p. 135.

31 Moss and Skinner, pp. 133–4; *The Times*, 'Midland Circuit, Lincoln, December 8,' 10 December, 1860.

32 'probably the earliest . . .' History by the Yard (online source); *The Morning Post*, 'The Murder at Dalston,' 23 August, 1884; *The Echo*, 'The Murder of a Constable at Dalston,' 22 August, 1884; *The Evening Standard*, 'Execution of Orrock and Harris at Newgate To-Day,' 6 October, 1884.

33 Starr, p. 46.

34 Ibid.

35 Ibid., pp. 46–47.

36 Moss and Skinner, pp. 137–8.

37 Ibid.; Wilson and Wilson, p. 322.

38 'the revolver in two parts . . .' Moss and Skinner, p. 140; 'by guns – and by murder . . .' Wilson and Wilson, p. 321.

39 'to illustrate the pattern . . .' Fido and Skinner, p. 142; 'as the Spilsbury of ballistics.' Wilson and Wilson, p. 323.

40 Berrett, p. 21.

41 Ibid., 15, 17.

42 Shore, p. 3; Honeycombe, p. 194.

43 Shore, p. 3; 'stealing and altering motor cars,' Ibid., p. 3; Honeycombe, p. 194.

44 Shore, pp. 4–5.

45 'He seemed to be . . .' Barker trial testimony. Ibid., p. 75.

46 'a stockingette mask . . . I'm done for now.' Barker report. Moss and Skinner, pp. 145–6.

47 'They were quite . . .' Browne trial testimony. Shore, p. 129; 'fully loaded Webley . . .' Barker report. Moss and Skinnger, pp. 145–6.

48 Berrett trial testimony. Shore, p. 98.

49 'Why should I tell you . . .' Ibid; 'I heard most about it . . .' Browne statement to police. Shore, 12.

50 Donnely (Kindle edition); Shore, p. 6; Berrett, pp. 17–18.

51 Honeycombe, p. 196; Thomas trial testimony. Shore, p. 92.

52 Thomas trial testimony. Shore, p. 92.

53 'had no intention'. Thomas trial testimony. Shore, p. 92; 'tired and afraid of Kennedy'. Liverpoolcitypolice.co.uk.

54 Kirschner trial testimony. Shore, p. 97.

55 Mattinson trial testimony. Shore, pp. 92–3.

56 Kirschner trial testimony. Ibid., p. 97.

57 Mattinson trial testimony. Ibid., p. 94.

58 Berrett, p. 18.

59 Berrett trial testimony. Shore, p. 99.

60 See Kennedy's statement. Shore, pp. 14–19.

61 Berrett, p. 5.

62 'You are charging me . . .' Berrett trial testimony. Shore, p. 101; Honeycombe, p. 201.

63 Honeycombe, pp.194, 202; 'into a pigskin target'. Churchill trial testimony. Shore, p. 107; 'Conceivably two grooves . . .' Berrett, p. 21; Moss and Skinner, p. 146.

64 'the cap of the cartridge . . .' Churchill trial testimony. Ibid., p. 107; 'from a cartridge . . . constable's head'. Crown's opening argument at trial. Shore, pp. 43, 44.

65 See Browne's trial testimony. Ibid. pp. 115–16, 118.

66 The Hartlepool Northern Daily Mail, '"G.B.S." on Browne's Trial,' 7 May, 1928

67 The Weekly Dispatch, 'Hanged by a Microscope,' 22 November, 1931; The Yorkshire Evening Post, 'The 'Personality' of Firearms,' 28 May, 1928.

68 'opening of the first . . .' Ramsland (Kindle edition); 'brought legitimacy to . . .' Platteborze, L. Peter (20 December21), Crime Magazine, 'The Birth of Forensic Ballistics,' (online at https://www.crimemagazine.com/birth-forensic-ballistics-0).

69 Berrett, p. 19.

70 Ibid., pp. vi, vii.

Epilogue: Fingerprints from Yesteryear

1 'the world's first . . .' Fido and Skinnger, p. 68.

2 The Evening Standard, 'Girl Found Strangled on a Lonely Path,' 12 April, 1937.

3 Ibid.

4 Honeycombe, p. 215.

5 The Evening Standard, 'Girl Found Strangled on a Lonely Path,' 12 April, 1937; 'The impression was . . .' Ibid., 'Important Statement by Girl in Murder Hunt,' 13 April, 1937.

6 The St. Louis Post-Dispatch, 'Convicted of Silk Murder by a Silk Thread,' 1 August, 1937.

7 Ibid.

8 'When that sentence . . .' Ibid.

9   'For the first time . . .' The *Guardian*, 'Saliva as Clue to Identity,' 13 October, 1839; Burt, p. 135.

10 'The smoker was . . .' Burt, p. 137.

11 Ibid., pp. 137, 140.

12 Williams's protestations in court. Burt, pp. 142–3; Cherrill, pp. 168, 171.

13 The conversation between Rae and Williams is quoted in Burt, p. 144 and Cherrill, p. 171.

14 Summerscale, p. xxii.

15 David, p. 179.

16 'the first, the longest . . .' Ibid.; 'impeccable . . . *The Moonstone* set the standard.' Collins, p. vi.

17 'the insistent rise . . .' David, p. 177; 'When it comes to . . .' The *Los Angeles Times*, 'Scotland Yard may move its famous headquarters,' 30 October, 2012.

18 *The New York Times*, '15 Were Injured By Bomb Blasts,' 23 January, 1957; 'the greatest individual . . .'; Cannell, Michael (April 2017), 'Unmasking the Mad Bomber,' *Smithsonian Magazine* (online at https://www.smithsonianmag. com/history/unmasking-the-mad-bomber-180962469/).

19 'probably very neat . . .' Cannell, Michael (April 2017), 'Unmasking the Mad Bomber,' *Smithsonian Magazine* (online at https://www.smithsonianmag. com/history/unmasking-the-mad-bomber-180962469/)

20 'constituted an important . . .' Neil Pemberton (2013) 'Bloodhounds as Detectives,' *Cultural and Social History*, 10:1, 69-91, DOI: 10.2752/ 147800413X13515292098197

21 'contamination and cross-transference . . .' Williams, p. 171.

22 'publicly funded, organized.' *Time Magazine*, 'How the U.S. Got Its Police Force,' 18 May, 2017.

23 'the most important . . .' *Time Magazine*, 'A Case for Scotland Yard,' 6 August, 2008.

24 Details of skull found in Attenborough's garden. *The Telegraph*, 'Head found in David Attenborough's garden was murder victim,' 5 July, 2011.

25 BBC News, '"Barnes Mystery" of Attenborough skull solved,' 5 July, 2011 (online at https://www.bbc.com/news/uk-england-london-14034969).

Bibliography

General Reading

Bailey, James Blake, *The Diary of a Resurrectionist* (London: Swan Sonnenschein & Co., 1896)

Begg, Paul and Skinner, Keith, *The Scotland Yard Files: 150 Years of the C.I.D. 1842-1992* (London: Headline Book Publishing PLC, 1993)

Bell, Suzanne, *Oxford Dictionary of Forensic Science* (Oxford: Oxford University Press, 2012)

Bondeson, Jan, *The Ripper of Waterloo Road: The Murder of Eliza Grimwood in 1838* (Stroud, UK: The History Press, 2017), Kindle edition

Boys, William Fuller Alves, *A Practical Treatise on the Office and Duties of Coroners in Ontario* (Second Edition), (Toronto: Hart & Rawlinson, 1878)

Browne, Douglas G., *The Rise of Scotland Yard: A History of the Metropolitan Police* (Westport, CT: Greenwood Press, 1973)

Browne, G. Lathom, and Stewart, C.G., *Reports of Trials for Murder by Poisoning* (London: Stevens and Sons, 1883)

Burney, Ian, and Pemberton, Neil, *Murder and the Making of English CSI* (Baltimore, MD: Johns Hopkins University Press, 2016), Kindle edition

Chisum, W. Jerry, and Turvey, F. Brent, *Crime Resurrection* (Burlington, M.A.: Elsevier Academic Press, 2007)

Collins, Wilkie, *The Moonstone* (London: J.M. Dent & Sons, Ltd., 1944)

Colquhoun, Kate, *Mr. Briggs' Hat: A Sensational Account of Britain's First Railway Murder* (London: Abacus, 2012)

Cornwell, Patricia, *Portrait of a Killer: Jack the Ripper Case Closed* (New York: G.P. Putnam's Sons, 2002)

Cunningham, Peter, *Handbook for London: Past and Present, vol. 2* (London: John Murray, 1849)

David, Deirdre (ed.), *The Cambridge Companion to the Victorian Novel* (Cambridge: Cambridge University Press, 2001)

Décharné, Max, *Capital Crimes: Seven Centuries of London Life and Murder* (London: Random House, 2012)

Dickens, Charles, *Christmas Books and Reprinted Pieces* (New York: John B. Alden, 1883)

—*Reprinted Pieces: The Lamplighter, To Be Read at Dusk, and Sunday Under Three Heads* (New York: Charles Scribner's Sons, 1911)

Donnelley, Paul, *Essex Murders* (Barnsley, UK: Wharncliffe Books, 2007), Kindle edition

Douglas, John, and Olshaker, Mark, *Mindhunter: Inside the FBI's Elite Serial Crime Uni* (New York: Gallery Books, 2017)

Doyle, Arthur Conan, *The Penguin Complete Adventures of Sherlock Holmes* (London: Penguin Books, 1988)

Evans, Stewart P., and Skinner, Keith, *The Ultimate Jack the Ripper Sourcebook* (London: Robinson, 2001)

Evans, Colin, *The Father of Forensics: The Groundbreaking Cases of Sir Bernard Spilsbury, and the Beginnings of Modern CSI* (New York: Berkley Books, 2006), Kindle edition

Fido, Martin, and Skinner, Keith, *The Official Encyclopedia of Scotland Yard* (London: Virgin Books, 1999)

Fitzgerald, Percy, *Chronicles of Bow Street Police-Office, Vol. II* (London: Chapman and Hall, 1888)

Gordon, Michael R., *Murder Files from Scotland Yard and the Black Museum* (Jefferson, N.C.: Exposit, 2018)

Gribble, Leonard, *Great Manhunters of the Yard* (New York: Roy Publishers, Inc., 1966)

Griffiths, Arthur, *Mysteries of Police and Crime: A General Survey of Wrongdoing and its Pursuit, vol. I* (London: Cassell and Company, Limited, 1899)

— *Mysteries of Police and Crime: A General Survey of Wrongdoing and its Pursuit, vol. II* (New York: G.P. Putnam's Sons, 1899)

Harman, Claire, *Murder by the Book: The Crime That Shocked Dickens's London* (New York: Vintage Books, 2018)

Holder, E. H., et al, *The Fingerprint Sourcebook* (Washington, D.C.: U.S. Department of Justice, 2011)

Honeycombe, Gordon, *Murders of the Black Museum 1875–1975* (London: John Blake Publishing, 2011)

Howe, Ronald, *The Story of Scotland Yard: A History of the CID From the Earliest Times to the Present Day* (London: Arthur Baker, 1965)

Huish, Robert, *The Life of James Greenacre* (London: William Wright, 1837)

Hurd, Douglas, *Robert Peel: A Biography* (London: Phoenix, 2008)

Innes, Brian, *Body in Question: Exploring the Cutting Edge in Forensic Science* (Kettering, UK: Index, 2005)

Jackson, Lee, *Dirty Old London: The Victorian Fight Against Filth* (New Haven: Yale University Press, 2015)

James, P. D., and Critchley, T. A., *The Maul and the Pear Tree* (New York: Warner Books, 1971)

Jobb, Dean, *The Case of the Murderous Dr. Cream: The Hunt for a Victorian Serial Killer* (Chapel Hill: Algonquin Books, 2021)

Johnson, Steven, *The Ghost Map: The Story of London's Most Terrifying Epidemic—and How It Changed Science, Cities, and the Modern World* (New York: Riverhead Books, 2007)

Kirby, Dick, *Whitechapel's Sherlock Holmes: The Casebook of Fred Wensley, OBE, KPM, Victorian Crime Buster* (Barnsley, UK: Pen & Sword True Crime, 2014)

Lancet, The, The Influence of Railway Travelling on Public Health (London: Robert Hardwicke, 1862)

Larson, Erik, *Thunderstruck* (New York: Crown, 2006)

Lock, Joan, *Scotland Yard's First Cases: The World of Detective Inspector 'Jack' Whicher* (Borough, UK: Lume Books, 2011)

— *Scotland Yard Casebook: The CID 1865–1935* (Endeavour Press Ltd., 2014)

McKay, Sinclair, *Murder at No. 4 Euston Square: The Mystery of the Lady in the Cellar* (London: Aurum, 2021)

McLaren, Angus, *A Prescription for Murder: The Victorian Serial Killings of Thomas Neill Cream* (Chicago: University of Chicago Press, 1993)

McCrery, Nigel, *Silent Witness: The Often Gruesome but Always Fascinating History of Forensic Science* (Chicago: Chicago Review Press Incorporated, 2014)

Melville, W. L. Lee, *A History of Police in England* (London: Methuen & Co., 1901)

Moss, Alan, and Skinner, Keith, *The Scotland Yard Files: Milestones in Crime Detection* (Kew, UK: The National Archives, 2006)

— *The Victorian Detective* (Shire Publications, 2013), Kindle edition

Murphy, Paul Thomas, *Pretty Jane and the Viper of Kidbrooke Lane: A True Story of Victorian Law and Disorder* (New York: Pegasus Crime, 2016) Kindle edition

Notes and Queries: A Medium of Intercommunication for Literary Men, General Readers, Etc. (Eleventh Series—Volume 1, January–June, 1910), (London: John C. Francis and J. Edgar Francis, 1910)

O'Brien, R. Barry, *Fifty Years of Concessions to Ireland, vol. II* (London: Sampson, Low, Marston, Searle, & Rivington, 1883)

Phillips, Watts, *The Wild Tribes of London* (London: Ward and Lock, 1855)

Quincey, Thomas de, *On Murder Considered as One of the Fine Arts* (Profundis Publishing, 2019) Kindle edition

Ralebitso-Senior, Komang T. (ed.), *Forensic Ecogenomics: The Application of Microbial Ecology Analyses in Forensic Contexts* (London: Academic Press, 2018)

Ramsland, Katherine, *Beating the Devil's Game: A History of Forensic Science and Criminal Investigation* (New York: Berkley Books, 2007), Kindle edition

Read, Simon, *In the Dark: The True Story of the Blackout Ripper* (New York: Berkley Books, 2006)

Rhode, John, *The Case of Constance Kent* (New York: Charles Scribner's Sons, 1928)

Robins, Jane, *The Magnificent Spilsbury and the Case of the Brides in the Bath* (London: John Murray, 2010)

Rose, Paul, *The Manchester Martyrs: The Story of a Fenian Tragedy* (London: Lawrence & Wishart, 1970)

Rowland, John, *Poisoner in the Dock: Twelve Studies in Poisoning* (London: Arco Publications, 1960)

Shelley, Mary, *Frankenstein, or The Modern Prometheus* (London: Colburn and Bentley, 1831)

Shpayer-Makov, Haia, *The Ascent of the Detective: Police Sleuths in Victorian and Edwardian England* (Oxford, UK: Oxford University Press, 2011)

Simpson, Keith, *Forty Years of Murder* (London: Granada, 1980)

Starr, Douglas, *The Killer of Little Shepherds: A True Crime Story and the Birth of Forensic Science* (New York: Vintage Books, 2011)

Storey, Moorfield, and Hoar, Samuel (eds.), *The American Law Review, 1877–1878. Vol. XII* (Boston: Little, Brown, and Company, 1878)

Stow, John, *A Survey of London Written in the Year 1598* (London: Whittaker and Co., 1842)

Summerscale, Kate, *The Suspicions of Mr. Whicher: A Shocking Murder and the Undoing of a Great Victorian Detective* (New York: Bloomsbury, 2009)

Thompson, Laurence, *The Story of Scotland Yard* (New York: Random House (no date))

Thomson, Basil, *The Story of Scotland Yard* (Librorium Editions, 2020)

Thornbury, Walter, *Old and New London: A Narrative of its History, its People and its Places* (London: Cassell, Peter & Galpin, 1873)

Tullett, Tom, *Murder Squad* (London: Granada, 1981)

Walker, Samuel, and Katz, Charles M., *The Police in America: An Introduction* (6th edition) (Boston, MA: McGraw Hill, 2008)

Watson, Katherine D., *Crime Archive: Dr. Crippen* (Kew, UK: The National Archives, 2007)

Weinreb, Ben, et al., *The London Encyclopedia* (London: Macmillan, 2010)

Williams, Andy, *Forensic Criminology* (London: Routledge, 2015)

Wilson, Colin, and Wilson, Damon, *Written in Blood: A History of Forensic Detection* (New York: Carroll & Graf Publishers, 2003)

Wise, Sarah, *The Italian Boy: A Tale of Murder and Body Snatching in 1830s London* (Metropolitan Books, 2014), Kindle edition

Worsley, Lucy, *A Very British Murder* (London: BBC Books, 2014)

Scotland Yard Memoirs

Andson, Robert, *The Lighter Side of My Official Life* (London: Hodder and Stoughton, 1910)

Berrett, James, *When I Was At Scotland Yard* (London: Sampson Low, Marston & Co. Ltd., 1932)

Burt, Leonard, *Commander Burt of Scotland Yard* London: Heinemann, 1959)

Cherrill, Fred, *Fingerprints Never Lie* (New York: The Macmillan Company, 1954)

Cornish, G. W., *Cornish of Scotland Yard* (New York: The Macmillan Company, 1935)

Dew, Walter, and Connell, Nicholas (ed.), *The Annotated I Caught Crippen* (London: Mango Books, 2019)

Howgrave-Graham, H. M., *Light and Shade at Scotland Yard* (London: John Murray, 1947)

Lansdowne, Andrew, *A Life's Reminiscences of Scotland Yard: In One-and-Twenty Dockets* (London: Leadenhall Press, 1890)

Macnaghten, Melville. *Days of My Years*. London: Edward Arnold, 1914

Neil, Arthur Fowler, *Man-Hunters of Scotland Yard: The Recollections Of Forty Years Of A Detective's Life* (Garden City, NY: The Sun Dial Press, Inc., 1938)

Savage, Percy, *Savage of Scotland Yard* (London: Hutchinson & Co. Ltd., 1935)

Sweeney, John, *At Scotland Yard* (London: Grant Richards, 1904)

Wensley, Frederick Porter, *Detective Days* (London: Lewisham Press, 2020)

Trial Transcripts

The following transcripts, listed chronologically, are available through the website of the Central Criminal Court of England and Wales (the Old Bailey):

Old Bailey Proceedings Online (www.oldbaileyonline.org, version 9.0), April 1837. Trial of JAMES GREENACRE, SARAH GALE (t18370403-917). Available at: https://www.oldbaileyonline.org/record/t18370403-917

Old Bailey Proceedings Online (www.oldbaileyonline.org, version 9.0). June 1840. Trial of FRANCOIS BENJAMIN COURVOISIER (t18400615-1629). Available at: https://www.oldbaileyonline.org/record/t18400615-1629

Old Bailey Proceedings Online (www.oldbaileyonline.org, version 9.0). May 1842. Trial of DANIEL GOOD (t18420509-1705). Available at: https://www.oldbaileyonline.org/record/t18420509-1705

Old Bailey Proceedings Online (www.oldbaileyonline.org, version 9.0), October 1849. Trial of FREDERICK GEORGE MANNING, MARIA MANNING (t18491029-1890). Available at: https://www.oldbaileyonline.org/record/t18491029-1890

Old Bailey Proceedings Online (www.oldbaileyonline.org, version 9.0). October 1864. Trial of FRANZ MÜLLER (23) (t18641024-920). Available at: https://www.oldbaileyonline.org/record/t18641024-920

Old Bailey Proceedings Online (www.oldbaileyonline.org, version 9.0), July 1871. Trial of EDMUND WALTER POOK (20) (t18710710-561). Available at: https://www.oldbaileyonline.org/record/t18710710-561

Old Bailey Proceedings Online (www.oldbaileyonline.org, version 9.0), July 1871. Trial of AGNES NORMAN (t18710710-569). Available at: https://www.oldbaileyonline.org/record/t18710710-569

Old Bailey Proceedings Online (www.oldbaileyonline.org, version 9.0), June 1879. Trial of HANNAH DOBBS (24) (t18790630-626). Available at: https://www.oldbaileyonline.org/record/t18790630-626

Old Bailey Proceedings Online (www.oldbaileyonline.org, version 9.0), October 1892. Trial of THOMAS NEILL (38) (t18921017-962). Available at: https://www.oldbaileyonline.org/record/t18921017-962

Old Bailey Proceedings Online (www.oldbaileyonline.org, version 9.0), May 1905. Trial of ALFRED STRATTON (22), ALBERT ERNEST STRATTON (20) (t19050502-415). Available at: https://www.oldbaileyonline.org/record/t19050502-415 (Accessed: 27 December 2023).

Enterprising publishers released trial transcripts as pamphlets to capitalize on infamous crimes. Pamphlets referenced include:

The Trial, Sentence, and Confessions of Bishop, Williams, and May at the Old Bailey, London, on Friday, December 2, 1831, for the Murder of Carlo Ferrari, An Italian Boy (London: C.F. Pitman, 1831). Available at: https://archive.org/details/trialsentencecon00bish/page/n5/mode/2up

The Trial of J. Greenacre and Sarah Gale for the Willful Murder of Hannah Brown (London: J. Duncombe & Co., 1837). Available at: https://nrs.lib.harvard.edu/ urn-3:hls.libr:1019203

The Bermondsey Murder: A Full Report of the Trial of Frederick George Manning and Maria Manning for the Murder of Patrick O'Connor, at Miniver-Place, Bermondsey, on the 9th of August, 1849 (London: W.M. Clark, 1849)

The transcripts of many sensational trials were published back in the day in book format – often as part of the Notable British Trials series. These volumes include not only edited versions of the transcripts, but detailed case summaries, reproductions of witness statements, and other material valuable to researchers. Volumes referenced include (alphabetized by editor):

Knott, George, *Trial of Franz Müller* (Sydney, Aus.: Butterworth & Co., Ltd., 1911)

O'Donnell, Elliot, *Trial of Kate Webster* (London and Edinburgh: William Hodge & Company, Ltd., 1925)

Shore, W. Teignmouth, *Trial of Thomas Neill Cream* (London and Edinburgh: William Hodge & Company, Ltd., 1923)

—*Trial of Frederick Guy Browne and William Henry Kennedy* (Sydney, Aus.: Butterworth & Co., Ltd., 1930)

Young, Filson, *Trial of Frederick Bywaters and Edith Thompson* (London and Edinburgh: William Hodge & Company, Ltd., 1923)

—*The Trial of Hawley Harvey Crippen* (London and Edinburgh: William Hodge & Company, Ltd., 1920)

Wallace, Edgar, *The Trial of Patrick Herbert Mahon* (New York: Charles Scribner's Sons, 1928)

Watson, Eric, *Trial of George Joseph Smith* (London and Edinburgh: William Hodge & Company, Ltd., 1922)

Scotland Yard Case Files

The following are available through the British National Archives at Kew:

Murder of Thomas Briggs by Franz Müller (The North London Railway Case). 1864 July. MEPO 3/75

Murder of Edward Edwards at Duddlewick Mill, near Bridgnorth. 1866 Jan. 14. MEPO 3/80

Attempted Murder of Charles Parfitt by Agnes Norman. 1871. MEPO 3/102

Murder of Mrs Cora Crippen (known as Belle Elmore) by 'Dr' Hawley Harvey Crippen at 39 Hilldrop Crescent, Camden Town on 1 February 1910. 1910–1911. MEPO 3/198

Murder of Minnie Alice Bonati by John Robinson at Rochester Row, SW, on 4 May 1927. 1927–1929. MEPO 3/1628

Journals and Magazines

July 1850, 'The Modern Science of Thief Taking', *Household Words*. https://www.djo.org.uk/household-words/volume-i/page-368.html

July 1929, 'Scotland Yardsman', *Time Magazine*. https://content.time.com/time/subscriber/article/0,33009,732630,00.html

July 1934, 'Sherlock Spilsbury', *Time Magazine*. https://content.time.com/time/subscriber/article/0,33009,754317,00.html

May 2018, 'Were St. Louis police the first in the U.S. to use fingerprinting?' *St. Louis Magazine*. https://www.stlmag.com/history/st-louis-sage/were-st-louis-police-the-first-in-the-u-s-to-use-fingerprint/

Cannell, Michael, 'Unmasking the Mad Bomber', *Smithsonian Magazine* (April 2017). https://www.smithsonianmag.com/history/unmasking-the-mad-bomber-180962469/

Dalrymple, B. E., 'Fingerprints', in: Mozayani, A., and Noziglia, C. (eds), *The Forensic Laboratory Handbook* (Forensic Science and Medicine. Humana Press, 2006). https://doi.org/10.1385/1-59259-946-X:117

Dewis, John, 'Comparative Tests for Occult Blood in Gastric Contents and Feces, with Especial Reference to Benzedine Test', *Boston Medical and Surgical Journal* (August 1907), 157:6, 169–78. https://zenodo.org/records/2023931

Gupta, S., 'Criminology: Written in blood', *Nature* (2017), 549, S24–S25. https://doi.org/10.1038/549S24a

Mayer, Catherine, 'A Case for Scotland Yard', *Time Magazine* (August 2008). https://content.time.com/time/subscriber/article/0,33009,1827868,00.html

Milne-Smith, Amy, 'Shattered Minds: Madmen on the Railways, 1860–80', *Journal of Victorian Culture* (2016), 21:1, 21–39, DOI: 10.1080/13555502.2015.1118851

Mitchell, Piers D., 'The study of anatomy from 1700 to the early 20th century', *Journal of Anatomy* (2011), 219:2. https://doi.org/10.1111/j.1469-7580.2011.01381.x

Pemberton, Neil, 'Bloodhounds as Detectives', *Cultural and Social History* (2013), 10:1, 69–91, DOI: 10.2752/147800413X13515292098197

Pietila, Antero, 'In Need of Cadavers, 19th Century Medical Students Raided Baltimore's Graves', *Smithsonian Magazine* (October 2018). https://www.smithsonianmag.com/history/in-need-cadavers-19th-century-medical-students-raided-baltimores-graves-180970629/

Platteborze, Peter, 'The Birth of Forensic Ballistics', *Crime Magazine* (December 2018). https://www.crimemagazine.com/birth-forensic-ballistics-0

Simpson, Keith, 'Sir Bernard Spilsbury', *Medico Legal Journal*, (1961); 29(4):182–9. DOI:10.1177/002581726102900402

Taylor, A. S., 'On the Processes for Detecting Blood in Medico-Legal Cases', *Guy's Hospital Reports* (1870), 15(3):273–4. https://books.google.com/books?id=PS1TAAAAcAAJ&lpg=PA273&ots=YpXcsrFUbb&dq=%22freshly%20precipitated%20resin%20of%20guaiacum%22&pg=PP2#v=onepage&q&f=false

Tulchinsky, T. H., 'John Snow, Cholera, the Broad Street Pump; Waterborne Diseases Then and Now', *Case Studies in Public Health* (2018): 77–99.

DOI: 10.1016/B978-0-12-804571-8.00017-2. Epub 2018 Mar 30. PMCID: PMC7150208.

Waxman, Olivia, 'How the U.S. Got Its Police Force', *Time Magazine* (May 2017). https://time.com/4779112/police-history-origins/

Wilton, G. W., 'Finger-Prints: The Case of Kangali Charan, 1898', *Judicial Review*, 49:4, 417–27. HeinOnline.

Winterman, Denise, 'World War One: How 250,000 Belgian refugees didn't leave a trace', *BBC News Magazine* (September 2014). https://www.bbc.com/news/magazine-28857769

From the BBC

BBC News, 'Q&A: Human Tissue Act', 30 August 2006. http://news.bbc.co.uk/1/hi/health/4944018.stm

BBC News, 'Manchester to Liverpool: The first inter-city railway', 23 July 2009. http://news.bbc.co.uk/local/manchester/hi/people_and_places/history/newsid_8165000/8165208.stm

BBC News, "'Barnes Mystery' of Attenborough garden skull solved", 5 July 2011. https://www.bbc.com/news/uk-england-london-14034969

BBC News, 'The macabre world of books bound in human skin', 20 June 2014. https://www.bbc.com/news/magazine-27903742

Parliamentary Records and Legislation

The Murder Act 1751
Available at: https://statutes.org.uk/site/the-statutes/eighteenth-century/1751-25-geo2-c37-murder-act/

Metropolitan Police Act 1829
Available at: https://www.legislation.gov.uk/ukpga/Geo4/10/44/contents

Metropolitan Police Act 1839
Available at: https://www.legislation.gov.uk/ukpga/Vict/2-3/47/contents

Fenianism—The Attack on Clerkenwell Prison
Hansard: HC Deb 9 March 1868, vol. 190 cc1215–8; available at: https://api.parliament.uk/historic-hansard/commons/1868/mar/09/fenianism-the-attack-on-clerkenwell

General Websites

Dictionary of Irish Biography (Barrett, Michael)
https://doi.org/10.3318/dib.000415.v1

Friends of the Metropolitan Police Heritage Charity
    https://fomphc.com/
Human Tissue Authority (Legislation)
    https://www.hta.gov.uk/guidance-professionals/hta-legislation
Liverpool City Police (P.C. Gutteridge killing)
    https://www.liverpoolcitypolice.co.uk/murders/pc-gutteridge-killing/
The University of Edinburgh Anatomical Museum (William Burke)
    https://www.ed.ac.uk/biomedical-sciences/anatomy/anatomical-museum/
    collection/people/burke
The Unsolved Murder of Robert Westwood
    https://davidkiddhewitt.wordpress.com/2017/12/04/the-unsolved-murder-
    of-mr-westwood/

Newspapers

Newspapers proved a tremendous source of information for *Scotland Yard*. Most often they printed, verbatim, trial and inquest testimony, and in-depth eye-witness accounts to provide a detailed view of crimes and the resulting investigations. Articles referenced in the book are listed below in chronological order.

The Leeds Intelligencer, 'Leeds, January 27', 27 January 1784
The London Courier and Evening Gazette, 'Horrible Murders', 9 December 1811
The Morning Chronicle, 'Horrid and Unparalleled Murders!' 9 December 1811
The Star, 'Murder of Mr. Marr and Family', 10 December 1811
The Evening Mail, 'The Murders in Ratcliffe Highway', 11 December 1811
The Star, 'The Murders in Ratcliffe Highway', 11 December 1811
The Globe, 'Interment of Mr. and Mrs. Marr, and Infant Son', 16 December 1811
The London Chronicle, 'More Murders at Ratcliffe', 20 December 1811
The News, 'More Murders', 22 December 1811
The National Register, 'Another Murder!' 22 December 1811
The London Chronicle, 'Coroner's Inquest', 23 December, 1811
The Stamford Mercury, 'More Horrid Murders!' 27 December 1811
The Star, 'The Late Murders', 28 December 1811
The Birmingham (UK) *Journal*, 'The New London Police', 3 October 1829
The (London) *Times*, 'To the Editor', 7 October 1829
The (London) *Times*, 'The New Police', 14 October 1829
The Englishman, 'The New Police', October 1829
The Northampton Mercury, 'Preservation of the Dead', 27 February 1830
Drakard's Stamford News, 'Resurrectionists', 26 November 1830
The Scotsman, 'Opening of the Liverpool and Manchester Railway', 15 September
    1830
The (London) *Times*, 'POLICE', 7 November 1831
The Evening Mail, 'An Inquest on the Italian Boy', 9 November 1831
The Globe, 'Inquest on the Italian Boy', 9 November 1831

The Public Ledger and Daily Advertiser, 'The Italian Boy-Adjourned Inquest',
     11 November 1831
The Public Ledger and Daily Advertiser, 'Alleged Murder of the Italian Boy',
     12 November, 1831
The Morning Advertiser, 'The Murder of the Italian Boy', 12 November 1831
The Berkshire Chronicle, 'The Italian Boy', 12 November 1831
Bell's Weekly Messenger, 'Alleged Case of Horrid Murder by Burking an Italian Boy',
     13 November 1831
Bell's Weekly Messenger, 'Alleged Case of Horrid Murder by Burking an Italian Boy',
     14 November 1831
The (London) *Times*, 'The Murdered Italian Boy', 21 November 1831
The London Courier and Evening Gazette, 'The Murdered Italian Boy', 21 November
     1831
The (London) *Morning Herald*, 'Final Examination of the Parties Charged with the
     Murder of the Italian Bo', 26 November 1831
The Public Ledger and Daily Advertiser, 'Trial of the Three Resurrection Men for the
     Murder of the Italian Boy', 3 December 1831
The (London) *Times*, 'The Trial of Bishop, Williams, and May for the Murder of the
     Italian Boy', 3 December 1831
The Preston Chronicle, 'The Trial of Bishop, May, and Williams for the Murder of the
     Italian Boy', 10 December 1831
The Berkshire Chronicle, 'A Knowledge of Anatomy obtained without the assistance
     of Burkers or Resurrectionists', 31 December 1831
The London Courier and Evening Gazette, 'The Meeting of the National Union',
     14 May 1833
The Hampshire Advertiser and Salisbury Guardian (no headline), 24 January 1835
The Morning Post, 'A Mutilated Human Body Found', 30 December 1836
The (London) *Times*, 'Suspected Murder', 30 December 1836
The Public Ledger and Daily Advertiser, 'The Mysterious Affair in the Edgware
     Road', 2 January 1837
The (London) *Times*, 'Discovery of the Head of a Female', 8 January 1837
The (London) *Times*, 'The Late Mysterious Murder in the Edgware Road', 10 January
     1837
The Morning Post, 'The Late Mysterious Murder in the Edgware Road', 12 January
     1837
The Chelmsford Chronicle, 'The Edgware Road Murder', 13 January 1837
The Weekly True Sun, 'The Edgware Road Murder', 14 January 1837
The Weekly True Sun, 'The Edgware Road Murder', 15 January 1837
Bell's Weekly Messenger, 'Discovery of the Legs of the Woman', 5 February 1837
The Morning Post, 'The Edgware Road Murder', 6 February 1837
The Evening Standard, 'The Edgware-Road Murder', 13 February 1837
The Windsor and Eton Express, 'Diabolical Murder', 25 February 1837
The Northampton Mercury, 'The Edgware Road Murder', 18 March 1837
The (London) *Morning Herald*, 'The Edgware Road Tragedy', 28 March 1837

The Evening Standard, 'The Edgware Road Murder – Examination of Two Persons and Extraordinary Confession of One of Them', 28 March 1837

The English Chronicle and Whitehall Evening Post, 'The Execution of Greenacre', 2 May 1837

The Morning Post, 'Greenacre', 4 May 1837

The Morning Chronicle, 'Another Murder of a Female', 10 May 1837

Freeman's Journal, 'Another Murder of a Female', 10 May 1837

The Morning Herald, 'Another Woman Murdered', 10 May 1837

The Morning Chronicle, 'The Late Murder in Laxton-Place, Regents Park', 12 May 1837

Bell's Weekly Messenger, 'Another Woman Murdered', 14 May 1837

The Weekly True Sun, 'The Frederick-Street Murder – Additional and Latest Particulars', 14 May 1837

The Morning Advertiser, 'The Frederick Street Murder', 16 May 1837

The Evening Chronicle, 'Another Dreadful Murder', 28 May 1838

The Morning Post, 'The Murder at Lambeth', 30 May 1838

The Cambridge Chronicle and Journal, 'The Murder of Eliza Davies', 2 June 1838

The Examiner, 'The Murder of Eliza Grimwood', 3 June 1838

The London Courier and Evening Gazette, 'The Murder and Arson in Princes Street', 5 June 1839

The Evening Mail, 'The Murder of Mr. Westwood', 7 June 1839

Bell's Weekly Messenger, 'The Dreadful Murder', 9 June 1839

The (London) *Times*, 'Murder of Mr. Westwood – Additional Particulars (from the *Observer*)', 10 June 1839

The Globe, 'The Murder in Soho', 11 June 1839

The Morning Herald (no headline), 13 August, 1839

The (London) *Times*, 'Horrible Murder of Lord William Russell, Uncle to Lord John Russell, Secretary of the Colonies', 7 May 1840

The (London) *Times* (no headline), 8 May 1840

The (London) *Times*, 'Murder of Lord William Russell', 9 May 1840

The (London) *Times*, 'To The Editor of The Times', 30 May 1840

The Morning Chronicle, 'The Trial of Courvoisier for the Murder of Lord William Russell', 19 June 1840

The (London) *Times*, 'Horrible Murder and Mutilation of a Female', 8 April 1842

The Morning Post, 'Horrible Murder and Mutilation of a Female', 8 April 1842

The (London) *Times*, 'The Murder at Roehampton', 12 April 1842

The (London) *Times*, 'The Roehampton Murder', 16 April 1842

The York Herald, 'Horrible Murder and Mutilation of a Female', 16 April 1842

The Planet, 'Conduct of Police', 17 April 1842

The Evening Standard, 'Apprehension of Good the Murderer', 18 April 1842

The Morning Post, 'New Police Arrangement', 12 July 1842

The (London) *Times*, 'Extraordinary Discovery of a Murder', 18 August 1849

The Illustrated London News, 'The Police Offices of London', 22 August 1846

The (London) *Times*, 'The Bermondsey Murder', 25 August 1849

The Morning Post, 'The Bermondsey Murder', 20 August 1849

The Globe, 'The Bermondsey Murder', 20 August 1849

The Evening Standard, 'The Murder in Bermondsey – Inquest on the Body', 20 August 1849

The Evening Standard, 'The Bermondsey Murder', 24 August 1849

The (London) *Times*, 'The Bermondsey Murder', 28 August 1849

The Stirling Observer, 'The Bermondsey Murder', 30 August 1849

The Globe, 'Bermondsey Murder – Arrest of Manning', 30 August 1849

The Morning Chronicle, 'A Visit to the Cholera Districts of Bermondsey', 24 September 1849

The Evening Mail, 'The Bermondsey Murder', 29 October 1849

The (London) *Times*, 'To the Editor of The Times', 14 November 1849

The Illustrated London News, 'The "City of Manchester" Screw Steamer', 19 July 1851

The Bath Chronicle and Weekly Gazette, 'Horrid and Mysterious Murder', 5 July 1860

The Wiltshire Times and Trowbridge Advertiser, 'Horrid and Mysterious Murder', 7 July 1860

The North Devon Gazette, 'Barbarous and Mysterious Murder', 10 July 1860

The Morning Post (no headline), 10 July 1860

The *Frome Times*, "The Murder at Road," July 18, 1860

The Leeds Times, 'The Mysterious Frome Murder', 21 July 1860

The London Express, 'The Late and Mysterious Murder at Road, Near Frome', 21 July 1860

The Reading Mercury, 'The Mysterious Murder Near Frome', 28 July 1860

The Ulverston Mirror and Furness Reflector, 'The Road Murder', 28 July 1860

The Morning Advertiser, 'The Frome Murder', 30 July 1860

The *Frome Times* (no headline), 1 August 1860

The *Frome Times*, 'The Road Murder', 1 August 1860

The Devizes and Wiltshire Gazette, 'The Road Murder', 2 August 1860

The Portsmouth Times and Naval Gazette, 'The Road Murder', 4 August 1860

The *Frome Times*, 'The Road Murder', 8 August 1860

The (London) *Daily News*, 'The Road Murder', 13 August 1860

Bell's Weekly Messenger, 'House of Commons – Wednesday', 18 August 1860

The (London) *Times*, 'Midland Circuit, Lincoln, Dec. 8', 19 December 1860

The Leeds Mercury, 'Horrible Murder in a Railway Carriage', 12 July 1864

The (London) *Times*, 'Murder in a First-Class Carriage on the North London Railway', 11 July 1864

The Evening Standard, 'The Atrocious Murder in a First-Class Carriage on the North London Railway', 12 July 1864

The (London) *Morning Herald*, 'Horrible and Atrocious Murder in a First-Class Carriage of a Train on the North London Railway', 12 July 1864

The (London) *Times*, 'The Murder on the North London Railway', 12 July 1864

The Daily Telegraph (no headline), 13 July 1864

The Bradford Review, 'Horrible Murder in a Railway Carriage', 14 July 1864

The Belfast Morning News, 'The Murder on the North London Railway', 15 July 1864

The Evening Standard, 'The Atrocious Murder in a Railway Carriage', 14 July 1864

The Evening Standard, 'To the Editor', 14 July 1864

The Evening Standard, 'The Atrocious Murder in a Railway Carriage', 15 July 1864

The Evening Standard, 'The Atrocious Murder in a Railway Carriage', 16 July 1864

The Saturday Review, 'Railway Imprisonment', 16 July 1864

The Preston Herald, 'The Railway Murder', 16 July 1864

The York Herald, 'Horrible Murder in a Railway Carriage', 16 July 1864

Reynolds's Newspaper, 'Latest Particulars of the Atrocious Railway Carriage Murder', 17 July 1864

The (London) *Times*, 'Letter to the Editor', 18 July 1864

The (London) *Times*, 'The Murder on the North London Railway', 18 July 1864

The (London) *Times*, 'The Murder on the North London Railway', 19 July 1864

The (London) *Times*, 'The Murder on the North London Railway', 20 July 1864

The Globe, 'The Murder on the North London Railway', 20 July 1864

The Morning Advertiser, 'The Murder on the North London Railway', 20 July 1864

The Morning Post, 'The Murder on the North London Railway', 21 July 1864

The (London) *Daily News*, 'The Murder on the North London Railway', 21 July 1864

The (London) *Times*, 'The Murder on the North London Railway', 21 July 1864

Reynolds's Newspaper, 'Suspected Discovery of the Murderer of Mr. Briggs', 24 July 1864

The Evening Standard, 'Müller in Liverpool', 17 September 1864

The New York Times, 'Great Britain: The Mysterious Murder. Supposed Discovery of the Perpetrator. His Flight to America. Further Particulars', 4 August 1864

The Brooklyn Eagle, 'Murder Will Out', 6 August 1864

The New York Daily Herald, 'The London Railway Murder', 26 August 1864

The New York Times, 'The Arrest of Müller, the English Railway Murderer', 26 August 1864

The *Chicago Tribune*, 'Müller, the Fugitive Criminal, Caught', 28 August 1864

The New York Daily Herald, 'Müller, the Alleged Railway Murderer, on his way to England', 4 September 1864

The Evening Standard, 'Müller in Liverpool', 17 September 1864

The New York Times, 'The Tallahassee', 29 September 1864

The (London) *Times*, 'The Murder on the North London Railway', 31 October 1864

The (London) *Times* (no headline), 15 November 1864

The (London) *Times*, 'Müller's Execution', 15 November 1864

The (London) *Times* (no headline), 27 April 1865

Bell's Weekly Messenger, 'The Road-Hill Murder', 1 May 1865

The (London) *Daily News*, 'Marlborough-Street', 31 July 1865

The Evening Standard, 'Shocking Murder in Shropshire', 17 January 1866

The Oswestry Advertiser, 'Murder in Shropshire', 24 January 1866

The Morning Advertiser, 'The Mysterious Murder in Shropshire', 29 January 1866

The Chelmsford Chronicle, 'The Mysterious Murder in Shropshire', 2 February 1866

The Shrewsbury Free Press and Advertiser for Salop, 'The Shocking Murder at Duddlewick', 3 February 1866

The Shrewsbury Free Press and Advertiser for Salop, 'The Duddlewick Murder', 24 March 1866

The Preston Chronicle, 'The rescue of two Fenian Head-Centres and the Murder of Sgt. Brett', 21 September 1867

The Dundee Courier, 'Execution of the Murderers of Brett at Manchester', 25 November 1867

The Evening Standard, 'Capture of 'Colonel Burke'', 25 November 1867

The Dublin Evening Mail, 'The Outrage at Clerkenwell', 14 December 1867

Saunders's News-Letter, 'Attempt to blow-up the prison and Clerkenwell', 14 December 1867

Reynolds's Newspaper, 'Attempt to blow up Clerkenwell Prison by Alleged Fenians', 15 December 1867

The Shields Daily News, 'The Clerkenwell Fenian Outrage', 21 December 1867

The New York Times, 'Affairs in England', 29 December 1867

The Morning Post (no headline), 28 April 1868

Freeman's Journal, 'The Execution of Barrett', 27 May 1868

Reynolds's Newspaper, 'Calcraft's Purveyors', 31 May 1868

The Evening Standard, 'Extraordinary Disclosures', 18 April 1871

The Morning Advertiser (no headline), 19 April 1871

The (London) *Daily News*, 'The Mysterious Tragedy at London', 1 May 1871

The (London) *Daily News*, 'The Eltham Murder', 2 May 1871

The Irish Times, 'Agnes Norman', 2 May 1871

The Evening Standard, 'The Eltham Tragedy', 5 May 1871

South London Chronicle, 'Extraordinary Charge of Child Murder', 6 May 1871

Reynolds's Newspaper, 'The Murder of a Servant Girl at Eltham', 7 May 1871

The Morning Advertiser, 'The Charge Against a Girl of Murdering Children', 19 May 1871

The Bristol Mercury, 'The Extraordinary Charge of Murdering Children', 20 May 1871

The (London) *Daily News*, 'The Eltham Murder', 17 July 1871

Freeman's Journal, 'Mrs. Davey, Agnes Norman, and Pook', 17 July 1871

The Daily Telegraph (no headline), 18 July 1871

The (London) *Times* (no headline), 18 July 1871

The (London) *Times*, 'Double Murder at Hoxton', 11 July 1872

Lloyds's Weekly Newspaper, 'Terrible tragedy in Hoxton', 14 July 1872

Reynolds's Newspaper, 'Double Murder at Hoxton', 14 July 1872

The (London) *Times* (no headline), 20 July 1872

The (London) *Times*, 'Supposed Murder', 26 December 1872

The (London) *Times*, 'The Coram-Street Murder', 27 December 1872

The Ipswich Journal, 'Horrible Murder in Great Coram Street, London', 28 December 1872

The Manchester Times, 'Shocking Murder in London', 28 December 1872

The Bristol Mercury, 'The Great Coram-Street Murder', 25 January 1873

The (London) *Times* (no headline), 31 January 1873

The Globe, 'The Charge Against Detectives', 19 October 1877

The Pall Mall Gazette, 'The Metropolitan Police', 8 April 1878

The Daily Telegraph, 'Extraordinary Discovery', 10 March 1879

The Penny Illustrated, 'A Parallel to the Waterloo Bridge Mystery', 15 March 1879

The Croydon Times, 'Extraordinary Discovery', 19 March 1879

Lloyd's Weekly Newspaper, 'The Barnes Mystery', 23 March 1879

The Daily Telegraph, 'The Barnes Mystery', 26 March 1879

The Manchester Evening News (no headline), 27 March 1879

The Dublin Evening Telegraph, 'The Barnes Mystery', 29 March 1879

The (London) *Times*, 'The Supposed Murder at Richmond', 29 March 1879

Freeman's Journal, 'The Barnes Mystery', 31 March 1879

The Daily Telegraph, 'The Barnes Mystery', 31 March 1879

The (London) *Times*, 'The Alleged Murder at Richmond', 31 March 1879

The (London) *Times*, 'The Murder at Richmond' 1 April 1879

The (London) *Times*, 'The Richmond Murder', 2 April 1879

The Evening Standard (no headline), 28 May 1879

The Wolverhampton Express and Star, 'The Richmond Murder', 3 July 1879

The Dundee Evening Telegraph (no headline), 9 July 1879

The Pall Mall Gazette, 'The Richmond Murder', 9 July 1879

The New York Times, 'A Woman on the Gallows', 30 July 1879

The (London) *Weekly Dispatch*, 'Justice at Fault', 17 August 1879

The Echo, 'The Murder of a Constable at Dalston', 22 August 1884

The Morning Post, 'The Murder at Dalston', 23 August 1884

The (London) *Times*, 'Dynamite Outrages in London', 31 May 1884

The Evening Standard, 'Execution of Orrock and Harris at Newgate To-Day',
    6 October 1884

The Referee (no headline), 25 January 1885

The Daily Telegraph and Courier (no headline), 26 January 1885

The Evening Standard, 'The Rainham Mystery', 13 June 1887

The Shields Daily Gazette, 'The Battle of Trafalgar Square', 14 November 1887

The Evening Star, 'The Trafalgar Square Demonstration', 14 November 1887

The Northern Echo, 'Trafalgar-Square', 14 November 1887

The (London) *Echo*, 'Why Mr. Monro Retired', 31 August 1888

The (London) *Times*, 'The Whitechapel Murder', 3 September 1888

The Dundee Evening Telegraph, 'The Whitechapel Horrors', 6 September 1888

The Morning Post, 'Another Woman Murdered in Whitechapel', 10 September 1888

The (London) *Times*, 'A Thames Mystery', 12 September 1888

The New York Times, 'Dismay in Whitechapel', 1 October 1888.

The (London) *Times*, 'To the Editor of The Times', 2 October 1888

The (London) *Daily News*, 'The Atrocities at the East End', 3 October 1888

The Daily Telegraph, 'The Whitehall Murder', 3 October 1888

The Evening Standard, 'Shocking Discovery in Westminster', 3 October 1888

The Evening Standard, 'The Shocking Discovery in Westminster', 4 October 1888

The (London) *Times*, 'The Murder in Westminster', 4 October 1888

The Globe, 'The East-End Murders', 9 October 1888

The Evening Standard, 'Another Arrest', 18 October 1888

The Morning Post, 'The Whitehall Mystery', 18 October 1888

Reynolds's Newspaper, 'The Whitehall Mystery', 21 October 1888

The Daily Telegraph, 'The East-End Tragedies', 10 November 1888

Lloyd's Weekly Newspaper, 'The Murders and Sir Charles Warren', 13 November 1888

The Morning Post, 'Resignation of Sir Charles Warren', 13 November 1888

The (London) *Times*, 'The Whitechapel Murder', 13 November 1888

The Evening Standard, 'Horrible Discovery in the Thames', 5 June 1889

The (London) *Times*, 'The Thames Mystery', 11 June 1889

St. James Gazette, 'The Thames Mystery', 17 June 1889

The Evening News, 'The Thames Horror', 26 June 1889

The Globe, 'The Thames Mystery', 26 July 1889

The Pall Mall Gazette, 'The Whitechapel Tragedies', 4 November 1889

Ally Sloper's Half Holiday, 'Harry Benson, Prince of Swindlers', 14 December 1889

The (London) *Times*, 'Electric Lighting at New Scotland-Yard', 6 June 1891

Lloyd's Weekly Newspaper, 'Poisoning Mystery in Lambeth', 18 October 1891

The Evening Standard, 'The South London Poisoning Cases', 23 June 1892

The Evening Standard, 'Mysterious Poisoning in South London. Inquest Today', 13 April 1892

The Evening Standard, 'The South London Poisoning Case', 14 April 1892

The Quebec Morning Chronicle, 'Thomas Neill Executed', 16 November 1892

The North Devon Gazette, 'Remarkable Evidence', 9 September 1902

The Dundee Evening Post, 'Identified by Finger-Marks', 15 September 1902

The South London Mail, 'The Recent South London Burglaries', 20 September 1902

The *Weekly Dispatch*, 'Finger-Prints', 21 September 1902

The Shields Daily News, 'The London Trunk Tragedy', 29 March 1904

The Portsmouth Evening News, 'Murder Mystery Solved', 29 March 1904

The Witney Gazette, 'Body in a Cemented Box', 2 April 1904

The Cavan Weekly News, 'The London Tragedy', 2 April 1904

The *St. Louis Post-Dispatch*, 'Impression of Chief Desmond's Finger Tips and the Man Who Took Them', 12 June 1904

The *St. Louis Post-Dispatch*, 'To Identify Crooks By Fingerprints', 29 October 1904

The Woolwich Gazette, 'The Deptford Mask Murders', 12 May 1905

The Edinburgh Evening News, 'Masked Murderers Executed', 23 May 1905

The Uttoxeter New Era, 'Murder of a Cripple', 4 November 1908

The Salisbury Times, 'The Meadow Road Tragedy', 6 November 1908

The Salisbury Times, 'The Meadow Road Tragedy', 11 December 1908

The Wiltshire Times and Trowbridge Advertiser, 'Who Killed Teddy Haskell?' 3 April 1909

The Dundee Courier, 'Jury Finds Mrs. Haskell Not Guilty of Murder', 5 April 1909

The *Daily Telegraph*, 'North London Crime', 16 July 1910

The New York Times, 'Crippen Dressed as Woman?' 19 July 1910

The Dundee Evening Telegraph, 'STILL AT LARGE', 20 July 1910

The *Observer*, 'CHASE ACROSS THE ATLANTIC', 24 July 1910

The Dundee Evening Telegraph, 'INSPECTOR DEW IS ON CRIPPEN'S BACK', 25 July 1910

The Ottawa Free Press, 'Detective is Catching Up with Crippen', 26 July 1910

The *Daily Telegraph*, 'Chase of Crippen – Position of the Steamers To-Day', 27 July 1910

The *Montreal Gazette*, 'Inspector Dew Arrives in Canada', 30 July 1910

The *Montreal Gazette*, 'Crippen Caught', 1 August 1910

The (London) *Times*, 'Captain Kendall's Message', 1 August 1910

The *New York Times*, 'Crippen, I Want You', 1 August 1910

The *New York Times*, 'Crippen Caught Admits Identity Girl Collapses', 1 August 1910

The *New York Times*, 'The Crime and the Pursuit', 1 August 1910

The (London) *Times*, 'Crime and Science', 1 August 1910

The (London) *Times*, 'The Story of the Flight', 1 August 1910

The *Aberdeen Evening Press*, 'Crippen', 14 September 1910

Lloyd's Weekly Newspaper, 'Miss Le Neve and the Crippen Case', 13 November 1910

The *Globe*, 'SECOND EXHUMATION', 10 February 1915

The *Evening Mail*, 'THE DROWNED BRIDES', 12 February 1915

The (London) *Weekly Dispatch*, 'Triple Charge of Wife Murder', 28 March 1915

The (London) *Weekly Dispatch*, 'Brides Case Ends at Bow-Street', 16 May 1915

The *Lancashire Evening Post*, 'Dr. Spilsbury's Evidence', 29 June 1915

The *Irish Independent*, 'Death Sentence', 2 July 1915

The *Daily Mirror*, 'Death Sentence in Brides Case', 2 July 1915

The *New York Times*, 'Noted Detective Dead', 26 September 1916

The *Globe*, 'Little Victims of Kaiser's Hatred' , 15 June 1917

The (London) *Times*, 'Bloomsbury Murder Mystery', 3 November 1917

The *People*, 'Diabolical Murder in London', 4 November 1917

The (London) *Times*, 'Murdered Woman Identified', 6 November 1917

The *Sheffield Independent*, 'Murder Mystery', 6 November 1917

The *Daily Mirror*, 'Sack Victim Wife of French Soldier', 6 November 1917

The (London) *Times*, 'Bloomsbury Murder Mystery', 7 November 1917

The *Scotsman*, 'The London Murder Mystery', 7 November 1917

The *Liverpool Echo*, 'The London Crime', 12 November 1917

The *Birmingham Daily Post*, 'The Bloomsbury Mystery', 13 November 1917

The (London) *Daily News*, 'The Bloomsbury Murder', 13 November 1917

The (London) *Times*, 'Murder Mystery', 13 November 1917

The *Scotsman*, 'The London Murder', 16 November 1917

The *Western Evening Herald*, 'The London Murder", 16 November 1917

The (London) *Times*, 'Murder Mystery', 21 November 1917

The (London) *Times*, 'The Murder of Mme. Gerard', 17 January 1918

The (London) *Times*, 'The Murder of Mme. Gerard', 18 January 1918

The (London) *Weekly Dispatch*, 'The First Air Raid Murder', 3 March 1918

The *Pall Mall Gazette*, 'Mrs. Thompson Executed', 9 January 1923

The (London) *Daily Chronicle*, 'London Woman Identified as Bungalow Victim', 6 May 1924

The *Yorkshire Post and Leeds Intelligencer*, 'Before the Magistrates', 7 May 1924

The *Yorkshire Post and Leeds Intelligencer*, 'The Bungalow Crime', 7 May 1924

The *People*, 'The Horror In Our Midst', 11 May 1924

The Dundee Evening Telegraph, 'Patrick Mahon's Amazing Story of Bungalow Tragedy', 22 May 1924

The Northern Daily Mail, 'Crumbles Case', 4 June 1924

The St. Louis Post-Dispatch, '"The Bungalow Murder" at Which "Crimeless England" Stands Aghast', 13 July 1924

The Western Evening Herald, 'The Crumbles Trial', 15 July 1924

The Western Evening Herald, 'Opening of the Crumbles Trial at Lewes Assizes: "Herald" Special', 15 July 1924

The Daily Mirror, 'Mahon Trial Begins Afress After the Collapse of a Juror', 15 July 1925

The Coventry Evening Telegraph, 'The Crumbles Tragedy', 18 July 1924

The Dundee Evening Telegraph, 'Miss Ethel Duncan's Ordeal at the Bungalow Trial', 17 July 1924

The Western Daily Press, 'Mahon on Miss Kaye's Fondness for Him', 18 July 1924

The Yorkshire Post and Leeds Intelligencer, 'Bungalow Murder Surprise', 17 July 1924

The Dundee Courier, 'Last Scene in the Crumbles Trial', 21 July 1924

The Dunstan Times, 'My Race with Crippen', 7 February 1927

The Western Daily Press, 'Warm Days', 9 May 1927

The Nottingham Journal, 'Diary of a Londoner', 9 May 1927

The Sheffield Daily Telegraph, 'London Day by Day', 9 May 1927

The (London) *Daily Herald*, 'Woman's Body in a Trunk', 11 May 1927

The Shields Daily News, 'Trunk Mystery: New Clue', 11 May 1927

The Gloucester Citizen, 'London Trunk Sensation", 11 May 1927

The (London) *Times*, 'Sale of Trunk Traced', 12 May 1927

The Dundee Evening Telegraph, 'Police Unravelling Trunk Mystery', 12 May 1927

The Sheffield Daily Telegraph, 'The Trunk Mystery', 13 May 1927

The Nottingham Evening Post, 'Midnight Police Talk', 13 May 1927

The Daily Herald, 'Woman in Trunk Identified', 13 May 1927

The (London) *Times*, 'Body in Trunk Mystery', 14 May 1927

The Sheffield Daily Telegraph, 'The Trunk Mystery', 14 May 1927

The Belfast Telegraph, 'Trunk Murder Arrest', 24 May 1927

The Dundee Evening Telegraph, 'Alleged Confession in Trunk Crime', 24 May 1927

The Hull Daily Mail, 'Trunk Crime', 15 June 1927

The Dundee Evening Telegraph, 'Robinson on Trial at Old Bailey', 11 July 1927

The Coventry Evening Telegraph, 'Trunk Murder Trial', 12 July 1927

The (London) *Daily News*, 'Trunk Trial: Robinson's Story', 13 July 1927

The Birmingham Gazette, 'Robinson to Die', 14 July 1927

The New York Times, 'Trunk Murder Case Solved in London', 25 May 1927

The Belfast Telegraph, 'Murder of P.C. Gutteridge', 28 September 1927

The Londonderry Sentinel, 'English Murder Mystery', 29 September 1927

The Dundee Courier and Advertiser, 'Abandoned Motor Car', 29 September 1927

The Belfast Telegraph, 'Essex Murder Mystery Developments', 29 September 1927

The Westminster Gazette, 'Net for Men Who Shot Policeman', 29 September 1927

The Sheffield Daily Telegraph, 'Murdered Constable', 29 September 1927

The Sheffield Independent, 'Clues in Shot Policeman Mystery', 29 September 1927

The Weekly Telegraph, 'The Murdered Constable', 8 October 1927

The Sunday Post, 'Shot Constable Riddle', 2 October 1927

The Hartlepool Northern Daily Mail, ' "G.B.S" on Browne's Trial', 7 May 1928

The *Yorkshire Evening Post*, 'The "Personality" of Firearms', 28 May 1928

The New York Times, 'Crime Expert Quits at Scotland Yard', 26 June 1929

The Birmingham Daily Gazette, 'Detective Retires', 28 September 1931

The *Weekly Dispatch*, 'Hanged by a Microscope', 22 November 1931

The *Chicago Tribune*, 'The Mystery of Mme. Gerard', 24 May 1936

The Evening Standard, 'Girl Found Stranded on a Lonely Path," 12 April, 1937

The Evening Standard, 'Important Statement by Girl in Murder Hunt', 13 April 1937

The *St. Louis Post-Dispatch*, 'Convicted of Murder by a Silk Thread', 1 August 1937

The New York Daily News, 'When Justice Triumphed', 8 May 1938

The *Guardian*, 'Saliva as Clue to Identity', 13 October 1939

The (London) *Daily News*, 'Wensley the Great Detective is Dead', 5 December 1949

The Aberdeen Press and Journal, 'Death of a "Yard" Man Who Knew No Fear',
    5 December 1949

The New York Times, '15 Were Injured By Bomb Blasts', 23 January 1957

The *Guardian*, 'Forensic Science: Secrets of the Case Against Crippen', 16 August
    2008

The *Telegraph*, 'Head found in David Attenborough's garden was murder victim',
    5 July 2011

The Scotsman, 'Dressed to Kill: Burke Trial Gown Found After 200 Years', 6 August
    2012

The *Guardian*, 'Largely Forgotten: A Manchester Police Officer Who Gave His Life
    on Duty', 26 September 2012

The *Los Angeles Times*, 'Scotland Yard may move its famous headquarters',
    30 October 2012

The *Independent*, 'Vital clue ignored for 50 years', 9 December 2012

The *Guardian*, 'The world's first hack: the telegraph and the invention of privacy',
    15 July 2015

The Gazette, 'Cholera epidemics in Victorian London', 1 February 2016

The *Mirror*, 'The secret life of Victorian killer Dr. Crippen's mistress revealed 107
    years after wife's murder', 13 October 2017

The *Irish Examiner*, 'Soldier, Fenian, and Patriot: Recounting the life of Cork's
    Ricard O'Sullivan', 27 April 2018

The Irish Times, '150 years ago today, a Fenian became the last person to be
    publicly executed in England', 26 May 2018

The *Guardian*, 'Madame Tussaud: the astounding tale of survival behind the
    woman who made history', 4 October 2018

The (London) *Times*, 'The Tragic Affair of the Milliner and the Murderer',
    4 November 2018

South London Press, 'Jane was 16, pregnant, and brutally murdered', 23 April 2021

Index